Personnel Interviewing

Personnel Interviewing

THEORY AND PRACTICE

Felix M. Lopez

WITHDRAWN

SECOND EDITION

McGRAW-HILL BOOK COMPANY

New York   St. Louis   San Francisco   Auckland   Düsseldorf
Johannesburg   Kuala Lumpur   London   Mexico   Montreal
New Delhi   Panama   Paris   São Paulo   Singapore
Sydney   Tokyo   Toronto

Library of Congress Cataloging in Publication Data

Lopez, Felix M
  Personnel interviewing, theory and practice.

  Bibliography: p.
  Includes index.
  1. Employment interviewing. I. Title.
HF5549.5.I6L6   1975   658.4′52   75–1047
ISBN 0–07–038726–5

1234567890   BPBP   78321098765

*The editors for this book were W. Hodson Mogan
and Robert Braine, the designer was Naomi Auerbach,
and the production supervisor was George E. Oechsner.
It was set in Primer by Monotype Composition Co., Inc.*

It was printed and bound by The Book Press.

To my wife Jean

Contents

List of Illustrations   ix

Preface   xi

Part 1   SOME BASIC CONSIDERATIONS **1**

  1. *What Is an Interview?*   3
  2. *Human Communication*   14
  3. *The Dynamics of Interviewing*   30
  4. *The Complete Interviewer*   53

Part 2   DECISION-MAKING INTERVIEWS **73**

  5. *Selection Theory*   75
  6. *Selection Strategy*   89
  7. *The Employment Interview*   108
  8. *The Assessment Interview*   133
  9. *Selection Interview Variations*   163

Part 3   PROBLEM-SOLVING INTERVIEWS **177**

  10. *The Dimensions of Job Effectiveness*   179
  11. *The Performance-Evaluation Process*   200
  12. *The Performance-Evaluation Interview*   222
  13. *The Career-Counseling Interview*   245
  14. *The Problem-Employee Interview*   262

Part 4   INFORMATION-EXCHANGE INTERVIEWS . . .   **281**

  15. *Information-Getting: The Employee Survey Interview*   283
  16. *Information-Giving: Orientation and Coaching Interviews*   302
  17. *The Termination Interview*   317

Selected Readings   335

Name Index   339

Subject Index   345

List of Illustrations

FIGURE	TITLE	PAGE
1	*The Basic Model of Communication*	16
2	*The Basic Model of Interview Communication*	26
3	*Normal Frequency Distribution*	81
4	*Sources of Human Trait Data*	83
5	*The 33 Traits*	102
6	*Principal and Supplemental Trait Measures*	103
7	*Definition of Trait Levels*	104
8	*Threshold Traits Analysis Selection Plan*	105
9	*The Decision-Making Employment Process*	106
10	*Completed Employment Interview Record*	129
11	*Completed Assessment Interview Report*	158
12	*Completed Page 3—Assessment Interview Report*	159
13	*Campus Interview Report Form*	166
14	*Supervisor's Interview Report Form*	168
15	*Job Effectiveness*	191
16	*Managerial Evaluation Program*	217
17	*Analysis of Managerial Styles*	219
18	*Computer Print-Out*	220
19	*Evaluation Record—Standards*	234
20	*Barrier Situation*	240
21	*Improvement Plan*	242
22	*Counselor's Report: Career Counseling Interview*	258
23	*Counselor's Report: Problem Employee Interview*	276
24	*Four-Phase Interview Checklist*	314
25	*Supervisor's Report of Termination*	324
26	*Interviewer's Checklist of Termination*	326

Preface

The ten years following the appearance of the first edition of this book have been marked by many new and important developments in the field of personnel management, particularly in the areas of employee selection and evaluation. Most importantly, equal employment opportunity legislation and adjudication have forced employers to examine carefully their selection, promotion, and evaluation techniques and procedures.

This book has been completely revised to reflect these events and my own intensive research and practice during this period. While the basic premises and the underlying theories that occasioned the original volume remain unchanged, I have found it necessary to make major and extensive revisions in the text.

First, the book's structure has been reorganized to give more prominence to the selection interview and to present the material in a more logical sequence from employment through termination. In Part I, the former Chapters 2, 3, 4 and 19 have been consolidated. In Part II, a new Chapter, 6, dealing with selection strategies and equal employment opportunity requirements, particularly with respect to job analysis, has been added. In Part III, another new chapter on the performance-evaluation process has been added which includes a model managerial performance-evaluation program. In Part IV, the former Chapters 5 and 8 have been combined into one chapter.

Second, I have added a great deal of new material besides that in Chapters 6 and 11. In Chapters 3 and 4, the more recent research findings on interviewing techniques are presented. Chapters 7 and 8 have been rewritten completely, new interview report forms have been presented, and the interview content has been expanded and emphasized. Chapter 10 has been rewritten to reflect the great interest in job satisfaction theory and research in the recent past and to deal with the critical issue of the criterion problem. The remaining chapters have been thoroughly updated to include the growing importance of personnel interviews in the Human Resources Personnel Program.

Third, I have changed the book's writing style to make it more interesting and readable for the practitioner. I have addressed myself to the personnel administrator and the supervisor rather than to the professional behavioral scientist and have adopted a more direct personal approach. To that end, I have also added a number of illustrations taken from the everyday experiences of real companies.

Nevertheless, the ideas and the techniques in this current revision are still based on the assumptions of the first volume, assumptions derived from my years of active practice and teaching in universities and management seminars.

My first assumption is that the purpose of personnel management is to assist employees in utilizing their talents most effectively in and on the job and, at the same time, to help them derive a substantial measure of self-esteem out of the job. The interviews described herein, therefore, are neither employer- nor employee-centered, and the style, technique, and methodology recommended for each type of personnel interview are always directed at this two-factor goal.

My second conviction is that personnel interviewing skills are best acquired by examining the interview in its context as an essential tool of the personnel function. To be most effective, therefore, a personnel interviewer must not only master the skills of interpersonal communication but also appreciate the underlying rationale, the immediate purposes, and the setting in which the interview takes place.

These assumptions have dictated the choice of subject matter, determined its treatment, and guided the organization of this book. Because of this focus on the interview as a direct personal confrontation between management and the employee, you, the reader, will obtain a "bottoms up" review of personnel administration. This approach is particularly valuable because it will give you a more realistic view of personnel management than the traditional overview of most textbooks.

My third assumption is that the maintenance of sound employee relations is the joint responsibility of the personnel administrator and the operating supervisor. This has determined the style in which I have chosen to write this book. It is my conviction that because interviewing is a badly neglected managerial skill, it deserves a more prominent place in the curriculum of supervisory and management development programs.

I have written this book, therefore, with several reader groups in mind—those actively engaged in the field of personnel management, those preparing to enter it, and the supervisors and operating managers.

Most of the ideas.and assertions contained in the succeeding pages are based on fairly substantial documentary evidence in management and behavioral science literature. To have enumerated all the sources on which I have drawn, directly, or indirectly, would have been tedious and superfluous. I have, however, included enough references to suggest the principal books and articles that have influenced my conclusions.

I must thank the people who have influenced the writing of this book. I am indebted to the many writers, scholars, and managers whose works I have referred to or quoted, even though I realize that perhaps they will not always agree with my interpretation of their ideas. I am also grateful to the very many students, colleagues, and friends who have helped me in one way or another by encouragement, advice, or material assistance. I would like to acknowledge publicly the assistance of Mrs. Terry Davidson and Mrs. Margaret Jones who have helped me prepare the manuscript.

Felix M. Lopez

Personnel Interviewing

Some Basic Considerations

Interviewing is very much like piano playing—a fair degree of skill can be acquired without the necessity of formal instruction. But there is a world of difference in craftsmanship, in technique, and in finesse between the amateur who plays "by ear" and the accomplished concert pianist. The self-instructed player mechanically reproduces on the keyboard certain melodies that have been committed to memory; the artist, by skillfully blending mastery of musical theory, countless hours of practice, and personal interpretation, creates an effect that is technically precise, pleasing to the audience, and expressive of the pianist's inner feeling.

The professional interviewer, too, differs from the amateur in an appreciation of the principles of interview theory, and like the pianist, translates that understanding into a skillful performance. Like the concert artist, an interviewer reaches this point only after frequent, intensive, and diligent practice. As with piano playing, interviewing skill comes so slowly and painfully at first, that the learner experiences frustration and a continual sense of inadequacy. If the person persists, however, these newly acquired techniques will almost imperceptibly become a part of unreflective behavior until, one day, the interviewer realizes the ultimate satisfaction of knowing that the technique has been mastered.

There is, however, a point where our analogy between piano playing and interviewing breaks down. A novice pianist approaches the learning task with a decided advantage over the novice interviewer. The beginning pianist has never performed a task similar to piano playing before, realizes it, and can freely admit it. There is, therefore, nothing to unlearn, no poor habits to erase, and no convictions about the level of skill to defend. So the learning task becomes that much easier.

The beginning interviewer, on the other hand, has years of conversational experience during which he or she may have acquired many unconscious habits that are detrimental to effective interviewing. Interviewers must therefore expect that the chief learning problem will be to avoid the well-worn conversational habits already acquired.

1

Part I is designed to give the reader clear understanding of the interview. It warrants careful study because it is the foundation for the other parts of this book. In it, the rationale of the interview as a transactional communication medium between human beings is thoroughly analyzed.

This approach may, at first, seem somewhat artificial and, perhaps, a trifle overdrawn. But a thoughtful reading of Part I will give you a frame of reference within which you can understand the application of the interview to specific situations in the occupational world. This should pay rich dividends, and an effective interview in a delicate situation may be your ultimate reward.

chapter 1

What Is an Interview?

> Look to the essence of a thing, whether it be a point of
> doctrine, a practice, or of interpretation.
> —MARCUS AURELIUS, *Meditations*

As humans have become increasingly civilized, they have devised many
conventions to enable them to exchange information speedily and accurately with each other. One particularly common device called the *interview* is the subject of this book. Originally, the word "interview" referred
to a conversation held with a person whose views were sought for publication. In this limited sense, the remark attributed to Oliver Wendell
Holmes that "the interviewer is a product of overcivilization" is probably
correct.

But since its origin as a journalistic technique, the interview has
risen in respectability, if not in esteem, as it has been applied to a
diversity of purposes and situations in human affairs. The interview is
now an indispensable tool of physicians, lawyers, educators, social
scientists, and business managers. Our concern here is with the *personnel interview,* that is, with the use of the interview as a management
device to facilitate the effective selection, placement, motivation, and
personal adjustment of employees.

What Interviews Are Not

Logically, the first step in learning to interview properly is to define our
subject. The systematic consideration of any subject requires, first, that
the investigator define the precise boundaries that mark it off from
other areas of learning. When the field of inquiry is as ambiguous and
as controversial as the interview, the need for a definition becomes
critically important. Because there are many varieties of human communication that appear to be interviews but really are not, we must

begin by defining precisely what we propose to discuss in such detail in the following pages.

The Need for a Definition   The fact that the interview is one of commonest personnel-management techniques has not prevented it from being considered by some as a weapon rather than a tool. Even though most personnel and operating managers believe they conduct highly effective interviews with employees and subordinates, the evidence is so mixed that researchers have concluded that, at best, the personnel interview is useful only as an expression of good intentions.

The selection interview has been particularly singled out for criticism. As long ago as 1922, the futility of the interview was exposed by an investigator who found very little agreement and some astonishing discrepancies in evaluation.[1]

Another comprehensive review of the literature on interviewing reported in 1949 that very little evidence had been obtained testifying to the effectiveness of the employment interview.[2]

In 1960, another pair of investigators surveyed the state of the interview during the 1950s and suggested that a moratorium on books about interviewing be called until more empirical support for its use was developed.[3] But by 1964 another investigator, while agreeing for the most part with the prior criticisms, suggested some starting points for basic research on the selection interview.[4]

The introduction of the interview into other management situations has fared no better than interviewing in general in the eyes of its critics. The performance-evaluation interview between a supervisor and a subordinate has become a cause célèbre in personnel literature. Everyone seems to agree that subordinates have the right to know how well they are doing in their jobs, and nearly everyone agrees that it is the immediate supervisor's obligation to so inform them. But only a small minority seem to believe that the performance-evaluation interview is the way to do it.

Disciplinary, counseling, survey, and termination interviews have also come in for their share of criticism, mainly on the grounds of inconsistency and subjectivity. The nearly universal judgment of behavioral scientists is that, as practiced in government and industry,

[1] H. L. Hollingsworth, *Judging Human Character* (New York: Appleton-Century Crofts, Inc., 1923), p. 268.
[2] R. Wagner, "The Employment Interview: A Critical Summary," *Personnel Psychology*, 2:17–26, 1949.
[3] G. W. England and D. G. Patterson, "Selection and Placement: The Past Ten Years," in H. G. Heneman, Jr. et al. (eds.), *Employment Relations Research* (New York: Harper & Row, Publishers, Incorporated, 1960), p. 62.
[4] E. C. Mayfield, "The Selection Interview—A Reevaluation of Published Research," *Personnel Psychology*, 17:239–260, 1964.

interview results should be treated with utmost caution until further research and refinement warrant greater confidence in them.

But, however much it is justified, criticism does not solve a problem— it only identifies it. The interview problem lies in the core fact that in most personnel transactions there simply is no practical alternative. All the complaints and denunciations boil down to the argument that the *interviewer*, not the interview, is the heart of the problem. In the hands of an unskilled amateur, the most useful and valuable tool is worthless and even harmful. The evidence has repeatedly demonstrated that trained, knowledgeable interviewers, as few as they may be, *are* effective. The vast amount of negative data concerning the reliability and the validity of the interview serves only to underline the obvious, that most interviewers do not understand the subtleties of this complex process.

To arrive at a workable understanding we shall travel a circuitous route by defining first what an interview is *not*. By examining various communications media that simulate but do not constitute interviewing, we can cut away the conceptual underbrush in order to view the essentials of correct interviewing clearly.

Communications Media It is evident that an interview is a medium of communication between people. In daily business life, there are many ways to communicate, and depending on the immediate situation, some are more effective than others. You can, for example, speak directly to another person, or write letters, memoranda, or formal reports; you can hold small group discussions or staff meetings; you can address large groups in an auditorium or over a public address system. Each of these methods is a legitimate communications medium, but obviously each is not an interview, for then interviewing would merely be synonymous with communicating.

An interview is a unique form of communication. Etymologically, the word "interview" means a viewing between people, an oral interchange in a face-to-face confrontation. This narrower interpretation excludes immediately all written communications and all telephone conversations. This definition still leaves us with a number of face-to-face encounters that common sense tells us are decidedly not interviews. A closer examination of those situations that are oral *and* face-to-face but are not normally considered interviews will help clarify the interview concept in two ways: first, it should identify those elements that are essential to the definition of a genuine interview; second, a review of oral, face-to-face communications that do not fit the precise definition of an interview will expose the common practices of those who believe they are interviewing when, in fact, they are not.

Let us consider four face-to-face situations that resemble interviews in some respects but upon closer scrutiny are found to lack the appropriate specifications: the lecture, the group discussion, the conversation, and the interrogation.

THE LECTURE.   A speaker delivering an address from a platform to a large group, a teacher in a classroom lecturing to a group of students, or a supervisor explaining the workings of a piece of equipment to a single employee are all examples of oral communication among humans in face-to-face encounters, but none of them fits our interview model. After only the briefest reflection, you will recognize that an essential element is missing—opportunity for the listener to talk back to the speaker, to tell the speaker how the message is being received, or to ask for clarification.

This idea may appear to be quite elementary, but it is surprising how often it is overlooked by some interviewers. If you do all or most of the talking, you may be communicating but you will not really be interviewing.

THE GROUP DISCUSSION.   In a small group of people gathered to exchange ideas or to discuss a problem, there is ample opportunity to talk back to one another. In fact, the power of the small-group mode of communication stems from its potential for interaction and feedback. But you will readily agree that group discussion does not represent an interview, and in such recognition you can discover another important interview element—it is exclusively a function of two people, interacting and exchanging ideas like a pair of tennis players hitting a ball back and forth across the net. Tennis is quite different from soccer or hockey, and interviewing is quite unlike group discussion.

THE CONVERSATION.   Two bus riders deep in conversation are involved in a thoroughly satisfying exchange of ideas, enjoying one of life's greatest pleasures. There is communication, and there are only two people. But such a conversation is not an interview. Why not? Because the pleasure obtained from the verbal interplay with another person is its purpose and its reward. The end of the dialogue is usually the end of the matter.

On the other hand, while pleasure is often a side effect, an interview's purpose is something more than the interaction and the verbal exchange. Some implicit or explicit goal of either the interviewer, the interviewee, or both characterizes and determines its occurrence.

You must attend to this very significant idea when you prepare to interview. Skilled though you may be in the art of conversation and adept at the conventions of idle chatter, an interview demands much more of you because of the goals that must be served. If you forget this element, you will merely be conversing when you believe you are interviewing. And because you are only conversing, you may not achieve your objectives. As an interviewer, you must know what you are doing and why. As a conversationalist, you will be no more effective in situations requiring skilled interviewing than a duffer playing in a professional golf tournament.

We have now excluded from our interview model many types of human discourse and, in the process, have clarified your perception of what an interview really is. So far we have seen that an interview involves two people speaking to each other for some purpose other than the pleasure of the conversation. But these elements do not round out the complete picture of the interview because there is one other situation that comes to mind that involves a "conversation with a purpose" but hardly fits our definition of an interview.

THE INTERROGATION.   A witness on the stand in a court of law is certainly engaged in an oral exchange with either the prosecuting or the defending attorney, and a prisoner suspected of a felony may interact very intensively with an inquiring detective. These "conversations" certainly have extrinsic purposes, but the question remains: Are they interviews? Most of us would deny quickly that such oral exchanges in a face-to-face situation comply with our interview model, but we might find it difficult to explain why.

An interview requires some spontaneity of response and freedom of interaction between the two parties. They meet in privacy and in a climate of mutual respect, and each is free to end the encounter at any time. In a courtroom the interchange between a witness and an attorney is neither private nor spontaneous.

In practice, a suspected felon is not usually free to speak or to remain silent as he chooses or to determine the conversation at his pleasure. While few of us would consider such events as interviews, many so-called interviews really are nothing more than interrogations. You must always remember that an interview is *not* an interrogation, and, whatever the circumstances, the interviewee is never on trial. A genuine interview, therefore, is conducted in a climate of spontaneity and mutual respect.

What Interviews Are

A review of what we have said so far indicates that indirectly we have already identified the elements of the interview. First, we stated that the interview is a tool; this implies that it is a means to an end and not an end in itself. If the interview is but a means, then there are certain contexts in which its use is appropriate and others in which it is inappropriate. To utilize an interview effectively, therefore, we must first identify the situations that make its employment advantageous.

We have also said that the interview is a medium for the transmission of information from one person to another. Unlike the conversation, the interview focuses upon a specific subject that is *relevant* to its situation. We shall refer to the situation and the subject matter as the interview structure, to which we will devote most of this book. We call these elements *structural* because they represent the more objective components of the interview that emanate from the organizational milieu itself and are reasonably independent of the interview participant.

We have also asserted that an interview requires the participation of two people who interact freely with one another. This specification constitutes not only the essence of the interview but also its source of error. Because the parties bring to the interview unique backgrounds, experiences, ideas, and behavioral patterns, every interview becomes an unreproducible encounter. We shall refer to these aspects as *functional* because they are determined by the parties to the interview and are, therefore, subjective.

The structural and the functional elements are considerably interdependent, but to further our understanding of interview dynamics, we shall explore each element separately.

The Structure of the Interview   An interview is initiated to achieve one or several objectives, takes place in a particular physical and social setting, and occurs as part of a procedural sequence of events. Further, it focuses on the present, past, or future behavior, beliefs, opinions, attitudes, or convictions of the interviewee. We call the setting, the sequence, and the objectives of the interview its *context* and the substance around which the conversation centers its *content*.

The context of an employment interview, for example, includes the job under consideration and the place where the interview is conducted (setting), the other selection procedures the applicant has already completed or will undergo (sequence), and the decision to be made when the interview is completed (objectives). The content of this interview includes the applicant's previous experience, education, vocational aspirations, and behavior during the interview.

INTERVIEW CONTEXT.   An interview is not an isolated event but rather is embedded in a complex social matrix and constitutes but one of a sequence of events. As an interviewer, therefore, you cannot perform very effectively if you fail to take into account the total situation and your immediate objectives. If in an exit interview, for example, you see your task as merely the dissemination of factual information and a final paycheck to a departing employee, you will not achieve the real purpose of the interview. However, when you are aware of your main job of obtaining useful information about the exiting employee's attitudes, you will get maximum value from this technique.

The context of the personnel interview will always relate to some function of personnel management—selection, performance evaluation, attitude assessment, termination control, or career counseling. But between the broad purpose and the actual interview lies an awareness of immediate intentions. Each personnel interview falls into one of three groups according to these immediate intentions: *information-exchange, problem-solving,* or *decision-making.*

Since the interviewer's intentions will almost always determine the interview content and its functional aspects, it will be helpful to consider briefly what we mean by each category of interviewing.

THE INFORMATION-EXCHANGE INTERVIEW. In certain personnel situations, the immediate intention of the interviewer is solely to give or to obtain information. The interview is employed in such a context to facilitate the exchange of this information, and as far as the interviewee is concerned, the termination of the interview ends the matter.

The fact-finding interview of the census taker is a clear-cut illustration of a simple information-exchange interview. It is not merely an oral questionnaire—true enough, the functional factors are so insignificant that the information exchange can be carried on at a most impersonal level—but, even in this unemotional, matter-of-fact encounter the interviewer will still have to evaluate the interviewee's behavior to ascertain the reliability of his or her responses. The employee attitude survey interview lies at the opposite end of the spectrum of complexity because it requires very skillful interaction to identify the largely unverbalized attitudes of the employee toward the work environment.

The information-exchange interview is the most elementary of personnel interviews because its purpose is the simple acquisition or dispensation of information. This does not deny the complexity of some such interviews but merely establishes the principle that the range of complexity is relatively lower than that of other interview types and that its basic techniques are easier to master. The information-exchange interview is most effectively adapted to opinion sampling and to market research activities; it is used extensively in sociological and anthropological research. In personnel administration, information-giving interviews are useful for employee orientation and on-the-job coaching; information-getting interviews are used chiefly for termination control and for employee attitude surveys.

THE PROBLEM-SOLVING INTERVIEW. Interviews are frequently initiated for the explicit purpose of resolving some kind of employee problem. Usually the problem stems from the employee's lack of capacity to do something he or she wishes to do or from the fact that mutually antagonistic goals are causing inner conflicts. In such situations, the interviewee enters the interview not so much with the intent of giving or getting information, but with the expectation that the interviewer has the insight or the authority to help resolve the conflict and to effect any necessary behavioral changes.

Although fact finding and information exchange may form an integral part of the problem-solving process, the immediate intention of this interview is to develop a relationship between the two parties that will enable the interviewee to adopt a more satisfactory behavior outside the interview. The problem-solving interview, therefore, is primarily a learning experience for the interviewee.

Since the complexity of the problem-solving interview depends on the nature of the problem, some may be quite simple and easy to handle and others may require years of education and experience for their successful execution. The psychotherapeutic interview is considered to be one of the most difficult and challenging interviews, not because of the skills required to conduct it, but because of the nature of the problem. In the personnel field, major problem-solving interviews include the performance-evaluation interview in which the job behavior of the interviewee is explored for developmental purposes, the counseling interview in which the job satisfaction of the interviewee is examined for career guidance purposes, the grievance interview with a dissatisfied employee, and the placement interview with the problem employee. Each interview is directed at the proximate goal of changing the employees' behavior by helping them to develop clearer insights into personal needs, attitudes, and current behavior.

THE DECISION-MAKING INTERVIEW.   The most commonplace personnel interview is the employment interview, as a result of which the interviewer must make a decision about the interviewee. This decision-making function of the employment interviewer presupposes three separate and prior steps: description, evaluation, and prediction. The selection interviewer must first elicit sufficient information from the applicant (description) to compare with a set of preestablished job requirements (evaluation) in order to draw a conclusion about the probable future behavior of the interviewee in a specific set of circumstances (prediction). On the basis of this prediction, the interviewer then makes a decision to refer or not to refer, to reject or not to reject, to employ or not to employ.

Because you, as an employment interviewer, possess something sought by the interviewee, you clearly have the advantage. You conduct the interview on your terms, set the tone, establish the norms, and otherwise call the turn on the behavior demanded of the applicant. This advantage makes the employment interview appear to be simple to conduct, but it is actually the most difficult because the description, evaluation, and prediction of human behavior is subject to gross errors.

INTERVIEW CONTENT.   After the situation, the broad objectives, and the immediate intentions have been clearly delineated, the interviewer must next decide what to talk about, what information is needed, and what information must be conveyed. The context of the interview will naturally prescribe these items for you, but you, the interviewer, must also know something about the information capacity of the interview. Interview content can be considered in terms of its *sources* and its *levels*. The sources of information consist of the interviewee's self-report and interview behavior. Applicants will tell a lot about themselves such as their age, education, marital status, and even, if asked, their food preferences. As an interviewer, you can observe the applicant's conduct during the interview for diction, personal appearance, and general emotional tone.

There are also levels of information discussed or transmitted during the interview: *factual* data such as address, employment dates, and salary; *subjective* data, including conclusions, opinions, feelings, and beliefs; or *subconscious* data, including values, convictions, and attitudes. The meaning of and the distinctions among these three data levels are more fully explained in Chapter 2.

An interview that focuses upon facts alone is called a *primary* interview. The employment interview, which concentrates almost exclusively on facts, is a good example of a primary decision-making interview. The census interview is an example of a primary information-exchange interview.

An interview concerned with a combination of factual and subjective data is called a *secondary* interview. The assessment interview is an example of a secondary decision-making interview; the performance-evaluation interview is an illustration of a secondary problem-solving interview.

An interview concerned with the deeper subconscious values and attitudes of the interviewee is called a *tertiary* or depth interview. A depth interview with a consumer to find out why he or she purchases a particular soap powder is an example of a tertiary information-exchange interview; a therapeutic interview by a psychiatrist can be classified as a tertiary problem-solving interview.

The Function of the Interview   Let us suppose that as an interviewer you plan to talk to thirty people applying for a particular job. If you are fairly well versed in selection techniques, you will prepare a standard set of questions, establish a precise time schedule, and adopt a uniform pattern of behavior during each interview to make sure each applicant is considered impartially. In spite of your efforts, each interview will differ from the rest in hundreds of subtle ways ranging from each applicant's interpretation of your questions to his or her reactions to your personality. No matter how hard you try, these variations may be quite wide because in each interview, one party is always different. Therefore, in each interview you, too, are "a different person."

Each of us possesses our own unique set of perceptions, motivations, attitudes, previous experiences, and emotions that specify the nature of the interaction that will occur in the interview. But to complicate the matter still more, the interaction between each of us and our role plays a significant part in the quality of the interview.

ROLE INTERACTION.   During the interview, both parties really enact roles as they see them. A *role* is defined as a pattern of behavior performed to justify a person's occupancy of a position. The actions are linked to the position and not to the person who is temporarily occupying the position and include not only the person's ideas of how the role should be played but, more importantly, how other people feel the person should behave in the role. Thus, role enactment is limited not only by your own perceptions but also by other people's expectations.

The interaction between your perception of your role as an interviewer and the other person's expectations influences the progress of the interview. In all fairness, it would be unreasonable to expect an interviewee to behave any differently than in everyday conversations. On the other hand, as an interviewer you should be fully aware of the actions appropriate to your role and should have at your disposal a repertoire of behavior to implement it most effectively. Also, your appreciation of the interviewee's understandably inadequate role perception should prompt you to coach and to guide the person.

There are three sets of actions that guide the way you play this role. First there are the *task* behaviors that are intended to accomplish the main objectives of the interview; then there are the *rapport* behaviors that help the interviewer to establish a bond of communication with the interviewee; and finally there are those unique *self-centered* actions that constitute your response to your personal needs. In Chapter 3, we shall say more about the dimensions of role behavior.

PERSONALITY INTERACTION.   The last element in our definition of an interview is the most elusive and yet the most significant. The term "personality" has many meanings and various implications. We shall use the word to mean those distinguishing qualities that set a person apart from all other persons and that are the result of genetic, constitutional, social, and cultural influences.

In an interview, two persons meet for a common purpose, each with an individual view of the world and an individual set of needs. These needs move each of them toward goals that each perceives as satisfying his or her own special situation. Each sees the interview differently; each views the other in a light illuminated by an individual perception; each acts and reacts to the other in accord with a combination of personal characteristics. This is what we mean by personality interaction, and it is this aspect that makes each interview so different and so challenging.

To exploit this personality interaction successfully, you may choose one of three *styles* of interview behavior: directed, nondirective, or probing. The style employed influences the way in which the two personalities conflict or converge and determines the degree to which you can probe the more sensitive, subtle areas of the interviewee's personality.

chapter 2

Human Communication

> Most of those I converse with, speak the same language
> I here write; but whether they think the same thoughts,
> I cannot say. —MONTAIGNE, *Selected Essays*

The principal event that takes place in an interview is an exchange of information. Because it is such an ordinary, everyday event, the transmission of an idea from one person to another is accepted as a rather simple, uncomplicated transaction. At least, most people behave as though it were so. There is, however, a surprising amount of evidence in scientific literature, if not within the average person's experience, to support a contrary assertion—that complete and accurate communication between people is quite uncommon. And when an emotional factor accompanies the communication, as it very often does, the probability of transmitting an idea, intact and undistorted, to another person is considerably reduced.

There was a manager of a small food processing plant, for example, who wished to communicate his feelings of good will to his subordinates on Christmas Eve. Accepted by them as a stern taskmaster the year round, they nonetheless gravely shook hands with him and exchanged the season's greetings on that one day of the work year. The manager returned to his office after this annual ritual quietly satisfied that he had convinced them of his deep regard for them. Yet, all of his employees were certain that he was really checking to see whether any of them had been drinking on the job!

To improve your interviewing skills, you must first become deeply aware of the complexities and the pitfalls of the communication process. What may make the task more difficult, however, is your assumption that since you have been conversing since childhood, you are quite good at it. Your conversational habits, unfortunately, can inhibit your interviewing effectiveness by misleading you into the belief that every time you converse with another person, you both really understand one another. The facts are often otherwise. Only when you appreciate what is involved in the communication process will you begin to lay aside your everyday conversational patterns and adopt the more difficult but effective style of exchanging ideas with another person.

To understand fully what is involved in an interview, we must first examine separately its two essential elements, communication and human interaction, and then explore how they combine to create a powerful, dynamic vehicle of human communication.

Understanding Communication

The word "communication" is one of the most overused and misused in the English language. Sometimes it is used to mean something imparted or sent, like a letter or a telegram; sometimes as a transportation route for supplies; and other times as a passage way from one place to another. For our purposes, we have to do better. We must agree on a clear and precise understanding of what communication really is.

What is Communication? The word "communication," derived from the Latin, holds a common ancestry with words like "community" and "communion." It means, therefore, much more than sending, or transmitting, or receiving. It implies a sharing of something with another human being, and this something is neither money, nor ancestry, nor citizenry but information and ideas.

In the same way that Milton spoke of good, "the more communicated, the more abundant grows," the sharing of an idea is much more than the mere process of giving or getting something—it enriches both parties to the transaction. From this concept of sharing, then, we can infer two principles central to the idea of the interview as a communication medium.

First, in the strictest sense of the word, communication can occur only between and among human beings. We know that most animals have the ability to attract the attention of other beings, whether animal or human, by means of such rudimentary signs as grunts, groans, squeals, barks, or chirps, but this activity in no sense constitutes communication in the limited sense we use here. In this sense, communication refers to a complex process of idea sharing that is not limited to the here and now, can be carried on across a thousand miles or years, may have no reference to the real or the concrete, and may employ as its vehicle of meaning an extensive repertoire of abstract symbols. Since such a process is possible only for human beings, the phrase "human communication" is really redundant.

Second, the most effective medium of communication is the interview. This principle will take the remainder of this chapter to explain, but in so doing, we should get a clearer insight into the dynamics of the interview process.

Information Theory   Until the middle of the nineteenth century, studies of communication were devoted exclusively to its philosophical and artistic applications. With the invention of the telephone, telegraph, radio, television, and ultimately, the computer, engineers developed a discipline known as *information theory* to specify precisely the capacities of various telecommunications systems. This theory is concerned mainly with the correct transmission of signals or the electric representations of messages and not at all with their content or their purposes. The fact that information theory is much too complicated for this presentation does not preclude us from borrowing its basic model and a few of its terms.

Conveying a message from one place to another implies an information source to emit a signal, a channel to carry it, and a destination to receive it. These three essential elements of the process are illustrated in Figure 1, but as the diagram indicates, there is more to it than this.

The message emanating from the information source must first be encoded, then transmitted via signals over a channel to a receiver specifically engineered to pick up these signals, then decoded, and passed on to the destination.

To inform the information source of how completely and accurately the message was received, the destination must respond in some way.

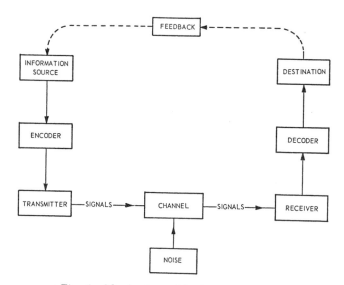

Fig. 1   The basic model of communication

This response or feedback to the information source closes the loop in the information system. An effective communication system must always provide this "closed loop" which permits continuous feedback from destination to information source so that increasingly accurate data are transmitted. This function of feeding information signals back from the output or receiver end of the communication loop to the input or transmitter end is illustrated by such error-correcting or "goal-seeking" systems as guidance mechanisms in intercontinental ballistic missiles. The human body has many feedback mechanisms to regulate such activities as heartbeat, body temperature, and blood pressure. The thermostat on the wall in a living room is a common example of a feedback servomechanism that informs the input apparatus (the furnace) of its output (the room temperature).

Information is transmitted over a system by means of signs and codes. A sign is any physical event used to represent something else in the communication process. A code is an agreed upon transformation of one set of signs to another. Human language, for example, constitutes a specific set of signs that can be expressed in many codes, such as the alphabet, and even transformed from one code to another, as in the Morse code that translates the alphabet into a series of dots and dashes. Communication requires that both sender and receiver use the same set of codes and signs. If a highway department wishes to warn drivers of a particularly dangerous highway intersection, it posts a "sign." On that sign are placed a number of codes to indicate danger, such as a cross representing an intersection or the unique shape of the sign or the use of the color red or all three. None of these codes, however, will communicate the message to the driver unless he knows the meaning of what they represent.

Coded information is projected via special equipment called a transmitter over a particular medium, termed a channel, to a specially constructed receiver. In television, for example, the transmitter, an expensive, complicated camera located in a central studio, sends wave signals over a channel to specially constructed antennas that receive the waves and pass them on to the decoder, the television set, which converts the message from waves into electronic impulses which are, in turn, transformed into light and sound stimuli.

While passing from transmitter to receiver over a channel, the signal can be weakened by outside interference called *noise*. "Snow" on a television screen or static on the radio are examples of noises that weaken the reception of the desired signal. If the noise is sufficiently intense, the message will be received in a distorted or incomplete state, or it may not get through at all.

To overcome noise and to make certain that there is no error in the message reception, the information source usually builds *redundancy* into its transmission. In other words, the sender overcommunicates by including in the message information not strictly necessary. For example, the highway department was redundant in representing danger in three ways—by the cross, by the shape of the sign, and by the color red.

At zero redundancy, the communication loop is perfectly efficient, but any errors in transmission or reception owing to noise or other disturbances in the "loop" will go undetected by the receiver. For example, if an employee receives a letter erroneously instructing him or her to report for work on the tenth instead of the eleventh of the month, the person will have no way of knowing that the message is inaccurate unless it redundantly includes the day of the week. The possibility of reception error is materially reduced by redundancy.

The ideal communication system provides a minimum of noise, a maximum of immediate and continuous feedback, and sufficient redundancy to eliminate reception error. It takes only the briefest reflection to realize that the interview is the communication medium with the most potential for noise reduction, feedback, and redundancy. When people earnestly desire to communicate with one another, when they really want to make certain that they understand and are understood, they meet and converse face-to-face and in private. Since this is a precise definition of an interview, our second principle, that the interview is the most effective interpersonal communications medium, is confirmed.

Human communication, however, is far more complicated than the basic engineering model might imply because there are many more variables to deal with than signs, codes, noise, redundancy, and feedback. These additional variables represent the psychosocial influences that affect the outcome of every human communication encounter far more than the physical elements.

Understanding Human Behavior

The pattern of interaction that permits the two participants to act upon, to influence, and to modify each other's perceptual world distinguishes the interview as a communications medium. To utilize it effectively, we must examine this interactional pattern more closely. While personal interaction is a rather ordinary event in our daily life, the interaction that occurs in an interview is not ordinary.

As an interviewer, you have the somewhat conflicting assignments of not only stimulating and responding to the interviewee's behavioral cues but also of observing, describing, evaluating, and reporting what takes place. To perform this multidimensional task, you must not only master the interview technique but also know a good deal about the complexities of human behavior.

The fact that in every interview you conduct at least one of the parties will always be the same—you—is a point in your favor, provided that you have an awareness of your needs, motives, and attitudes. Without this self-insight, you can never really be certain how much of yourself is subconsciously woven into the interview outcome. When you interview, the Socratic dictum "Know thyself" applies very literally.

Since the other party to the interview will nearly always be different, you must have a general idea of what makes people tick. In the next few pages, we shall try to provide you with a brief introduction to human behavior. Since our treatment can only skim the surface of this complex subject, we suggest that you consult other references for additional insights and information.

What Makes People Tick? Even the most casual observation of the countless ways in which people behave daily inclines us to agree with Sophocles, who wrote over 2500 years ago "Wonders are many and none is more wonderful than man." Human behavior, though wonderful, is really not so mysterious. It is often difficult for people to fathom the actions of others simply because they do not see the situation in the same way and are unaware of each other's motives.

People act for reasons which are usually, but not always, best known to themselves. When they do not know, they may require the careful, patient assistance of a professional therapist to help uncover their inner motives. The fact remains that reasons do exist. Underneath every human action lies a complex series of motives. A *motive* is simply a connection between a felt *need* and a perceived *goal*. A boy turns on a water faucet to fill his glass. We can assume that he feels a need called thirst resulting from a lack of moisture in his body. His goal is the restoration of his bodily water balance by drinking the water. His motive, therefore, in acting the way he does, is to quench his thirst. This presumes, of course, that he actually drinks the water. He might pour it down his brother's back, in which case another need was operative and, perhaps, a far more satisfying goal was achieved.

Behind every action, however obscure and ulterior it may be, are felt needs and perceived goals, linked in a chain of activities that is called a *drive*. Some drives, such as hunger and thirst, are inborn; others, like the drive for power or position, are learned from the culture in which a person matures. The first set of drives is called *primary*; the second is called *secondary*. Usually, human behavior is a manifestation of secondary or *social* drive. But these drives nearly always represent the bare surface of human motivation. When we peel off layer after layer of social behavior, we encounter the real motivating forces underlying them: the primary needs, both physiological and psychological.

PHYSIOLOGICAL DRIVES. There is a set of drives that originate in the undeniable physiological needs of the human body and motivate behavior toward goals that will lead to their satisfaction. Prolonged failure to satisfy physiological needs results ultimately in impaired health, disease, and even in death. These drives are often called "animal" because human beings share them with the animal kingdom.

Although these drives are primary motivators in every human being, civilization has so gratuitously rearranged matters that they are taken for granted by the average adult, and their satisfaction is subordinated to a host of ancillary social needs. In most segments of Western society, people are able to satisfy most physiological needs without much effort. But wherever they are satisfied at the price of a hard, bitter struggle, as in the developing areas of the world and in the lower socioeconomic groups in Western countries, they remain powerful motivators. And even among the affluent, when primary needs are threatened, as in a fire or a shipwreck, they will quickly reassert themselves as major determinants of behavior.

PSYCHOLOGICAL DRIVES. Another complex set of needs is strictly human because these needs stem from a person's unique position in nature as a rational, volitional creature. These *psychological needs* have to do with a person's desire for knowledge and experience, for understanding and mastery of things in the world at large, for appreciation and recognition from other people, and ultimately for self-realization.

Whether these needs are primary is a matter of contention among philosophers and behavioral scientists, but it is quite clear that the way in which they are satisfied is a function of learning and maturation. Although people are occasionally overwhelmed by other needs, the satisfaction of their "human" needs, as we prefer to call them, is essential to healthy development and functioning. The persistent thwarting of these needs leads eventually to emotional disturbances and to physical illnesses.

SOCIAL DRIVES. Since people are also social animals, they have a set of needs that have been taught them by various political, social, cultural, religious, and economic organizations with which they identify. These needs, therefore, are definitely acquired after birth.

The manner in which people express their social drives depends on their environment and on their particular stage of physical, emotional, and intellectual development. As experience widens, an individual's social drive becomes increasingly complex, expanding from the desire for parental effection to the need for esteem of particular peer groups and finally to approval from society in general. This drive expresses itself in various social patterns and mores that dominate life: in the need for a college degree, for promotion, for a larger house in a better neighborhood.

All the affairs of people—the business activities, the political crises, the domestic tangles—all the strife and struggle can be viewed in terms of people working to achieve individual goals that will satisfy the complex needs with which they have been endowed by birth or which have been taught them by society.

In Chapter 10 we shall discuss the ways in which work satisfies the animal, human, and social needs of each employee and how the interview plays its part in contributing to that satisfaction. Some types of human behavior are marked by integrated, self-enhancing activities that are purposive, logical, and persistent. Most occupational activities are of this sort, and when they characterize a particular work group, there is harmony, efficiency, and usually productivity. But experience tells us that there are many instances of human behavior that are not quite so orderly or rational.

Sometimes people's actions are emotional, pointless, and self-destructive. The question is, therefore, what are the motives here? What prompts perfectly intelligent people to do things that can only hurt them, and, even more mystifying, what makes them keep on doing them? The answer to these pertinent questions will require us to examine another human quality, the self-concept.

The Self-concept   All people have ideas, feelings, and opinions about themselves that are of the utmost importance to them. This self-image, referred to by psychologists as the *concept of self*, forms a person's innermost sanctuary to be guarded with the strictest surveillance. People's behavior can be explained in terms of the enhancement or the defense of this self-concept.

To clarify this assertion, let us look at the need-goal sequence again. All behavior, we said, is motivated, that is, it constitutes a response to some felt need. But, unfortunately between the need and the goal, there occur with most distressing frequency all kinds of obstacles and barriers. When an obstacle appears in the path of an activity that is directed toward a goal, the activity must be altered in some way, however slight. The resulting behavior is now not merely motivated, but frustrated, and, as such, tends to become more emotional, less constructive, and, therefore, less rational.

FRUSTRATION.   Frustration is an external circumstance or an act of some other person that prevents the attainment of a goal. It can be relatively minor, such as failure of a picture tube in a television set, or catastrophic, like a severe illness or death of a loved one. The resulting behavior is no longer directed at a goal but at the tension within the person that is causing the discomfort and distress.

It is apparent that most people can tolerate frustrations brought about by things or circumstances much more readily than those caused by other people. A person will be quite philosophical if it rains and prevents him or her from playing golf, but if the spouse forgets to put gas in the car, the same person may explode with anger. Most people can handle the ordinary disappointments that crop up daily, but the immature, maladjusted person will react violently to even the mildest frustration. Again, even well-adjusted people have those days when they feel blue or depressed and their frustration "threshold" is so low that they will respond to a petty disappointment in a manner quite out of proportion to it.

Frustrated behavior, in contrast to goal-oriented behavior has three distinguishing characteristics. It tends, first of all, to be *aggressive* in a physical way, such as kicking the wall or slamming a door, or in a verbal way, such as shouting, raving, joking maliciously, or using sarcasm or irony. It will also tend to be *regressive*, that is, reverting to a more immature level of behavior, such as resorting to pouting or temper tantrums that are more appropriate to children. It will also be *fixated*, or tend to persist despite its uselessness.

Frustrations, of course, are not always harmful because in the form of challenges they can arouse a person to activity that will serve him better in the long run.

CONFLICT.   A conflict is the arousal of two incompatible drives at the same time. The analysis of typical responses to conflict will be discussed in more detail later when we review anxiety.

Interviewers encounter conflicted and frustrated behavior in many situations often without realizing it. Knowing what the block is can often serve to explain what is otherwise mystifying interview behavior. For example, the employment interview itself is a frustration for an applicant because it represents for the person a hurdle that must be surmounted to achieve the desired goal of employment. Within the interview, an answer to a question may induce a conflict when the interviewee wishes to tell the truth but fears a negative reaction from the interviewer. Each conflict builds up within the interviewee feelings of disequilibrium that we call *tension* and will be in direct proportion to the intensity of the forces working upon him or her.

Now tension, in and of itself, is not necessarily an undesirable condition. Without it a person would be powerless to act since a tension-free organism is a dead organism. It is only a particularly unpleasant type of tension that people try to avoid as much as possible, a tension termed *anxiety*. To understand behavior in response to conflict, we must examine this condition more thoroughly because it is present in most interviews to some degree.

ANXIETY. Anxiety is a vague apprehension or dread of some ambiguous, ill-defined danger that can be acutely uncomfortable and personally distressing. Physically it is quite similar to fear, being accompanied by trembling, heart palpitation, sweating, or other reactions of the autonomic nervous system. But anxiety is quite different from fear because it is sensed as personal and persuasive and arises from within the self. Fear is a response to a real danger; anxiety is a response to an undetermined threat.

Mild anxiety is a useful drive when it moves a person to correct minor personal difficulties, to mix more socially, or to work harder on the job. But if the conflicting motives within the person are so ambiguous or so unrecognized that the anxiety becomes extremely intense, the resulting drive will dominate his total behavior to the exclusion of all other motives. The person will then adopt behavior patterns that have anxiety reduction as their sole objective. To a less perceptive observer, such actions might appear to be wholly irrational because they are unrewarding and contrary to the person's best interests. The executive who, despite the fact that he is wrecking his career, continues to drink heavily is responding to an anxiety drive.

The interview situation is an anxiety-inducing process for an interviewee because of its ambiguity and because of the conflict in motives that it so often arouses. This anxiety can be relieved through the empathy of the interviewer. If the interviewer is also tense and anxious, as is often the case in supervisor-subordinate interviews, he or she will only increase the interviewee's anxiety. There is research evidence to support the hypothesis that a person who interacts with a more anxious person will also become more anxious.[1] There is less substantial evidence for the opposite effect of communicating comfort. It seems to be much more difficult for an interviewer to reduce the tension of an interviewee's anxiety than to increase it.

TRANSACTIONAL ANALYSIS. As part of the maturational process, people learn to protect themselves against extreme distress stemming from situations that might undermine their feelings of self-worth. They gradually acquire persistent, largely unconscious ways of behaving called *defense mechanisms*, which become so unconscious and involuntary that people perform them even when they no longer require them. These defense mechanisms are often referred to as "games." The latter term is derived from a model of interpersonal transactions developed by Eric Berne[2] called Transactional Analysis. This system is based on the idea that every human communication, verbal or nonverbal, is a good

[1] P. O. Mattson, "Communicated Anxiety in a Two-person Situation," *Journal of Consulting Psychology*, 24:488–495, 1960.
[2] Eric Berne, *Games People Play*, (New York: Grove Press, 1964).

or bad transaction between people. Transactional Analysis proposes that each person is a total system which operates from three components or subsystems—parent, adult, child.

The parent subsystem is judgmental, critical of the self and others, tradition-bound, and paternalistic. The adult is logical, nonemotional, fact-oriented, and oriented to the here and now. The child is spontaneous, fun-loving, curious, and self-centered.

All three subsystems have a place in the practices and feelings of the total person, so that each of us acts, at times, like a parent, adult, or child. Your self-concept determines to what degree and in what situations you will use behavior that is predominantly parental, adult, or child-like.

LIFE POSITIONS.   During childhood and adolescence, you develop a perception of yourself as a distinct person, as a *self* separate and distinct from all other objects and people in the world. Just as you form attitudes toward these other objects and people, you form an attitude toward yourself that may or may not be realistic. As you pass through life, you continually test this idea of yourself in numerous situations and in diverse activities. You retain those ideas that please you, and you reject and replace those ideas that do not meet the test of reality as you perceive it.

Almost every specific goal of behavior, therefore, has the more distant objective of increasing feelings of self-esteem. Since this need is so basic, its thwarting will generate tensions and anxieties in a person.

If, for example, a young girl has difficulty developing a concept of herself characterized by adequacy and self-respect or if those whom she loves and depends on convince her of her unworthiness, she will spend the remainder of her life and a good deal of her available energy trying to establish a defense against what she has come to believe is an inadequate self. By the time she becomes an adult, she will probably have acquired a highly specific set of behavioral mechanisms to cope with any situation, most of which will be ill-suited to the purpose for which they are employed.

All people experience moments of insecurity in early life, but fortunately because of opportunities to try them out in a number of "real world" encounters in the home, in the neighborhood, in school, and in the community, they will develop reasonably stable, healthy images of themselves.

The highly respected vocational psychologist Donald Super in his theory of vocational adjustment underscores the importance of the self-concept in the world of work. The choice of an occupation, he says, is one of the principal points at which you are called upon to state rather explicitly your concept of yourself and to say definitely, "I am this or that kind of person."[3] In holding and adjusting to the job, he asserts, you find out whether that job permits you to play the role you want to play, whether the role the job makes you play is compatible with your self-concept, and whether in this process of testing your self-concept against reality, you can actually live up to this picture of yourself. In choosing an occupation, Super concludes that one is, in effect, choosing a means of implementing a self-concept.[4]

Harris[5] has defined four basic states of the self-concept that he refers to as "life positions." He characterizes the "I'm OK—you're not OK" and "I'm not OK—you're OK" as pathological. The "I'm not OK—you're OK" position first adopted in childhood, he says, is highly defensive and dependent. Through the maturational process, this position can be transformed into the last and healthiest, the "I'm OK—you're OK" position.

The personnel interview, as we shall point out in the next two chapters, represents an excellent medium for giving other people a strong feeling that you think they are OK, and that you value them as human beings. In Chapter 3, we shall examine some specific ways of doing this by giving the interviewee "positive strokes," which are acts or words of consideration that make the other person feel "all right."

The Interview as a Communication Medium

We are now ready to pull together the separate ideas of human interaction and communication into a single model that will illuminate the personality dynamics that serve as the principle vehicle of communication in the interview.

Psychosocial Influences   The information theorist focuses on the signal transmission and ignores its meaning. Those who are concerned with the psychosocial aspects of communication must deal with such psychological variables as human perception, needs, motivation, attitudes, and the social and cultural context in which the information exchange occurs.

The social scientist is concerned with the answer to the question "Who said what to whom, with what effect?" Since the general purpose of communication is to share ideas, the message input is represented

---

[3] Donald E. Super, *The Psychology of Careers* (New York: Harper & Row Publishers, Inc., 1957), p. 191.

[4] *Ibid.*, p. 196.

[5] Thomas A. Harris, *I'm OK—You're OK* (New York: Harper & Row Publishers, Inc., 1969).

by the intention of the information source, that is, by the person speaking. The clear understanding of the sender's intentions represents the output. The perceived behavior of the receiver provides the sender with feedback concerning the accuracy with which the message has been received.

In Figure 2 we have modified the basic model of communication to reflect the interaction of interview communication. The information source is now a person with an intention of transmitting a message for some reason. This message is encoded into words, gestures, or other physical events that are transmitted by means of the vocal cords, the lips, or the general body musculature. The signals are audio-visual stimuli that are picked up by the other person's sensory organs, and through the perceptual mechanisms are decoded into meaningful ideas that enable the receiver to understand and to share the sender's ideas and intentions. The receiver, then, by means of appropriate behavioral *cues*, feeds back to the sender confirmation of the fact that the message has been received. This feedback can be almost anything from an imperceptible nod to a vehement retort. A blank or puzzled facial expression indicates that the message did not get across, that the idea was not shared. If I ask a man, for example, to close the window and he smiles or nods or tips his hat, I understand immediately that he did not get my message, that perhaps we are not sharing the same signs, and therefore that he cannot comprehend my language. I must therefore

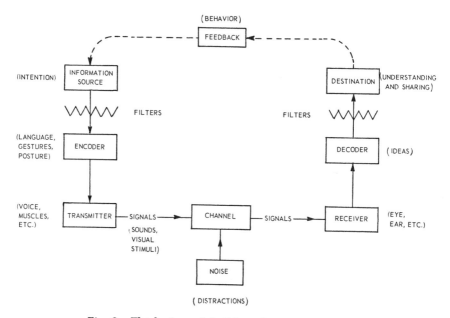

Fig. 2   The basic model of interview communication

resort to other signs, gestures rather than words, and when I see him close the window, I know for sure that my idea that the room would be better off with the window shut has been shared by him.

In communications among people, noise takes on proportions of greater significance and amplitude than in the engineering model. The strength of a signal can be reduced materially not only by such physiological phenomena as sound, light, heat, a hard chair, a high carbon dioxide content in the air, or a low blood sugar level in the receiver, but also the psychological effects of nervous tension, anxiety, emotional stress, and insecurity and by the social and cultural impact of ethnic differences, class consciousness, social customs, and individual habits.

Psychosocial noises are often much more distracting and block communication more effectively than physical noises. Since there is no way that they can be eliminated completely, you must rely heavily on feedback mechanisms and redundancy. You must learn to develop sensitivity to the subtle but distinct cues given to you by the interviewee that enable you to gauge how accurately you are transmitting and receiving information.

Figure 2 introduces another element into the basic model of interview communication: *filters* between information source and encoding, and between decoding and destination. These filters deserve a little closer scrutiny. Despite the physical excellence of the information system, the receiver may not receive the message in the way intended by the transmitter. Such a communication breakdown is usually due to the perceptual screens of each person through which all incoming and outgoing ideas must pass.

This filtering mechanism consists simply of the sum total of an individual's felt needs, prior experiences, attitudes, and his life position. Every message sent or received is always referred to this psychological field for meaning and relation to the self, and unless a message can be so related, it will be treated as ambiguous or meaningless.

If *A* desires to transmit an idea to *B*, he must pass it through his own filters first, even before he converts the idea into language or into another sign. *B* then picks up the transmitted signals, decodes them through his perceptual apparatus, and organizes them meaningfully in terms of his own past experiences. As a result of this complex process, *A*'s original idea may be twisted beyond recognition, and even with the most imaginative redundancy and a high degree of sensitivity to feedback cues, *A* may never share his idea with *B*.

Personality Interaction   The interaction that occurs between two people in an interview is also diagrammed in Figure 2. It starts in the upper left part of the diagram within the box labeled "Information Source" and continues counterclockwise around the page. As an interviewer, your life position determines your attitude toward the interviewee and your preliminary expectation of what should occur in the interview. This combination of life position, then, prescribes the game you will play in conducting the interview based on the goals that you perceive as satisfying the complex set of needs you feel, needs that include both the explicit purpose of the interview and your implicit personal drives.

Suppose, for example, that to cope with some deep-seated feelings of not being OK, the interviewer plays the game of aggression, masked under its more socially acceptable form, condescension. To satisfy this need for ego support and the employer's need (to consider an applicant for employment), the interviewer's behavior will be directed not only at information exchange but also at securing deference and submission from the interviewee. This outward behavior may be officious, impersonal, and abrupt.

This particular outward behavior represents an "input," that is, the interviewer's contribution to the interview interaction. It may not facilitate the attainment of the explicit goal of the interview, employment consideration, and it may even hinder it, but it will, hopefully, satisfy a more pressing need, a need that stems from the innermost recesses of the interviewer's life position, from a feeling that all is somehow not OK.

Now let us examine what happens when the message is picked up by the interviewee. The input passes first through the perceptual screens, or filters, and is referred immediately to the memory drum for recall of how to deal effectively with such "inputs." This perceptual organization is in turn referred to the interviewee's life position and is processed there to form subsequent behavior toward the interviewer. These intentions are translated into outward behavior that constitutes feedback to the interviewer.

The condescending behavior described above might have been interpreted as "businesslike," "cold," or "hostile," depending on the interviewee's previous experiences, expectations, and, in the last analysis, self-concept. The behavior of the interviewee will reflect this interpretation and also previous experience in coping with businesslike, cold, or hostile people. If it is decided that the behavior is hostile and experience has taught the interviewee that the best way to meet hostility is by counteraggression, then the response to the condescension may be sarcasm, another form of oral aggression. This output undermines further the interviewer's feelings of inadequacy and stimulates even stronger defense mechanisms. It also reinforces the interviewer's basic life position that most people feel "You are not OK" and act accordingly.

This feedback therefore launches another cycle of behavior input, perception, evaluation, reaction, and feedback, modified to some extent by the previous feedback each of the parties in the interview has received. In the case we have described, the resulting interview interaction leads to a cold, impersonal encounter marked by overcontrol, formality, and little communication. If this pattern continues throughout the interview, the explicit goals of the interview will never be reached.

The communication diagram, then, is completed with the addition of these filters. It is now much more complex than the model of the information theorists. There are many points in the system where errors can occur or where the message can be distorted or lost altogether. The interview, as communication, as an information sharing system, is the most effective medium precisely because it enables the information source and destination to so interact that the "leaks" in the system, the noise interferences, the blocks, the gaps, and the filter distortions can be overcome by continuous feedback, by redundancy, and by the social functions of empathy and rapport. This will be discussed further in the next two chapters. But the difficulty of effective interviewing can now be appreciated. Each interview is an engagement of self-concepts and life positions, and since our perception of ourselves is largely unconscious, the outcome of every interview is influenced strongly by factors of which we are unaware.

chapter 3

The Dynamics of Interviewing

> All the world's a stage,
> And all the men and women merely players.
> They have their exits and their entrances;
> And one man in his time plays many parts.
> —WILLIAM SHAKESPEARE, *As You Like It*

An assembly plant manager became concerned with the performance of the assistant manager whose usually fine work and friendly attitude had slipped noticeably. The manager arranged a meeting with the subordinate for an open and frank exploration of the situation. While the assistant manager acted surprised, hurt, evasive, and indignant in the early part of the interview, the manager reacted patiently and understandingly, listening carefully for clues suggesting the real problem.

From the bits of information obtained, the manager began to piece the puzzle together. Because of preoccupation with personal matters, the superior had created an erroneous but plant-wide impression that the assistant manager was in disfavor. When coupled with rumors that the manager was shortly to be promoted to general manager, the idea had demoralized the subordinate. During this interview the manager not only reassured the assistant, but together they developed a plan to dissipate the false impression of plant personnel. If this manager had not been a skillful interviewer and had simply laid the law down to the assistant, the problem would have been aggravated rather than solved.

To be an effective interviewer, you have to be a very good listener. Whether you function as a fact finder, a counselor, or a decision maker, you are continually enacting the role of *participant-observer*. In the first place, you must participate actively in the interview; you must initiate the appropriate behavior designed to achieve interview goals; you must question the interviewee; you must guide the course of the conversation over the ground that must be covered; and you must respond quickly to the interviewee's leads and behavioral cues. You must also listen attentively, sensitively, and empathically; you must be astutely observant;

you must be aware constantly not only of what is being said but also of what is happening during the meeting; and you must take notes so that you can report fully and accurately exactly what occurred during the interview or describe in detail the personal traits of the interviewee.

To play this role of participant-observer, you must be familiar not only with the complexities of personal interaction and the intricacies of the communication process but also with the dimensions of the interviewer role.

You must accept the idea that you are essentially a leader, and that you are fully accountable for the outcome of the interview. You cannot divest yourself of this accountability nor can you attribute interview failure to the interviewee. It is completely up to you to assure a smooth flow of conversation along lines that are congruent with both the implicit and the explicit purposes of the interview. You must employ techniques that will enable the interviewee to follow your leads, to express himself or herself freely, and to participate actively in the interaction process.

To implement this participant role, you must have at your command a variety of actions that facilitate the development of a relationship between you and the interviewee that is likely to accomplish interview objectives. The actions that you must initiate will, of course, be most effective if they conform to your unique combination of personality characteristics and also to the structural aspects of the interview. You would accomplish little if your manners were obviously artificial and out of character, or if you used techniques in an employment interview that were more appropriate to a counseling interview.

Since interview interaction is basically a special form of group interaction, a classification of interview-role dimensions which describes the different roles played in well-functioning, cohesive groups seems appropriate. The system that we shall use is a modification of that originally presented by Benne and Sheats and by others associated with the National Training Laboratories at Bethel, Maine.[1]

According to this system there are three sets of dimensions to the interviewer's role: task, rapport, and self-centered.

TASK DIMENSIONS. Since an interview always has a purpose, you have to ask appropriate questions and say things that enable you to accomplish it. The things you say or do to fulfill your purpose are called *task behaviors*. You initiate the action, seek and give information, clarify, test, and summarize. These are the rational aspects of the interview.

RAPPORT DIMENSIONS. You must also adopt a pattern of behavior that will facilitate communication, that will build a bridge between you

[1] K. D. Benne and P. Sheats, "Functional Roles of Group Members," *Journal of Social Issues*, 4:42–45, 1948.

and the interviewee over which ideas can cross. The things you do and say to create a climate of warmth and support represent the *rapport* dimensions of the interview. Because they represent the emotional aspects of the interview, rapport skills are more subtle. Being the basis of successful interviewing, these skills consist of encouraging and releasing emotions, dealing with tension, and keeping the conversation flowing smoothly.

SELF-CENTERED DIMENSIONS. When your interview actions or conversations are intended solely to satisfy your own needs, you will build an effective barrier between you and the interviewees. These *self-centered* behaviors are to be avoided. You cannot respond to the interviewees' anger with anger, or to their sarcasm with sarcasm. You cannot put applicants down, you cannot make sure they know you are doing them a favor by interviewing them, nor can you make them feel sorry for you. If you do any of these things you will create an impossible climate, and you will get little information.

Task Role Behavior

In an interview you always have a purpose—to secure information, to help solve a problem, to decide whether to hire or not hire. To accomplish these tasks you have to give and get information. You do this in two distinct ways, by direct communication—asking questions and listening—and by indirect communication—that is, by the use of such techniques as silence and restatement.

But before considering the techniques of direct and indirect communication, we must first consider the problems inherent in the transmission and reception of information via the interview. Also, we must examine ways of regulating and controlling the interview to insure that reliable data are assembled with which correct and valid decisions may be made. Only after an understanding of the potential information capacity of the interview and modes of communication can we define its role dimensions.

The Information Capacity of the Interview
To determine the information capacity of the personnel interview, we must first define what we mean by the word "information," and that is a task not completed merely by reference to a dictionary and not fully explained by information theory alone. At the end of an interview, you will have collected a veritable storehouse of items or bits of information. You may have recorded various events in the interviewee's past life, dates, places, people, institutions; you may recall certain expressed feelings and opinions—political leanings, religious convictions, preferences for food, music, books, or companions; you may remember certain behavior—

outward demeanor, poise, nervous mannerisms, or voice inflection; and you may have already formed some tentative conclusions about the intellectual capacity, social skill, or general character of the applicant. This accumulated information forms the stuff of the interview, the raw material out of which are hewn the generalizations that lead to evaluation, prediction, and decision. To work this raw data correctly, you must temper your treatment with an awareness of their validity as objective information.

Any bit of information lies along a spectrum extending from hard, concrete, almost self-evident sense data to vague, generalized, subconscious data. Between the factual and subconscious extremes of the spectrum lies a middle ground composed of subjective, cognitive data.

Since there is really no clear-cut dividing line to mark each data area off from the others, it is the responsibility of the interviewer to appreciate their differences by keeping in mind that, in the words of Bertrand Russell, "what is actually given in sense is much less than most people suppose, and that much of what, at first sight seems to be given, is really inferred."[2]

FACTUAL DATA.   We refer to interview data as factual when they represent sensible events or actions in the present behavior or past life of the interviewee. A person's date of birth, for example, is a fact. Height, weight, color of hair, shade of blouse or necktie, and grammatical expression are facts. Smoking a cigarette, perspiring freely, or drumming one's fingers on the desk are also facts. The conclusion that the interviewee is "ill at ease" because of them is not a fact but a conclusion about the probable cause of such behavior. Applicants will report many facts about themselves which will be false, but insofar as the interviewer is concerned, the reported data continue to be factual until proved otherwise.

The task of an effective interviewer is, like the investigating officer in detective fiction, "to get the facts" and to discern the difference between facts and nonfacts. For factual data you need rely only upon your senses; you add nothing from your own experience, and you make certain that the interviewee adds nothing from opinions, feelings, or beliefs.

Facts, however, being purely descriptive, are by themselves of little or no possible value until other information is joined to them and a relationship is perceived. The instant the observer perceives a relationship and combines two separate and distinct events into a proposition, he or she has moved into the logical or subjective area of the informational spectrum.

---

[2] B. Russell, *Our Knowledge of the External World,* A Mentor Book Edition (New York: New American Library, 1960).

SUBJECTIVE DATA. Logic deals with the orderly and the correct relationships between separate phenomena and ideas. The observer is no longer involved with external reality, with a series of discrete events that other observers can describe in nearly identical terms. Now the observer is coping with the *noumena,* with events and apprehensions that go on only in the head, and while they may be just as important and valid in their own right, they are not facts or *phenomena.*

The subjective area of the spectrum can be divided into subcategories ranging from near factual to near psychological information. Closest to the factual sector of the scale are the demonstrable *conclusions* about the observable relationships between events, such as the deduction that all people are mortal, and *feelings* that describe the inner emotional state, the sentiments, the desires, the cravings, involving the individual's affective state. If a patient says, "I feel sad," he or she is reporting an event that, at least to that person, is real, concrete, and factual. The conclusion that two and two equal four is also verifiable to the senses and this too approximates factual information.

During an interview, the applicant will frequently precede a statement with the phrase "I feel," "I think," or "I believe," phrases that are inevitable signals of the forthcoming expression of an *opinion* or a *belief.* Opinions as verbal responses to questions are difficult to verify because they involve the interviewee's preferences and tastes. One employee, for example, may express the opinion that the supervisor is far too strict; another may feel that the same supervisor is too lenient, and both may be quite truthful.

A belief is much stronger and more enduring than an opinion, is less subject to change, and refers to an idea that is of some importance to its holder. An employee's opinion about the food in the cafeteria is more subject to change than a personal belief about a man's right to join or not to join a labor union.

SUBCONSCIOUS DATA. Moving a step beyond the level of beliefs, we encounter the most durable organization of a person's mental world, an area not necessarily within conscious awareness or subject to voluntary recall. Here, where the cognitive powers and the volitional forces meet to form the personality, the observer encounters the subconscious data referred to as a person's *values* and *attitudes.* Values constitute the most firmly held and the most deeply felt convictions and occupy a position halfway between the conscious and the preconscious life. Because they are so fiercely held and defended, they are almost impossible to change and for most people difficult to verbalize.

Attitudes refer to those implicit personal responses that are oriented toward approaching or avoiding a given object, person, group, or symbol in the environment. In popular use, opinions and attitudes are used interchangeably, but for the professional interviewer, a vital distinction must be made between the two. Opinions are verbalizable, changeable, and refer to non-ego-involving situations; attitudes are unconscious, very stable, and represent a deep personal commitment. As noted in Chapter 2, attitudes govern a person's style of life, influence the choice of an occupation or spouse, determine the reaction to any event or stimulus perceived or encountered, and form the integrative and organizing component of a personality.

In an interview, you must discriminate carefully among the three levels of data. You must recognize when you are observing facts, when you are recording feelings or opinions, and when you are attributing attitudes or values to an interviewee. As you progress along this information spectrum from the purely factual to the broadly subconscious, you will tend to insert more and more of yourself into the interview data. Since attitudes are largely unconscious and unverbalizable, their identification requires you to make broad inferences from the discrete items obtained. In this inferential process, you must integrate your observations with your psychological field. Unless you have acute perceptual skill and intimate self-knowledge, you will assign attitudes and convictions to the interviewee that are really your own. Unless you are a highly trained interviewer, do not venture into the interviewee's subconscious world to draw conclusions about values, inner drives and attitudes. It is much safer to stay in the world of facts, conclusions, opinions, and feelings, and besides, there is plenty to be done here; there are plenty of hazards involved in the way factual information is communicated.

Modes of Communication   While language is the principal vehicle or mode of interview communication, it is not the only one. People can share information in nonlanguage terms by means of subverbal cultural cues, body language, and intuitive processes.

LANGUAGE.   Since language is the chief means of sharing information in an interview, the interviewee and interviewer must not only speak the same tongue but also understand the precise meanings of the words used. First, there is the problem of semantics, a subject whose aim is, in the words of Stuart Chase, "to achieve a better understanding inside our heads of what goes on outside them, by helping us to clarify meanings in much the same way as a good pair of glasses can clarify a landscape to one suffering from astigmatism."[3] One of the principal hazards of language is its emotional content which can give a different meaning to the same word depending on the hearer's personality.

You have to be acutely conscious of the symbolic value of your words.

---

[3] Stuart Chase, "Executive Communication: Breaking the Semantic Barrier," *Management Review*, **46**:58–66, April 1957.

The word "foreigner," for example, while meaning merely "noncitizen" to you may be quite offensive to an interviewee. The word "bosses" to an employee may stand for something to be feared, while it represents for you nothing more than an amiable reference to members of top management.

Second, you must remember that words are not absolute things, that they are only conventions used by men to represent ideas, events, or concrete facts. Since each person is unique in his inheritance, previous experience, and existence at a given point in time and space, words take on such a myriad of subtle nuances in meaning, that, in truth, every word used in conversation has a meaning for the listener that is slightly different from the one intended by the speaker. So when Humpty Dumpty said to Alice, "When I use a word . . . it means just what I choose it to mean—neither more nor less," he was speaking for the whole human race. To counteract this problem, you must rid yourself of the assumption that because the interviewee and you speak the same tongue, you share the same interpretation of the words spoken. You must apply yourself consciously to the effort of gauging the precise meaning of the other person's words.

CULTURE.   Each personnel interview takes place in a particular social setting and in a specific culture, and culture is, as the anthropologist Edward T. Hall noted, the "silent language."[4] Since culture represents a people's way of life, the sum of their learned behavior, customs, and material goods, Hall says that culture is communication and communication is culture. Your dress, style of behavior, demeanor, posture, and emotional control—all communicate nonverbally to the interviewee.

The values, commitments, and orientations of the parties to the interview constitute a significant part of this communication process. The cultural impact on the interview outcome is very evident in anthropological and sociological fieldwork; it is not so evident in employment and attitude research in American society, but its effect is still there. When you seek information from an inhabitant of a culture totally different from your own, you may find that although the person comprehends and speaks your language fluently, he or she will have great difficulty understanding or interpreting the ideas transmitted.

Whether you realize it or not, you belong to a subculture that is, in many respects, quite different from that of the worker with whom you converse in the personnel situation. The value commitments and orientations may be so different that each is bewildered by the other's words. When the two meet to exchange information, the cultural barrier may

---

[4] Edward T. Hall, *The Silent Language*, A Premier Publication (Greenwich, Conn.: Fawcett Publications, Inc., 1959), p. 93.

be so dense and so impenetrable that communication and comprehension are almost impossible.

BODY LANGUAGE.   Besides words and the silent language of culture, another important mode of communication consists of the facial expressions, postures, gestures, and other physical characteristics of the interview participants. Referred to as "body language," these mannerisms convey a good deal of information. For example, simply by smiling and nodding your head when applicants use a particular word will stimulate them to repeat it frequently throughout the interview. Raised eyebrows communicate disbelief, tapping a pencil implies impatience, and a yawn demonstrates boredom. By using approving body language such as smiling and nodding your head, you show your acceptance of the interviewee. These are not necessarily insincere gestures; they simply indicate that you are trying to understand your interviewees, to see the situation from their points of view. This body language communicates to them that you are an empathic interested listener, and they will talk more freely.

INTUITION.   Besides language and cultural conventions, there is the possibility of one more mode of communication that may occur without the mediation of sensory experience or without recourse to inference or reflective thinking. This form of communication, referred to as *intuition,* abounds in the romantic literature as "love at first sight" and is also referred to as "a sixth sense of impending danger," "communing with nature," and mental telepathy.

Whether this mode of information exchange, which admittedly is more appropriate to Oriental metaphysics, actually occurs in interviews and whether the parties come to an intuitive sharing of ideas in a "unity of identification" is certainly a question of more interest to students of parapsychology. There is little doubt, however, that intuitive communication, devoid of any mediating sensory experience, is little understood or recognized in Western thought. We mention it as a possible mode of information-sharing simply because it seems to be manifested sometimes in the form of "hunches" that less systematic interviewers rely on to form impressions of the interviewee.

Direct Communication   Direct communication refers to those interview-role dimensions that are explicitly and obviously intended to get or give information to the interviewee. To communicate directly with another human being, you must ask questions and listen to the answers. Task behavior includes, first of all, the dimensions of initiating, getting information, and giving information. And to enact each of these, you must be skilled at the art of asking questions.

ASKING QUESTIONS.   Since it is up to you to take the lead in the interview, you must ask questions which suggest what you want to know. The art of interviewing depends upon the way you ask questions. If you ask too many and too direct questions, the interview will become just an interrogation, like the third degree; if you ask too few and too broad questions, your interview will assume the rambling quality of a mere conversation. Questions, of course, will vary according to the interview context, and we shall deal with these more specifically in the other three parts of this book. Here are a few general questions that apply to all types of interviews:

- It is best to phrase your questions in a *declarative form*. The suggestion "Tell me about your present job" is preferable to the question "What kind of work do you do?"

- *Use open-ended questions*, that is, questions that cannot be answered with one or two words. Closed or dead-end questions usually can be answered with a "yes" or a "no."

- Your questions should not *telegraph* the answer you want. For example, "How did you feel about mathematics in high school?" could be phrased better as "What courses were of most interest to you in high school?"

- *Comprehensive introductory* questions such as "Tell me about yourself" are excellent stimulants for interviewees because such questions suggest to them that they are expected to do most of the talking.

- Questions that are based on what interviewees have *just said* show that you are listening carefully and encourage them to continue to talk.

- Start with *easy-to-answer questions* and move toward more difficult or sensitive questions later in the interview.

- When asking a *difficult or sensitive question* try to present a reason for asking it that the other party will accept.

- *Self-evaluation questions*, that is, asking people to talk about themselves, or rate themselves, or tell you how they think, act, or believe, often are the most revealing.

Asking questions is designed primarily to enact the three task role dimensions of initiating, getting information, and giving information. To define each dimension more clearly, we shall add a few excerpts from different types of personnel interviews as illustrations of the verbal behavior encompassed by each dimension.

INITIATING.   The lead is always up to you, the interviewer. It is your responsibility to get the interview started and head it toward the goals specified by its context. You can do this by proposing a procedure, by defining the problem to be solved, or by suggesting ideas to be explored. While initiating usually takes place at the beginning of the interview, it may be introduced at any time to steer the course of the conversation to new ground.

- Attempting to get things started . . .

"Suppose you tell me why you're here."

"I've asked you to drop in for a chat today so that we can review your performance over the past year."

■ Defining the problem to be solved . . .

"As I understand it, and correct me if I'm wrong, you and your supervisor do not see exactly eye to eye on how your job is to be done."

"Our purpose here this morning is to decide whether you are the man for this job and whether this job is right for you."

■ Suggesting new ideas or steering the interview to a new topic . . .

"If you were the supervisor, how would you handle this matter?"

"Well, I guess we've covered your experience pretty well. Tell me about your education."

INFORMATION SEEKING. Seeking information is an essential part of all interviews, of course, but too many interviewers assume that it is the *only* task. Analysis of many employment interviews, for example, reveals that 90 percent of interview activity can be classified as information seeking. Such an interview becomes so unbalanced that, paradoxically, less information is obtained.

Even when information-seeking behavior is properly utilized, the interviewer must deliberately direct his attention to the level and the source of the information he requires: facts, opinions, or attitudes and observed or reported data. Correct information-seeking behavior includes gathering data pertinent to the interview goals, asking for verifiable facts, for suggestions and ideas, for feelings and opinions, for values and attitudes, and observing the interviewee's physical appearance and responses during the interview.

■ Requesting authoritative facts . . .

"How many times has your supervisor spoken to you about this?"

"What was your major subject in college?"

■ Asking for the opinions or feelings of the interviewee . . .

"Do you think your supervisor has been fair to you?"

"What type of work are you most interested in?"

"How do you feel about the food in the cafeteria?"

■ Observing interviewee appearance and actions . . .

(Noticing facial expression, body movements, voice pitch, vocabulary, diction, varying eye contacts, or perspiration.)

INFORMATION GIVING. To help interviewees evaluate a situation properly and to aid them in arriving at a better understanding of the total context, it is desirable and frequently necessary to *give* them information—facts, opinions, and ideas. At appropriate points you can do this by offering relevant information, by making suggestions, or by stating a belief or feeling that may be pertinent to the discussion.

- Offering relevant facts . . .

> "There is nothing in your personal folder on that matter."

> "All our employees are required to phone in on a day when they are absent because of illness."

- Offering suggestions or ideas . . .

> "If I were you, I would talk this over with your spouse before making as drastic a move as you plan."

> "Why don't you jot down some of the facts about this job as I describe them for you."

- Stating a belief or expressing a feeling . . .

> "I feel that you might not be very interested in this position once you have tried it out for a while."

> "I have known your supervisor for a long time and have the greatest respect for his word."

LISTENING.   Listening is a critical component of your skill as an interviewer. Many interview errors are due to differences in this area. Because it is so important and applies to other aspects of the interview-role discussion, we will discuss it in more detail in the following chapter.

Indirect Communication   Indirect communication refers to those inter-view-role dimensions that subtly and subverbally suggest to the inter-viewee the information you want. This style of communicating, also referred to as *nondirective,* is characteristic of the skilled interviewer. It includes essentially two basic techniques, the effective use of both silence and restatement. The task behavior involves the dimensions of clarifying, hypothesis testing, and summarizing.

SILENCE.   In our culture, silence during a conversation represents an unpleasant vacuum that has to be filled instantly. A few moments of silence during an interview can create an unconscious impulse in the interviewer to speak, to fill in the break in an otherwise uninterrupted pattern of verbal exchanges. When a few seconds elapse between question and reply, the impulsive interviewer will jump in with another question and effectively interrupt the client's train of thought, perhaps take the person off the horns of a significant dilemma, or block the flow of important information.

After asking an open-ended question, *pause,* give the interviewee time to think and reply. Don't panic because no one is talking. Remember that a few seconds can seem like a long time, but really isn't. After the interviewee has answered your question, don't jump in with another question too quickly. Use the intelligent approach—*wait*. Remember in an interview, *silence is golden!* Keep this rule in mind, that an interviewee will often give you the most significant information after a period of silence.

RESTATEMENT.   Restatement simply refers to the art of repeating, reflecting, rewording, or summarizing what the interviewee has told you. This technique can be your most effective tool because it will enable you to give feedback to the interviewee using the information you have gathered during the interview. While it is a most difficult skill to learn, it is valuable for five reasons:

1. *Aids listening.* To restate accurately what a person has just said to you requires that you listen carefully and attentively.

2. *Shows interest.* Restatement shows the other person that you are really interested and that you are trying to understand what is said. Most people are pleased when another person shows genuine interest in what they have to say.

3. *Chance to modify.* Sometimes we say things we don't really mean or don't say them in just the right way. Restatement gives interviewees an opportunity to hear what they have just said and to correct or modify it if you did not hear them accurately.

4. *Chance to clarify.* Restatement gives interviewees a chance to clarify or to elaborate their thoughts, to talk things out. The result is a much deeper level of communication between you and your interviewees.

5. *Shows acceptance and understanding.* Restating applicants' ideas is the best way of showing them that you accept their ideas and are trying to understand them as people. It often gets you out of an argument or a debate because by accepting what interviewees say, you avoid an indication of disapproval or concern and merely continue the conversation.

Restatement is accomplished by clarifying, hypothesis testing, and summarizing. Keep in mind that whether your restatement is *precisely* correct, whether you accurately feed back what the interviewee meant, the technique helps you to make sure that you are obtaining clear and correct information in the interview.

CLARIFYING.   Clarifying is designed to give interviewees feedback on how they are communicating by enabling them to hear what they have said. Such feedback helps them to develop insight into their own ideas, feelings, or attitudes or enables them to correct any erroneous impression that may have formed in your mind. You clarify the interviewees' statements by reflecting feelings and attitudes, by restating content, or by clearing up confusing or ambiguous terms.

■ Reflecting feelings and attitudes . . .

    EMPLOYEE: "I just can't get these sheets out on time."

    SUPERVISOR: "It's really discouraging for you the way they pile up."

■ Restating content . . .

EMPLOYEE: "Well, I'm trying to improve, but the machine is so darn old, that it breaks down two or three times a week."

SUPERVISOR: "You haven't shown any progress because of the poor condition of the machine?"

■ Clearing up confusing or ambiguous terms . . .

EMPLOYEE: "Management doesn't appreciate me."

SUPERVISOR: "By management are you referring to your immediate supervisor?"

TESTING.   During the interview, you will be mentally drawing conclusions about the interviewee. These "conclusions" must be considered to be *hypotheses* until they have been confirmed by further questioning or by other evidence obtained from sources outside the interview. Throughout the conversation, test your inferences about the interviewee's feelings, attitudes, or attributes.

■ Testing hypotheses . . .

"You are really not resigning, then, only because of the higher salary in the new job?"

"I get the impression then, that most of your experience has been in staff work."

■ Testing conclusions . . .

"You feel, then, that your work could stand improvement?"

"We are in agreement, then, that this job is not the one for you?"

SUMMARIZING.   Toward the end of the interview, it is highly desirable to summarize its main trends and to establish unequivocally what will follow thereafter. The interviewer performs this task by pulling together related ideas, by summarizing what has occurred and what has been said, by defining the main conclusions, and by enumerating the actions that will follow the interview. This action then becomes a signal to the interviewee that the interview is about to end and thus provides a convenient way of terminating it gracefully.

■ Rephrasing the main ideas of the interviewee to ensure mutual agreement . . .

"In other words, if I have heard correctly, you are interested primarily in work involving public contact, but you are not interested in door-to-door selling?"

■ Pulling together related ideas and summarizing what has occurred . . .

"Well, now to sum up, you have told me that you are dissatisfied with the treatment you have been receiving, but since you like your job and your coworkers, you don't want to leave the company, and now you want to find out what I can do to help you."

■ Defining main conclusions and enumerating future actions . . .

"OK then, it's agreed. We'll both try to work more closely together in the future. I'll keep you informed every day of changes in your work schedule, and you will let me know directly of any problems that you may have and not keep them bottled up within you."

You will note that the task-role dimensions focus directly upon interview purposes and upon getting the main job done, whether it be to survey employee attitudes, to discuss a subordinate's job applicant, or to evaluate a job applicant. The achievement of each interview objective depends on the degree to which communication takes place in the interview. Hence, you must adopt the pattern of behavior that will facilitate communication. You must somehow establish a bridge between the other person and yourself.

If the purpose of the interview is such that areas of an intimate or delicate nature must be explored, it is even more important to establish a relationship that will encourage informative sharing on a deeper, more sensitive level. An interviewee will not confide in a person in whom he or she has no confidence.

Rapport Role Behavior

The acquisition of effective rapport skills is the most challenging and demanding aspect of the interviewer's role. Rapport itself is difficult to define precisely, but most authorities describe it as the maintenance of a comfortable and unconstrained relationship between interviewer and interviewee. Rapport skills deal with the emotional aspects of the interview, with the attraction between the two participants, with the warmth and the support developed, and with the ability of the interviewer to function as a mature, responsible person.

Rapport behavior consists, in the language of transactional analysis referred to in the preceding chapter, of giving interviewees "positive strokes." It can be as simple as smiling at them or it can be subtle, such as making them feel you are interested in them and what they have to say. It creates a warm, friendly feeling in other people; it is supportive, creative, and appreciated, and it, therefore, invites candor and trust.

ESTABLISHING A CLIMATE.   Besides initiating and getting movement started toward interview goals, you must also inform the interviewee of the ground rules, establish acceptable norms and standards for behavior during the interview, and define a goal toward which you both should direct your energies. By so doing, you create a mood in which the interview can be conducted most pleasantly. In most encounters between two people, unspoken rules of conduct that bind both are always understood implicitly. In some interviews, however, the interviewee may not be sure of the assumptions on which the conversation is to be based. It is up to you to indicate not only what kind of behavior is permissible, but also what is expected. If a climate of amiability and sincerity is established from the outset, for example, if you demonstrate that everything said or done will be treated with the utmost confidence, if you give assurance by an air of quiet self-confidence that you know what you are doing, the interviewee cannot fail to sense this atmosphere of support, permissiveness, and encouragement that will allow a full and free exchange of ideas; and this, after all, is the essence of an interview.

■ Expressing standards . . .

"Let's both talk frankly and honestly without pulling any punches."

"If you don't agree with me at any point during this interview, please say so."

■ Establishing norms . . .

"How do you think we ought to conduct this interview?"

"Just what did you expect to accomplish in this interview?"

■ Applying standards to interview results . . .

"We cannot expect too much of a change in your outlook as a result of only one interview."

"Do you mind if I take some of these matters up with your supervisor?"

ENCOURAGING.   Interaction between people is usually facilitated by a warm, friendly, mutually supportive atmosphere. To create this climate, you must be encouraging by being openly responsive to the interviewee; you must accept your client's problems, ideas, and suggestions; you must lend emotional support through casual remarks, through an attitude of undivided attention, through facial expressions, and through a generally approving demeanor.

■ Being friendly, warm, or responsive . . .

"How are you today?"

"I'm awfully sorry to hear that."

Smiling!!! (whenever appropriate)

■ Accepting his problems, ideas, and suggestions . . .

"That's a good point you make, and I see your difficulty."

"There are many ways of looking at this situation, and yours is certainly one of them."

"I think that is a fair statement to make."

■ Attempting to give emotional support by remarks, facial expression, by listening . . .

"This is very interesting. Please tell me more."

"Please continue, I am interested in what you are telling me."

■ Indicating approval in various ways . . .

"Good. Fine." (Nodding, smiling, etc.)

RELEASING EMOTION AND FEELING. The behavior of some interviewees will be marked by suppressed emotion or intensity of feeling. The interview will be of great importance to most interviewees: they may be seeking new jobs that they want very much; they may have problems that are bothering them gravely; they may have grievances that have built up within them intense feelings of hostility. To achieve explicit interview goals, to open up a deeper level of communication, or to obtain more specific data from the here and now, it may be desirable to permit interviewees to display their emotions safely within the confines of the interview environment. To release emotional feeling, you must first sense the respondents' moods and then by sharing your own feeling suggest that you will tolerate any emotional overflow that might occur. When this emotional tension has been permitted to boil over without recrimination, a more intimate relationship can usually be, at least tenuously, established between you and your interviewees. In short, they become friends and can communicate more deeply thereafter.

■ Sensing feeling and mood . . .

"I gather that you are not quite yourself today."

"You seem to be quite unhappy over this."

■ Tolerating emotional overflow . . .

"I can see that you feel deeply about this matter. Why don't we talk it over from the beginning."

"I understand your bitterness. It is good to get these feelings off your chest. Now, why don't we review the whole matter together."

(Not running away from anger, tears, hostility, and, above all, not responding in kind.)

■ Sharing one's own feelings . . .

"You certainly showed a good deal of courage in that situation."

"That was very interesting. I am really astounded."

REDUCING TENSION. Sometimes, however, since discretion is often the better part of valor, it may be wiser to steer the conversation to less turbulent water when it becomes apparent that the interviewee may be approaching an anxiety threshold. While the interview atmosphere becomes charged with emotion, you must move to reduce the tension. Such a situation can occur while an employee is discussing a bitter conflict with a supervisor or when an applicant is relating a private event which appears acutely distressing or embarrassing or which possibly will place the applicant in a distinctly unfavorable light.

Tension may be reduced by changing the subject, by attempting to minimize or to reconcile the conflict, or by playing down unfavorable information.

- Changing the subject . . .

> "Well, let's come back to this subject later on."
>
> "Perhaps we can move on to another topic now."

- Reconciling external conflicts . . .

> "It really appears to me that basically the two of you are not very far apart on this matter."
>
> "Perhaps, if I were in your shoes, I would see the matter in a different light."

- Playing down unfavorable information . . .

> "Well that happens to everybody sooner or later."
>
> "How do you patch things up with your boss?"
>
> "Considering the strain you were under, I can understand your decision."

UNBLOCKING.   Sometimes conflicts between interviewer and interviewee, stemming from different points of view, varying degrees of information, or even from the client's negative attitudes, are unavoidable and block communication. It is up to you to remove such blocks by offering to compromise your own position. You can do this by admitting error if, in fact, you were mistaken, by offering to come halfway to reach agreement, or finally, by exercising self-discipline. Regardless of the provocation, it is useless to engage in an argument or a debate with an interviewee. Frequently if you really listen you will detect many points of agreement and find ways of reducing conflicts between you and the interviewee.

- Admitting error . . .

> "Oh, excuse me, I completely misunderstood you."
>
> "Obviously, we made a mistake in the letter that we wrote you."

- Offering to compromise own position by coming halfway . . .

> "Well, perhaps I was a little hasty in my conclusions."
>
> "I suppose I have been somewhat thoughtless in the way that I have supervised you. But do you think that completely accounts for your behavior?"

- Disciplining self to maintain harmony . . .

> (Keeping an even temper or suppressing inner feelings of resentment.)

GATEKEEPING.   Gatekeeping is one of the most important ways to establish rapport and to keep the channels of communication open. To facilitate the participation of the interviewee in the conversation, you use open-end questions, that is, questions that must be answered in more than one or two words, build questions on the previous answers of the interviewee, and tolerate periods of silence during the conversation to let the interviewee think the answers through completely before replying. Gatekeeping, therefore, is the art of keeping the conversation door open at all times.

■ Using open-end questions . . .

"Tell me about your work with Ajax."

"What would you like to talk about today?"

■ Building questions on previous answers . . .

Q. "What do you do in your free time?"

A. "Oh, all sorts of things, but mainly I read."

Q. "Tell me what you read."

A. "Oh, newspapers, magazines, and books."

Q. "What kinds of books do you read?"

A. "Mainly popular fiction, novels, best sellers."

Q. "What is it about fiction that appeals to you?"
(and so on)

■ Facilitating the interviewee's participation in the interview . . .

(Keeping one's own participation down to 20 to 30 per cent of the talking.)

(Keeping silent—*waiting!!!*)

Not all of these rapport role dimensions are employed in every interview. Some such as tension reduction and emotional release are more appropriate to problem-solving interviews. The rapport skills themselves have their greatest application in the less structured, that is, in the nondirective interview. All of them can contribute to the development of an interview climate because they permit the interviewer to exercise participant role behavior more effectively.

Self-centered Role Behavior

Every interview is initiated for a purpose that is in some way related to the needs of the interviewee and of the employer. Your job is to satisfy both sets of needs. This is your mission; this is the obligation that you undertake when you assume your role. You are, in a sense, no more than an instrument by means of which an employee or a prospective employee can directly address the management for the benefit of both parties. This objective—hiring an employment applicant, helping an employee to improve job performance, assisting another in dealing more effectively with a problem, or merely finding out what someone thinks of the cafeteria food—is the heart of an interview.

Even though as an interviewer you are an instrument, a communication medium, you are not a piece of copper wire, a printed page, or a tabulating card. You are flesh and blood, possessed of a highly developed nervous system, a complex repertoire of emotional responses, and a varied range of unique needs. You bring these possessions with you into every interview, and somehow they keep cropping up in the conversation. If they are not controlled, they will so dominate the dialogue that at the end of the interview, the only one really satisfied by the encounter will be you!

Self-centered behavior usually is expressed through negative strokes. A negative stroke is a putdown, a criticism. It is anything you might do or say to belittle interviewees, make them feel less worthy, uncomfortable, ill at ease, or guilty. It tells them that they are not OK with you.

Often, without meaning to, we give negative strokes—when we are tired, preoccupied, or just acting out of habit. But that does not lessen the pain we cause or the damage we do.

Learning to interview begins by becoming aware of negative strokes. The fact that you behave in ways designed, perhaps subconsciously, to satisfy your own needs should humble you but not discourage you. The situation becomes serious only if you ignore the fact that your actions dominate the interplay. By reviewing some of the more common types of self-centered interview behavior, you can analyze your own actions and perhaps identify your putdowns.

Displaying Aggression   To cope with your own anxiety, you may psychologically attack your interviewees. You can do this by countless, subtle putdowns—by deflating them, by expressing disapproval of their feelings, actions, or values, by joking, or by showing envy.

- Deflating the interviewee . . .

   "I always enjoy chatting with one of my subordinates."

   "It is highly unlikely that you'll qualify for a position with us."

- Expressing disapproval . . .

   (Feelings) "There is no reason to become emotional at this point."

   (Actions) "I'm sure by now you have regretted your uncouth behavior."

   (Values) "We don't need any idealists in this company."

- Joking aggressively . . .

"Well, if this keeps up, we'll have to elect you president of our 'boob-of-the-month' club."

■ Showing envy toward the interviewee . . .

"Don't let your college degree give you any big ideas. I may not have a degree but I am still the supervisor around here."

BLOCKING. Some interviewers seem to find the greatest satisfaction in frustrating interviewees by being especially negative or by placing serious obstacles in the conversational path. Blocking behavior, as it is termed, is generally exemplified by a strongly negative or stubbornly resistant adamancy in which the suggestions or the recommendations of interviewees are opposed without or beyond reason. It can be done by interrupting interviewees frequently and thus preventing them from expressing themselves adequately or by attempting to maintain an issue or to bring it up again long after respondents have exhausted the subject or indicated that they would rather not discuss it.

■ Negativism . . .

"I disagree with you completely."

"I don't care how reasonable it seems to you. We just cannot go along with it. It is not company policy."

■ Opposing without or beyond reason . . .

"No, the answer is no!"

"I cannot explain it to you, but I just cannot buy it."

■ Interrupting or preventing the interviewee from speaking . . .

"Sorry to break in, but I just thought of something that I wanted to ask you."

"Never mind answering, it wasn't important anyway. Let's go on to something else."

■ Maintaining an issue interminably . . .

"I would like you to tell me once more why you failed to carry out my orders."

"I know we have already discussed this, but I would like to hear once again the reasons why you resigned from your last position."

SEEKING RECOGNITION. Some interviewers are attracted to the interview atmosphere because it constitutes an ideal arena in which to obtain reassurance. The deference won from another person counteracts their deeply seated feelings of inadequacy. The interview context offers such a person an unparalleled opportunity in which to report on personal achievements, to behave with an air of importance and dignity, and to act out a fantasy of prestige, eminence, and power without fear of contradiction.

- Reporting personal accomplishments . . .

  "When I was your age, I was supervising ten men."

  "Let me tell you about the time I was elected president of my sorority."

- Behaving with an air of importance . . .

  (Pacing the floor, ostentatiously taking notes, shuffling obviously important papers.)

- Overuse of the telephone or intercom during the interview . . .

  "Excuse me, London is calling."

  (To secretary) "Miss Jones, set up a luncheon appointment at Antonio's for me and the president."

SELF-CONFESSING.   Some interviewers have a strong need to win interviewees' sympathy by telling them of personal difficulties. This is done in many subtle ways, but it is most frequently engaged in by supervisors during performance-evaluation interviews with subordinates. The most common practice includes the expression of irrelevant feelings or complaints.

- Expressing irrelevant personal complaints . . .

  "You don't realize the work I have to do after you leave."

  "I've had a very trying day."

  "Your troubles are nothing compared with what I have to put up with."

DOMINEERING.   A very common interviewer game is the assertion of superiority over interviewees. Many employment interviewers enjoy the temporary advantage afforded by the selection situation. The encounter becomes a cat and mouse game in which the interviewer toys with interviewees by interrogating them or by keeping them in a state of suspense.

- Interrogating . . .

  "Tell me, Jones, what makes you think you can sell appliances?"

- Domineering or controlling . . .

  "If I want any information I'll ask for it. Just answer my questions."

- Keeping the interviewee in a state of suspense . . .

  "At the end of the interview, I'll let you know what is going to happen to you."

There are many other interview techniques that have as their object the satisfaction of interviewers' needs and alleviation of their anxieties. Space precludes further description here, but the few we have cited should underscore our main point. For individual growth and development as an interviewer, you must understand your own hangups, control them, and minimize their impact on the outcome of the dialogue.

Styles of Interviewing   One final word remains to be said concerning role behavior. The degree to which the different dimensions are employed in combination to form a specific conversational pattern is referred to as the style of the interview. *Interview style* refers to the pattern of interaction used to converse with the interviewee, to project questions, to respond to leads, and to establish a mutual bond. The literature identifies three styles of interviewing that can be followed in whole or in part, depending on the time available, the interview objectives, and the personalities participating. In some cases, an interview may be conducted in one style only, but in others, the interviewer shifts from one style to another to suit his purposes.

THE DIRECTED INTERVIEW.   The most common style of interviewing in the personnel situation is the directed style, sometimes referred to as the patterned or the standardized interview. It is usually the most efficient for employment purposes. The format is highly structured, including a precise interview plan, a pattern of direct questions, a set time limit, and a preprinted checklist to record the applicant's responses and the interviewer's evaluation. This particular format delimits considerably the applicant's response freedom.

In initial or primary interviews, an interviewee's responses are drastically limited so that the interview may be completed in no more than twenty or thirty minutes. Since the directed interview is so controlled, personality interaction is somewhat inhibited and more subtle levels of communication are inaccessible. The task dimensions are utilized almost exclusively and little rapport is, therefore, established. The exclusive use of this interview style is advantageous only when purely factual information is sought.

THE NONDIRECTIVE INTERVIEW.   The nondirective style was originally developed by Carl Rogers for use in his "client centered" therapeutic interview. In this style, interviewers remain nondirective in the sense that they do not take the responsibility for deciding the subjects to be discussed, the goals that the interview should attain, or the solution to interviewees' problem.

Interview topics, goals, and solutions are seen as the prime responsibility of interviewees, and it is the function of the interviewer only to help them assume this responsibility by creating an atmosphere of acceptance and permissiveness that guarantees security and protection against recrimination, reprisal, and retaliation.

The nondirective style is most applicable to problem-solving interviews, but it has its place, within limits, in other types of interviewing as well. Besides creating a supportive attitude, you, as an interviewer, can facilitate communication in the interview by clarifying and reflecting the feelings and the ideas that the respondent expresses. By emphasizing particularly the task dimensions of clarification and testing, you permit your interviewees to hear what they have been struggling to say. If they find that the reflection does not represent accurately or completely the meaning which they wish to convey, they are in a position to make modifications. This procedure may also serve to change their own thinking on a subject by permitting them to hear what they have been saying.

Although it is extremely effective, the nondirective technique is time-consuming. Since it requires considerable skill and insight, it can also be risky. The most obvious danger is that your opinions, prejudices, and feelings will inadvertently influence your attempts to summarize or to reflect the respondents' words and attitudes. If your reflections are inaccurate or distorted or if your interviewees feel anxious in an unstructured situation, it can stimulate defensive or hostile reactions in them.

STRESS INTERVIEWING.   Stress interviewing refers to the use of such methods as deliberately interrupting your interviewees, frequently questioning their opinions, remaining silent for extended periods, or adopting a hostile, unfriendly posture to intimidate them and put pressure on them. When used intentionally by an extremely skillful and experienced interviewer under carefully controlled conditions, the stress style may have some advantages in a particular selection context, e.g., considering an applicant for a door-to-door salesman position. Obviously, the method must be applied cautiously. It cannot be used on an interviewee who in nonstressful situations shows signs of low anxiety control. It cannot be used at the beginning of an interview because it would be impossible to compare the subject's normal behavior with behavior under stress. It cannot be used at the end of an interview because a period of time must elapse to enable the interviewee to be "depressurized" and return to normal composure.

It is well to bear in mind that more often than not the interview is so implicitly full of stress that there is little need to apply it deliberately.

chapter 4

The Complete Interviewer

> Let knowledge grow from more to more,
> But more of reverence in us dwell . . .
> —ALFRED, LORD TENNYSON, *In Memoriam*

There was a manager of a systems department who was convinced that he was an excellent judge of character. Since, in his eyes he had selected the programmers and systems analysts in his department for years without a mistake, he had accumulated a set of almost "infallible techniques" to appraise an applicant. One was gauging the amount of eye contact between him and the applicant; another was offering the applicant a cigarette but providing him no ashtray; a third was asking him embarrassing questions to see how he would react. His selection standards were equally "precise and objective." Among others, each applicant had to be male (women were too emotional), clean shaven (mustaches and beards were a sign that the applicant was devious), at least six feet tall (authoritative), and, above all, must possess a firm handshake (a clue to his sincerity).

After two serious equal employment opportunity complaints and his enthusiastic selection of a senior programmer who turned out to be a psychopathic impostor, company officials decided to relieve him of the burden of employment interviewing.

The complexity of the interview makes it obvious that competency in its practice does not come with experience. The question that logically occurs, therefore, is how to acquire the proficiency required to move artfully through an interview.

There have been several classic answers to this question—all represented by the usual interviewer "training program." While the theory and methods of these instructional programs have varied greatly, they have a common tendency to stress adherence by the learner to specific behavioral patterns. Traditional training manuals and pamphlets on how to conduct an interview consequently list a series of ideal questions and include a set of sample interviews accompanied by explanatory comments by the author.

Another school of thought holds that this approach to interviewer development fails to consider too many variables to be practical. Since an interview is really the spontaneous interplay between your unique personality traits and the demands of your role, to employ the interview proficiently you must adopt your own behavioral pattern, a pattern quite unlike anyone else's but effective simply because it is as authentic as it is correct. There is, therefore, no "royal road" to learning this approach because it requires, above all, a knowledge of yourself.

Interviewer Problems

Effective interviewing, however, takes more than self-knowledge. To show you how to develop into an accomplished interviewer, we must describe briefly some common interviewer errors, besides the self-centered behaviors discussed in the previous chapter. Then we will explore the sources of these errors.

Interviewer Errors   As mentioned earlier, the interview has been the subject of repeated criticisms that have centered principally on the interviewer rather than the technique of interviewing itself. Research by various investigators over the past twenty-five years has produced little evidence to show that the average interviewer does the job effectively. The reasons for this state of affairs can be summed up in the following paragraphs.

UNTRAINED INTERVIEWERS.   Since most average interviewers have never been exposed to formal interview training, they are usually unprepared to conduct an interview properly. Without realizing it, they are likely to obtain so little relevant information that, at the end of an interview, they have to fill in their sketchy impressions with information from their own heads.

CONTENT VARIABILITY.   The interview content is covered haphazardly and indiscriminately. Most interviewers tend to question the applicant on areas that are of interest to them or which they deem to be most relevant. In the employment interview, for example, there often is little uniformity in the information covered by interviewers speaking to several applicants for the same job, nor even by the same interviewer from one interview situation to the next.

QUESTION VARIABILITY.   Interviewers vary considerably in the way they ask questions and often fail to realize that the form of the question affects its answer. Interviewees, therefore, usually try to give the answer they believe the interviewer wants rather than the true one.

UNEVEN INTERPRETATION.   Even when interviewers obtain the same information, they are likely to interpret or weigh it differently. One investigator found that interviewers differ widely on how much certain items of information impressed them. The same items created quite favorable impressions on some interviewers and unfavorable impressions on others.

PREMATURE DECISIONS.   In employment interviews, most interviewers tend to make their decisions early and thereafter look for information to support that decision. Their initial interpretations of information derived from application blanks or an applicant's personal appearance usually are decisive. The often-stated observations "I sized him up the minute he walked into my office" or "I liked her style the moment I saw her" are examples of this error.

NEGATIVE APPROACH.   The attitudes of untrained interviewers affect the information obtained. The fact that they are more likely to be influenced by unfavorable than by favorable information or to change their originally favorable impressions to unfavorable impressions might suggest that their purpose is to search for negative information.

UNRELIABLE DECISIONS.   The decisions made as a result of an interview are often unreliable and inconsistent. As usually conducted, the interview has been shown to be so inconsistent that the results depend more on the interviewer than on the interviewee. An applicant who is interviewed by two different persons for the same job can be judged qualified by one and unqualified by the other.

POOR INTERVIEWING CONDITIONS.   Interviewing conditions may be something less than ideal. On a typical day, an interviewer may have to see dozens of people. Time being a critical element, the interview is hurried and what might be critical areas of information are disregarded. In addition, there may be little chance for privacy in the interview, and this, therefore, reduces the level and the amount of information that can be obtained.

IMPROPER INFORMATION.   Interviewers often ask for information that is improper because it constitutes an invasion of the privacy of the interviewee or violates federal, state, or local regulations with respect to equal employment opportunity.

TELL AND SELL APPROACH.   In the performance-evaluation interview, superiors do most of the talking in an effort to sell subordinates on the need for improvement. The more the subordinates are criticized, the more defensive they become and the less likely they are to improve.

Sources of Error   Serious contemplation of the information capacity of the interview, with its varicolored spectrum of data and its complex modes of transmission, will serve to suggest the main sources that lie hidden in this list of errors. These error sources arise out of the inherent ambiguities of the information itself and the confusion over the manner in which it is obtained.

INTERVIEWER'S BACKGROUND.   Studies have demonstrated that such background characteristics as the age, sex, class, or ethnic group of the interviewer tends to influence both the quantity and the quality of the information collected. An early study showed that there were significant differences in the responses of persons interviewed by working-class and by white-collar interviewers. In another investigation, it was reported that interviewers belonging to different ethnic groups would elicit significantly different responses to questions involving racial issues.

The conclusion is inescapable that cultural factors affect the way information is shared and that, therefore, dress, speech, and the appearance of the investigator are important variables that must be controlled in using and interpreting data gathered by the interview technique.

INTERVIEW QUESTIONS.   The type of information sought, the selection of questions, and the way they are asked have a great deal to do with the validity of the replies. Interviews in which factual information is sought have the greatest validity, but there have been many instances where interviews concerned only with such items as length of employment, job title, and pay received have reported erroneous results. When the inquiry is directed at subjective and subconscious data, the margin of error increases greatly.

The questions selected to be asked can bias an interview result before it even starts. Many an employee opinion survey, by asking the wrong questions and by leaving the employee little room to volunteer information, overlooks important answers to management problems.

Even when a standardized interview style is adopted, differences in elicited information due to the way the interviewers word their questions are still possible. A number of studies have been reported of interviews recorded without the interviewers' knowledge. The results suggest that the considerable variations in question techniques, in follow-up or probing questions, in suggestions to the interviewee on ways of responding, were serious enough to cast clouds of doubt on the data collected.

INTERVIEWER ATTITUDES.   In previous chapters, we have discussed how your attitudes can influence both the extent and the nature of elicited information. There are three major ways you can do this: first, you can project your attitudes into your interviewees' responses and ascribe those attitudes to them; second, your attitude can cause you to so anticipate your interviewees' responses that what you hear will reflect what you expected rather than what was actually said; third, your attitude as reflected by your behavior can stimulate your interviewees to respond in ways really at variance with their true beliefs, feelings, or opinions.

VARIATIONS IN TECHNIQUE.   The extent to which interviewers press individuals to respond differs considerably from interviewee to interviewee, and the responsiveness of those included in the study constitutes another variable that can effect the validity of the information collected. Since some investigators undoubtedly probe considerably more than others, the amount and quality of the information assembled from an interview may be due as much to the zeal and the interest of the interviewer as to the extent and depth of the interviewee's knowledge.

The interest and the cooperation of the interviewee must be considered in analyzing the results.

RECORDING THE RESULTS.   The last major error source lies in the way interview results are recorded. Researchers have reported that the way this task is performed is a major concern in the analysis of interview data and poses a problem to which we must give considerable attention in our explorations of each type of personnel interview. We merely wish to point out here that besides stimulating the interviewee to respond in a way sure to yield the desired data, you should record it accurately, objectively, uniformly, and completely. A major obstacle to faithful recording is the fallibility of the human memory. Unless you make notes promptly, much interview material will escape you, and your report may be so full of gaps that it will convey an impression quite at variance with the real facts.

Techniques of an Effective Interviewer

To minimize the effect of these unconscious sources of error, you must develop skills that will enable you not only to elicit appropriate information from the interviewee but also to observe it objectively, attend to it, remember it, and interpret it. To do this systematically, you must first be aware of the interview sequence.

Interview Sequence   In every interview, no matter how long or short, there is a definite sequence or flow of the ideas discussed. This sequence does not have to be apparent to the interviewee, but you must pay close attention to it. For one thing, it will help you to organize and use your time efficiently, and, for another, it will facilitate the orderly achievement of your interview objectives. There are four sequences to an interview: establishing a climate, getting information, giving information, and summarizing.

ESTABLISHING A CLIMATE.   The opening sequence is designed to create a comfortable atmosphere in which the interviewee can easily talk to you. This sequence should take about 15 percent of your total interview time budget. If you do this properly, you will establish a communications bridge between you and the interviewee over which information will flow freely. You will also convey the impression of being sincerely interested in the interviewee. In later parts of this book dealing with specific types of interviews, we will make suggestions as to how to establish a proper interview climate.

GETTING INFORMATION.   The information-getting sequence varies with the type of interview. In most interviews, it will require about 55 percent of your total interview time. There is no set way of entering this phase. Ideally, you move into it without realizing it by building your questions on the interviewee's remarks during the opening sequence. If the introductory conversation goes well, the interviewee will be talking freely and comfortably.

Details are important, even though the interview must move along fairly rapidly. Little things—casual remarks, faulty memory—are often significant. When you pick up these details, follow them up carefully but unassumingly or note them for future checking.

You must not hesitate to discuss sensitive topics if they arise, but you should avoid showing any outward sign of disapproval or distress if unfavorable information is brought up. If you project an understanding and an accepting attitude, you are likely to obtain more information than by displaying displeasure or disbelief. And you must avoid probing into areas that are irrelevant, no matter how interesting they may be.

GIVING THE INTERVIEWEE INFORMATION.   Another important task of the interviewer is to give information to the interviewee. This sequence should require about 15 to 40 percent of your time, depending upon the type of interview you conduct.

SUMMARIZING.   When the interview reaches the 85 percent mark, you must begin to bring it to a close. By that time, both you and the interviewee should have a clear idea of what the interview intended to convey. To double check this understanding, at that point give the person a chance to ask questions. Then terminate the interview with a brief summary of what has been discussed and what the next steps will be.

Listening   Most conventional interviewing manuals pay considerable attention to the business of asking questions and to the way in which the conversation can be directed toward the specific interview goals. Consequently, many beginners devote their efforts solely to the techniques of asking questions and to ways of stimulating the interviewee to talk. Although this behavior *toward* an interviewee is important, it should constitute less than half of your skill. Your effectiveness should lie in your ability to listen attentively, perceptively, and, hence, meaningfully. Skillful listening requires, first, concentration upon relevant behavior; second, meaningful perception of what you have focused on; and third, accurate assimilation and analysis of what you have perceived.

PERCEPTION.   Accurate listening depends to a great extent upon the first link in the chain, perception. Perception is the process by which you internalize and organize the sensations to which you have attended and which enable you to know where you stand in relation to the objects and conditions of the external world.

Perception is affected by two sets of influences, one objective and the other subjective. The objective influences refer to the characteristics of what is perceived and the situation in which it is embedded. Physical appearance, dress, social status, ethnic origin, organizational affiliation, and place of residence are elements that can determine the way in which you perceive an applicant for employment because taken together they tend to form a total pattern. These objective perceptual influences, however, can create an illusion that misleads as well as helps you.

Subjective perceptual influences refer to what you *expect* to see or what you would like to see. *Selective perception* as it is called is an important variable which must be controlled rigorously. Unless you are careful, you will perceive only events in your interview that confirm your existing values and beliefs. When, for example, biased interviewers prepare to interview a member of a minority group, they usually expect to confront a person with unkempt dress, boorish manners, an accent, and possibly carrying a dangerous weapon. If, on the contrary, they are introduced to a well-dressed, neat, polite person with perfect diction and manners, they will continue to search diligently for those characteristics previously associated with the minority group stereotype.

Each of us has an irresistible tendency to "fill in the gaps" in what we perceive, to see what we want to see and to hear what we want to hear, not realizing that many of the details in our perceptual field are assumed rather than real. Our social and cultural backgrounds combined with the objective and the subjective perceptual factors determine not only the direction of our attention but also the way in which we organize our experiences. Experienced anthropological field interviewers or skilled social investigators exploring slum conditions will constantly neutralize the effect of their own cultural and social values and customs on what they are recording and interpreting in their interview investigations. Personnel interviewers, too, must recognize and accept their own special cultural biases if they are to prevent the distortion of interview results.

Becoming a skillful listener, therefore, takes practice, especially since you have to ask questions, direct the interview sequence, and take notes. Yet if you learn to control both the situation and yourself (the most common obstacles to effective listening) and follow six positive rules, you can become a "good" listener.

Obstacles that Hinder Effective Listening

INTOLERANCE. The cultural, social, ethnic, or religious background of an interviewee can be a source of substantial "noise" for you and thus reduce your listening acuity. If you are intolerant of the speech, the physical appearance, the dress, or the mannerisms of your client, you will find it difficult to concentrate. Since some of your attention will be devoted to mental criticism of the other (one definition of intolerance), the meaning of the message that gets through will be incomplete, distorted, and probably influenced by stereotypes.

IMPULSIVITY. Poor impulse control is one of the greatest enemies of good listening. All interviewers should have the four-letter word *wait* stamped indelibly upon their consciousness. Anxiety, discomfort, and inability to tolerate silence may cause you to break into the interviewee's speech or train of thought without allowing time to formulate a complete answer, cause you to answer the question yourself or to suggest an acceptable answer, or prompt you to change the subject.

ANTICIPATION. Intolerance and impulsivity lead to a third source of poor listening—the anticipation of what will be said by the interviewee. When anticipation is reinforced by the speaker's first words or actions, intolerance and impulsivity are so confirmed that further interviewing becomes totally unnecessary. This is the basis of the frequent interviewer error of "sizing up" an applicant at first sight.

Anticipation forms the basis of most social arguments and debates. Two people will engage in an animated, lengthy conversation in which neither listens to the other but merely anticipates what the other will say and replies to this expectation. Finally, one of the combatants may exclaim: "Will you please let me finish a sentence!" In poorly conducted interviews, anticipation occurs in a more polite and more subdued form but with the same result—little true information sharing.

INDOLENCE. Proper listening takes hard mental effort. If the interview dwells on a subject that is abstract, complicated, or difficult, the natural inclination is to rebel by becoming bored or distracted or by changing the subject to simpler, more interesting material. Ineffective listening may constitute nothing more than sheer mental sloth. To control this tendency to evade the hard or the complex, you must develop a keen interest in the subject matter, a little self-confidence, and a willingness to apply yourself.

SUGGESTIBILITY. To maintain your objectivity, you must avoid the suggestibility of emotional or ambiguous terms by constantly asking for clarification. Such adjectives as "extremely," "awful," or "terrible" are emotionally loaded; phrases like "all the time" or "the whole office" are ambiguous. Unless you clarify them you can be misled easily. When you hear such words, you should ask for a concrete example to obtain a clearer and a more precise idea of the speaker's meaning and of the factual basis on which it is based.

Positive Steps toward Effective Listening

PREPARATION. You must be fully informed about the substance and the objectives of the interview. To facilitate this, you must acquire as much advance information as possible. A "cold" interviewer listens under a severe handicap because he has few "bench marks" to appreciate fully the significance and the implications of the speaker's remarks. The nature of the position involved, company policy, rules and regulations, and the personal background of the interviewee constitute areas of information with which you ought to be familiar before the interview in order to increase your listening power during the interview. In our description of the different personnel interviews, you will note that each is preceded by instructions on preparation.

Often you have very little time to prepare for an interview. Either you are presented with a filled-out application and must start interviewing immediately, or a grieved employee walks into your office and sits down in front of you with a complaint, or a subordinate drops in and asks how he or she is doing. These unexpected interviews require that your preparation occurs *before* the interviewee seats himself in front of you. A big part of this "instant" preparation involves your qualifications and training, as we shall discuss later in this chapter.

But the place where the interview is conducted must be arranged carefully. Without exception an interview must be conducted in private, which means a closed office with no interruptions. It is poor practice to conduct an interview in an open area or even in semiprivacy. It is discourteous and distracting to permit interruptions in the form of phone calls or personal visits during an interview.

Privacy and courtesy also mean that your interview area is neat and tidy, that your desk is clear of papers and books, and that you are dressed appropriately. An untidy desk or a disheveled interviewer creates the impression that the interviewee is either intruding or being treated indifferently.

INVOLVEMENT. Lack of interest is one of the chief enemies of listening because it dilutes attention. To listen effectively you must first convince yourself that the interview is important. Unless you become personally involved, at least to the extent that you desire a successful outcome, you will find it difficult to focus your attention properly. Even in the most routine employment interview, you must not only sustain your interest but also develop a sense of *commitment* to the applicant that will enable you to give your utmost attention to the business at hand. If it is not important to you, it most certainly is to the applicant, and a person who undertakes even the most casual interview assumes the responsibility for being vitally interested in a successful outcome.

The direction of your attention, that is, the particular sensations you focus upon, is a function of the power of the stimulus to attract your attention and of your internal motivations. An applicant's particularly odd manner of speech might have sufficient power to attract your attention. If you then become too interested in his diction, you will be unable to concentrate on the content of what he says.

CONCENTRATION. Interest and personal involvement alone are not quite enough to insure keen, attentive listening. Without attention there can be no perception, and the chief enemy of attention is distraction. Distraction can be caused by opposing stimuli, such as loud noises, glaring lights, pain, or physical discomfort, that have the power to shift attention from the matter at hand. Prevention and control of physical distractions in the interview are usually fairly simple. This does not eliminate distraction altogether, however, because the chief cause of human inattention is boredom, fatigue, or lack of interest.

To get the most from an interview, then, you must first facilitate close attention by eliminating potential sources of distraction. You must control not only such factors as noise, light, physical movement, temperature, fresh air, and physical comfort, but you must also develop an interest in your subject, know what to focus on in the interviewee's behavior, and recognize the debilitating effect of prolonged attention.

The diversions that occur within you are far more disruptive than those from outside because they dissipate attention almost imperceptibly. In normal conversation, the average person speaks at the rate of between 150 and 200 words per minute, while you can comprehend at *four* times this rate. Add to this disparity between speaking and listening rates the repetitious pattern of ordinary speech, and the result is an irresistible tendency in you to shift your attention from the speaker's words to your own thoughts. In this way, distractions are generated and listening is reduced.

Nervous or inexperienced interviewers, especially, will tend to think of their next question, to worry about what is being said, or to ponder over the impression they are making on the interviewee when they should be listening carefully. Experienced interviewers will so focus their attention and mental energy on the words, the voice inflection, the gestures, and the underlying meaning of what is being said as it is being said that they will have little time to think of themselves or to refer to their own conscious thoughts. Complete concentration affords no opportunity to consider what to say next.

LINKING. If you prepare adequately, if you are sufficiently interested, and if you concentrate intently, your interview will flow along smoothly and unaffectedly. The natural link between questions, answers, and subsequent questions will thus form a chain of interconnected ideas stretching from the beginning to the end of your interview. You will need only to glance at your outline from time to time to make sure you cover all the areas in your interview plan.

You can begin with a broad introductory question, then build your subsequent questions on the interviewee's replies and, in this way, cover most of the ground naturally. Freed from the conscious effort required to formulate questions, you can devote your whole attention to listening, observing, and remembering. This step, linking, is therefore the reciprocal of "gatekeeping."

INTEGRATION. Preparation, interest, concentration, and linking enable you to listen in depth, which is your whole objective. While you may ask for details, facts, and figures, you will really listen for the main ideas, for patterns, and for trends. Attention, perception, and retention are often overwhelmed by a simple catalogue of unrelated facts. Intelligent comprehension requires assimilation and interpretation by which isolated facts are related, a pattern of relationships is delineated, and meaning is given to the entire sequence of ideas presented by the interviewee.

By organizing what you hear and by searching for behavioral trends, you "hear" a great deal more than is spoken. Gaps in the overall pattern become evident, and further questions and additional areas to be explored are suggested.

Retention   While the problems of perception and listening make interviewing an extremely tentative enterprise, the frailties of the human memory make it almost impossible. Most of us are unable to recall even a small portion of our experiences, observations, and thoughts shortly after they occur. Things that you may want very much to remember are beyond your ability to retain for any length of time, and those that you do retain are so changed by faulty memory that they sometimes are almost unrecognizable.

This phenomenon of recall is referred to by psychologists as *the embedding process*. It proceeds in three stages: leveling, sharpening, and assimilation. Since the number of details that you can retain from a witnessed event is quite small and declines rapidly over time, a leveling out of details occurs that changes the actual event in the direction of greater brevity and conciseness. This leveling, however, does not occur at random. Items that are of particular interest to you, facts that confirm your expectation and help support your attitudinal structure, are retained for indefinite periods.

But you do more than get rid of what you consider to be extraneous details. You will unconsciously exaggerate or "sharpen" the limited number of details that you have retained. Items that become sharpened most readily are those that stand out, such as numbers, slogans, labels, symbols, or any reasonable explanation that gives meaning to the story. A $10 win at cards grows to $100 when the story is repeated; a nail file becomes a dagger; a minor tiff becomes a bitter struggle. And finally, your attitudes, interests, and beliefs affect what you remember and, by the influence of your stereotypes, expectations, and prejudices, enable you to give meaning and understanding to both what you perceive and what you can later recall.

You must be concerned with your ability to recall interview events as they happen, and you must constantly reexamine your conclusions and evaluations. The only effective way to do this is to take notes *during* the interview. It is effective, first, because it helps your memory, which is a very fragile thing. Second, it helps you organize the information you get into logical categories for comparison to job requirements.

It is most desirable to record interview judgments and observations while the interview is in progress. There is little danger that you will distract the interviewee by writing during the interview. If you wait until afterwards, you are apt to forget many important details. There is always a chance that interruptions may prevent the completion of this task for an hour or even a day. Naturally, the later the task is postponed, the less reliable your observations will be.

Immediately after the interview, therefore, you must complete your notes and make a final summary of your impressions. This summary, written while the interview is still fresh in your memory, is invaluable later if there is an occasion to review your final evaluation and the reasons for it.

Interpreting Interview Data   The most difficult problem in taking action after an interview stems from properly interpreting the facts and data obtained. Sometimes we forget that the interview is only a tool to help evaluate, predict, and decide. Information is sterile in and of itself. It is what we do with the information that counts!

Most interviewers have difficulty in effectively interpreting interview information because of four common errors:

1. They do not listen for facts.
2. They do not remember the facts.
3. They draw invalid conclusions from facts.
4. The conclusions they draw may be valid in some cases, but they fail to realize that there are other equally plausible explanations of the same set of facts.

Or, to put it another way, they often tend to draw conclusions from a bit of information and then accept it as being true and valid, rather than considering it as a hypothesis or idea that is to be tested against further evidence. Scientifically speaking, a hypothesis is a tentatively unproved explanation of a set of data or facts. But it may surprise you to know that you use hypotheses everyday in ordinary situations. Your supervisor scowls at you in the morning and you jump to the conclusion that it is because of a bad mood. But it is only a hypothesis based on the facial expressions of the supervisor.

We form hypotheses about everything we see and hear. But unless we go one step further, we may just jump to unfair or incorrect conclusions. The hypothesis must be confirmed or rejected by testing. The process of hypothesis testing or interpreting data, as we shall discuss it again in this book, depends on the purpose of the interview. But its fundamental objective is to keep us from jumping to erroneous conclusions.

The Traits of an Effective Interviewer

These techniques when combined with the role dimensions described in the preceding chapter give us a clear picture of the traits of an effective interviewer: knowledge, empathy, and communication skills.

Knowledge Since knowledge must precede action, you as an effective interviewer must be aware of the context of the situation in which you are expected to function. This truism is often ignored in practice. Inexperienced personnel representatives are first assigned to employment interviewing to train them for "more responsible" positions later. Similarly, supervisors are expected to conduct performance-evaluation interviews, counseling interviews, and even employment interviews with no instructions or preliminary guidelines on what they are expected to do and with no thought given to whether they have the knowledge or skill to do it.

As an interviewer, you must first have a deep understanding of human motivation and personal adjustment. This knowledge, acquired by a formal education or years of meaningful experience in dealing with people, provides you with an appreciation of the way people behave and why.

Second, you must have a broad knowledge of personnel administration as a vital part of the management effort. In particular, your grasp of management science should give you an appreciation of how the personnel interviewer can help attain corporate objectives.

Third, you must know your organization, its internal relationships, its products, its policies, and its practices, so that within the interview, you can serve as a useful resource person.

These, then, are the ability factors that permit the interviewer to operate successfully within the framework of the personnel program. With them and appropriate intellectual and personality characteristics, anyone, regardless of education or experience, can learn to conduct effective interviews.

Empathy Since interviewing is so psychologically complex, the primary qualification of a skilled interviewer should be quite obvious. Above all you must be reasonably well-adjusted, in sound mental health, with substantial insight into your own personality and behavioral dynamics. You must have the ability to empathize with the other person in the interview. Empathy seems to be a reflection of your acceptance of yourself and of your basic self-regard that enables you to express warmth and genuine sincerity toward the interviewee. You must accept yourself and others in such a way that those with whom you interact can do the same thing.

While empathy has been variously defined and may even be a multidimensional trait, it generally is interpreted to mean the ability to understand, to feel along with, to anticipate, or to predict what another person will do.

We shall use the term in a more restricted sense, not shared by all psychologists, to mean the imaginative *participation* in the feeling or state of mind of the interviewee *without* necessarily experiencing the same emotion. By this definition, we distinguish empathy from *sympathy*, a form of behavior that implies feeling the same emotion as the other person. When you empathize with sick people, for example, you can appreciate their suffering and understand how they feel; in sympathizing with them, on the other hand, you not only appreciate their suffering but suffer along with them and feel the same aches and pains.

To be helpful, you must always be empathic, but you can never be sympathetic because you then become so emotionally involved that your thought processes are blocked. You must appreciate keenly the feelings and the outlook of the other person but only in a helpful, understanding manner. You may, for example, understand vividly an interviewee's nervousness without feeling the slightest bit nervous yourself. You can listen attentively to a grieving employee's tale of indignation without becoming indignant yourself.

If you are unable to respond sensitively and imaginatively to an interviewee's feeling or, conversely, if you find yourself becoming emotionally implicated, you will be seriously handicapped. Empathy, then, describes all skillful interviewers, whether they are employment managers, supervisors, or counselors.

But the question is, how does one acquire empathy or develop it to its maximum extent? This is a hard question, largely unanswered by present-day research and certainly beyond the scope of our discussion. The answer is bound up with the development of self-insight and with the possession of a sense of self-regard which we have referred to earlier.

Communication Skills   The principal vehicle of human communication is language. It is not the only vehicle, but others such as facial expression, gestures, and voice inflection normally accompany language by accentuating or supporting the verbal structure. Without language, human communication becomes extremely difficult, if not impossible.

There are many different types of language such as mathematical signs, telegraphic codes, scientific symbols, and even customs and conventions, but our concern is with the most ordinary of languages, that which involves words, spoken or written, and understood by the majority in a given community. It is this language that is the principal vehicle of communication in the interview.

From the standpoint of its structure alone, language has an indefinitely large capacity. There are only twenty-six letters in the English alphabet, but they form over 500,000 words. Despite the large number of words in existence in any civilized language, the average person understands only a few. Children at the age of seven understand about 24,000 words; by the time they graduate from high school, they have a *passive* vocabulary of about 80,000 words, the same amount as the average adult.

This vocabulary consists of an ability to recognize the general meaning of a word when it is used in a specific context. A person's active vocabulary, that is, the number of words he uses in conversation, is far fewer. Vocabulary size depends upon a person's intelligence, education, and cultural background. You must be careful to use words that can be understood by your listener, or your message simply will not get across. In turn, by listening carefully to your interviewees' vocabulary range, you can get a fair idea of their intellectual ability, education, and social background.

But the problem of language is much more than quantitative. In most modern tongues, but particularly in English, one word can have many meanings. The word "fast," for example, can describe a horse that is either securely tied to a hitching post or running away; it can also refer either to going without food or to a color that won't fade when a garment is washed. You must make certain that you and your partner in the interview are using words in precisely the same way. No word has a really unique meaning but takes its exact significance from the context in which it is employed. The inherent ambiguity of language, even when articulated carefully, should give you pause and prompt you to take no meaning for granted.

Words are not merely symbols for ideas, they also convey emotions. Some words have far more emotional overtones than others. The word "black" to describe a night is much more emotional than the word "dark." Poets draw heavily upon the emotional content of words to establish moods or to share emotional effect with their readers. Some words, too, are emotionally relevant only for certain groups of people and are quite neutral for others. The word "profit" is just another economic variable to an economist, but to a businessman it stands for his reason for risking his capital, and to a labor leader it has a highly charged content associated with exploitation and injustice. The word, therefore, is quite different in that it stimulates a unique response in each of the three.

In choice of words, the effective communicator must pay attention to the range of the listener's vocabulary, to the meanings assigned to words, and to their possible emotional impact.

Interviewer Development

The final and most important point in our survey of the basics of interviewing concerns the way to teach the skill and develop effective interviewers. Since interviewing is a psychomotor skill, it cannot be acquired merely by reading this book. It requires observation of effective techniques, practice in applying them, and helpful coaching. To understand this, we need to know more about how people learn and what constitutes effective interviewer training.

How People Learn   Learning does not consist in the rote memorization of a few platitudes or conventions. Learning occurs only when there is a permanent change in students' habitual response patterns resulting from a reorganization of their perceptual field. Without an observable change in behavior, there is really no learning.

If, for instance, upon completion of this book, you, reader, change none of your interviewing habits or if you never interview anyone, you cannot possibly have learned anything. You may have been entertained, amused, or edified, but you have not been taught.

Changing an adult's behavior in any respect is no easy task. Because in outward appearance it simulates normal conversation so closely, interviewing is doubly difficult to teach. Programs designed to teach such an intricate skill must take into account the motivation of the learner, the rate of learning, and the individual's ability to learn.

MOTIVATION is a primary aspect of the learning situation. People must come to an instructional situation prepared to learn. Unless they are sincerely convinced that they must change their behavior in some degree, they will, consciously or unconsciously, resist the attempt to teach them new tricks. So you, the interviewer-learner, must feel a need to acquire or to improve your interviewing skills. If you are secretly convinced that you are already an interviewer, you are so disposed that all instructional efforts will prove fruitless. Unless you appreciate your present inadequacies and the advantages of remedying them, you will not submit to the slow, painful effort required to learn new ways.

The supervisor, for example, who has been conversing with subordinates—instructing them, coaching them, and telling them how their performance will be appraised—will not submit willingly to a session on interviewing skills, unless, first, the supervisor is sold on the idea that improvement is necessary and, second, that it will pay benefits in the long run.

The *rate* at which people learn varies widely from individual to individual and within the same person. It depends on the nature of the task to be learned, the time span over which the learning must occur, and previous learnings related to the new task to be acquired. Some interviewers become quite adept in a few short weeks of instruction, and others, despite intensive coaching, never succeed at the task. And for the same person, some simpler aspects of interviewing can be acquired in a matter of a few hours, while the more complex may take years to master.

All student-interviewers must undergo a learning program suited to their needs. The entire program should incorporate intensive sessions of *massed* learning and more widely spaced sessions of *distributed* learning in which students can internalize and apply this new learning. One-week interviewer training courses are of less value than the same amount of instructional hours spaced over several months.

An ideal program combines short intensive theory sessions, consisting of lectures, readings, study, and discussion, followed by role playing and actual interviewing placed not too far apart but distributed over a longer period of time. Unless this sequence is followed scrupulously, regression to older, more firmly fixed habits and consequent loss of learning is likely to ensue.

Each student's particular interviewing aptitude is influenced by a general *capacity* to learn as determined by such factors as overall intelligence, retentive powers, age, and previous learning experiences. Because of positive attitudes toward the educational process, some people are more teachable than others, a fact that has significant implications for interviewer selection.

Interviewer Training vs. Development   You will have noted by now that we have carefully avoided the use of the word "training" to describe the education of interviewers. This word, derived from the earlier phrase "manual training," refers to the teaching of mechanical skills to people. It is unfortunate that, by extrapolation, it now refers to the total teaching-learning process in industry. It is a particularly noxious term when applied to the learning of interview skills because it implies a routine, automatic type of conditioning pertinent to animal training or to the acquisition of the correct golf swing. Interviewers cannot be "trained"; they are "developed." Development implies growth and the realization of a person's potential. It signifies self-initiation and a voluntary, purposeful maturation of the whole person.

We shall use the term "interviewer development" to describe not only activities helpful to the person's education but also specifically to the changes, conscious or unconscious, in the person that improve capabilities and that make for increased capacity as well as improved performance.

The erroneous assumption of learner passivity, that people change if someone does something to them, has dominated interviewer development so that it is indeed viewed as "interviewer training."

In this teaching approach, emphasis is placed so heavily on passivity and on a stereotyped pattern of behavior, that most personnel interviewers fail to rise above a low level of mediocrity. They continue to conduct interviews that are masterpieces of conformity, decorated with a patter of clichés and meaningless chatter having little or no true relevancy.

More recent approaches have stressed the view that highly skilled interviewers are the result, not so much of what happens to them from without, but rather of what happens to them within, involving the whole person and not merely the perception and enactment of a specific role. Appropriate interviewer development is not only a program but a dynamic, internal, and ongoing process that must conform to the needs of each learner assigned to this function.

How to Teach Interviewing To impart interviewing skills effectively requires a skilled teacher, the proper learning aids, and on-the-job coaching.

A TEACHER. In the introduction to Part 1, we mentioned that learning to interview is like learning to play the piano. This task is a far cry from learning to swim; learners cannot be thrown into water over their heads and be expected via the floundering process to master the art. Learners require a competent teacher to explain the principles of interviewing, to demonstrate them, and to analyze their performance by pointing out areas to be developed and strengths to be emphasized and sharpened.

LEARNING AIDS. Interview learning is facilitated by visual, auditory, and participatory aids. These learning aids will include audio and videotape recordings to enable learners to critique their performance in actual interviews: filmstrips, timing devices, charts, and one-way mirrors for teacher observation.

The audio-tape workbook cassette program has proven to be an effective aid in interviewer training. This approach combines the most advanced method of audio program instruction with maximum participation and involvement of each group taking the program.[1]

Role playing is by far the principal learning tool. By this method, the student actually participates in a specific situation and acts out in an

---

[1] See for example F. M. Lopez, *Employment Interviewing Workbook/Cassette Training Program,* F. M. Lopez & Associates, Inc., 1973.

"as if" manner the dimensions of the interviewer role. Maier and his associates report that the interview behavior of students of a human-relations course could be significantly improved by role-playing training, particularly by experiences in nondirective counseling. The authors' conclusions about human-relations training seem to be applicable to interviewer training—that the typical course is "neither long enough nor does it include enough skill training to enable trainees to develop skills that will change their behavior significantly."[2]

Role playing, however, seems to be ineffective without *impact* as Lawshe and his associates discovered.[3] Impact, they suggest, as a characteristic of a learning experience, allows learners to criticize their own performance, provides them with adequate feedback regarding their performance, and emphasizes a learning factor in a strong emotional manner.

When combined with the video or audio tape recorder, role playing becomes a laboratory for learners in which they can test a variety of responses and acquire the equally important skill of critiquing their own reactions by noting unconscious mannerisms that tend to weaken interview continuity.

On-the-job Coaching Role playing, however, is but a prelude to real-life interviewing, without which there can be no true acquisition of interview skills. Again, this cannot be performed haphazardly by tossing the interviewee into a situation and hoping for the best. Interview learning in an on-the-job setting requires first, a coach who is not only an accomplished interviewer but who is also cognizant of the responsibilities of a teacher. After the initial program of lectures, films, laboratory exercises, and role-playing sessions and when the learner is sufficiently familiar with the rudiments of interviewing, the coach conducts a real-life interview in the presence of the learner and records the interview on tape. (As an ethical obligation, permission from the interviewee must be obtained first.) Usually this will not inhibit the interviewee at all, but the practice is not recommended in delicate situations.

To avoid any embarrassment or dilution of interaction that might occur with the presence of a third person in the interview, some teachers place the interviewer-learners outside the room, and with the aid of one-way windows, permit them to observe an actual interview. This, however, is not nearly as effective a teaching device as the previous method cited.

Tapes of several such interviews are replayed and analyzed according

[2] N. R. F. Maier, L. R. Hoffman, and L. N. Lanholz, "Human Relations Training as Manifested in an Interview Situation," *Personnel Psychology*, 13:11–30, 1960.

[3] C. R. Lawshe, R. A. Bolda, and H. L. Brune, "Studies in Management Training Evaluation: II. The Effects of Exposure in Role Playing," *Journal of Applied Psychology*, 43:287–292, 1959.

to the method described below. The coach explains why the things recorded on the tape were said and done. The learner discusses the interviewee's reactions to the leads of the coach and suggests alternative ways of producing the same results.

The next step is to reverse roles. Now the learner conducts the interview, and the coach observes; interviews are also taped, and later analyzed, and the entire interview critiqued.

When, in the opinion of the coach, the interviewer-learners have progressed sufficiently, they are ready for a "solo" performance. They now conduct interviews on their own, although they are still taped and analyzed until the teacher feels that the learners have reached a stage of development where the instructional phase can be terminated and the students "graduated."

The length of time this program requires will vary from person to person and depends upon the type of interview to be learned. For personnel interviews, it is recommended that the learning process begin with the simplest interview, the initial employment interview, because this interview is so highly structured that personal interaction is minimal. After, say, six months, novice interviewers can progress to minor employee advisory interviews. Then they can move to orientation and termination interviews and then to the more complex counseling and grievance interviews. By the end of another year, they should be ready to conduct opinion-survey or assessment-selection interviews at which point they will have attained the status of *journeyman* interviewer. Progression beyond this point requires much more intensive study, practice, self-analysis, and personal development. Normally, about five years of experience is required to achieve the level of a highly skilled professional interviewer who is qualified to conduct counseling interviews with problem employees, to coach supervisors in the conduct of performance appraisal interviews, and finally to conduct selection interviews in depth.

part 2

Decision-making Interviews

During the journey from infancy to old age in our highly complex
society, the average person is exposed repeatedly to formal and
informal evaluations based on ability, character, and achievements.
For social purposes, informal and spontaneous person-to-person
appraisals present few real problems, are engaged in all the time,
and lead usually to congenial personal associations and even to
lasting friendships.

But in the more serious tasks of operating a business or a government agency, subjective, interpersonal assessments based on individual tastes are, at the very least, impractical because they are meant
to predict behavior in situations where camaraderie plays only a
minor role. More formal, more systematic, and more realistic techniques are therefore essential. One such technique is the decision-
making interview.

The decision-making interview is simply a measuring tool, and as
such, its utility consists of its ability to meet a simple test. It must
predict some future event or series of events by indicating the probable future behavior of the interviewee under a given set of job
conditions. The only way that this can be accomplished is by assessing the interviewee in a fashion that is consistent, objective, and
quite independent of the interviewer's personal values and of the
time, the place, or the circumstances surrounding the interview.

The failure of most selection interviews to meet these standards of
consistency and predictability has not deterred the average personnel
manager or supervisor from relying almost exclusively on them as
instruments of employee choice. The reason for this state of affairs
is not hard to find. Most average personnel managers or supervisors
are accustomed to judging people in all types of situations for a
variety of purposes ranging from the selection of a spouse to the
election of a president without ever bothering to examine the accuracy of their assessment. If, perchance, later events do demonstrate
incontrovertibly the error of the original evaluation, they can fall
back on the comforting rationalization that human nature is really
unpredictable anyhow!

In modern times, however, the evidence of the fallibility of subjective, interpersonal judgment has been so overwhelming that considerable research effort has been devoted to the development of more scientific approaches to the problem of the selection and placement of employees. To improve the quality of the selection process and hence the employment decision, emphasis has been placed on a more objective approach to the description, the evaluation, and the prediction of job performance. Aptitude tests, self-descriptive personality inventories, projective personality tests, situational games, weighted biographical questionnaires, and structured interviews have been developed as more appropriate and more reliable measures of an employment prospect's abilities, achievements, attitudes, and social skills.

Despite overly optimistic claims in some quarters, no single one of the aforementioned instruments has proved to be the final answer to the selection question. As a matter of fact, no matter how objective or how scientifically constructed, it is fairly certain that a particular selection instrument can adversely affect the chances of members of some ethnic and racial groups to obtain fair employment opportunities.

In Part 2, we shall be concerned with one selection tool—the interview. This interview is, by far, the most widely practiced of personnel interviews. Indeed, when one refers to the personnel interview, many people think automatically of the selection interview. To reduce the many errors that creep into its use, it is necessary to understand, first of all, some basic principles of selection theory. Then we shall consider the fundamentals of selection strategy. Only after reviewing these fundamentals can we consider how the interview can contribute to the goal of a substantially reduced margin of error in selection decision-making.

chapter 5

Selection Theory

> Then it will be our duty to select, if we can, natures which are fitted for the task of guarding the city?
> It will.
> And the selection will be no easy matter, I said; but we must be brave and do our best?
> We must.
> —PLATO, *The Republic*

Since the beginning of human social history, mankind has been continually preoccupied with finding suitable approaches to the equitable division of labor. The obvious fact that some people can perform some tasks better than other people and that nobody can do all things well has prompted princes and philosophers of every age and culture to seek a quick, convenient, and accurate method of estimating human ability without undergoing the sometimes painful, always wasteful process of trial and error. Historians have recorded the rich and colorful variety of selection techniques that have been invented, ranging from the examination of a bird's entrails and the casting of lots to plain kidnapping and outright enslavement. Although each of these methods undoubtedly had its value in certain contexts and in appropriate cultures, the more progressive inhabitants of this planet have suggested from time to time that there may be more effective ways of choosing people for particular positions.

As long ago as 350 B.C., in *The Republic,* Plato described a number of tests that could be administered to young men to screen out the "smiths" and to choose the guardians of the city. About the same time, the always inventive Chinese had devised a system of examinations to judge candidates for various magisterial positions. And heredity had been and still is considered to be a most logical method of designating people for such occupational roles as king, queen, president, or even plumber.

Sometimes the choice presents no problem because either the job to be filled is easy or the labor supply is extensive. But in a democratic society that frowns on nepotism, divination, or chance as instruments of job appointment and when the positions to be filled are complex and the supply of competent labor is rather tight, it becomes a matter of paramount concern to avoid the prohibitive financial cost of continually hiring inadequate employees.

The interview, which is the most widely used selection technique of modern society, must constitute a valid method of choosing people for specific jobs. If it does not, it is no better than the older and more interesting methods of selection mentioned earlier. As we have already indicated, the evidence for interview validity is not readily apparent. The most recent survey of research on the selection interview concludes that much more study is needed because of the many variables involved.[1] The results reported in the literature are mixed and inconclusive partly because of the varying methodologies employed and partly because of the lack of appreciation of the entire setting in which the selection interview is employed.

The selection interview involves a decision. The value of the decision made can be optimized and the probability of error minimized by applying a correct strategy at the major points of the selection process. This process consists of four stages: description or assessment of the applicant, evaluation of qualifications by comparison to a predetermined set of standards, prediction of probable success on the job in question, and the decision whether to select or not to select. For their successful accomplishment, these stages depend on what we shall call the components of a theory of selection: human resources planning, three basic selection principles, seven selection tools, and five major selection phases.

Human Resources Planning

Since the selection process is an artifact of the culture in which it is embedded, the one that we shall describe occurs only in a free economy with a free labor market in which workers sell their services to the highest bidder, employers must meet the competition in bidding for these services, and workers may move freely from employer to employer as they see fit without regard to an individual employer's needs or to the national interest. We shall review the elements of a selection program in a society where employers are strictly on their own and must figure out their own needs for the immediate and the long-range future. Under such a set of circumstances, selection, as Albert Maslow has so succinctly put it, is a reductive process by which an applicant population that presumably contains a representative proportion of the people with the skills and the abilities required by employers is separated out from

---

[1] Orman A. Wright, Jr., "Summary of Research on the Selection Interview Since 1964," *Personnel Psychology*, 22:391–413, 1969.

a universe of workers.[2] If the labor market is such that employers happen to skim off the "cream" and separate out no one but highly qualified workers, they can simply choose as they see fit on a random basis. If they happen to strike the bottom of the talent barrel, the selection process will again be unnecessary, because no matter what instruments they use, they will inevitably end up with inferior or unqualified workers. But if, as is most often assumed, they happen to extract a representative cross section of the labor universe, from the bottom to the top, it then becomes the proper object of the selection process to sort out, to classify, and to identify those workers with the requisite skills and abilities.

An effective selection interview presupposes careful human resources planning, based upon a manpower information system consisting of a set of corporate policies, a comprehensive career plan, well-defined selection standards, and a forecast of future personnel needs.

The company should know *right now* what kinds of employees it has, what kinds it needs, what kinds, in numbers, it will probably need in the next five years or even as far ahead as the next ten years. For the next five years, it should even forecast specific individuals who are to fill these openings, not just numbers, but real people.

Defining Employment Policies The first task is to establish a realistic set of employment policies and to communicate them widely throughout the company. These policies must be based on an underlying management philosophy with respect to the value of the corporation's human resources. They must also state clearly the company's position with regard to hiring the best qualified among a group of applicants, its positive recruitment efforts, and its willingness to commit resources to valid selection techniques and to meeting its community and social obligations.

In particular, the personnel policies must conform to current governmental guidelines with respect to equal employment opportunities. In 1964, the Congress adopted the Civil Rights Act which affected many aspects of modern life, including voting qualifications, equal access to public facilities, desegregation of public education, community relations, and equality of employment opportunity. Title VII of this act dealing with employment made it the avowed objective of the federal government to eliminate all employment discrimination based on race, color, religion, sex, or national origin in all industries affecting interstate commerce.

Above all, the policy must be articulated, published, and supported

---

[2] A. P. Maslow, "Measurement in the Selection and Development Process," in *Behavioral Science Research in Industrial Relations*, Industrial Relations Monograph No. 21., Industrial Relations Counsellors, Inc., New York, 1962, pp. 121–148.

by a program that guarantees its implementation. As we shall indicate in the following chapter, pious statements of management's good intentions are no longer acceptable in the courts.

Developing the Career Plan   After establishing its basic policies, the company must develop a comprehensive career plan. This plan should define job functions, relate jobs to one another, vertically and horizontally, and present a reasonably accurate and objective description of the duties and demands of each job.

Every position in the company should be placed in a two- or three-way matrix consisting of level of complexity and job family and location. The term "job," as used throughout this book, refers to a group of positions with the same title and function. A "job family" refers to a group of jobs that are related by function and personal requirements. The "level of complexity" refers to the degree of skill required to perform the job functions.

Establishing Selection Standards   After obtaining a reasonably clear picture of job requirements, the next step is to establish selection standards that give a relatively accurate evaluation of the abilities, skills, and attitudes required to perform each job effectively.

Most organizations have available certain techniques to enable them to develop precise job descriptions. But the ordinary job description says little about the traits a person must possess to perform a job effectively. It usually concerns itself with the technical competence, that is, with the education and experience of the incumbent. Social or cultural associations are often ignored because it is assumed that they play only a minor role in job performance. Yet, analyses of the reasons why employees terminate jobs show that the motivational and social characteristics, work habits, and ability to get along with others are often more important than levels of education or lack of job knowledge.

Thus, the first order of business in an employment program is to write a job and trait description in clear, unequivocal language that specifies what is required to perform a job effectively. It is difficult to conceive of an effective employment program that is not based on a rather rigorous analysis of the traits required for effective job performance.

Forecasting Employment Needs   Finally, management must create a system of forecasting manpower needs which gives reasonable advance notice of how many and what type of workers will be required to keep the organization fully and competently staffed. Since good selection takes time, it is understandable that many employers become bogged down by the need to fill vacancies on short notice. Forecasting is not an exact science, but there are certain types of information available which enable an employer to put together a clear projection of personnel requirements.

Employment forecasting requires an extension of present personnel trends and a prediction of external factors, over which the employer has no control, that will effect personnel needs.

Taken together, the four elements of defining employment policies, developing the career plan, establishing selection standards, and forecasting employment needs will enable managers to develop an integrated human resources plan. This plan can represent a master strategy in shaping the character and the quality of the corporate labor force.

The Three Selection Principles

The selection program by which the human resources plan is implemented is a complex of methods, procedures, techniques, and instruments. Underlying these activities are three fundamental principles: the selection ratio, individual differences, and prediction.

The Principle of the Selection Ratio By definition, selection implies a choice. If you have thirty vacancies and only thirty-five prospects, your selection ratio, that is the proportion between applicants and hirees, will be so high that you might just as well place the thirty-five applicants' names in a hat and hire the first thirty whose names are drawn out. No other method can improve appreciably this cheap and simple procedure.

The principle of the selection ratio states, therefore, that the wider your choice, the better your chance of making a valid selection. A low selection ratio, such as one out of fifty, sharply increases your chances of making a correct selection decision, assuming, of course, that within the group of fifty there are at least some persons who can do the job. On the other hand, if all fifty applicants are qualified, selection is unnecessary, and you may use the hat profitably once more.

Your first selection task, then, is to attract a sufficient number of quality applicants to make your selection efforts worthwhile. Merely lowering your selection ratio will not help you unless you are aware of how people differ and how these differences relate to job effectiveness.

The Principle of Individual Differences The principle of individual differences simply refers to the nature, extent, and significance of the ways in which people differ. For our presentation, we have chosen to group the ways people differ into five arbitrary and not necessarily exclusive classifications.

1. *Physical differences.* Obviously, people differ in such physical characteristics as height, weight, sex, age, and outward appearance.

Other important physical differences that are not so obvious include heart functioning, blood pressure, visual acuity, and reaction time.

2. *Mental differences.* People differ in mental capacity; in individual ability to learn specific skills, such as typing, piano playing, and basket weaving; in problem-solving ability; and in such other cognitive processes as memory, discrimination, and abstraction.

3. *Learned differences.* People differ in environmental experiences that lead to the acquisition of specific attributes based on the cultural or social group in which they have matured. Such differences include education, work experience, craft knowledge and skill.

4. *Motivational differences.* People differ in their adaptability to environmental conditions, in their self-control, and in their ethical standards.

5. *Social differences.* Finally, people differ in social behavior, customs, and emotional reactions to other people.

The principle of individual differences implies, therefore, that effective selection requires the assessment of the whole person in relation to the total job. To ignore one category of individual differences is to invite future problems in the form of inefficiency, maladjustment, absenteeism, or low job satisfaction. To overemphasize one category, such as mental ability at the expense of another, such as adaptability to repetition or discomfort, is to invite high turnover.

The Principle of Prediction   Merely to recognize that differences exist among people is insufficient; it is also essential to know to what extent and with what significance these differences relate to job performance and job satisfaction. The answers to these questions lie in the principle of prediction. The procedures required to answer them are so involved and complex that you are invited to consult a good text dealing with this subject.[3]

Since employment specialists deal with intangible human traits that do not permit direct, sensible measurement—intellectual capacity, accounting knowledge, or emotional stability—they face a difficult but not altogether unsolvable problem when they attempt to determine how much of what trait an employment applicant possesses. By comparing the individual's performance to the average performance of a specific group on certain well-defined tasks, they can derive a set of numerical terms that imply "below average," "average," and "above average" performance on these tasks and in terms of this group. When the tasks and the group are relevant to some aspect of the job situation, the derived information is quite meaningful. To describe what is meaningful information, we

[3] See, for example, Marvin D. Dunnette, *Personnel Selection And Placement* (Belmont, Calif.: Wadsworth Publishing Co., 1966).

must briefly consider its three characteristics: normality, reliability, and validity.

NORMALITY.   Sometimes a number is derived that describes the applicant's relationship to a particular group and is expressed as a "percentile," or "intelligence quotient," or "standard score"—arbitrary terms adopted by statisticians to communicate complex ideas more conveniently. Such numbers must be treated with caution because they can be quite misleading. Since many human attributes are distributed in the population in the form of a "normal" probability distribution (or it is assumed that they are), these numbers describe an individual's position on that frequency curve by specifying what percentage of the group scored higher and lower. When these relationships have been summarized numerically, psychometricians can do many things with them, one of which is quite important to the idea of prediction. Figure 3 shows graphically what a normal frequency distribution looks like.

RELIABILITY.   Any measurement will contain some degree of error, no matter how infinitesimal, as in measuring the distance between two continents. Two sets of measures of the same features of the same person will never duplicate each other exactly, but repeated measures of the same person under the same circumstances will ordinarily show some consistency. This tendency toward consistency is referred to technically as *reliability*. If a person achieves a test score of 50 on one day and a score of 100 on the next, the test results are inconsistent and, therefore, unreliable. Putting it another way, it can be said that reliability is the extent to which a measurement is free of error. An unreliable measure has little merit because it is as undependable and as inconsistent as an elastic ruler.

VALIDITY.   When a tool such as a ruler, a micrometer, or an aptitude

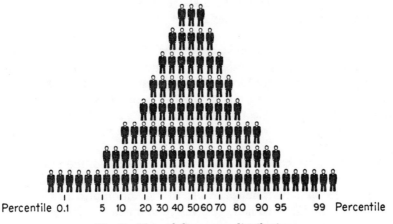

Percentile 0.1   5   10   20 30 40 50 60 70 80   90 95   99 Percentile

Fig. 3   Normal frequency distribution

test measures what it is intended to measure, it is valid. But validity implies more than this, and it depends on the answers to three questions that can be asked of any selection measure:

1. Does it really measure the personal trait it purports to measure?
2. Is the trait it measures possessed by an effective job performer?
3. Does the trait it measures predict future performance?

An affirmative answer to the first question is called *construct validity,* which indicates the extent to which the measurement factor defines the performance in question. An affirmative answer to the second question is referred to as *concurrent validity,* which indicates the extent to which the measurement factor represents effective *present* job performance. An affirmative answer to the third question is called *predictive validity.*

For example, suppose a company develops a test to measure "supervisory skill" to help select and promote effective supervisors. Before using this test in the selection process, *it must meet four distinct criteria*:

1. Employers must determine that the test consistently yields the same results with the same people. They do this by showing that each applicant obtains the same score each time the test is taken, and that the test score is independent of the person administering or scoring it.

2. Employers must determine the *construct validity* of the test by finding out whether it really measures "supervisory skill" rather than intelligence or verbal fluency. They do this by showing that the people who have supervisory skill score higher on this test than people who lack it.

3. Next, employers must determine the *concurrent validity* by administering the test to a group of supervisors some of whom have been evaluated as excellent, some as average, and some below average. If the excellent supervisors obtain the highest scores on the test and the below average supervisors obtain the lowest scores, the test is concurrently valid.

4. Finally, employers must determine the *predictive validity* of the test. They must administer the test to a number of applicants for supervisory positions who are hired without regard to their test scores. After a suitable period of time has elapsed, the supervisors' performance is compared to their test scores. If the effective supervisors turn out to be high scorers and the ineffective supervisors low scorers, the test is predictively valid.

Although in practice it is much more complicated, the procedure just described constitutes the essence of the notion of validation.

One major difficulty, however, lies in the notion of construct validity. For unlike the thermometer or the micrometer, such psychological measures as an interview or a test depend on the environment and the circumstances in which they are used. While we know that a thermometer measures nothing more or less than the degree of heat in an object, we are never really sure what a psychological instrument is measuring if its constructors rely only on concurrent and predictive validity to demonstrate its usefulness. Consequently, an instrument that is valid in one company or one geographical area or among one racial group may not be valid for another. *This gives rise to the measurement problems that plague those that approach the selection process without adequate analysis of the job for which it is designed.*

The Seven Selection Tools

There are three major sources of information available to personnel administrators to enable them to obtain the information necessary to make a relevant prediction of an applicant's chances of job effectiveness: the self report, the direct observation, and work samples. Although the lines of distinction between one source and another can be fuzzy, by and large, they are tapped by seven basic selection tools. Figure 4 illustrates how the various selection tools flow from the sources of human trait data.

Self-report Measures   The most obvious source of information about people is the people themselves. Only they can tell you about their inner feelings, their likes and dislikes, and the details of their life experiences. Naturally this source of information is invaluable, but it can be quite unreliable. Through self-deception or deliberate distortion, an applicant may convey erroneous information to you. Therefore, self-

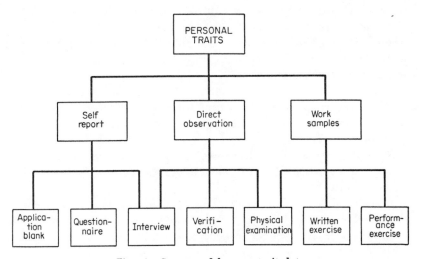

Fig. 4   Sources of human trait data

report information must be treated cautiously and subjected to confirmation by direct observation or by behavioral samples whenever possible.

Self-report information can be obtained in three ways: the biographical information blank, the self-report questionnaire, or the interview.

THE BIOGRAPHICAL INFORMATION BLANK (APPLICATION BLANK). The biographical information blank is a systematic way of ordering factual life history information about an applicant to facilitate comparison with job standards and with other people. While apparently quite simple in appearance, the design of an application blank is rather complex. It must *include* information that is relevant to the requirements deemed to be important for effective job performance, and it must *exclude* information that is unnecessary. Properly used, this tool is far more than a record of biographical data. Job effectiveness scores can be computed from application blank data by weighing such items as location of residence, distance to place of employment, previous experience, occupational stability, and salary history. Because the biographical questionnaire is such an integral part of the interview, it will be discussed in detail in Chapter 7.

THE SELF-REPORT QUESTIONNAIRE. Another way to obtain information about people's traits is to ask them to complete a standardized questionnaire containing statements about their interests, habits, and preferences. While an inventory is really a written interview, the content, scoring procedures, and interpretive guides are so highly standarized that it is usually referred to as a "personality" test.

THE INTERVIEW. Another way to obtain information about people is simply to talk to them. Of all the methods used to appraise job qualifications, the interview is the oldest and the most widely practiced; and as we have already suggested, it can also be the most abused. The interview has severe limitations if it is used as the sole tool of selection, but when it is employed correctly by a trained interviewer in conjunction with the other tools, it can constitute a highly relevant instrument of selection decision making.

As a source of information, the selection interview has two functions:

1. It enables applicants for a position to give information about themselves to the interviewer. As such, it constitutes a self-report measurement device.

2. It also enables the interviewer to observe certain aspects of applicants' behavior. In this fashion, it serves as a direct observation measurement device.

Direct Observation Measures Some traits are measured best by direct observation of an applicant's behavior. *Personal appearance* and *oral* *expression* are two such traits that can only be evaluated effectively in this way. There are other traits such as *creativity* that are judged best by directly examining some product of the applicant's talent. For other traits, such as *integrity,* the applicant's qualifications can best be evaluated by reference to independent records or to the observations of other people.

There are three ways of obtaining information by direct observation:

THE INTERVIEW. As we have already indicated, the interview is a measurement device for directly observing certain aspects of an applicant's behavior.

VERIFICATION. Verification is a process of establishing the possession of certain traits by directly observing some product or piece of work that an applicant has done in the past or by asking other people who know the person well to tell you about the applicant. Usually, verification techniques are used to confirm information already obtained about an applicant by self-report. This process, referred to as a background investigation, is often the last step in the selection process.

PHYSICAL EXAMINATION. To ascertain an applicant's physical traits, the principal sources of information are either an examination by a physician or the performance of physical exercises. The former is a direct observation measure; the latter is a work sample exercise.

Work Samples Probably the most accurate way of measuring the possession of a trait is by sampling an applicant's behavior under controlled conditions. Because the sample is truly representative of a particular job function and the result is independent of the observer or measurer, the behavioral sample is the most reliable and accurate indicator of the possession of a trait. Typing speed, for example, is best measured by a typing work sample, provided that the administration of the exercise is standardized, the typewriter and other external conditions are controlled, and the scoring is objective.

There are three ways of obtaining trait information through behavioral samples:

PHYSICAL EXAMINATION. As we have already indicated, such psychophysical exercises as finger dexterity and reaction-speed tests give accurate information about the physical traits of an applicant.

WRITTEN EXERCISES. Work samples that involve paper-and-pencil exercises can give information about craft knowledge, decision-making, and other traits. A stenographic dictation test, an accounting test, or an in-basket exercise are examples of written work-sample exercises.

PERFORMANCE EXERCISES. Performance exercises are work samples that require the applicant to act out a particular job function. A road test for driving skill is an example of a performance exercise. A typing test or a leaderless group discussion test are examples of performance work-sample exercises.

The Five Selection Phases

The art of selection consists in the use of the appropriate selection tool at the right phase of the selection sequence. Since the selection process involves a sequence of five interdependent phases—recruitment, classification, qualification, synthesis, and probation—inadequacies in one phase will disrupt the entire sequence or cycle. Each selection tool and procedure in the program has not only an objective based on one of the three selection principles but also a correct phase in which it is best employed.

Recruitment   The primary goal of the recruitment phase is to ensure a satisfactory supply of quality prospects. The caliber of the selected applicant will depend as much on the quality of the recruitment effort as on the effectiveness of the selection techniques used because the task of selection is to appraise and to choose, not to attract people. The attraction of a mediocre group of applicants will result inevitably and unavoidably in the selection of mediocre employees, no more and perhaps a lot less. Many complaints about the irrelevancies of interviewing or testing should more properly be directed at the ineptness of the recruitment effort.

This is not to say, however, that recruitment is simply a matter of waiting for people to submit applications. The recruitment effort must be well planned; it must be imaginative and aggressive and deliberately aimed at those sources in the labor market that produce the best people. There are basically two groups of recruitment sources: the natural and the artificial. Artificial recruitment sources are distinguished from the natural "spontaneous" sources in that they require active efforts by employers to stimulate a flow of job seekers, a flow that is not otherwise forthcoming. To the extent that employers have to resort to artificial recruitment methods, they must be prepared to accept limitations on applicant quality.

The company's own staff is the most fruitful natural source of candidates for high-level positions. Unless a recruitment program is based on this concept, the external sources described later will be much less fertile. Conversely, recruitment will be more active because an employer gives his turnover a sharp boost when he bypasses promotion channels.

Assuming, then, that internal sources are tapped first, the second-best source consists of applicants referred by employees or by others who know the company well. The third-best source consists of those who are entering the labor market for the first time, recruited directly from schools and colleges.

The fourth-best natural source consists of those who have made voluntary application by dropping into the employment office, by writing a letter, or by submitting a resume through the mail.

Perhaps the principal artificial recruitment sources are employment agencies, commercial or public. In some locations, for some occupations, and for some industries, the state employment agency is indispensable—the prospective employee population is accustomed to filing for employment there and nowhere else. In such instances, the state agency is as effective a recruitment source as some of the natural sources listed earlier. In large metropolitan centers, commercial agencies attract applicants who tend to be job shoppers and hoppers, who are highly mobile, and who seek to advance themselves by moving from one company to another.

Direct advertising in newspapers, professional journals, and trade magazines is the last and most artificial recruitment source. Being the most expensive and the least rewarding recruitment technique, it should be used only as a last resort.

Despite their relative value none of these sources will be fruitful if applicants are treated inefficiently or discourteously when they visit the prospective employer's establishment. If it is well laid out, tastefully furnished, and staffed by competent, well-trained personnel who believe it desirable to be pleasant and courteous to every applicant, then the employment office itself becomes a major recruitment aid. When applicants are treated well, they are bound to be impressed and to develop a feeling that this is a company with which they would like to be associated.

Finally, some type of tasteful recruitment literature should be made available to applicants to inform them of the many details of company employment that they will be curious about. Not the least of these will be the details of the company employment program, including the steps required to obtain a job. Such literature is an absolute prerequisite in the employment interview because it saves the interviewer valuable time in explaining to an applicant employment policies, programs, and benefits.

Classification When the problem of an adequate supply of applicants has been solved, the next problem is to sort them into broadly homogeneous groups. This task, normally a routine function of the employment office, is best accomplished by the application blank and the employment interview.

Qualification   In this phase, applicants are sifted further to single out those with the desired ability to do the job under consideration. Since this task requires more precise measures, placement exercises have their chief applicability in this phase.

Synthesis   After qualification, the next step is to select from a small, relatively homogeneous group (e.g., all qualified) the person deemed to be the *best* employment risk. Since it is assumed that more than one person has qualified, the object now is to pick the most qualified by a synthesis of all the information accumulated about the applicants to describe them fully in relation to the job requirements. The assessment interview is the most appropriate tool to utilize in this phase, but for less complex jobs it may not be necessary.

Probation   The classification, qualification, and synthesis phases of the selection sequence are really successive screens through which pass only those likely to do the job effectively. The end product, however, is not always an effective employee. As with any decision process, an error-correcting procedure must be incorporated into the system, and in the selection sequence, this is called probation. Provision must be made for a period of time, varying in length according to job complexity, during which the appointees can prove themselves. If the selection techniques have been effective, a high but not necessarily perfect success ratio will be achieved here. The important point to emphasize is that the only way to determine whether people are capable of doing a job is to let them do it. The probation phase, then, represents the final selection step and is also a controlling aspect of the selection process because it permits the vital feedback to the selection planning stage described earlier in this chapter.

chapter 6

Selection Strategy

Swift decisions are not sure.

—SOPHOCLES, *Oedipus Tyrannus*

A major American corporation, a leader in its industry, was disturbed to learn that one of its employment tests was found to be invalid. Since the company's personnel and operating managers had placed great faith in its predictability over a fifteen-year period, they had administered this widely accepted test to well over a million employment applicants. But analysis of the job for which this test had been used to select incumbents showed that one of the test's main components, arithmetic skill, was unnecessary to perform the functions of the job satisfactorily. In effect, the company had for years been disqualifying thousands of employment applicants because they could not do what they would not have to do on the job!

This situation is by no means unique; it describes the employment programs of a substantial number of American employers. It is not merely a case of an invalid instrument, however. It is a prime example of an inadequate selection strategy that is not only unfair to employment applicants but is also wasteful and costly for the employer.

Selection strategy, as distinct from selection theory, consists of the specific procedures and standards used to choose people to perform the work of an enterprise. This strategy facilitates the decisions that have to be made at different choice-points along the critical path extending from the population universe through the labor market to the personnel roster of the company.

To understand what a selection strategy implies, that is, the significance of the sequence of events employed to transform a member of the community into a company employee, we must consider briefly some aspects of a theoretical system around which we have structured our consideration of the selection-interview context—decision theory.

Decision theory constitutes an attempt to put decision making on a mathematical basis by considering various alternatives in a decision situation, the consequences of possible error in each, and the choice of a course of action. According to the theory, it is always possible to find the probabilities for the various options and to compute a number called the "value of the game" which is roughly the minimum outcome one can expect from playing the game blindly by basing the outcome on pure chance. The strategy that assures the player the value of the game or better is therefore a good strategy.

Much of the work in decision and game theory has been applied by operations-research specialists to economics and production to aid in making financial, operating, and sales decisions. It can provide a useful frame of reference, also, for the selection program. Selection can be viewed as a very complex game involving a number of variables that require many decisions at appropriate points. Some are leading or anticipatory decisions, that is, of a "maybe" nature that lead to other decisions, and others are concluding or terminal decisions because they are of "go–no go" variety that end the game. To improve these decisions, objectives must be clearly defined, data must be collected and analyzed, principles must be elaborated, the proper tools must be employed, alternative strategies must be analyzed, and the consequences of each must be evaluated.

But first, the rules of the game must be set down. That is, the selection strategy must be planned according to certain basic assumptions and management standards concerning the equal employment opportunity movement, the notion of what constitutes and predicts job effectiveness, and the practical aspects of processing employment applicants.

The Equal Employment Opportunity Movement

With the passage of the Civil Rights Act of 1964, American employers were confronted with two new but critical questions concerning their selection strategy. Was it possible for employers to discriminate unfairly against specific subgroups of an applicant population simply by the selection strategy they adopted to recruit and select people for positions in their labor force? Could their selection standards and procedures, no matter how impartial and objective, effectively bar eligible females and members of minority groups from the better paying jobs?

Two Explanations   By the 1970s, affirmative answers to these questions appeared to be the norm with nearly every employer in the public and private sectors of the American economy. What was unique about this situation was that while the architects of these selection plans knew about the adverse impact upon women and minority groups, they resolutely maintained that they were fair and economically necessary.

Since people in our society are not recruited, selected, and placed in occupations randomly, the distribution of workers by sex and race in the labor force of employers is a direct outcome of their selection strategy and the structure of their labor markets. There are, therefore, two possible explanations for an uneven and inequitable distribution of women and minority groups on a company payroll:

EXPLANATION A. The labor market does not contain a sufficient number of females and/or minority group members qualified to perform effectively in the positions where the underrepresentation has been observed.

EXPLANATION B. The firm's selection strategy operates, deliberately or not, to create a pattern of sexual and ethnic segregation and discrimination.

The burden of proof is on every employer to support Explanation A. This proof has to consist of a demonstration that the employer is vigorously pursuing a recruitment and selection strategy based on the concept of business necessity as defined by the Supreme Court in the Griggs decision.[1]

To comply with the law, it appears that employers are on the horns of a very unpleasant dilemma. They can initiate expensive, time-consuming research efforts that may or may not produce the evidence needed to support Explanation A. Or they can adopt a straight quota system that may very well reduce overall standards of employee effectiveness.

There is, however, a way out of this dilemma. By adopting a decision-making selection strategy based on a worker-oriented job analysis, positive, aggressive recruitment and business-related selection tools, employers can meet both their legal obligations and their business objectives. What the equal employment opportunity movement has done in effect, therefore, is to force employers into a more rational, sensible employment strategy.

The Civil Rights Act of 1964 The year 1964 represented a landmark year in equal employment opportunity. Title VII of the Civil Rights Act, which became law that year, imposed upon employers, labor unions and employment agencies a new set of obligations, gave employees, job applicants, and members of minority groups new rights, and set up machinery for enforcing those rights.

One of the principal objects and effects of the act was to create the Equal Employment Opportunity Commission (hereafter referred to as

[1] *Griggs et al. vs. Duke Power Company*, No. 124, October Term, 1970 (March 8, 1971) 401 U.S. 424 (1971).

EEOC) to supervise and enforce the provisions of Title VII. Although it had very little actual power in the beginning, it has acquired more and more as time has progressed.

The principal impact of the Civil Rights Act was to extend the protection of the government to minority groups throughout the country and to take out of the hands of individual states the responsibility for passing and enforcing their own employment-practices legislation.

By 1970, the separate streams of fair employment-practices research, legislation, and litigation had converged into law and national social policy. In a civil rights case, it was no longer a sufficient defense to show that your employment practices were impartial and objective. And if employers were found guilty of unlawful discrimination, they were no longer merely "slapped on the wrists" and urged to do better. The courts put teeth into their decisions in the form of heavy financial penalties and the federal agencies developed rigorous standards with which to evaluate selection programs. In April 1972, Congress passed an amendment to Title VII of the 1964 Civil Rights Act giving expanded powers to EEOC. This amendment extended the coverage of the law to employers with at least fifteen employees and authorized the commissioner to bring suit to end the pattern or practice of discrimination by a union or an employer without resorting to the Justice Department.

Affirmative Action Programs   On February 5, 1970, the Office of Federal Contract Compliance, Equal Employment Opportunity, Department of Labor issued Order No. 4 calling for affirmative action programs on the part of federal nonconstruction contractors.[2] This order directed contractors with more than fifty employees or a contract of more than 50,000 dollars to develop a written affirmative action compliance program for each of their establishments.

Briefly stated, an affirmative action program requires employers to develop a plan for increasing the distribution of minority groups in the various occupations and levels within their own work forces. This requirement of establishing precise goals to develop and maintain equality of employment has become quite controversial. This is because it appears to resemble the quota concept which is repugnant to the American ideal of employment based upon merit. But a genuine affirmative action program does not have this effect. An affirmative action goal is nothing more than an estimate of what constitutes a reasonable distribution of minority-group employees in specific jobs in the employers' labor force. This estimate is derived from the actual distribution of minority groups in the recruitment population for each specific job. It

---

[2] Office of Federal Contract Compliance, "Affirmative Action Programs," *Federal Register,* 35(25):2586–2590, 1970.

is up to employers, of course, to prove what the actual minority group distribution is in their recruitment populations.

The established goals were intended to assist employers in planning corrective action and not to determine whether they were discriminating against certain groups. The difficulty is that if employers establish goals without realistic programs to achieve them, they are unlikely to succeed and thus open themselves to the possibility of an imposed quota system. In other words, employers must realize that the *goals* established by their affirmative action programs will indeed become *quotas* unless they really establish constructive programs of equal employment opportunity.

In 1972, the OFCC revised Order No. 4 requiring federal contractors to include women in their affirmative action goals for more equitable distribution of workers in their labor force.

The EEOC Testing Guidelines   On August 1, 1970, EEOC issued a new set of "Guidelines on Employees Selection Procedures"[3] establishing standards on four key issues.

1. *What is meant by a test?* The *guidelines* defined a "test" to mean not merely a paper and pencil or performance measure but any formal, scored, quantified, or standardized technique of assessing job suitability. This includes personal background, educational- or work-history requirement, a scored interview, or a biographical information blank. This prescription applies to any technique designed to measure eligibility for hire, transfer, promotion, training, referral, or retention.

2. *What constitutes discrimination?* The *guidelines* explicitly state that any instrument that adversely affects the hiring, promotion, transfer, or any other employment opportunity of classes protected by the Civil Rights Act of 1964 constitutes discrimination *unless* that instrument demonstrates:

   (a) a high degree of utility in—

   (b) *predicting* important elements of the work behavior—

   (c) *relevant* to the job for which the applicant was evaluated.

In addition the *guidelines* require that this utility must be demonstrated for each minority group to whom the instrument is administered. This provision incorporates two important requirements:

   (a) If the instrument does *not* have an adverse impact on a "protected class," no evidence of validity need be produced because, in fact, there is no discrimination

   (b) If the instrument has an adverse impact on a protected class, the relationship between the instrument and job performance must be clearly demonstrated.

[3] Equal Employment Opportunity Commission, "Guidelines on Employee Selection Procedures," *Federal Register*, 35(149):12333–12336, 1970.

3. *How do you demonstrate validity?* The most controversial aspect of the *guidelines* is the prescription for demonstrating the validity of a selection instrument. EEOC bases its requirements on standards published by the American Psychological Association.[4] These standards prescribe that *predictive* validity is the most desirable method of demonstrating the business necessity of a selection instrument. The fact is, however, that this validation method is difficult, costly, and time-consuming and, for most employers, is simply impracticable. The *guidelines* provide, however, that, where predictive validity is not feasible, *content* or *construct* validity will be acceptable. Information from job analyses sufficient to demonstrate the relevance of the content or the construct has to accompany these validation efforts.

4. *What is differential validation?* Perhaps the most controversial aspect of the *guidelines* is the requirement that the validity of an instrument must be shown for each minority group for which it is used as a selection device by stipulating that "where a test is valid for two groups but one group characteristically obtains higher test scores than the other without a corresponding difference in job performance, cut-off scores must be set so as to predict the same probability of success in both groups." The *guidelines* accept the notion of differential validity. We shall return to this issue later.

Since the implications of the *guidelines* were so sweeping and the requirements so stringent, a court test was inevitable. The first confirmation of the legality of the *guidelines* came in 1971 when the Supreme Court of the United States announced its decision in *Griggs vs. Duke Power Company.*

Griggs vs. Duke Power Company   On March 8, 1971, the U.S. Supreme Court reversed a September 1968 decision of the U.S. District Court in North Carolina in the case of *Griggs, et al. vs. Duke Power Company.*[5] In its decision, the Supreme Court struck down the personnel policies of Duke Power Company's Dan River Power Station by which laborers could advance only if they had a high school diploma or passed two standard commercial tests.

Lawyers for the NAACP Legal Defense and Educational Fund, Inc., showed that because black laborers could not pass the company's tests, they were frozen into the lowest rung of the job ladder. By unanimous vote, the justices ruled that such promotion practices were unlawful under the 1964 Civil Rights Act and that permission in that law to use tests applied only to those with direct relevance to the job to be done.

[4] American Psychological Association, *Standards For Educational and Psychological Tests*, Washington, D.C., 1974.
[5] *Ibid.*

In rejecting the particular testing practices at issue in this case the court's opinion made it clear that the use of tests or testing procedures was not ruled out. The decision directed that the defendant no longer require the passing of a standardized, general intelligence test as a condition of employment. By this decision the court settled four issues:

1. It defined a professionally developed test and asserted that if it screens out minority group members, it must be justifiably related to job performance.

2. It put to rest the good faith argument that as long as employers meant well and were trying to be fair, they could not be found guilty of discrimination.

3. It dismissed the so-called objectivity argument. The court said that if a test has an adverse impact on minority groups, it must be related to job performance regardless of whether or not it is objective.

4. It disposed of the issue of whether or not tests were inherently biased. The court said that this was of no interest because the only issue was whether or not the test predicted effective job performance.

Continuing Legal Developments   In the years following, a number of court decisions and the expansion of the EEOC's and OFCC's jurisdictions established a fairly clear pattern with respect to equal employment opportunity. In a series of cases, the federal courts, in addition to remedying employment standards, required large national employers to pay damages to complainants in fair employment cases. These damages were substantial and these awards made clear that the government was prepared to take a hard line on a broad spectrum of discrimination issues involving race, sex, and national origin against even the most progressive employers in the country.

In effect, employers were required to take a new and searching look at their selection strategies.

Elements of a Selection Strategy

To understand the notion of what we mean by a selection strategy, it will be helpful, first, to consider certain controversial issues: differential validity, the criterion problem, and applicant-processing models.

Differential Validity   It has been observed that a selection instrument can be valid for one group in an applicant population but not for another. Studies have shown, for example, that a test may be valid for white applicants but not for those from minority groups. If such is the case, the instruments will underpredict the minority applicants' job performance. Thus, it is unfair because, as Guion has defined it, "unfair discrimination exists when persons with equal probabilities of success on the job have unequal probabilities of being hired for the job."[6]

When differences in the relationship of test scores to job performance between minority and non-minority groups were first reported, efforts were made to explain them by the notion of the *moderator variable.* It is known that some selection instruments can predict job performance more accurately for persons who have been preselected by another standard. This latter standard is referred to as a moderator variable because it determines how well the tests predict actual performance. It was suggested originally that race might be a moderator variable because the predictive efficiency of a test seemed to be enhanced or attenuated by the racial factor. But this theory did not explain sufficiently why racial or ethnic membership affects the relationship between a predictor and a criterion variable. Psychologists began to examine the notion of differential validity more closely.[7] Most of them concluded that psychological tests did not discriminate unfairly against minority-group applicants when they were administered correctly. While expressing their doubt about the existence of differential validity, these psychologists pointed out the need to pay more attention to the criterion problem.

The Criterion Problem   Of particular interest in the differential validity issue is the fact that most studies are based on a multiple-regression equation between a set of selection variables (e.g., test scores, interview ratings) and a single criterion of job performance (e.g., supervisor's performance-evaluation, training school success). In multiple regression analysis, an equation is computed from the correlations of each variable with the criteria and their intercorrelations. Each predictive score in the equation is weighted according to how much it contributes to the prediction of the criterion score.

The dependency of most studies on a single index of job performance constitute their "Achilles heel." To begin with, it is imprecise to speak of *job performance* because this term represents only one aspect of what the employer really seeks, *job effectiveness.* The other and equally important aspect is *job satisfaction.* As we shall discuss in more detail in Chapter 10, *job performance* refers to the value of employees' efforts to a company, while *job satisfaction* refers to the extent to which employees' efforts meet their personal needs. Job-performance criteria measure how well persons are doing their jobs, while job-satisfaction criteria measure how long they will continue to do them well.

These aspects strongly imply that job effectiveness has many dimensions. Some will refer to the quantity and quality of output; some will

[6] Robert M. Guion, "Employment Tests and Discriminatory Hiring," *Industrial Relations,* 5(2):20–37, 1966.

[7] See, for example, Virginia R. Boehm, "Negro-White Differences in Procedures: Summary of Research Evidence," *Journal of Applied Psychology,* 56(1):33–39, 1972.

refer to adherence to organizational policy on such matters as attendance, neatness, punctuality, and honesty; some will refer to relations with superiors, coworkers, subordinates, and customers; some will refer to ability to progress to higher levels of responsibility; and some will refer to willingness to put up with hazardous, uncomfortable, or trying working conditions.

It is also apparent from even a cursory review of published criterion research that these effectiveness dimensions relate to each other in varied ways: some correlate positively with other dimensions, some are independent of all of the other dimensions, and some correlate negatively with other dimensions. It is impossible, therefore, to combine them all into a global index of effectiveness.[8]

In employment strategy, employers must specify, therefore, the best configuration of *job effectiveness* they need to meet the demands of their business. They may accept a lower *task* performance level to maintain job stability, or they may accept a high turnover rate in exchange for low training costs and wage rates. They can rarely acquire high task performance, job stability, and low training costs and wages with a uniform set of selection standards simply because the personal attributes necessary to achieve these three effects do not occur often in the same person.

Applicant Processing Models   The problem is further compounded by the applicant processing model the employer adopts. The idea that applicants must undergo a screening process to save both them and the employer time and money is accepted unquestioningly by a majority of American employers. This strategy, known as the "successive hurdle approach," requires applicants to hurdle a series of progressively *more* difficult obstacles in the form of application blanks, tests, and interviews on the way to job selection. Applicants are automatically eliminated as soon as they fail a hurdle even though it measures only a minor portion of their total job qualifications.

The varied and multidimensional nature of job effectiveness, however, makes this traditional selection strategy inadequate. Those eliminated early in the game often represent the most effective employees in the long run. Noted authorities in selection theory have pointed out that the traditional employment model of multiple regression analysis by no means constitutes the only one and is, in fact, subject to serious limitations.[9, 10]

[8] See Frank L. Schmidt and Leon B. Kaplan, "Composite vs. Multiple Criteria: A Review and Resolution of the Controversy," *Personnel Psychology*, 24:419–434, 1971.

[9] L. J. Cronbach and G. C. Gleser, *Psychological Tests And Personnel Decisions*, (Urbana: University of Illinois Press, 1965).

[10] Cameron Fincher, "Testing and Title VII," *Atlantic Economic Review*, 15(6): 15–19, 1965.

A much more effective strategy requires employers, through appropriate job analysis, to determine the personal traits relevant for clearly acceptable performance of the essential job functions. Then they must design the instruments to measure these traits and to define the threshold points that indicate clearly acceptable levels of them.

In effect, employers must adopt a decision-making selection strategy that emphasizes those criteria of effectiveness that guarantee the most satisfactory achievement of business objectives. If they need to increase job stability, they can select measures that emphasize this dimension of job effectiveness. If, however, they need promotable employees because of an expanding operation or expected retirements, they can choose measures that predict this criterion. To adhere to the goals set forth in an affirmative action program, for example, they can emphasize those job-performance criteria that will favor minority groups and women *without* reducing overall job effectiveness. This is not discrimination in reverse, but rather an example of effective managerial decision making. In essence, the employer evaluates the whole person for the total job and does so on the same basis for each applicant.

The Decision-making Employment System

The basic principles of the employment process described above are translated into action through what we refer to as *the decision-making employment system*. This system is based on management's basic function of making decisions for the organization. One of these key decisions is to select men and women for vacant positions.

The decision-making approach to selection is not only logical and practical, but it also simplifies the complexity that surrounds the employment process. Properly conceived and implemented, it meets and even surpasses current governmental requirements for establishing equality of employment opportunity for all applicants.

The *decision-making employment system* incorporates the following features:

1. It is based upon a worker-oriented job analysis method.
2. It includes an affirmative action recruitment program.
3. It uses performance-related selection instruments.
4. It provides for an employment-applicant processing flow designed to evaluate the whole person for the total job.
5. It includes continuous monitoring of the program's operation for updating and adaptability to the labor market.
6. It is designed to integrate smoothly with the other components of the organization's manpower system.

Job Analysis   The first step in the development of an effective selection strategy for a particular job is to analyze its major and critical functions in order to identify the personal traits necessary to perform a job effectively. American management has produced a number of techniques to enable it to analyze jobs for a variety of purposes. The oldest approach consists of those traditional work-requirement systems designed by industrial engineers to provide measures of work, time study, production standards, and work results. Closely related to these techniques are the work flow analyses used in some manufacturing and process studies. Other methods vary from a minute task analysis approach used in human engineering to the broad narrative job descriptions prepared by salary analysts for compensation purposes.[11]

None of these techniques, however, represents a format suitable to the requirements of a decision-making selection strategy. Work flow or process analysis cannot be applied readily to people. Task analysis provides data that are difficult to synthesize into a form that makes the construction of measuring instruments practical. And none of them provides an indication of the psychological and social demands of the job.

Their use as a basis for selection can lead to an overemphasis on traits that may only partially predict job effectiveness. To offset this possible error and to comply with governmental guidelines, companies must adopt a job analysis method that identifies job related employment standards. Such a technique contains the following characteristics:

1. It is based on what workers have to do (tasks) in their jobs and on what they have to put up with (demands). A task is a specific duty to be performed, like typing a letter, driving a truck, designing a dress, or selling a car, that usually requires *ability*. A demand is a condition surrounding a job, like working in the cold, or meeting a deadline, or avoiding stealing, that usually calls for either *adaptability* or *self-control*.

2. It relates each task and demand to the personal trait needed for it. A trait is a set of personal characteristics by which one person is distinguished from another. There are a great many traits, as we shall list later.

3. It focuses on primary traits. A primary trait is one which is in the person, such as strength, creativity, or knowledge of physics. Traits that refer to a group, such as sex, race, educational level, or years of experience are secondary. The basic idea is to judge a person on his or her own merits and not on those of family or friends.

---

[11] For a comprehensive analysis of these methods, see E. P. Prien and W. W. Ronan. "Job Analysis: A Review of Research Findings," *Personnel Psychology*, 24:371–396, 1971.

4. It takes into account the varying levels of trait strength possessed by people. Trait levels are either *unique* or *common*. If the level of a trait, such as vision, required by a job is possessed by the vast majority of employable people, it is common; if it is not, it is unique. A job analysis system should tell the employer what primary, unique traits are required of an effective (clearly acceptable) incumbent.

Threshold Traits Analysis   A number of methods have been developed to analyze positions for the purpose of identifying worker requirements.[12] In Threshold Traits Analysis, the method developed by the author, analysts use a list of thirty-three primary traits to help them determine the requirements of each job.

First, they have to determine exactly which of these thirty-three traits an applicant must possess to perform a job in a clearly acceptable manner. Then, they have to decide whether the level of that trait is unique or common, and if it is unique, they have to specify the precise level. For example, if they determine that the job requires *numerical ability*, they have to determine whether the ability required is at a level possessed by most applicants. If it is not, they have to specify the acceptable level, let us say the ability to divide, extract square roots, solve algebraic equations, etc.

Space does not permit us to go into the details of this fairly complex method, but basically it identifies those unique trait levels that are necessary to perform certain unique position functions effectively. It does not attempt to identify such functions as being present for work, following work rules, or refraining from stealing or destroying property because these functions are common and are assumed to be present in all positions. They are not, however, excluded from consideration in the employment process.

Threshold Traits Analysis does try to identify traits that are possessed by nearly everyone in the labor market. When these traits are identified, they are classified as common traits and are considered only in the classification phase of the employment program.

THE THIRTY-THREE TRAITS. The important question is how to identify and classify human traits. Theoretically, the number of possible human traits that one can describe is limitless. In Threshold Traits Analysis, a compromise was struck between precision and practicality to identify thirty-three traits grouped under the five major classes of individual differences described in Chapter 6. Admittedly, this classifica-

[12] E. J. McCormick, P. R. Jeanneret, and R. C. Mecham, "A Study of Job Characteristics and Job Dimensions as Based on the Position Analysis Questionnaire (PAQ)," *Journal of Applied Psychology*, 56(4):347–368, 1972; J. K. Hemphill, *Dimensions of Executive Positions*, Ohio Studies in Personnel (Columbus: Ohio State University, 1960); E. S. Primoff, *Test Selection By Job Analysis*, U.S. Civil Service Commission Assembled Test Technical Series No. 20, 1953.

tion scheme is somewhat arbitrary, and there is some overlapping among the classes.

Figure 5 on page 102 lists the traits and their definitions under each of the five categories of individual differences.

TRAIT MEASURES.   For each of the thirty-three traits described in Figure 5, at least one of the seven measures described in Chapter 5 has been designated as the principal way to obtain information about it. By *principal way*, we mean not only that it is the *best* way of measuring the trait but the *essential* way. It is not the *only* way, however. There are usually many ways to measure human traits besides the one designated as the principal measure. These other ways of measuring are referred to as *supplemental* measures for the trait in question.

To assure the accuracy of a measurement result, it is desirable to use the hypothesis approach. In this approach, the conclusion derived from one measure is considered to constitute a hypothesis that has to be confirmed by information from other sources or data categories. For example, the score on a paper and pencil exercise measuring *numerical expression* will lead to the assumption that the applicant is competent at that level. If his background information offers evidence that he has completed certain academic courses in arithmetic satisfactorily and has held positions involving arithmetic skill successfully, the hypothesis would be confirmed.

Sometimes it is not feasible to develop a principal measure for a specific trait. In such cases, supplemental measures have to be used. But when supplemental measures are used for a particular trait, it is important that those making the final selection decision keep this fact in mind.

Figure 6 presents the appropriate sources of information to measure each of the thirty-three traits. The capital letter P stands for the principal measure and capital letter S for the supplemental measure. Notice that the principal measures for the *physical, mental,* and *learned* traits are work-sample exercises. The interview and the application blank are the principal measure of the *motivational* and *social* traits.

It is important for you as a personnel interviewer to understand how to measure these traits and which ones you can evaluate during an interview. If you fail to measure them accurately, you cannot make a valid employment decision.

TRAIT LEVELS AND DEGREES.   A trait level signifies the amount of complexity or intensity of a trait as determined by job analysis. The degree of proficiency or adaptability within a trait level is another matter. There are many degrees of proficiency in addition, for example. There are fast adders and slow adders, and the degree of proficiency might make a difference in job performance. Degrees of proficiency are almost always determined by trait measures after they are carefully

	TRAIT	DEFINITION
PHYSICAL	1. STRENGTH	Ability to lift, pull or push physical objects such as packages or pieces of equipment.
	2. STAMINA	Ability to expend physical energy over significant time periods without loss of efficiency.
	3. AGILITY	Ability to react quickly to stimuli and/or dexterity and coordination of fingers, hands, arms, feet.
	4. VISION	Ability to see details and color of nearby and distant forms, objects and symbols.
	5. HEARING	Ability to recognize and differentiate loudness, pitch and tone quality of sounds.
MENTAL	6. PERCEPTION	Ability to observe and differentiate quantitative, qualitative and other details and/or relationships of objects, forms, symbols or events.
	7. CONCENTRATION	Ability to pay attention to details of work amid distractions.
	8. MEMORY	Ability to retain and recall details, ideas and directions well enough to carry them out when working alone.
	9. COMPREHENSION	Ability to recognize and understand readily spoken, written, numerical, graphic, symbolic or behavioral material.
	10. PROBLEM SOLVING	Ability to analyze information and by inductive reasoning to arrive at a specific conclusion or solution.
	11. CREATIVITY	Ability to combine information from various sources to produce new ideas, products or solutions.
LEARNED	12. NUMERICAL EXPRESSION	Ability to solve arithmetic and mathematical problems.
	13. ORAL EXPRESSION	Ability to speak clearly, grammatically and effectively.
	14. WRITTEN EXPRESSION	Ability to write clearly, grammatically and effectively.
	15. PLANNING	Ability to project a course of action based on a relatively complex set of variables and foreseeable events.
	16. DECISION-MAKING	Ability to choose courses of action in uncertain situations on the basis of policies and guidelines but without specific instructions.
	17. CRAFT KNOWLEDGE	Possession of unique and specialized information normally acquired by formal training.
	18. CRAFT SKILL	Ability to perform a complex set of psychomotor activities acquired by formal training and practice.
MOTIVATIONAL	19. ADAPTABILITY-CHANGE	Adaptability to interruptions in work routine or to changes in work situations, rules, standards, or assignments without dissatisfaction or loss of efficiency.
	20. ADAPTABILITY-REPETITION	Adaptability to highly pre-determined and repetitive activities that vary little over time without dissatisfaction or loss of efficiency.
	21. ADAPTABILITY-PRESSURE	Adaptability to critical and responsible work activities — rapid work flow, constant deadlines, minimum tolerance for error — without dissatisfaction or loss of efficiency.
	22. ADAPTABILITY-ISOLATION	Adaptability to work situations with little contact with other people or frequent travel away from home without dissatisfaction or loss of efficiency.
	23. ADAPTABILITY-DISCOMFORT	Adaptability to cold, hot, crowded, smelly, cramped, noisy and/or dirty work situations.
	24. ADAPTABILITY-HAZARDS	Adaptability to work situations where danger to life or limb is present and real.
	25. DEPENDABILITY	Self-controlled sufficiently to work with a minimum of supervision and follow-up.
	26. PERSEVERANCE	Self-controlled sufficiently to stick to a task despite frustration — discouragement, boredom, difficulties.
	27. INITIATIVE	Self-controlled sufficiently to act on own, to take charge, to take moderate risks in situations not covered by existing procedures.
	28. INTEGRITY	Self-controlled sufficiently to adhere to recognized standards of moral and ethical behavior.
	29. ASPIRATIONS	Self-controlled sufficiently to limit aspirations for promotion.
SOCIAL	30. PERSONAL APPEARANCE	Ability to meet specific standards in physical appearance, dress and/or grooming.
	31. TOLERANCE	Ability to deal effectively with many types of people — fellow employees, customers, general public — in delicate, frustrating or tense situations.
	32. INFLUENCE	Ability to influence people to act in desired ways in situations where they have freedom to act otherwise.
	33. COOPERATION	Ability to work effectively with people in situations where actions are interdependent.

Fig. 5 The thirty-three traits (Copyright © 1974 by Felix M. Lopez & Associates, Inc.)

Area	Trait	Self report		Direct observation		Work samples		
		A	Q	I	V	MX	WX	PX
Physical	1. Strength	S		S		P		P
	2. Stamina	S		S		P		P
	3. Agility	S		S		P		P
	4. Vision	S		S		P		P
	5. Hearing	S		S		P		P
Mental	6. Perception	S		S	S		P	P
	7. Concentration	S		S			P	P
	8. Memory	S		S			P	P
	9. Comprehension	S		S	S		P	F
	10. Problem-solving	S	S	S	S		P	P
	11. Creativity	S	S	S	P		S	S
Learned	12. Numerical Computation	S		S	S		P	
	13. Oral Expression	S		P				P
	14. Written Expression	S		S			P	
	15. Planning	S		S	P		P	
	16. Decision-making	S		S	S		P	P
	17. Craft Knowledge	S		S	P		P	
	18. Craft Skill	S		S	P			P
Motiva-tional	19. Adaptability - Change	P	S	P	S			
	20. " - Repetition	P	S	P				
	21. " - Pressure	P	S	P	S			
	22. " - Isolation	P	S	P	S			
	23. " - Discomfort	P		P		S		
	24. " - Hazards	P	S	P		S		
	25. Control - Dependability	S	S	S	P			
	26. " - Perseverance	S	S	S	P			
	27. " - Initiative	S	S	S	P			
	28. " - Integrity	S	S	S	P			
	29. " - Aspirations	P	S	P				
Social	30. Personal Appearance	S		P				
	31. Tolerance	S	S	P	P			S
	32. Influence	S	S	P	P		S	S
	33. Cooperation	S	S	P	P			S

Fig. 6 Principal and supplemental trait measures (Copyright © 1971 by Felix M. Lopez & Associates, Inc.)

validated by use on effective employees. Figure 7 shows how a trait is divided into levels.

The Selection Plan   Through job analysis, a selection plan is developed for each job title. This plan, as exemplified in Figure 8 (page 105), indicates the level, its relative weight in the final hiring decision, the appropriate measuring instrument, and the degree of proficiency or adaptability required for each relevant trait. With this information, it is possible to design the final applicant-processing flow.

The purpose of this applicant-processing flow is to identify applicants' suitability for the position in question for each trait that has been demonstrated to be relevant for a specific job function. In terms of the

```
                                          NUMERICAL EXPRESSION 12

TASK              Quantitative Computation.

DEFINITION        Ability to solve arithmetic and mathematical
                  problems.

LEVEL  0          Can handle simple mental arithmetic.

LEVEL  1          Can add, subtract and multiply.

LEVEL  2          Can divide, do fractions and figure percentages.

LEVEL  3          Can compute square roots, solve algebraic equations
                  and geometric problems.

DEGREES           Speed and accuracy.

© FELIX M. LOPEZ & ASSOCIATES, 1972
   All Rights Reserved
```

Fig. 7   Definition of trait levels (Copyright © 1971 by Felix M. Lopez & Associates, Inc.)

applicants' possession of the trait, it is possible to describe them in four categories.

1. *Unacceptable.* They do *not* possess a minimum degree of proficiency or adaptability at the level required for clearly *effective* job performance.

2. *Marginal.* They possess a questionable degree of proficiency or adaptability at the level required for clearly effective performance.

3. *Acceptable.* They possess more than the minimum degree of proficiency or at the level required for clearly effective performance.

4. *Superior.* They possess either or both of the following:

   (a) a *superior degree* of proficiency or adaptability at the level required for clearly effective performance, or

   (b) more than the minimum degree of proficiency or adaptability required for a *superior* level of performance.

Applicant Flow   The selection sequence described earlier in this chapter represents a theoretical framework for the employment process. Any such scheme, naturally, is susceptible to exceptions and modifications based on operational needs. By combining the final selection plan with the seven selection measures and the five phases of the selection sequence, we can develop the basic steps in the employment process. Each step is designed to measure certain specific trait levels required by the position for which the applicant is being considered. The steps constituting the applicant-processing flow from labor market to labor force is depicted in Figure 9.

STEP 1. COMPLETING THE APPLICATION BLANK. All applicants take the first step when they apply for employment. The application blank that is completed in this step is geared to common traits. STEP 2. EMPLOYMENT INTERVIEW. After completion of the application blank, the applicant is administered the employment interview, which is geared primarily to lower-level traits. After this step, interviewers make one of three decisions: they can disqualify the applicant on the basis of interest or suitability for the position; they can refer the applicant for further testing or a departmental interview; or they can,

THRESHOLD TRAITS ANALYSIS SELECTION PLAN

JOB TITLE _Instrument Man A_ ANALYST _Jon Weitzman_
DEPARTMENT _Power Plants_ DATE _December 17, 1973_

AREA	TRAIT	LEVEL A	S	WT	INST P	S	MEASURING INSTRUMENTS
Physical	1. Strength	2	2	6	M	I	Medical Examination
	2. Stamina	1	1	4	M	I	" "
	3. Agility	1	2	5	P	M	Performance Exercise
21 %	4. Vision	1	2	4	M	I	Medical Examination
	5. Hearing	1	1	2	M	I	" "
Mental	6. Perception	1	2	4	W	V	Placement Exercise PMC-4
	7. Concentration	1	1	4	W	V	" " "
	8. Memory	1	2	4	W	V	" " "
	9. Comprehension	1	1	3	W	V	" " "
21 %	10. Problem-solving	1	1	?	W	V	" " "
	11. Creativity	1	1	3	W	V	" " WE-9/10
Learned	12. Numerical Computation	1	2	5	W	V	" " NC-6
	13. Oral Expression	1	1	4	I	A	Employment Interview
	14. Written Expression	1	1	2	W	A	Placement Exercise WE-9/10
	15. Planning	1	1	2	W	V	" " PD-8
21 %	16. Decision-making	1	1	3	W	V	" " PD-8
	17. Craft Knowledge	1	1	2	V	I	Verification Report
	18. Craft Skill	1	1	3	V	I	" "
Motiva-tional	19. Adaptability-Change	1	1	3	I	V	Employment Interview
	20. " -Repetition	2	2	6	I	V	" "
	21. " -Pressure	1	1	2	I	V	" "
	22. " -Isolation	1	1	2	I	V	" "
	23. " -Discomfort	2	2	4	I	V	" "
	24. " -Hazards	1	1	2	I	V	" "
	25. Control-Dependability	1	1	2	V	I	Verification Report
	26. " -Perseverance	1	1	2	V	I	" "
	27. " -Initiative	1	1	3	V	I	" "
30 %	28. " -Integrity	0	1	2	V	I	" "
	29. " -Aspirations	1	1	2	A	I	Application Blank
Social	30. Personal Appearance						
	31. Tolerance	0	1	2	I	V	Employment Interview
5 %	32. Influence						
	33. Cooperation	1	2	3	V	I	Verification Report

TTA-5
M5833
© FELIX M. LOPEZ & ASSOCIATES. 1971

Fig. 8 Threshold Traits Analysis Selection Plan (Copyright © 1971 by Felix M. Lopez & Associates, Inc.)

in the case of a qualified applicant, file the person's application for additional processing later as openings become available.

STEP 3. PLACEMENT EXERCISE.   In this step, the applicant takes one or more placement exercises or tests, as required by the selection plan. When this step is completed, one of four decisions is made: applicants can eliminate themselves through their lack of interest or qualifications; their applications can be filed for later consideration; the applicants can be referred for a departmental or an assessment interview; or the applicants can be offered employment. In the last case, Step 4 is omitted and the process moves to Step 5.

STEP 4. ASSESSMENT INTERVIEW.   This step is geared to the more complex levels and traits indicated by the selection plan. In this step, an assessment interview may be conducted.

STEP 5. THE EMPLOYMENT OFFER.   When an employment offer has been made, applicants are requested to complete a detailed personal history form on which the *verification* process in Step 6 is based.

STEP 6. VERIFICATION.   In this step, geared to all trait levels, applicants' backgrounds are verified, and their health is checked through medical examination.

STEP 7. PROBATION.   In this final step, applicants are appointed to the position and go through a probationary period. The purpose of the probationary period is to determine whether applicants are, in fact, qualified for the position and to determine whether the work suits them. As a consequence of this step, applicants are either eliminated through lack of interest or qualifications or they are given permanent status in the organization.

DECISION-MAKING EMPLOYMENT MODEL.   This integrated system constitutes the decision-making employment system on which all the interview procedures described in the next three chapters are based. It will be noted that this model superficially resembles the successive-hurdle model, but this similarity is more apparent than real. Its underlying philosophy and end products are quite different. The flow is

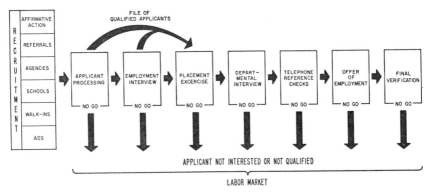

Fig. 9   The decision-making employment process

designed primarily to save an unqualified or disinterested applicant considerable time, rather than to make the selection task simple and quick. The *decision-making employment system* enables an employer to evaluate the whole person in relation to the total job in an economical, practical way. It is applicant-centered from the very first recruitment step. People are considered for employment for as long as they are interested or until it becomes firmly established that there is no vacancy for which they can qualify. In making that final employment decision, the employer considers all of the applicants' traits that are relevant to effective performance of a job.

The Role of the Interviewer   There are three types of decision-making interviews, each designed to elicit the level of information required about the applicant—factual, subjective, or subconscious. The primary interview, that is, the employment interview, as we already suggested focuses on facts, is of fairly short duration, and comes early in the selection sequence. It represents the applicant's first contact with the employer and results in a contingent, "maybe" decision whether to continue considering the applicant. It is administered to all applicants for employment and will be considered in the next chapter.

The secondary selection interview, that is, the assessment interview, focuses on factual and subjective information, probes beneath the surface, and is conducted toward the end of the selection sequence when applicant and interviewer know a lot about each other. It leads to a final employment decision. It is usually reserved for management and professional positions and will be discussed in Chapter 8.

The tertiary interview, that is, the in-depth interview, focuses on subconscious information, requires intensive probing techniques, is of extended duration, and is conducted usually by qualified psychologists. It leads to a hiring decision and is usually reserved for very sensitive positions. It will be briefly discussed in Chapter 8.

Besides grouping based on the data that is to be explored, decision-making interviews can be grouped according to the administrative strategy with which they are employed. The most standardized and systematic selection interview that utilizes only a directed style is called a *patterned* interview. This interview involves careful preparation of questions in areas to be covered, the use of printed forms to record the information uniformly, and a manual of interview procedures to be followed.

Other administrative strategies include the *serial* interview, a technique involving successive interviews of a single applicant by several interviewers; a *panel* interview, a procedure consisting of several interviewers meeting with a single applicant; and the *group* interview, a situation where several applicants meet with one or more interviewers. These strategies will be discussed in more detail in Chapter 9.

chapter 7

The Employment Interview

> It has long been an axiom of mine that the little things
> are infinitely the most important.
> —SIR ARTHUR CONAN DOYLE,
> *The Adventures of Sherlock Holmes*

Some years ago, as personnel research results increasingly indicated that the employment interview was an inept, useless tool of selection, there was an inclination in some quarters to abandon it altogether. This trend, still reflected in the comments on interviewing found in the behavioral science literature, resulted in an emphasis on the test as the primary selection instrument—an event that has, in turn, met with its own unfavorable reaction. In terms of public response, the test seems to be far more unpopular than the interview; and, in any case, despite the intensity of the criticism, there never was much of a rush by employers to eliminate the interview from their employment procedures.

For example, the author introduced the interview into a large-scale selection program for police officers. Later statistical studies yielded no significant coefficients of correlation between a numerical index of the interviewer's ratings and a supervisory evaluation index computed from the consensus of nine sergeants' appraisals of performance a year later. But the interview doubled the rate of medical acceptances of applicants during the selection program, thereby reducing the total number who had to be referred for medical examination by one-half; the number of applicants rejected after character investigation was reduced by one-third; and the termination rate in the police academy during the first eight weeks of employment was reduced from a customary 10 percent to zero. The overall caliber of the entire group selected was judged by instructors in the police academy to be superior to previous classes that had been selected on the basis of only tests, biographical questionnaires, and medical examination.

This is what we mean by relevancy and why we say that when used correctly, the interview is the most *relevant* and the most useful tool of the selection, decision-making program.

The truth is that the interview is indispensable, not only because of its information potential, which is considerable, but also because of its distinctly human aspects. No applicant wants to be judged for a position without an opportunity to discuss it face-to-face in a meeting with a company representative. The interview gives applicants the feeling that they matter, that they are being considered by another human being rather than by a computer. The interview also gives them a chance to ask questions about the job, about the company, and about its salary and employment benefits. It also gives you, the interviewer, an opportunity to do some selling if that is necessary, as it often is. Finally, because it gives applicants a chance to feel that they are the ones doing the deciding, it enables them to maintain their dignity in what can become a very impersonal process.

Instead of being relegated to the scrap heap of interesting but obsolete conventions, therefore, the interview has to be reexamined carefully with a view toward developing it into a useful and valid selection tool. The way to do this is to redefine and restructure it by capitalizing on the unique contribution it can make to the selection process and by neutralizing its natural limitations. In the preceding chapters, we have subdivided the selection interview into three types. The first, the employment interview, is the focus of this chapter. This type of interview is intended to eliminate obviously unqualified applicants, to assess more precisely the qualifications of those apparently qualified, and to interest definitely qualified applicants in employment. It is conducted at the beginning of the selection sequence and lasts from ten to thirty minutes.

The Components of the Employment Interview

In its structural and functional aspects, the employment interview is one of the simplest of personnel interviews. There is none of the rich interaction that characterizes a performance-evaluation interview nor is there much of the emotional content that marks a problem-employee interview. There is even less role definition and personality interaction than in such information-exchange interviews as the termination and orientation interviews. Stripped of its essentials, the employment interview is an oral application blank.

This stark simplicity can trap the uninformed and unwary interviewer because while the error potential is still very high, there is little chance for correction. The employment interview is a very decisive step in the selection program for the applicant who gets no further. When the interviewer admits an unqualified applicant to further consideration instead of rejecting him or her outright, the error involves nothing more than a loss of time and effort because it can be corrected later in the employment program. But when a qualified applicant is rejected, an irrevocable loss of a potentially valuable employee can occur.

While the employment interview seems simple because it is designed to emphasize facts, the outcome is of critical importance. Its very brevity is another hazard. Into the ten, twenty, or thirty minutes must be packed a host of information-seeking questions covering highly relevant areas of the applicant's background. A well-planned employment interview, then, is the base of departure for the effective implementation of a sound selection program.

The Structural Aspects of the Employment Interview   The employment interview constitutes the first personal contact that an employer makes with the applicant for the specific vacancy in question. In this context, this first step on the journey through the five selection phases prescribes the nature of this interview. First, it means that you and the interviewee are strangers, have not met before, and are likely to be unfamiliar with what each has to offer. In this interview, therefore, sufficient information has to be exchanged to initiate mutual interest.

Second, you are undoubtedly considering other applicants, a fact that introduces another important element—time. Since you must budget your time jealously, you cannot afford the luxury of speaking leisurely to any applicant, especially if a large number of applicants is waiting in a reception room. Any of the interviewing techniques described earlier in Part 1 will be inapplicable because of this time pressure.

Even though we structure the employment interview around a time allotment of thirty minutes, applicant volume, the employer's needs, and a heavy schedule can reduce this time allotment to as little as ten minutes. When the time available is reduced to this point, the interview no longer constitutes a bona fide interview but rather a variation that we shall consider in Chapter 9. For purposes of presentation, however, we shall describe a model interview of thirty-minutes duration which you can modify as the situation requires. But, and this is the point, this must be done with full awareness of the fact that you are modifying it.

Since time is such a factor and since the purpose is to make a contingent decision, the employment interview focuses almost exclusively on factual data and on the most overt interviewee behavioral traits. By factual data, we refer to age, marital status, physical condition, appearance, educational achievements, previous employment, and general character. Within the framework of these items, only the most elementary facts can be explored. There is no time to consider the applicant's philosophy of life, attitudes and convictions, motivations, social techniques, or ethical values. These questions are reserved for the assessment interview.

The interview focuses also only on the most obvious interview behavior, such as voice quality and tone, freedom from speech impediments or annoying voice pitch, overt mannerisms, nervous tension, general appearance, neatness, and cleanliness. You cannot explore the more subtle aspects of the applicant's behavior or probe the deeper areas of his or her personality. In your information-giving role, you must describe the job, the company, and the selection process only in the broadest outlines.

The Functional Aspects of the Employment Interview   Even though we did say it, it is not exactly true to state that the employment interview is nothing more than an oral application blank. Since two human beings spend time communicating face-to-face, there must be some role definition, however ambiguous, and inevitably there must be personality interaction.

You will concentrate on the task dimensions of role behavior, on giving and seeking information, and at times, on clarification and summarizing because you have no time to spend establishing rapport with the interviewee. Nevertheless, you will often encounter applicants such as high school graduates who are being interviewed for the first time who fail to understand your role and purposes. In such cases, you have to stimulate them to talk, to give information, and to coach them in proper interview behavior. Because of time limitations, this task becomes, even in the employment interview, a delicate art that some interviewers perform so smoothly and so deftly that even in a brief encounter they obtain a range of information and a depth of insight not acquired by less skilled interviewers conducting much longer interviews.

Employment interviewers can fall into the error of behaving so impersonally that they arouse the interviewee's defenses, increase anxiety, and thus very effectively shut off all communication. The personality interaction may be minimal, but you still must project a sufficiently warm, understanding, friendly demeanor to relax interviewees and to allay their anxieties.

How to Conduct the Employment Interview

Conducting an effective employment interview requires more than an appreciation of its structural and functional aspects. There are definite techniques and procedures that must be followed to make the entire encounter flow smoothly and yield a maximum amount of relevant information in the available time. Control of these factors, information and time, results in an effective interview. To conduct such an interview requires an interview plan and a deliberate sequence of interview events.

The Interview Plan   Like the football coach who always has a "game plan," you will conduct an effective interview when you follow a careful plan. A haphazard interview is not only disconcerting to applicants, it also inhibits the coverage of their qualifications and distorts your final decision.

The employment interview plan consists first of all of the information areas you wish to explore. These will be considered later in the interview-content part of this chapter. The employment-interview plan also includes such preliminaries as preparation, interview location, review of application blank, and ways of taking notes.

PREPARATION.   Often, you have very little time to prepare for an interview. You are presented with a completed application and must start interviewing immediately. This means that your preparation has to occur *before* the applicant sits down in front of you. A big part of this preparation involves your qualifications and training as we have mentioned in Part 1.

Preparation for the employment interview is a bit different from that of other personnel interviews. First, you must know thoroughly the requirements of the position for which you are interviewing; you must be familiar with the informal circumstances accompanying specific positions; you must know the background details of your company, its divisions, departments, and other organizational units; and you must be an authority on company personnel policy, salary structure, the duties and qualifications of many of its jobs, and even the personalities of its supervisors. You must also have a clear idea of the critical traits that mark the difference between effective and ineffective performance. Otherwise excellent interviewers can do a poor job if they are unfamiliar with the background of the occupational world they represent.

Second, preparation for the employment interview requires meticulous arrangement of the area in which the interview takes place. It is decidedly poor practice to conduct this interview in semiprivacy or in an open area. All interviews, without exception, must be conducted in privacy, and by privacy we mean not only in an area hidden from another's view, but also in an area where phone calls cannot be received and the conversation cannot be overheard readily by others.

The interview area should be neat and tidy and your desk kept clear of all papers, books, correspondence, and other claptrap. An untidy desk or a disheveled interviewer creates an impression on applicants that they are either intruding or being treated casually. To add to the "aura of quiet dignity," you must dress in good taste.

Third, preparation requires you to have a systematic way of covering the required information areas. A logical, neatly unfolding approach assures complete coverage of all the important aspects of the interview, makes sense to applicants, and convinces them that they are getting a fair hearing.

Fourth, you must take steps to see that you get at least a quick look at the application blank *before* the interview. This review is so important that the appointment hour for the interview should allow time for the applicant to complete the application form before the interview.

THE APPLICATION BLANK.   There are two indispensable aids to good interviewing, an application blank and an interview report form. The applicant should complete the application blank before the interview. Do not accept a résumé unless it is accompanied by an application form. Make sure that the applicant completes it rather than a friend because the completed form gives you an idea of literacy, attention to detail, neatness, and self-expression. Above all, do not try to conduct the interview without some written biographical information before you.

Later in this chapter, we shall discuss the application blank in more detail. It should be clear, uncluttered, and easy to complete. Take a few minutes to review it for completeness before starting your interview. A lot can be determined about an applicant by the way the blank is completed:

1. Are all blanks filled in?

2. Is the writing legible?

3. Is the spelling accurate?

4. Has the applicant correctly interpreted questions asked on the application blank?

5. Did he or she sign the application?

6. Does he or she seem to have a good idea of all the dates that were asked for on the application blank?

Answers to these questions reveal quite a lot about the prospective employee before the interview.

Later in this chapter, we shall list some specific details to examine on the application form. But the cardinal rule to follow is never to ask an applicant for information that is provided on the application form. Discuss it, ask for clarification, and summarize it, but do not repeat the facts contained in it.

TAKING NOTES.   To interpret interview information properly, you must remember it and organize it. The only effective way to do this is to take notes *during* the interview. It is effective, first, because it helps your memory, which is a very fragile thing. Second, it helps you organize the information you get into logical categories for comparison to job requirements. The Employment Interview Record, Figure 10 (page 129), has been designed to make this job fairly simple for you and will be explained more fully later.

There are a few simple rules to follow in taking notes during an interview:

1. Explain to the applicants why you will be taking notes. Tell them that you want to be sure you have complete and accurate information on them before making a final decision.

2. Cover your notes in such a way that applicants will not be able to read what you are writing. You do this, not because you will be jotting down unfavorable information about them, but to keep from distracting them or making them unduly self-conscious.

3. Stop taking notes while applicants are saying anything negative about themselves—personal problems, periods of unemployment, difficulties with a previous supervisor. Later, at a less tense moment in the interview, you can make a note of what was said.

4. Take only enough notes to capture a few key points. If you spend too much time writing, you won't spend enough time looking at and talking to the applicants.

Interview Sequence   In each interview, no matter how long or short, there is a definite sequence or flow to the ideas discussed. This sequence does not have to be apparent to applicants, but you must give close attention to it. For one thing, it helps you organize and use your time efficiently, and, for another, it facilitates the orderly achievement of interview objectives. There are four sequences to an interview:

First, *establish rapport* with applicants, a climate of friendliness and personal interest in them and get *base-line* (the minimum go–no go qualifications for the job or the company) from them.

Second, move into broader areas of *information getting* about their qualifications.

Third, *give them information* about the job and your company.

Fourth, *summarize* what you both have learned from the interview and *close* it by telling the applicant what the next step in the employment process will be.

There's another important feature of the interview sequence—*time*. So you must plan how much time to allow for each phase of the interview.

ESTABLISHING RAPPORT.   This opening sequence is designed to create a comfortable atmosphere for applicants so that they will be willing to talk to you, to establish a starting point for selection decision-making, and to create a mutual interest between applicant and employer. In this *base-line,* you must have ready a list of questions that will tell you whether applicants meet the bedrock requirements of any job in your organization and whether you can meet their minimum requirements with respect to salary and job interests.

These might be called the "go–no go" elements. They include such common traits as willingness to work the required hours or within a given salary range, physical fitness, or ability to read and write English. Applicants must meet *all* of them or they cannot be considered further. Consider these elements at the very beginning of the interview because it saves you time and it saves the applicant time.

This sequence should take about 15 percent of your total interview time unless the interview is terminated by applicants' answers to your base-line questions. If handled properly, it should establish a communication bridge between you and interviewees over which information can flow freely. You must convey the impression of being sincerely interested in your applicants.

Some interviewers have almost a compulsion to skip the amenities, get right at it, and start digging. This is a serious mistake because you need the applicants' good will and cooperation to get accurate information. That is likely to occur if you have established rapport with them.

The first step toward establishing a friendly interview climate is to be prompt at starting it. If the appointment is set for 9:30 A.M., it should begin precisely at that time. Of course, if interviewees have dropped in unexpectedly, then they must take their chances. But when you invite an applicant to appear for an interview at a specific hour, you must be prompt.

On entering your office, welcome an applicant warmly by name, call him or her "Mr.", "Mrs.", or "Miss", (or even "Ms." if it seems appropriate), shake hands, and introduce yourself. Then seat the applicant in a comfortable chair in full view so that you can observe physical appearance from shoes to headdress, style and taste in clothing, neatness, decorum, and personal cleanliness.

After you are both seated, give the applicant a chance to relax by saying politely, "If you don't mind, I'd like to take a minute or two to glance over your application." Even though you are familiar with the contents of the application form, you do this to divert your attention from the interviewee so that he or she can gaze around the room without being self-conscious, become more familiar with the surroundings, and get a good look at you. This reassuring bit of stageplay often helps an interviewee to gain composure and become more relaxed.

After a minute or two of reviewing the application, you open the conversation. Avoid the artificiality of talking about the weather. Since your task now is to establish rapport, your opening remark should refer to some facet of the applicant's background that is of mutual interest. Nearly always in a detailed application blank, you can find some item that you share with the interviewee, whether it be a hobby, a school subject, or a community activity. By discussing a topic of mutual interest, you establish immediately a bond between you and the applicant, who is then more apt to feel that he or she is talking to a friend.

If the opening subject is particularly interesting, you can continue it for three or four minutes, during which time you may mention your own background and confess that you also have hobbies and interests. Imperceptibly, however, you move into the main sequence of the interview.

GETTING INFORMATION.   The information-getting sequence requires about 55 percent of the interview-time budget. There is no set way of entering this phase. Ideally, you move into it without realizing it by building your questions on the applicant's remarks during the opening sequence. If your introductory conversation goes well, the applicant will be talking freely to you. Then in an unassuming manner you can bring up the subject pertinent to your interview purposes. If the introductory conversation has been particularly apropos, the conversation will slide naturally into the main sequence. If not, you may have to initiate it more directly.

The applicant's previous life history, education, work experience, and personal qualifications form the primary substance of the interview and are covered quickly but completely. Without resorting to the subtle probes required in an assessment interview, look for overt and observable signs of instability, of untruthfulness, or of physical or mental characteristics that would preclude employment. This review is greatly facilitated by sketching mentally a chronological outline of the applicant's life history. With the aid of the application blank and by adroit questioning, you can account for every day in the applicant's life from birth until the moment of the interview. In this way, you are more apt to uncover unexplained gaps in the applicant's history, clear up confusion of dates, and rectify other errors in the record.

To accomplish this result with brevity and dispatch, it is unnecessary to start with the applicant's birth and go step by step through elementary school, high school, college, and each job held. You can skip back and forth from one period of the applicant's life to another in an apparently casual review, but inwardly you will put it together in a logical pattern.

Details are important even though the interview must move along rapidly. Little things—casual remarks, confusion on dates, faulty memory, "minor" periods of unemployment—are all very important to you. While they are picked up in a casual manner, you should follow these little things up conversationally or note them for future reference.

Wherever possible, avoid direct questions. Instead of asking "Why did you leave the Ajax Company?," wait until the interviewee has completed a description of the job held at the Ajax Company, and then, in an encouraging voice, say "And then you decided to leave the Ajax Company." This approach constitutes a gentle lead for the interviewee to which a more spontaneous response is likely.

Do not let applicants ramble aimlessly or take you on a guided tour of their lives. If they dwell on a subject that is particularly interesting but totally irrelevant to your task, firmly but gently guide them back to the main point.

You must not be hesitant to discuss sensitive but pertinent topics when they arise. Avoid any sign of disapproval or distress when unfavorable information is discussed but attempt rather to project the feeling of understanding and acceptance. You will obtain much more information that way than by displaying symptoms of displeasure, disbelief, or dismay. Often, an applicant will test you by revealing some minor unacceptable incident of social behavior, such as getting a parking ticket. If you accept this without any apparent concern, the applicant may follow it up with more sensitive and important information.

It is not your function to dig too deeply into any area because the entire life history of the applicant must be covered in a short period of time. When questionable items are noted, they are recorded for later discussion and review.

GIVING INFORMATION. Another important interview task is to tell the interviewee about the job and your company. This sequence requires about 15 percent of your interview time. When someone comes to you for a job, he or she is looking for several things which all relate to the job but are not exactly the same as the job itself or even the money it pays. One of your responsibilities is to find out what a qualified person really wants and then show how he or she can get it by working for your company.

A good rule to follow is to have the applicant discuss his or her qualifications before you discuss the job and the company. If you present your information in a concise, complete, and understandable summary, it should take no more than five minutes or so. First, describe your company, its organization, products, and policy; then the job or jobs under consideration, the duties, qualifications, and promotion opportunities; finally, tell the applicant about the way employment is secured and the details of the selection program.

Keep in mind that there are good and bad features in every job. Stress the favorable aspects last, following the presentation of the less desirable elements. The fact that the job involves an off-hour shift, or requires considerable overtime or travel, or provides little opportunity for promotion must be mentioned, but immediately afterwards you should describe the more attractive features. Take care to overstress neither. Some interviewers dwell on the less desirable features of a job in a misguided attempt to protect themselves from later recriminations from an irate new employee.

The employment interview is neither the time nor the place to describe the intricacies of the pension plan or the overtime policy. Merely mention briefly that your company has many employment benefit programs, one of which is a pension plan. Give the applicant a rough idea of the salary unless it is quite fixed and not subject to negotiation, in which case you should mention the specific starting rate. This phase of the interview is facilitated by giving the interviewee a pamphlet prepared by your company that contains all the information required. Then, you can refer to it and to the portions you wish the interviewee to read later. Finally, give the applicant the chance to ask questions. Answer them as fully and as courteously as you would expect to be answered.

In giving information, your main objective is to give the applicant the facts needed to help make a decision. You don't want to hire someone who lacks a good commitment to the job. So, by helping the applicant determine interest in your company, you are helping yourself. Second, a clear picture of your company will impress on the applicant that working for you is better than working somewhere else. That will be important if you decide to hire the applicant.

SUMMARIZING AND CLOSING.   When the interview reaches the 85-percent mark, you should begin to bring it to a close. By now, you should have a clear idea of the applicant's basic strengths and limitations for the job under consideration and the applicant should understand your job opportunities and personnel policies. To double-check this understanding, at this point give the applicant a chance to ask questions. Then, terminate the interview with a brief summary of what has been discussed and what the next step in the employment process is to be.

If it appears that the applicant is qualified, make arrangements for testing, medical examination, or referral to a department. Immediately after the applicant leaves, review your notes and write a careful summary of your evaluation.

The interview is rarely concluded with an on-the-spot unfavorable decision, unless it is absolutely unavoidable. To reject the applicant out of hand may project you into an awkward and embarrassing explanation of why you deem the applicant to be unqualified. Ideally, you should inform applicants early in the interview that since a number of people are being considered or because there is no specific vacancy at the present time, they will be notified of their employment chances by letter or by telephone at a later date.

If you decide that the person is not qualified, you have several choices depending upon the situation. If the applicant lacks some specific skill, like typing or shorthand, you can easily mention this during the interview. When the disqualification is due to some more personal deficiency, such as personal appearance or a poor attitude, it is not a good idea to reject the applicant out of hand because it can prolong the interview unnecessarily. Instead, simply say that you will be in touch in a day or two. Of course, this commitment must be kept. To reassure the applicant further, you may suggest that if no reply from you is received by a designated date, you should be contacted directly. This will assure the interviewee that he or she is really being considered carefully, and that is all any applicant can expect. Also, you may often find that after seeing many other applicants, you may wish to modify your initial negative reaction to this particular interviewee.

While in most cases it is not a very good idea to go into detail about why the applicant does not qualify for a job, make sure you carefully record the reasons for your decision on your employment-interview report.

There is also this to consider. In an interview, both you *and* the applicant are comparing qualifications to job requirements. The decision-making employment program, of which this interview is a part, is not simply a process of finding the right peg for the right hole. It is a process of determining on which traits the applicant is *unacceptable, marginal, acceptable* or *superior,* and then determining whether the superior traits, if any, can compensate for marginal traits, if any, in the performance of a specific job. By the way you explore the relevant aspects of your applicant's background, he or she will recognize as well as you whether or not the qualifications for the job have been met. Now, this, obviously, will not happen all the time, but in many cases it will make the final decision a lot easier for both. And this approach will enable your applicants to maintain their dignity when it becomes apparent that they are not qualified for a job with your company.

In any event, when the interview has been concluded, your interviewees should know what action will take place next. You must be quite specific and avoid such generalities and ambiguities as "we'll let you know." Thank them for their time and interest and bid them goodbye. Then proceed immediately to write up the results of the interview according to the directions contained at the end of this chapter.

The Content of the Employment Interview

The purpose of the employment interview is to determine whether an applicant is qualified for a particular job. To qualify, the person must meet your common standards of employment and the specific requirements of a particular job. The content of the employment interview focuses on those common standards and a few unique requirements that can best be measured in this interview.

You need two tools to guide you in obtaining the appropriate information in the employment interview, the *application blank* and the *employment-interview record.* Both should be carefully designed to complement one another. The application blank should place great emphasis on the interview. Many questions normally found on application blanks can be omitted because they might violate the law or they can best be answered in an interview. Both tools should be directed at what we refer to as "life information areas" that provide the basis for drawing conclusions about the applicant's possession of the common and unique traits required by the job.

The Application Blank   Your application blank should be a streamlined form designed to be filled out by applicants and to be used only as part of the employment process. As soon as an offer of employment is made, the applicant will complete a much more detailed personal history record that will become part of his or her personnel file.

PURPOSE.   Your intent should be to make this form a friendly, easy-to-complete document because whether or not applicants are hired, you would like them to think well of you. Hence, you should begin with a statement telling them a little about yourself and what you do and assuring them that their applications will be considered on merit and on no other consideration.

The biographical questionnaire has two basic purposes: it permits applicants to present their qualifications to the prospective employer in a concise, convenient, uniform, and complete form; second, it also impresses applicants with the efficiency, the thoroughness, the objectivity, and the courtesy of the employer. Unfortunately, while only a few employers tend to overlook the first objective, a great many pay little heed to the second. When it is recalled that thousands of applicants will fill out application blanks without any real prospect of obtaining employment, it should be evident that a well-designed, interesting, and tasteful application blank is a distinct asset to the company's community-relations program. To effect this result, little notes of encouragement can be included, applicants can be informed that the information they give will remain highly confidential and that the need for the detailed and personal information is necessary to evaluate their qualifications fairly, and as a final touch, the form can include the company's trademark or symbol, a brief history of the company, and its products. The application blank should be well-designed, preferably laid out by a forms-design specialist, and printed on good-quality paper.

Because of the nature of the positions available, application forms may also differ in format and content within a company. Some corporations have three, four, and even five different application blanks that are distributed by a receptionist on the basis of the applicant's interest and general appearance. This procedure can lead to embarrassment and suspicion when an applicant observes different people receiving different forms to complete, or it can be cumbersome if the applicant has to fill out two or three forms within the same company.

Many organizations find one omnibus form quite practical for all their needs and a great convenience for the interviewer. Admittedly, applicants for lower-skilled jobs may find many of the questions to be irrelevant, but it does no harm to include them.

While we cannot discuss in detail the design, the content, and the processing of application forms, as a background for proper discussion of the employment interview we can make a few suggestions.

The main purpose of the form is to elicit information in a logical, orderly manner. The application form will contain certain relevant inquiries about an applicant's background and will exclude other information.

DESIRABLE CONTENT. The standard form includes the following areas of the applicant's background:

1. *Personal data:* Date of birth, citizenship, residence, telephone number, and position desired.

2. *Education:* Name and address and dates of all formal education from elementary school through graduate school; degrees, major courses, class standing; trade and correspondence schools.

3. *Work experience:* Names and addresses of present and past employers, dates of employment, position titles, brief description of duties, salary earned, name and title of immediate supervisors, reasons for leaving each position, and military experience, if any.

4. *Special skills and avocations:* Hobbies, interests, community activities, licenses, equipment operated, memberships in professional organizations, and other vocational or avocational information that more fairly depicts the applicant's qualifications.

UNDESIRABLE CONTENT. A well-designed employment application blank is direct and to the point and relevant to its purpose. The following miscellaneous "clutter" on many company application forms is better omitted:

1. *Biased information:* Questions concerning an applicant's sex, age, race, religion, national origin, arrest record, or any indirect reference to them if barred by law.

2. *References:* Personal references are of little practical value because applicants are likely to furnish only the names of persons who will recommend them favorably.

3. *Interview information:* Broad questions such as "What is your ambition?" or "Where would you like to be in ten years?" or "What subjects did you like least in school?" should not be included on an application blank because they are much better suited to the interview.

THE WEIGHTED FORM. Many investigators are convinced that the biographical questionnaire is more than a cold record of life facts; some see it as a projective personality test that provides important psychological information that the applicant unknowingly reveals. They take particular note of the manner in which the application form is completed—its neatness, misspelled words, erasures, strikeovers, characteristic check marks, response phrasing to questions, precision on dates and other numerical questions—seeing in these idiosyncrasies possible clues to personality traits. So far, however, little empirical evidence has been offered to substantiate the validity of this approach, so it must remain in the category of an interesting but intuitive venture.

A much more promising and fruitful method of analyzing a biographical questionnaire consists of the assignment of numerical weights to certain items such as age, marital status, and the like, to obtain a predictive score that will correlate with some aspect of successful job performance.

There is no doubt that the weighted analysis of biographical data is quite effective and can be developed wherever there are a relatively large number of employees doing the same kind of work for whom there are fairly adequate records available. In positions for which the turnover rate is high and where the volume of acquisitions is reasonably large, it becomes a most significant selection instrument and well worth the cost of the research necessary.

RÉSUMÉS.   One of the standard tools used to apply for a job, particularly for a semiprofessional, professional, or management position, is the prepared résumé or *curriculum vitae*. Purported to be a concise summary of an applicant's qualifications, it is prepared presumably for the employer's convenience. Although the format varies considerably, all résumés have one characteristic in common—they are written by applicants with their own interests in mind and are, therefore, nothing more than formal letters of application. They should be treated as letters of application and under no circumstances accepted as substitutes for the employer's application form.

Life-information Areas   There are two sources of information about applicants' qualifications for a particular job: their observed behavior and their self-reports. This information, for purposes of convenience, can be grouped into five major life-information areas: *personal, social, career orientation, education,* and *work experience.* By grouping them in this way, you can organize your interview and, as we shall point out, confirm inferences drawn from one area, such as *education,* using information obtained from another area, such as *work experience.*

It is erroneous to attempt to evaluate the possession of a trait directly. What has to be done is to accumulate a set of facts that will support an inference about the possession of a trait. For example, if you wish to evaluate adaptability to pressure, you must gather information concerning applicants' previous experiences under pressure plus your observations of their behavior during the interview.

In this chapter, we shall look at the life-information areas somewhat briefly because they are not probed very deeply in the employment interview. In the following chapter, we shall explore them in more detail.

PERSONAL-LIFE AREA. This area includes personal facts about the applicants' physical ability, ability to get to work regularly, the general state of their health, and their moral character. This area relates mainly to the physical and motivational traits.

Travel to work. The applicant's residence gives you a good indication of how long he or she will stay with you and the probable attendance record. You should find out how the applicant is going to get back and forth to work in locations where public transportation is 'difficult. Also, estimate the cost of the transportation in the light of the probable weekly salary.

Health. You should ask about the general state of the applicant's health. This, of course, will be checked by a medical examination, but you may save the applicant considerable time and inconvenience. If you have some indication that a health problem exists, advise the applicant that there is a medical examination and ask the following question: How many days have you missed due to illness in the past year? Good judgment is the best guideline in determining whether applicants meet minimum health requirements. When in doubt, refer them to the medical staff.

Moral character. It has been determined in a federal court that an arrest record alone is not a bonafide reason to reject a prospective employee; convictions are required for such rejections.

The most important action here is the use of common sense and good judgment. It would be extremely easy to compile a long list of offenses and say you would not hire people convicted of any of them. Such a list, however, would defeat the purpose of the employment program and would remove from the area of good judgment and common sense any kind of determination of the constructive potential of people's attempts to rehabilitate themselves. For example, a car-theft conviction would not preclude a person from employment if it did not involve a syndicate or organized crime, if the conduct has not been repeated, if the act occurred a long time ago, and if there is evidence of intent to reform.

Bear in mind, too, that in overpopulated communities where there is a high proportion of disadvantaged and minority-group people, it is not unusual for the police to bring in large groups of "suspects" for questioning. This fact alone, of course, would not necessarily reflect any wrongdoing.

SOCIAL AREA. This area covers the applicant's ability to get along with others. It is not enough to evaluate the applicant on the basis of appearance and behavior during the interview. Specific questions must be asked about family history, leisure-time activities, hobbies, and community interests to ascertain the person's degree of social adjustment.

This is one of the more difficult areas of exploration, and you just cannot make an accurate assessment of it in an employment interview. You judge the applicant's ability to get along with people mainly by the way he or she influences and gets along with you. A major aspect of the employment interview is the observation of the outward qualities of the applicant, including physical and facial characteristics, voice, diction, vocabulary, and general ability to communicate orally. It is important, of course, that these be related to job effectiveness. If, for example, successful job performance requires mere cleanliness and ordinary good manners in taste, dress, and comportment, you cannot look for high fashion, elegant behavior, and precise diction.

Since the interview is the only way to assess these traits, it is important that they be carefully described and noted. An alert interviewer develops a sharp eye for appearance and an acute ear for oral expression. When well-defined standards have been established for these qualifications, the appraisal will be much more meaningful.

Appearance.   Here, you should judge the applicant's neatness and personal cleanliness but also keep in mind cultural differences in what is appropriate dress and appearance.

Conversation.   The applicant should be able to converse in English well enough to be understood, unless he is being considered for a job where speaking English is not required at all. Conversation is also an indication of a person's mental and learned traits.

Behavior.   A major area of interview inquiry consists of a combination of the reported, observed, and inferred information—the interviewee's manner, poise, self-assurance, self-control, sincerity, and integrity. From the personal facts he or she has reported and the ease with which he or she relates to you, *inferences* are drawn about social skill, truthfulness, and general personality style — outgoing, extroverted, friendly, warm, responsive, shy, withdrawn, introverted, or introspective. Admittedly, these will be nothing more than rough first impressions, but they can prove valuable when assessed in the light of subsequent observations by other interviewers.

Avocations.   This factor refers to the applicant's social and recreational life. Look for indications of interest that involve other people as a key measure of social skill.

CAREER-ORIENTATION AREA.   This area covers the applicant's career aspirations, immediate and long-range goals, and potential for advancement. Like the *social-life area,* it is pretty difficult to judge in a short period of time. In the employment interview, nearly all you can do is consider the reasons the applicant applied for the job, his or her salary expectations, the hours of work being sought, and the short- and long-term ambitions of the applicant.

Information in this area is used exclusively to rate the *motivational* traits.

Reason applied. Here you will be concerned with the position applied for and the reason. Has the applicant indicated the position which his or her background and education merit? Or is he or she vague and just looking for a job, any job?

Hours. This factor gives you a clear picture of the applicant's availability and will help avoid a lot of problems that may occur if you do not have an accurate idea of when people can work. Raise questions about working evenings, weekends, and overtime. The more flexible a person is, the higher the rating you can assign. This question is of particular importance for applicants presently attending school or for married people with children. Find out also whether the applicant is seeking a full-time, part-time, or temporary position. If the position sought is in one of the latter two categories, you may not be able to accommodate the applicant.

Salary Expected. Is the salary requested appropriate to the applicant's

(a) qualifications?

(b) responsibilities (size of family, debts, etc.)?

(c) salary in previous positions?

If this figure is unrealistically high, the applicant will probably never become a satisfied employee in spite of what might be said about being willing to start for less.

Many applicants will probably either leave this question blank or use a fairly conservative figure. Do not hold an applicant to an expected starting pay that is less than the normal starting rate. Too many employers have done this in the past, and it is just not fair to the people applying for work.

Aspirations. This is a tricky factor. For some jobs, you want people who are really looking to get ahead. But for many jobs, you have very few promotion opportunities so that the applicant who is not looking for a career, who does not expect to get promoted in six months or so, is often the better prospect.

EDUCATIONAL-LIFE AREA. This area covers the type of schooling, the quality of grades, class standing, social activities, relationship with teachers, honors and awards, and athletic accomplishments of an applicant. Questions in this area can provide a good indication of an applicant's initiative, independence, reliability, intellectual competence, and emotional stability.

A high school education is not a hiring minimum because it can be discriminatory. If a person is to be disqualified due to lack of education, it has to be for specific reasons, such as writing legibility, ability to comprehend instructions, ability to do simple mathematics, etc. Do not reject an applicant solely because he or she is not a high school graduate.

For young applicants recently out of high school, it will be very helpful for you to ask them questions about high school because you have no meaningful employment history to help you with your employment decision. Such questions are listed below. This area is particularly useful in evaluating the *mental, learned,* and *motivational* traits of the applicant.

Highest grade.   This question refers to how far the applicant went in school—9th grade, high school graduate, or college. If an applicant has some college but did not graduate, find out why graduation was not achieved. Questions can also be asked about achievement in school and class ranking. Of course, sheer amount of schooling isn't always a good predictor. Knowledge, skill, and attitude are the traits that really count. But the highest grade reached does give some indication of a person's *mental, learned,* and *motivational* traits. For a person with a culturally deprived background, a high school diploma indicates self-discipline, determination, and ability.

Subjects.   This question refers to the pertinency to the job function of the subject matter the applicant has studied. For high school graduates, find out what kind of courses were taken: general, shop, commercial, or technical. For college graduates, discuss college major. For those with work experience, find out if they have participated in any in-company training programs or other specialized studies that are relevant to the job under consideration. Even if this section is left blank on the application form, you should ask the applicant what other training has been acquired.

Activities.   This is an important area of training and education to explore. For recent high school graduates, ask whether they worked while in school. What kind of honors, if any, did they obtain? This is another place to ask applicants what they did achieve while they were in school, especially if this portion of the application is blank. If applicants took no part in extracurricular activities, you should ask why.

Look for the applicant who will give you *honest* reasons for a lack of achievement while in school, if that was the case. Participation in many extracurricular activities is usually associated with a high drive and energy level.

If you are interviewing a college graduate you should go into some detail about the applicant's college record, such as:

    (a) What percent of the educational cost did the applicant pay personally? This question is important because if a young person has earned the majority of personal expenses while going to college and has managed to graduate, he or she has to be a person with a great deal of perseverance and drive.

(b) What kind of activities was the applicant in? If none, why not? There can be a number of valid reasons, e.g., working his way through school.

(c) Why did the applicant select the particular college(s) attended and how did he or she determine what to major in?

(d) Which subjects were hard or easy? Why?

Again, ask questions that give detailed information. The more information you receive, the better your hiring decision. We realize that in most employment interviews, you will not have time to explore these questions in detail, but you can get some brief ideas that will help with your final decision.

Current studies.   This factor refers to the applicant's present educational efforts. Generally, self-improvement efforts are indications of initiative, determination, and strong motivation. But in some cases, they can be a disadvantage for an employer. If the applicant attends evening college, ask how many evenings a week the schedule calls for and what hour the classes start. Is the college close enough to enable the applicant to work a full day and still get to class on time? Is the position he or she is applying for going to call for frequent overtime? Has the applicant recently attended a technical school which would indicate interest in an area for which he or she is not being considered?

WORK EXPERIENCE AREA.   This area provides the best opportunity to predict future performance except for those with no employment history. It must be fully explored. It highlights not merely an applicant's technical competence but also the level of responsibility and skill attained in previous jobs, the position level and salary progression achieved, and the reasons for leaving former jobs. Questions in this area should be directed at obtaining evidence of good judgment, stability, initiative, and ability to assume responsibility. In this regard, work history will also include military service, if any.

There should be space on the application to list the applicant's five or six most recent employers. Review this section carefully for it will enable you to explore past employment briefly but fully. Keep in mind that history tends to repeat itself. A person with a poor employment record tends to be a poor risk; a person with a solid achievement record is likely to continue to perform at a high level in subsequent employment. Adherence to this philosophy helps to predict future employment success or failure.

Relevancy.   This factor refers to the appropriateness of the applicant's experience for the job under consideration. You should carefully review job titles and duties listed by the applicant.

(a) *Job title.* Ask if this was the only job title held, and if not, write in other jobs held.

(b) *Describe your job duties.* Job titles can be confusing, so ask enough questions to be certain you understand the job functions performed.

Knowledge and skill. This factor refers to the degree of skill or knowledge required by the job. The applicant's previous experience should indicate a level of knowledge or skill appropriate to the job for which he or she is being considered.

Stability. This factor deals with the very important question of how long the applicant is likely to stay with you. The answers come from two areas, employment dates and salary.

Accuracy in dates is essential. Insist on accurate dates, because they can be very revealing. If the applicant's employment record is stable or the reasons for leaving other jobs are logical and convincing, he or she is likely to be a reasonably good employment risk.

Review the monetary progress an applicant has made throughout his or her employment history. Be wary of sharp upward or downward turns in salary as an applicant goes from employer to employer. Do not allow applicants to leave the salary section blank; everyone has at least a "ball park" idea of what the starting and final salaries were for previous jobs.

Stability is rated under the *motivational* and *social* traits.

Reason for leaving. This topic is one of the most important in the interview. Questions in this area should be reserved for the latter part of the interview and should deal not only with the applicant's reasons for leaving but also with his or her attitude toward previous supervisors.

You want the *exact reasons* for leaving. Get down to specifics. Do not accept general statements like "better job" (Why couldn't you get a better job where you were?) or "more money" (Why couldn't you make more money where you were?). By careful questioning, you can often develop the applicant's typical job-behavior patterns.

Get the names of previous supervisors because you may have an opportunity to speak to them about the applicant's job performance. A little digging in this area may very well uncover the applicant's attitude toward supervision in general.

Recording the Interview Findings   While there is some controversy over the question of when interview data is to be recorded, the best course of action is to record it while you are interviewing. If you wait until after the interview, you will lose about 50 percent of the detail through the unavoidable process of forgetting. The fear that by writing during the interview you will distract and disconcert the interviewee is offset by the impression you make of the seriousness with which you take your responsibilities. Recording information during the interview and following a precise interview plan is facilitated by a well-designed interview-report form.

THE EMPLOYMENT-INTERVIEW RECORD. Figure 10 illustrates a brief interviewer-report form completed on an applicant for a secretarial position. As you will note, it is designed to combine the five classes of traits included in the Threshold Traits Analysis with the five life-information areas.

The five life-information areas are listed along the left side of the page. Next to them are key factors that give information concerning the

EMPLOYMENT INTERVIEW RECORD

NAME *EILEEN PATRICIA McCARTHY* NO. *1245* DATE *9-23-75*

PAGE 1

INFORMATION AREAS		PHYSICAL				MENTAL				LEARNED				MOTIVATIONAL				SOCIAL			
		U	M	A	S	U	M	A	S	U	M	A	S	U	M	A	S	U	M	A	S
PERSONAL	STABILITY															✓	⊠					
	TRAVEL TO WORK															✓	⊠					
	HEALTH				✓																	
	INTEGRITY															✓	⊠					

NOTES: *HEALTH EXCELLENT -TRAVEL CONVENIENT*

SOCIAL	APPEARANCE																			✓		
	CONVERSATION						✓				✓											
	BEHAVIOR																					
	AVOCATIONS	⊠		✓	⊠					⊠				⊠				⊠				

NOTES: *VERY WARM AND FRIENDLY - WELL SPOKEN - PLAYS TENNIS - COMMUNITY ACTIVITIES*

CAREER	REASON APPLIED															✓						
	HOURS																✓					
	SALARY															✓	⊠					
	PROGRESSION															✓						

NOTES: *LIKES RECEPTIONIST WORK - VERY INTERESTED IN COMPANY - CAN WORK FLEXIBLE SCHEDULES*

TRAINING	HIGHEST GRADE						✓									✓						
	SUBJECTS										✓											
	ACTIVITIES	⊠		✓	⊠					⊠		✓	⊠				⊠				✓
	CURRENT STUDIES															✓						

NOTES: *GRADES GOOD; HIGH SCHOOL - CHEER-LEADER - STUDENT COUNCIL VICE-PRESIDENT*

WORK	RELEVANCY			✓				✓								✓				✓		
	KNOWLEDGE/SKILL							✓														
	EQUIPMENT															✓				✓		
	REASON LEAVING						✓									✓				✓		

NOTES: *MEDICAL CLAIMS PROCESSOR, INSURANCE COMPANY FOUND WORK TOO MONOTONOUS - WANTS TO WORK WITH PEOPLE.*

TTA-6B

Fig. 10 Completed employment interview record (Copyright © 1974 by Felix M. Lopez & Associates, Inc.)

applicant's possession of the required trait. Across the top are listed the five trait categories. Each trait category has four columns, headed respectively by the letters U, M, A, and S, representing the degree to which applicant meets the factor on the left—unacceptable, marginal, acceptable, or superior.

During the course of the interview, you discuss each factor in each informational area. You then place a checkmark in the appropriate box under the trait category measured by this factor. For example, if after discussing the applicant's health you decide that he or she is "acceptable," you place a check in the box under the letter A in the physical category. For some factors like "Avocation" in the social area and "Activities" in the training area, it is possible to make a judgment under all five trait categories. Use the "Notes" rows to elaborate on your checkmarks or to make any other comments you deem appropriate.

At the end of the interview you should not only have covered all the salient aspects of the applicant's background but you will have profiled her under each trait category. You can then summarize her qualifications on the back of the record more easily and make a better decision about her.

OVERALL RECOMMENDATION AND DECISIONS.   After the interview, review your notes and write a final summary of your impressions and evaluations of the applicant and indicate a tentative decision. If you wait until the interview is over to complete the interview report, and even if you have an excellent memory, there is still the chance of an interruption that may prevent you from recording the interview for an hour, four hours, or even twenty-four hours. The later the postponement, the less reliable will be the final evaluation decision

Your final decision is made in the light of two independent variables —trait requirements and the qualifications of the other applicants. The trait requirements are covered in the final selection plan. You must be careful, tolerant, and broadminded at this point. If the application blank is well constructed and if you have conducted a skillful interview, unfavorable information may have been uncovered—gaps in employment, unsatisfactory performance in previous jobs, inadequate social life, history of illnesses, emotional disorders, a record of previous convictions— these should not be considered as necessarily disqualifying. Indeed, to be intolerant is to encourage application falsification. High personal standards can be established and adhered to, and at the same time, careful consideration can be given to the circumstances surrounding each unfavorable event or detail of an applicant's qualifications.

The effectiveness of your decision will depend not merely on your ability to obtain relevant information about an applicant but also on interpreting it correctly. Interviewers sometimes tend to draw invalid conclusions from the bits of information they obtain because they accept them as positive truths rather than as mere hypotheses that must be confirmed by additional information. As we indicated earlier, interpretation of interview data consists of the ability to resist leaping to erroneous conclusions.

In Chapter 8, we shall explain how to use evaluation questions and the hypothesis approach to interpret interview information most effectively.

But in the last analysis, you must remember that each person has strengths and limitations and that for every limitation there is usually a counterbalancing strength. The most satisfactory interview approach, therefore, is to concentrate upon an applicant's strengths and compare them to the limitations to determine how compensatory they are.[1] This is the essence of the applicant-centered approach, by far the most effective interviewing technique. Basically, it consists of obtaining the facts, asking self-evaluative questions about the facts, formulating hypotheses, and then confirming or rejecting them by additional questioning.

In summary, there are three important guidelines to conducting an effective employment interview:

1. In obtaining and interpreting information about an applicant, you must always keep the job requirements in mind. No matter how socially desirable or undesirable a personal trait may be, it is of no significance unless it affects job performance.

2. You must wait until the interview has been completed before making a final decision. The biggest pitfall in interviewing lies in making an evaluation on the basis of facts or impressions formed early in the interview.

3. You must evaluate the *whole person* in relation to *total job performance*. As we have said, people have a way of compensating for their weaknesses by strengths in other areas.

If you follow these guidelines, you will surely find that your job is much more difficult and challenging than you imagined, but your overall judgments will be right far more often than they will be wrong.

Since all interview and application data must be carefully reviewed, a well-constructed report form is a distinct asset in making a final decision. You must make this ultimate decision, and in many cases it will be uncorrectable, but it will be yours to make. Your understanding of the decision standards is crucial at this juncture. Patricia Rowe reports[2] evidence to show that variance in interviewers' decisions can be accounted for by each interviewer's "category width," a general trait that refers to how broadly the interviewer views the selection standards.

---

[1] See Thomas D. Holloman, "Employment Interviewers' Errors in Processing Positive and Negative Information," *Journal of Applied Psychology*, 56(27):130–134, 1972.

[2] P. M. Rowe, "Individual Difference in Selection Decisions," *Journal of Applied Psychology*, 47:304–307, 1963.

Fortunately, since in an employment interview you can allow yourself considerable latitude in your judgment, you can afford to give the interviewee the benefit of a substantial doubt. At this stage of the selection process, a broad category width actually increases the reliability of your evaluation. Conversely, a narrow interpretation of standards will lead to a much greater uncorrectable error factor (many rejected who might have made desirable employees) and is therefore to be avoided.

You must also be wary of the "halo" effect, the undue influence of an irrelevant trait on your overall judgment. Careful consideration of an interview form such as that illustrated in Figure 10 (page 129) will tend to minimize halo and permit a careful, objective evaluation.

FINAL DECISION.   After the overall recommendation has been completed, you are ready to make a final decision about the applicant. This decision may have been made very quickly as a result of the base line questions asked early in the interview, or it may not be made until after the test results are in. Your decision may be to disqualify the applicant, hold his application for consideration at a later date, to refer for either testing, a departmental supervisor's interview, or an assessment interview, or to make an employment offer. Once your decision is made, you have only one thing left to do: place all your written records in the applicant's file. These include the two forms we discussed (the application blank and the employment interview report) and the results of any test score exercises the applicant has completed.

These records must be kept to meet federal requirements and perhaps those of your local government. They must accurately and completely reflect both your hiring decision and the reasons behind it. Write the reasons for disqualification on your interview-report form in an appropriate place. Be as specific as possible. "Better qualified applicants" is not a valid reason unless you state who was hired and are prepared to compare the qualifications of the rejected and accepted applicant.

If any of your employment decisions come under the scrutiny of government investigators, your records will help justify and substantiate your actions as being free from bias. They will show how you endeavor to match the applicant for a job to the traits required for that job. They will clearly show which applicants did not have those traits to the degree needed and so were rejected by you or the supervisor or the manager who also interviewed the applicants.

chapter 8

The Assessment Interview

What is character but the determination of incident?
What is incident but the illustration of character?
—HENRY JAMES, *The Art of Fiction*

With the completion of the employment interview and placement exercise procedures, the selection program moves into its final preemployment phase—synthesis. For a great many jobs, this phase consists solely of a medical examination and of verifying the facts already obtained about an applicant. An employment offer is made on the strength of the employment interview and exercise results. But when the position requires rather complex levels of mental, learned, motivational, and social traits, the applicant must go on to an assessment interview before a final hiring decision is made. The traits investigated in this interview, therefore, are much more subtle and call for more acute judgment and more intensive interviewing skill.

Since in the assessment interview you will explore areas that are both factual and subjective and, at the end, will measure the whole person against the total job requirements, you must prepare for and plan this interview carefully. Without meticulous attention, your interview decision may be based on little more than your personal opinion and may be solely a product of your own prejudices or assumptions.

Not long ago while conducting a training program for a company's campus interviewers, a psychologist listed on the blackboard the personal strengths and weaknesses of a hypothetical applicant for a managerial position in the company. He asked the participants to review the list of traits and then decide whether or not they would offer the "applicant" a job with the company. Not a single student decided to hire the applicant. The psychologist then disclosed to them that the list of traits was actually a profile obtained from a recent psychological assessment study of the company's most effective managers.

To conduct an assessment interview properly, that is, to obtain information that will produce a sound employment decision, it is necessary to know how to conduct the interview and what to look for.

The Components of the
Assessment Interview

Conducting the assessment interview is both an art and a science, but it is not quite either. Like all interviews, its outcome depends on the information exchanged. But to a considerable extent, the quality and the range of the information obtained in this encounter depend upon the personal interaction that takes place between you and the interviewee. While the basic format of this interview is much like the employment interview, the climate is quite different, and your final decision will be related much more to your interviewing skills.

The Structural Aspects of the Assessment Interview   Since the assessment interview is an extension of the employment interview, they are similar with respect to the areas of life information covered, the personal traits measured, and the division of time allotted to the various sequences. The employment interview, however, as the opening gambit of selection strategy, is essentially a fact-finding interview. Since you can sketch only a surface picture of the applicant—physical appearance, level of education, work history, and general interest in the position—your interview style must be direct, leading, and assertive as you initiate the questions and guide the conversation along clearly demarcated lines of inquiry.

The assessment interview is conducted in quite a different vein. You now possess a wealth of information about the applicant and may be meeting him or her for the second or third time. The interviewee, too, is by now familiar with the job and the company and is very definitely interested in both.

Your task is to penetrate the surface layer of factual data you have accumulated and to probe into the more subtle regions of the applicant's qualifications to identify strengths, to understand limitations, and to measure the applicant as a whole person against the total requirements of the job. The specific traits that you would explore are, for the most part, at higher levels of complexity. For some traits, your assessment will be their principal measure, and for others, it will be an important supplement to information already obtained from tests or to be obtained by verification.

The context of the assessment interview includes the final consideration of an applicant for a complex position involving substantial responsibility. Since this is the last step in the selection process, the candidate has already passed through a gamut of selection techniques—the completion of a detailed biographical questionnaire, the employment interview, testing, background investigation, and perhaps a complete medical examination. A veritable library of data has been accumulated about the applicant, and it is now your task to so synthesize them that the resulting portrait is not merely a sketch or even a mosaic but a three-dimensional, stereoscopic view of the applicant. The idea is to telescope ten years of experience with the applicant into an hour or so of "conversation."

The content of the interview focuses on the applicants' technical and professional knowledge, values, attitudes, convictions, interpersonal relations, and general view of the world. Since applicants cannot verbalize their innermost attitudes readily, the inferences that you make will take considerable time and a generous sample of the candidates' expressed thoughts. In forming these impressions, you must be extremely careful to prevent your own feelings, prejudices, and values from influencing what the interviewees tell you or what you hear.

The Functional Aspects of the Assessment Interview   Since the assessment interview is conducted in the qualification and synthesis phases of the selection sequence, it is a major tool of the selection program. Its primary goal is to choose the *best* qualified person from a reasonably homogeneous group of *qualified* applicants, and, therefore, you need a precise knowledge of position demands, an understanding of selection theory and practice, and a highly skilled interview technique. The interview is preceded by a careful study of the qualifications required of an effective incumbent, is conducted in a climate that brings into sharp focus the strengths and weaknesses of each candidate in relation to this specification, and concludes with a synthesis of the accumulated information, inferences, and insights. Conducting the assessment interview is like fitting a glass to a precise window frame where the glass is made up of many tiny, multicolored bits that must be painstakingly pieced together.

Consequently, the assessment interview is lengthier than the employment interview and its style is more nondirective. Your questions will have to be more comprehensive and evaluative. You must focus more on clarifying and testing the applicant's responses and on creating a climate of openness and trust, and you must listen very intently and interpret your information as objectively as possible.

There are, therefore, some important differences between this and previous selection interviews. First of all, you must remember that the assessment interview is likely to constitute a real anxiety-producing situation for the interviewee. If the anxiety level remains too high, neither you nor the applicant will function effectively. Some anxiety is desirable, however, because a relaxed, indifferent, or apathetic applicant will be insufficiently motivated to achieve interview goals.

Anxiety, as we pointed out in Chapter 2, requires a defense, and the most likely line of defense for either party is to engage in a carefully controlled intellectual conversation that produces a high verbal output but a minimum of communication. To counteract this tendency, you must establish an aura of quiet friendliness, warmth, and understanding without becoming overly familiar or too informal. Anxiety is so highly communicable that any defensive behavior such as condescension or rudeness on your part will trigger a reaction in the interviewee that will destroy spontaneity. To handle anxiety, the interviewee will either respond with hostility or extreme nervousness, or behave rigidly, impersonally, over-politely, and uncommunicatively.

You must work on the forces that hold the interviewee's behavior at an ineffective level of equilibrium. To influence it to the point where it becomes spontaneous yet purposeful, emotional as well as rational, warm as well as dignified, you must capitalize on the interviewee's desire to please you, to present a positive image, to hide personal factors which are thought to be weak, and to resist an invasion into the realm of personal privacy—all in ways that give the applicant the assurance that he or she is controlling throughout the interview what is projected. This dynamic interaction is the essence of the assessment interview.

In nine out of ten selection situations, the employment and assessment interviews will be sufficient to make a final decision about a person's promotability or employability. If the vacancy is one in which the occupant directly influences the job performance and the job satisfaction of other employees, however, a more intensive selection strategy is necessary. The selection interview in depth is one of the principal instruments of such a strategy.

When absolutely called for, the employment of true depth techniques must be left to the really expert person who has considerable professional education and experience, a sense of personal integrity, and a high regard for ethical conduct. The "depth" interview, which we shall describe in this chapter, is nothing more than a longer, more intensive and extensive assessment interview. For precision and clarification, we shall refer to this interview as an *in-depth* interview, the term being applied specifically to the evaluation of the whole person in terms of personality, ability, achievement, and experience.

We have included a brief exposition of the in-depth interview in this chapter partly to round out the discussion of the selection interview, partly to better illustrate certain interview techniques that can be applied in the assessment interview, and partly to describe another selection strategy. Ronald Taft, in a broad review of methods of personality assessment for predicting performance, distinguishes three types of assessment strategy: *naïve empirical,* in which inference proceeds directly from the predictor to the performance; *global,* in which the assessor relies upon intuition and empathy to make a prediction; and *analytic,* in which there is an inference made about the personality traits necessary to do a job successfully and then an assessment of the individual's possession of these traits.[1]

Thus, the employment interview is an instrument of the *naïve empirical* strategy because the variables measured by it are related directly to the success criteria. The ordinary assessment interview is an instrument of *global* strategy because it provides for an intuitive synthesis and a broad multidimensional prediction. The in-depth assessment interview is an instrument of the *analytic* strategy because its purpose is to describe certain personality variables that lie beneath surface behavior, with the assumption that whether they have been manifested overtly before or not, they will most certainly become manifest in performing the job in question.

Therefore, in this chapter we shall really be discussing two types of assessment interviews. The first, which addresses itself to professional and technical qualifications, to an evaluation of the higher levels of problem solving and decision making, to such personal traits as initiative, dependability, perseverance, and influence, is reserved for most professional and managerial positions. This constitutes the ordinary assessment interview that deals with factual and subjective information.

The in-depth assessment interview addresses itself to the underlying motivations of the applicant and, therefore, to subconscious levels of information.

The question, then, is what are the positions that require this more intensive, probing appraisal technique? Almost every position in an organization affects other people's performance, satisfaction, and tranquillity to some degree. But the majority permit the employer a reasonable margin of error in selecting incumbents. Even though a small percentage of those hired will turn out to be maladapted or maladjusted, the annoyance to other employees and the disruption of organizational efforts will be so relatively minor that the use of the more probing tools is warranted on neither economic nor ethical grounds.

Sensitive Positions   There are, however, two types of positions in which the penalties for error are high enough to require more penetrating assessments of a prospective incumbent's qualifications. Both classes of positions have a common dimension — human relations. Managers and

[1] R. Taft, "Multiple Methods of Personality Assessment," *Psychological Bulletin,* 56:333–352, 1959.

professional personnel positions directly involve their incumbents in important contacts with other people to the extent that these incumbents can materially affect the other people's personal contentment and peace of mind.

MANAGERIAL POSITIONS.   It is perhaps an oversimplification to say that the manager's job is to get a piece of work done through the efforts of other people. This popular definition places managers in the invidious role of overseer and gang foreman, two fairly anachronistic images of the modern manager. Research over the past twenty years has clearly shown that the so-called production-centered manager is not nearly as effective as the employee-centered manager, especially in positions where the subordinate has considerable latitude for independent judgment and initiative. In the current view, the manager is seen more as a decision and information center whose role is that of a consultant, coach, and team builder. And, most assuredly, if the manager is to enact the role spelled out in Chapters 11 and 12, his or her personal interaction with individual members of the team will have a deep effect on their feelings of self-worth and their effectiveness.

This perception of the manager demands that the people being considered for such positions be carefully scrutinized to determine whether, in fact, they do have the attributes of character, self-integration, and integrity necessary for success in this unique, influential role. Not everyone has the capacity, the sense of self-esteem, and the regard for the feelings of other people that is essential to the successful enactment of this new managerial role. And since the word "manager" is so all-encompassing, the need for intensive selection extends not only from junior manager to chief executive but also grows more acute as the level of accountability rises.

In the higher reaches of the organization, we encounter positions that, although the opportunity for face-to-face contact with other people may be less frequent, are even more socially sensitive. The behavior and the decisions of top executives and managers can have far-reaching impact on the lives of thousands and, in some cases, hundreds of thousands of workers. If, in such positions, the incumbents have little appreciation of the human consequences of their strategies and decisions and if they are obsessed by the legal, technical, financial, or economic aspects of their responsibilities, they can cause a great deal of havoc, grief, and pain to many people.

For management positions, therefore, the prospective employer has not only the right but the obligation to delve into a candidate's background to determine how personally fit that person is for the position sought. The man or woman who aspires to a position of great responsibility must be prepared to open up his or her personal life history for a tactful review by the agents of that institution in which he or she proposes to function. This is not an invasion of privacy—it is merely common sense and differs from the experiences of political candidates only in climate and audience.

Personnel-relations Positions   In the corporate structure, there will be some professional positions whose primary responsibility will be to deal with people as people. The most notable example is the personnel administrator himself, and by this term we are not referring to the purely technical personnel specialist such as the salary administrator, the research technician, the records supervisor, or the cafeteria supervisor. We mean the persons who meet employees on a face-to-face, ego-to-ego basis—the interviewer, the employment manager, the training coordinator, the guidance counselor, the social investigator, the employee benefit specialist, the recreational adviser, the medical officer, and even the labor relations negotiator. They too must be prepared to submit themselves to deeper assessment before assignment to responsible positions in the personnel management field.

The judgments personnel people make, the actions they take, and the advice they give are so inextricably interwoven into the lives and the psyches of other workers that they are truly in positions to help or to harm, to please or to hurt.

In a sense it really is a form of preventive medicine when an astute employer, realizing that there are millions of dollars invested in his or her human resources, makes certain that employees who occupy sensitive human relations positions have the personal qualities to perform their tasks effectively.

The necessity, then, for the use of in-depth assessments for certain positions seems irrefutable. But these interviews cannot be conducted indiscriminately just because the jobs applicants seek are highly imaginative or creative, require high technical capacity, or involve high-pressure performance. Applicants are perfectly within their rights to resist the attempt to force them to undergo elaborate assessment merely to determine whether they are self-starters, are in the right vocational field, or have creative ability. A less intensive assessment interview can do this job perfectly well and still keep the employment risk low.

Assessment Centers   Many companies use evaluations by professionally trained psychologists to assess managerial prospects. A confidential report is then prepared for management. The heart of this report consists of the insights and the conclusions drawn by the psychologists from the assessment interview. Psychologists have reported that the information from these interview reports contributes substantially to assessment-center evaluations.[2]

[2] Donald L. Grant and Douglas W. Bray, "Contributions of the Interview to Assessment of Managerial Potential," *Journal of Applied Psychology,* 53(1):24–34, 1969.

The effectiveness of these assessments depends mainly on the talent of the interviewer rather than on the validity of the instruments used to gather the information. Many companies, however, prefer an assessment method that does not depend on the expertise of a single person. They have turned in recent years to the assessment center. The assessment-center approach provides for the simultaneous assessment of a group of candidates by a team of evaluators. Candidates spend one day to a week in residence at a center where they go through a variety of assessment exercises, one of which is the in-depth assessment interview described in this chapter. Another technique, the leaderless group discussion will be examined in the following chapter.

Proponents of this approach contend that it is more effective than the normal employment procedure if all candidates have an equal opportunity to display their talents, are seen under similar conditions, and are evaluated by a team of trained assessors. While there are drawbacks to the assessment-center approach, it appears to have the most potential for capitalizing on the decision-making selection model we presented in earlier chapters.[3]

Conducting the Assessment Interview

A well-conducted assessment interview is the crowning skill in the art of personnel interviewing. To meet with people for the express purpose of exploring personal backgrounds, to journey with them through the byways of their lives, to speculate about the dynamics of their behavior, to formulate hypotheses about their character, to test them in conversation, and to accept or reject them during the course of the engagement is, indeed, an imposing challenge. But, to accomplish these objectives so unobtrusively and so considerately that the other parties reveal themselves without losing their dignity or right to privacy in those areas that are irrelevant to the job is a real triumph.

The usual assessment interview lasts about one hour depending on the job in question. Some will require more time and some less. As with other interviews, it really begins long before the applicant makes an appearance and it terminates a good while after he or she has departed. When it is determined that an assessment interview is in order, arrangements should be made to conduct it at an appropriate time and place. The format follows the same pattern as the employment interview; there is the usual preparation to make ready for the candidate—the opening phases of the interview, the middle game with its subtleties and complexities, the conclusion, and the write-up after the interview has been terminated.

---

[3] See James R. Huck, "Assessment Centers: A Review of the External and Internal Validities," *Personnel Psychology,* 26:197–212, 1973.

Preparation: Making Ready Every personnel interview requires adequate preparation, careful preliminary planning, and, of course, the assessment interview is no exception. As with the employment interview, you must be quite familiar with all the circumstances, formal and informal, of the job and particularly with the details of the final selection plan.

First of all, it is obvious that you cannot prepare for this interview merely by reading a job specification, for you are not interviewing the applicant for a class of positions or for a level of positions, but for a specific, unique job situated at a particular location. The essence of the assessment interview is that there is nothing abstract, academic, or hypothetical about what the prospective job incumbent will have to do or what traits are required to do it. You must familiarize yourself with the job so that you know it intimately; you must visit the job site and talk to the people with whom the incumbent will have to deal. You must understand the problems that occur in the job, the local color, and the cultural and social ground rules by which it is bounded and determined.

In addition, however, you must be familiar with the data accumulated about the applicant, consisting of prior interview reports, application form, test scores, and reference reports. You must analyze this information very carefully beforehand to obtain basic leads to the line of questioning that should be pursued during the interview.

You must also prepare a broad interview plan to follow, consisting of a series of general and specific questions to be answered by the applicant. There are many good plans available, our own preference being for the one described later in this chapter.

With a general plan of interviewing firmly established and supported by a well-designed report form, you are ready to conduct your interview. The physical conditions accompanying the initial interview—privacy, freedom from interruption, neatness of desk, punctuality—of course apply even more importantly to the assessment interview. It is also wise to advise the applicant beforehand that the meeting is likely to last an hour or so. It would certainly be very upsetting if a well-planned interview went awry because the interviewee had to leave after only thirty minutes for another appointment.

The Actual Interview The details of this interview follow the general pattern of any well-conducted interview that we have stressed repeatedly throughout this book. But there are some points that deserve repetition, and some that are unique to this situation. Also, for the reader's convenience, we list below some typical questions to ask.

The way the questions are asked, the interview plan followed, the importance of listening and of dealing with the unexpected, the formulation and the testing of hypotheses about the applicant, and knowing when and where to stop are the basic elements of the assessment interview.

When interviewees report for the interview, it is your job to put them at ease and to motivate them to respond unself-consciously. Regardless of their self-confidence and self-assurance, most interviewees will be anxious about this particular interview and will have a vague feeling of being on display, of being put under a microscope, or perhaps of undergoing analysis. At the outset, they will display defensiveness in the form of controlled, socially correct, stereotyped behavior.

You have to lower these defenses to win the interviewee's confidence by motivating him or her to speak and behave naturally and to be convinced that the interview will be helpful. Begin with the usual social amenities. Carefully establish a climate in which you will conduct the interview and in which the style of behavior you expect will be defined. To facilitate this, talk freely about yourself, describe your own feelings and attitudes, why you happen to be there, what your job is, and what you hope to accomplish. This presentation is developed more leisurely than in the employment interview. Sometimes it takes as much as fifteen or twenty minutes just to complete the opening phase, to set the appropriate tone, and to put the interviewee in a receptive frame of mind.

The basic idea to share is that since the position under consideration is so important, it is in the applicant's best interest to find out whether he or she is, in fact, suited for it and will be happy in it. If you convey the impression that the applicant is under a microscope for the employer's benefit, the interview will stay on an impersonal and over-controlled level, and its objectives will be unrealized. You must convince yourself that your job is to assist the interviewee, and that by helping him or her you perform a service for your employer. You must also convince the applicant that everything he or she says or does will remain strictly confidential, that any report that is recommended to your employer will be discussed with him or her too.

If you can convey these ideas to the applicant, the remainder of the interview should flow smoothly into meaningful areas. The odds are that the interviewee will then be anxious to cooperate and communicate. If he or she does not accept the ideas either because they were not conveyed sincerely or because the interviewee is emotionally unable to do so, you will have to form your own conclusions as to the reasons why.

After a sufficiently warm atmosphere has been established, move into the "middle game" or the main sequence of the interview. The conversation will turn to areas relevant to job effectiveness which normally would constitute the private and personal affairs of the applicant. The applicant will have to recount failures in previous jobs, describe an estimate of personal shortcomings and weaknesses, hopes and ambitions, narrate details of childhood and adolescence, relations with parents, brothers and sisters, teachers, friends, and former supervisors. Roughly speaking, the assessment interviewer covers many of the same areas described in the outline of the employment interview—personal characteristics, educational achievement, occupational experience, social skill, and career orientation—only the assessment interviewer pursues them more intensively and with one objective in mind, total evaluation.

To follow your plan and to get the information you require, you must know what questions to ask and how to ask them. To prevent breaking the thread of conversation, begin with a broad, general, declarative statement and build natural inquiries on the responses obtained, directing the conversational stream so that it winds back and forth across the applicant's personal landscape.

The broad general statement may be simply "Tell me about yourself." How and where the interviewee chooses to begin is always self-revealing. One person will unconsciously begin with what is considered to be the strongest area, a common response; another will start literally at the beginning and plunge into a tedious exposition of early childhood and adolescence; another will start with the present job and the reason why he or she is applying for a new job; another will discuss an avocation or a hobby; and the more cautious will counter with the question "What would you like to know?"

It is not desirable to lead the applicant into believing that you are unfamiliar with his or her background. It is much better to begin by explaining that you have studied the information gathered so far and have found it interesting and that since the applicant is now under serious consideration, in everyone's interest, it is best to converse candidly.

As the interview progresses, revert to a permissive nondirective, applicant-centered style that, depending on the time available, permits the interviewee to digress if he or she so desires. Most interviewees will cover the interview plan in their own style, and thus you will be free to observe and to record. This method will take you into areas that you may never have planned to explore if you had led the questioning. The more garrulous, disorganized applicant may require interruption from time to time to be brought back to relevant subjects. This can be done easily and naturally by a comment such as "This is all very interesting, but I wonder how it relates to our purpose here today?"

The assessment interview also requires intensive listening, listening with an inner ear to hear the subsurface resonances that suggest important topics for deeper probing or raise serious questions in your mind. Strict attention is required to hear these delicate undertones. Further, the steps toward and the hindrances to effective listening deserve rereading before an assessment interview.

Asking Questions   As indicated above, one way of encouraging the interviewee to talk is by asking questions. Your immediate task will be to determine what type of questions to ask.

Ultimately, you seek closure, that is, you wish to draw all the data together into one continuous whole so that the applicant's qualifications can be compared with the demands of the job. Questions, then, serve to fill in the gaps and to provide the missing elements in the pattern forming in your mind. These gaps suggest a style of asking the questions, as well as their intentions, sources, and the order in which they are posed.

STYLE OF QUESTION.   The first style of question is the closed question that allows a response of only a few words, usually nothing more than a "yes" or "no." This type of question tends to limit conversation so severely that its principal use is in the interrogation process. If you intend, however, to switch from a nondirective style to one of mild stress in order to note defensive reactions, and sometimes this is quite desirable, you can use closed-end questions for brief periods.

The opposite style of question is the open-end question which is usually broad, comprehensive, and indeterminate. It starts conversation going and keeps it moving.

Another style of question is the clarifying question that we have referred to repeatedly. Clarification and summarization are, of course, important role dimensions in this interview.

A fourth style of question is the probing question, a variation of the clarifying question except that its aim is to dig deeper beneath the surface of a previous answer to get at the attitudes or the motivations behind it.

And finally, you may ask speculative questions that pose a hypothetical situation based on a typical situation and ask the interviewees to describe what they would do. This approach is less desirable than finding out what the applicants have done. Its weakness lies in the opportunity it affords the applicants to describe what they would do on a pure fantasy level in terms of what they think you will accept as desirable.

Nevertheless, it is often useful to test an hypothesis about an applicant's traits by posing an assumed or real-life situation to solve. Even though the interviewee will attempt to solve the problem in a way believed to be most pleasing to you, the perceptions and reactions shown can give you additional insight into his or her thinking and values.

QUESTION INTENTIONS.   The questions asked are directed at defining or uncovering problems that will lead to a clearer impression of the applicant. In the employment interview where you are emphasizing facts, your task is to get the "what," the "where," and the "when." In the assessment interview, your task is more complex—to describe the applicant's underlying lifestyle and motivational patterns. Your questions, therefore, focus on the "why," the "who," and the "how."

The first question is the "who." You can ask the interviewee such questions as "who is the most important person in your life? Who helped you the most? Who advises you? Whose respect means the most to you? Whom do you advise, counsel, or help?" The way in which these questions are answered will prove most fruitful for the final assessment and may be an occasion for discovery for the applicant too. By gentle probing, you will obtain answers that reveal the candidate's degree of initiative, capacity for independent action, and sense of personal autonomy, all of which should be important for the job at hand.

The second group of questions deals with the time-space factor, the "when" and the "where." Here, you can ask such questions as "When did you first go to work and where? When did you first act independently and responsibly? In what type of situations? When did you first decide that you wanted a promotion or a change in your present position? Where do you think you are going now?" Timing gives you an indication of the applicant's maturity, independence, and self-reliance. The answers to "where" questions usually point to autonomy and inner drive and to the sense of achievement that the individual possesses.

The answer to the "how" and "why" tells you the typical mode of response of the candidate, as well as style of life, energy, and self-direction.

If you are inexperienced or untrained in assessment interviews, you will find it difficult to phrase "why" and "how" questions to elicit substantial information. As a result, your interview will degenerate into a monologue with you doing all the talking. Often, you will find yourself trying to sell the job to the applicant rather than ascertaining suitability for the job.

Naturally, it is often necessary to "sell" an applicant on the job. However, make sure you really want the applicant before you start selling the job. Keep in mind that there is no more satisfying experience than to be put through a searching interview and then be offered a job. To the extent that you do a good job of interviewing, you are selling. If the applicant turns out to be unsuitable, you are far better off not to have made a direct selling effort.

Good interviewing means good questions. In the assessment interview, good questions depend on your sources, on the order in which you ask them, and the extent to which they enable the applicants to evaluate themselves.

QUESTION SOURCES.   There are three sources of questions that you may use. One source consists of the application blank, employment interview, and test data. A study of this information usually suggests many points that can be phrased into questions for use in the interview. Another source lies in the answers the applicant gives to your questions. This type of follow-up question is most effective because the applicant feels that he or she is important to you and will tend to relax and furnish information more readily. By formulating follow-up questions, you are forced to listen more intently to the applicant.

A third source of questions may be called a "library" of questions that have been predetermined and prephrased. This is the least desirable source, but you will find it helpful until you gain the experience to use questions that have been the most productive for you.

A trait-related library of questions is provided in the interview-content part of this chapter. These questions are grouped by life-information areas and are indicative of the type that may prove helpful in drawing an applicant out. Each group of questions is preceded by a paragraph describing the particular topic to be explored.

No one is expected to use each question in the "library" with every applicant. The list is supplied to show you the possibility of using the interview as a data gathering method and to encourage you to develop the ability to conduct an interview in depth.

Before the interview starts, list the traits and the areas of information you have to cover and then work as many of these questions into the interview as you can. If a particular question would break the train of thought or destroy the rapport you have developed, do not ask it. When the interview is nearly completed, you can, in the applicant's presence, browse through your papers or notes to see if there are any questions you have left out. At this point, you can introduce a new question without the risk of destroying the relationship you have developed.

THE ORDER OF QUESTIONS.   Another way of making your questions more effective is to start with easy-to-answer questions and move toward more difficult or sensitive questions. Generally, the easiest to answer are questions that are factual or deal with recreational and social activities. The more difficult questions refer to career goals and programs, to reasons for leaving other jobs, or to the applicant's ideas about his or her strongest and weakest points. Save the difficult questions for the latter part of your interview when you have established a good relationship with the applicant based on mutual respect and trust. When you pose a tough question in a sensitive area, you might give a reason for asking it that explains its significance and importance to you.

SELF-EVALUATION QUESTIONS.   The richest source of interview material, especially for the motivational and social traits, is derived from answers to questions that require applicants to evaluate themselves.

Such questions as asking applicants to talk about themselves, to rate themselves, to tell you just how they think, act, or feel often reveal more data than any other single question.

A typical question, such as "What do you consider to be your biggest asset?," immediately stimulates an applicant to express his or her innermost feelings, attitudes, and aspirations. Facts, in and of themselves, mean very little. The fact that people achieve high grades in school tells you little about *how* they did it and what those grades meant to them. The question "What contributed most to your getting those grades?" invites applicants to tell you how they function and what they *think* they have going for them.

Self-evaluation questions tell you a great deal about a person's objectivity and ability for realistic self-assessment. A person who is unaware either of strengths or limitations may be shortsighted, immature, or anxious, or a combination of all three.

Hypothesis Testing In Chapter 3, we briefly noted that interviewers often fail in their final employment decisions because they tend to draw conclusions from different bits of information, accepting them as positive truths rather than as mere hypotheses that must be confirmed by additional information. In a sense, we said, interpretation of interview data consists of the ability to resist leaping to erroneous conclusions.

Interpretation is essentially a logical rather than an intuitive process. You elicit information about the applicant, put it together to establish a hypothesis that explains this information, seek confirmation of your hypothesis from other information about the person, and refer the whole to the traits and trait levels deemed essential for job performance. Basically, therefore, interpretation is a process of continuous generation of hypotheses from the applicant's life history as described to you and from the applicant's behavior during the interview. You may confirm or reject these hypotheses on the basis of other evidence obtained in the same interview.

We're using the word "hypotheses" in its scientific sense: a tentative conclusion based on preliminary observations.

By your questions during the interview, you obtain the material with which to generate your hypotheses. Obviously, the richer the material, the more fertile will be the hypotheses generated. The applicant's past history, of course, provides the best source for these hypotheses. However, the same sources can also be used to confirm or reject them. One approach is to use personal-life data or education as areas from which to generate ideas about the applicant and then to confirm them by questions concerning work experience. For example, if an applicant indicates that in high school and college he or she had difficulty with teachers, you might formulate the hypothesis that the person has a negative attitude toward authority. You confirm or reject this hypothesis by careful questions about relationships with past and present supervisors.

Another approach is to ask self-evaluative questions. For example, the question "What do you consider to be your chief asset?" is a straightforward self-evaluative query. But there are many other ways to ask the same question. Suppose an applicant says "I believe that I can become a manager in five years." An evaluative question might then be "What would you say you have going for yourself that will make that level of attainment possible?"

Answers to self-evaluative questions can confirm the hypotheses about an applicant's strengths and weaknesses that you have already formulated. The most interpretable information comes from self-evaluative questions.

Remember that in and of themselves facts mean very little. The fact that an applicant obtained low grades in school does not really tell you anything about how he or she functions as an adult. What you want to know is whether those school grades are consistent with present achievements.

The hypothesis-testing approach is reinforced or deterred by your basic attitude toward this task. Most interviewers follow the cautious approach of looking for an applicant's weaknesses because they wish to avoid the error of recommending an unqualified applicant for employment. But the opposite error of rejecting a qualified applicant can be, and often is, much more damaging to an organization because it is uncorrectable.

Concluding the Interview   The assessment interview generally runs for an hour but may last longer with a particularly articulate, interesting applicant who is being considered for an extremely important position. Occasionally you may ask the applicant to return for another session because you have not covered all the areas in the plan during the time available. But somewhere along the line, the interview has to end, and the question is how to stop it and when. The answer is simple enough. When you believe that you have come to definite conclusions about an applicant, that you really know and understand that person, can write a detailed and informative description of his or her qualifications and are confident of its accuracy, it is time to end the interview. This is done with dispatch, in a polite but firm fashion. You summarize the conclusions of the interview, describe what will happen next, how long before the interviewee will receive a decision and then ask if there are any further questions. When these have been answered, simply say, "Well, I guess that does it. Thank you very much." Stand up, help the applicant with packages, coat, briefcase, or umbrella, shake the person's hand, see him or her to the door or elevator, and say goodbye. Then go back to your desk to write up your impressions immediately.

Interview Problems Assessment interviewing is not nearly as smooth and as untroubled as we have indicated, no matter how skillful you may be. At times, you will run into sensitive situations, and with different applicants that will require more than the usual techniques.

SENSITIVE SITUATIONS. During the course of the discussion, you may encounter subjects, situations, or areas in the interviewee's background that are a source of anxiety and discomfort to you or the applicant. The two most common problems of this sort are the discussion of a subject of personal concern to the interviewee and the disclosure of unexplained gaps or inconsistencies in the applicant's presentation.

THE DELICATE SUBJECT. Frequently, you will encounter a subject that is touchy or even embarrassing to the interviewee, but it must be discussed because of its relevancy to job performance. Delicate, perhaps painful topics of conversation may include the reason why an applicant terminated a previous position, an incident in his or her personal life, or a health problem. You should be ready to deal with these topics when they are reached in the conversation. Sometimes you will stumble on one unexpectedly. It is important not to panic or "run away." Sometimes it may be more direct to change the subject for a while or to avoid it all together. If you have established the proper rapport and have been permissive and friendly, you can bring the matter up tactfully and help the interviewee discuss it. Carefully avoid any gesture or facial expression that would suggest disapproval of what is related. The applicant may disclose a very painful, embarrassing event in his or her life which taken in its entirety may not prejudice the chances for employment at all. But if you express shock or dismay, the conversation will be cut short and an incomplete story will be presented. In any event, your role is to listen, to describe, and to evaluate only after all relevant information has been gathered. You should make this responsibility evident to the applicant and also point out that you are not prying and not inquiring out of a sense of morbid curiosity. You must bear in mind, however, that your values and ethical standards are not universal, and that it is not your place to insist that everyone adhere to your norms of conduct.

GAPS. When it becomes obvious that there are periods of time unaccounted for in the applicant's background information, or inconsistencies in the person's story, inexperienced interviewers may become so unsure of themselves that they avoid further questioning. This will only leave large question marks in the final appraisal of the applicant. When a gap of more than a few weeks appears, ask the applicant directly "What were you doing between these dates? I don't see anything on your application form to account for this period." Your tone of voice may suggest that perhaps there has been an oversight. Additional probing will determine whether or not this is so or whether the gap relates to a period that the interviewee would rather not discuss. Usually, the latter explanation is closer to the truth.

Most adults do not make thoughtless mistakes on an application blank, nor are their memories as hazy as indicated by a confusion or vagueness of dates. You may file away such casual references to oversight or faulty memory for more thorough investigation later in the interview or afterwards when checking references. If the applicant states that the gap covers an experience or incident that he or she would rather not discuss, you can handle it as a delicate subject.

DIFFICULT APPLICANTS.   As an experienced assessment interviewer, you will find most applicants easy to talk to. They will take their cue from the interview climate established and will follow your lead. If you indicate that you want them to do most of the talking along reasonably well-defined lines of investigation, they will take it from there. But there are job applicants who, for one reason or another, have preconceived notions of just how an interview ought to be conducted and how they would like to conduct it. Given the permissive atmosphere of the assessment interview, they may behave in ways that can pose problems for you. Other applicants may not respond to your attempts to establish a warm, supportive climate. These variants in interview responses range over a broad spectrum, but a few of the chief "culprits" deserve mention.

1. *The Aggressive Applicant.* The most difficult people to control are aggressive talkers. Introducing a broad, comprehensive question to such people is like handing them the ball and asking them to run with it until they are tackled or fall down from exhaustion; and they neither tire easily nor are brought down without a struggle. Unless checked, they will talk on and on, roaming far from relevant topics, explaining each point in their lives in boring detail that suffocates you with triviality. For a while, such a response may be interesting as a significant display of character traits, but it will soon become tedious—and what is most disconcerting, it becomes time-consuming. Hence, you must exercise restraint to harness these verbal torrents. You will have to interrupt frequently to suggest firmly but politely that another subject be discussed. The particular applicant may have excellent qualifications and may have mistaken your nondirectiveness for a desire for lengthy discussion. When such a person is reminded discreetly that lengthy discourse is unnecessary, the subsequent conversation is apt to be more concise. Despite your permissive role, never be intimidated by aggressive behavior and, without becoming ruffled, suggest to the interviewee that the responses be shortened or, if necessary, cut in when you have heard enough.

2. *The Hostile Applicant.* Some applicants, because of their basic attitudes toward the world, resent being interviewed for a job. Others, because of real or imaginary slights received during the selection program, will have grievances. Still others, because of failure in previous interviews, will have a latent antagonism toward all interviewers. They approach the assessment encounter with expectations of threatening, condescending, or humiliating interviewer-role behavior. To defend themselves against their expectations, they will behave with rigidity, reticence, sarcasm, or ill-placed humor.

You must accept these "negative strokes" by treating the applicant with respect and concern. Try to bring the resentment into the open where you can both confront it. The reason for the hostility has to be found and ventilated before the interview can continue. Once the emotional pressure has been relieved, usually by encouraging the interviewee to "sound off" without fear of retaliation, the communication block will be so effectively removed that substantial progress can be made during the remainder of the interview.

3. *The Anxious Applicant.* Anxious applicants will display some signs of discomfort and lack of poise. They will find it difficult to express themselves or will exhibit such nervous mannerisms as drumming their fingers, laughing at the wrong time, or squirming in the chair. The resulting tension creates a sense of distance between the parties that will block communication. You can handle anxiety best by self-assurance and poise, warmth, friendliness, and understanding. Gently confront your interviewees with their nervousness and show them you understand and accept it. Once interviewees discuss this nervousness openly, they will usually relax because part of their anxiety stems from the effort to hide it from you.

4. *The Silent Applicant.* Sitting stolidly but mutely at the opposite end of the conversational continuum from that of the aggressive talker will be the strong, silent type who answers every question with one sentence of three or four monosyllabic words. Nontalkativeness can be due to intense anxiety, to resentment, to poor verbal fluency, or, in rare cases, to the fact that the interviewee is accustomed to saying very little. Since the truly strong, silent type is nearly impossible to "crack," you should not develop feelings of inadequacy when you encounter one. People who simply will not or cannot engage in a conversation are rare, but they are met, and no amount of cajoling, coaxing, pleading, or suggesting will induce them to speak up or to respond fluently to questions and leads.

The person who is not used to talking because of a limited vocabulary or pure inexperience will have to be dealt with tactfully and gently. You may have to fall back on the direct approach. Interaction under any of the above circumstances will be so limited that, in reality, the assessment interview will be largely ineffective.

The Content of the Assessment Interview

While the conversation may roam over a wide area, cover many subjects, and digress into many unanticipated byways, you, by using your notes and your interview-report form, must make certain that you cover the five life-information areas described in Chapter 7. To help get at these areas more completely, we have listed below some questions you can use. The main points of the assessment interview, of course, must be carefully recorded. Human memory is so fallible that the subtler aspects and even the mainstreams of the interview will soon be obliterated from your memory unless you get them down on paper. Once they are gone, your biases will take over as substitutes for recall and will distort the eventual outcome. The well-structured assessment interview always includes a prepared form which will retain the salient points.

Life-information Areas   The *Assessment Interview Report* (Figures 11 and 12) has been developed to help guide you through this difficult and challenging interview. This report combines the traits defined in Chapter 6 with the life-information areas described in Chapter 7. In the following pages, these life-information areas have been expanded in detail and a library of questions has been provided for each topic to help you obtain information necessary to measure relevant traits.

PERSONAL LIFE.   Admittedly, questions in this area call for tact and diplomacy. However, when phrased properly and accompanied by an explanation of why you need to know this information, it can be obtained without offense or embarrassment.

EARLY LIFE HISTORY.   Early life history refers to the relative economic, social, and emotional conditions in which the applicant grew up, and relationships with parents and other members of the immediate family. Consider the applicant's achievements with respect to the support and help received from his or her family and friends. If the applicant came from a poor family, started to work at age 10 or 11, worked all through school, and still managed to achieve some measure of success, this would be a strong indication of initiative, perseverance, and dependability.

TYPICAL QUESTIONS:

Was discipline at home strict, lenient, or what?

When did you first start to earn your own spending money?

How old were you when you started to choose your own clothing?

Looking back on your childhood, how happy was it?

PRESENT FAMILY SITUATION AND OBLIGATIONS.   Cover the applicant's current domestic and economic situations: marital status, dependents, style of living, residence, debts, and outside income.

TYPICAL QUESTIONS:

How does your wife (husband) feel about this job?

What, if any, outside sources of income do you have?

What plans have you made for your children's education?

How does your husband (wife) feel about travel?

HEALTH AND PERSONAL HABITS. Cover the personal health, energy, and personal habits of the applicant.

TYPICAL QUESTIONS:

In recent years, how has your health been?

When you have a cold or headache, what do you most often do?

What have you done to try to keep healthy in the past year?

PERSONAL ADJUSTMENT. Cover the way in which the applicant copes with the setbacks, frustrations, and other problems that are a daily part of life.

TYPICAL QUESTIONS:

Tell me about some problem you have had. How did you handle it?

When you make a bad decision, what do you do?

What is your biggest problem today?

SOCIAL LIFE. This area includes two "silent" topics in that you as an interviewer question yourself silently rather than asking questions of the applicant. This is often an excellent area in which to begin the interview. However, judgments made in this area are often the most difficult and unreliable. It is insufficient to make judgments simply on the basis of your reactions to the applicant. Look for confirmation of your impressions in the avocational and community activities engaged in by the applicant.

INTERVIEW BEHAVIOR. Assess the personal behavior of the applicant during the interview. How poised was the applicant? Did he or she become easily ruffled? Were you able to establish a relationship with the applicant in which he or she felt willing to confide in you? Were personal appearance and posture in keeping with the demands of the job?

ORAL EXPRESSION. How was the applicant's oral expression during the interview? Keep in mind that the interview is the principal measure of this trait. Look for organization and clarity, conciseness and completeness, grammar, diction, vocabulary, fluency and facility of expression, colorful and interesting language, cohesiveness, and persuasiveness.

AVOCATIONS. Note whether the applicant's leisure activities are spent alone or with other people. This will give you a good clue as to the interpersonal competence of the interviewee and to the type of job in which he or she will perform best. Leisure activities also provide evidence of intellectual skill, creative ability, physical condition, and motivation.

TYPICAL QUESTIONS:

Tell me about your hobbies.

What do you do with your free time?

What do you do for physical exercise?

What types of reading do you prefer?

COMMUNITY ACTIVITIES. Review the organized social and group activities in which the applicant participates.

TYPICAL QUESTIONS:

Do you get into any community or civic activities?

What is your role in the organization?

How much of your time is expended in this activity?

INTERPERSONAL RELATIONS. Cover the whole framework of the applicant's relations with other people. Do the interviewee's responses and social activities indicate that he or she can maintain an effective working relationships with superiors, subordinates, and customers?

TYPICAL QUESTIONS:

What kind of people do you get along well with?

What kind of people "rub you the wrong way?"

CAREER ORIENTATION. The topics in this area are all interrelated, but they form the heart of an applicant's qualifications. This area generally should be explored last in the interview after all the other areas have been discussed.

GOALS AND OBJECTIVES. Review the applicant's short- and long-range goals. A person with clear-cut and realistic goals that fit into company needs is an excellent prospect. However, goals must be broad enough to enable the person to modify them as circumstances arise.

TYPICAL QUESTIONS:

What kind of job do you want to work toward in the next five years?

What do you seek most out of a job—pay, prestige, or achievement?

How do you see this job fitting in with your career goals?

VOCATIONAL PLANNING. The applicant's orientation toward his or her present and future in the world of work is an important area to cover. The immature or disoriented person has given little thought to an immediate career beyond the requirement that it furnish a certain amount of income and security.

TYPICAL QUESTIONS:

What caused you to select _____ as a career?

How long have you been planning to do this kind of work?

Why do you feel this is a good plan for you?

SELF-EVALUATION AND IMPROVEMENT EFFORTS. The applicant's evaluation of personal strengths and limitations and his or her efforts to improve vocational qualifications are keys to job effectiveness. These efforts must be viewed, however, in the light of the resources available to the person and of environmental restrictions which are present.

TYPICAL QUESTIONS:

What abilities do you have that you feel will help you reach your objectives?

Looking over all the areas which we've covered, what would you say would represent your strongest single asset?

In what areas do you feel further improvement could be made? None of us is perfect; we all have ways of developing further.

REASONS FOR APPLYING. Ask for specific reasons why the applicant applied for this job. A person who is primarily interested in personal work content and in a chance to exploit personal potential is an excellent prospect.

TYPICAL QUESTIONS:

What prompted you to apply for this job?

What have you learned about this company?

What appeals to you about this job?

TRAINING AND EDUCATION. Questions in this area give more than an indication of a person's knowledge and intellectual ability. They lead to fruitful hypotheses about initiative, self-reliance, dependability, and emotional stability.

LEVEL AND CHOICE OF EDUCATION. The type and level of schooling, the reasons why particular schools were chosen, and the degree to which the applicant financed his or her own education are clues to initiative and perseverance.

TYPICAL QUESTIONS:

I see you went to _____ college (high school).

How did you pick that school?

What do you feel were the most significant things you got out of that school?

CURRICULUM RELEVANCY. The courses of study pursued by the applicant and their relevancy to career plans and goals, as well as the requirements of the job for which he or she is applying, are covered here.

TYPICAL QUESTIONS:

What type of program did you take?

How did you happen to concentrate in that field?

In which subjects were you the most interested?

SCHOLASTIC ACHIEVEMENT. Review the intellectual and scholastic achievement of the applicant, including grades, class standing, honors, etc.

TYPICAL QUESTIONS:

In what subjects did you do your best work?

With what subjects did you have the most difficulty?

What were your grades like?

Approximately where would you say you ranked in your class?

SOCIAL ACHIEVEMENT.   Ask the applicant about his or her role in extracurricular activities and also relationships with teachers and fellow students.

TYPICAL QUESTIONS:

How did your teachers generally regard you?

In how many social activities did you participate in school?

Were you ever chosen or elected class or group leader?

ATHLETIC ACHIEVEMENTS.   Participation in active competitive sports is usually a strong indication not only of stamina and strength but also of perseverance, initiative, and cooperation.

TYPICAL QUESTIONS:

What athletic activities did you engage in?

Were you ever chosen captain of any team you played on?

WORK EXPERIENCE.   Perhaps the most productive source of information regarding the possession of relevant traits comes from an exploration of an applicant's work history. This exploration, however, should not be devoted exclusively to a discussion of job duties and their execution. Technical incompetence is only a minor cause of job failure. Working habits, personal effort, and ability to work as part of a team are more important. Deficiencies in these areas are the major causes of job failure. In this area, you should include military history for discussion, treating it as a period of employment.

WORK STYLE AND HABITS.   Review the way the applicant approaches a job, emphasizing such factors as alertness, imagination, initiative, willingness to work, sense of responsibility, and priorities.

TYPICAL QUESTIONS:

I notice that you are working for _____.

Would you tell me a little about that job?

How did you happen to go to work for them?

What are the things you expect most from the company that hires you?

RELEVANCY OF PREVIOUS POSITIONS.   Compare the applicant's work experiences to the job functions for which he or she is being considered, particularly with regard to the knowledge and skill required.

TYPICAL QUESTIONS:

Tell me about what you did in your last job or jobs?

What experience have you had with _____? (Here mention a piece of equipment, a problem, a process, or a situation.)

How was planning involved in your job?

What speaking and writing responsibilities did you have?

OCCUPATIONAL ACHIEVEMENT.   Estimate the applicant's job accomplishments, position, and salary progression.

TYPICAL QUESTIONS:

What would you say were your major accomplishments on that job?

Would you describe any special methods, new techniques, or novel developments which you have designed on your own?

Looking back, what would you say were the two or three most difficult job problems you faced?

LEADERSHIP AND INTERPERSONAL RELATIONS.   Cover the applicant's relations with superiors, peers, subordinates, and customers.

TYPICAL QUESTIONS:

I see you worked for _____.

What kind of a person was he or she?

What kind of a relationship did you have with him or her?

How do you feel he or she would rate (or describe) you?

What kind of supervisor do you feel you work best for?

REASONS FOR LEAVING JOBS.   By the time applicants have applied for several jobs, they have developed socially acceptable reasons for leaving previous jobs. These stated reasons may or may not be true. Unless there is a clear and logical reason for the change in employment such as higher pay, or an opportunity to learn or apply a higher skill, serious consideration should be given to the validity of the reasons offered.

TYPICAL QUESTIONS:

Tell me your reasons for leaving your various jobs?

What were the circumstances leading up to your decision to leave that job?

What aspects of the job did you find most stimulating and satisfying?

What aspects, on a relative basis, did you care for less?

The Assessment Interview Report Form   Every assessment interview must be reported on a carefully designed form. There are many such forms for reporting the interviewer's final evaluation, ranging from precisely structured checklists to "free-response" report forms that allow for the uninhibited expression of the interviewer's reactions and judgments. Each has its proper use depending on the interview context. Desirably, however, a proper balance should be struck between a form that confines the interviewer too narrowly and rigidly and one that gives no guidelines whatsoever and thus makes comparisons among different interviewers and different applicants highly tenuous.

ASSESSMENT INTERVIEW REPORT

NAME _James P. Wilson_   NO. _2234_   DATE _7-1-75_

POSITION _Programmer Trainee_   LOCATION _Research Data Proc._

INTERVIEW SUMMARY

TRAIT			RESULT				TRAIT			RESULT			
NAME	P/S	WT.	U	M	A	S	NAME	P/S	WT.	U	M	A	S
Perception	S	7			✓		Influence	P	5				✓
Memory	S	6			✓		Cooperation	P	7				✓
Comprehension	S	7			✓								
Problem-Solving	S	7				✓							
Creativity	P	7			✓								
Planning	S	4				✓							
Decision-Making	P	4		✓									
Initiative	P	4				✓							

DECISION

ESTIMATE OF STRENGTH FOR PRESENT POSITION

☐ BELOW AVERAGE   ☐ AVERAGE   ☑ ABOVE AVERAGE   ☐ OUTSTANDING

ESTIMATE OF POTENTIAL BEYOND PRESENT POSITION

☐ BELOW AVERAGE   ☐ AVERAGE   ☑ ABOVE AVERAGE   ☐ OUTSTANDING

FINAL RECOMMENDATION

☐ DO NOT EMPLOY   ☐ FILE FOR FUTURE CONSIDERATION   ☑ MAKE EMPLOYMENT OFFER

SUMMARY COMMENTS:

Mr. Wilson is a strong prospect. His initial interview and placement exercise results place him in the superior category for programmer trainees. This interview confirmed these findings.

INTERVIEWER _Mary Brown_

FORM 7b

Fig. 11 Completed Decision–Assessment Interview Report (Copyright © 1974 by Felix M. Lopez & Associates, Inc.)

The *Assessment Interview Report* is a four-page form designed to enable you to cover the relevant portions of an applicant's qualifications systematically and completely. Page 1 is completed before and after the interview; pages 2, 3, and 4 are completed during the interview. A completed page 1 is shown in Figure 11 and a completed page 2 in Figure 12. Pages 3 and 4 are similar to page 2.

PREPARATION. Before beginning the interview, fill in the applicant's name, number, the date, the position, and department for which he or

	LIFE INFORMATION AREAS				
TRAITS	**PERSONAL**	**SOCIAL**	**CAREER**	**TRAINING**	**WORK**
	1. EARLY LIFE HISTORY 2. PRESENT FAMILY SITUATION 3. HEALTH AND PERSONAL HABITS 4. PERSONAL ADJUSTMENT	1. INTERVIEW BEHAVIOR 2. ORAL EXPRESSION 3. AVOCATIONS 4. COMMUNITY ACTIVITIES 5. INTERPERSONAL RELATIONS	1. GOALS AND OBJECTIVES 2. VOCATIONAL PLANNING 3. SELF EVALUATION 4. SELF IMPROVEMENT 5. REASONS FOR APPLYING	1. LEVEL AND CHOICE 2. CURRICULUM RELEVANCY 3. SCHOLASTIC ACHIEVEMENT 4. SOCIAL ACHIEVEMENT 5. ATHLETIC ACHIEVEMENT	1. STYLE AND HABITS 2. RELEVANCY 3. ACHIEVEMENT & PROGRESSION 4. INTERPERSONAL RELATIONS 5. REASONS FOR LEAVING
Creativity	1+4 ☒ HOME LIFE HAPPY EARLY SELF RELIANCE	3 ☒ HOBBIES PAINTING ELECTRONICS SHORT WAVE RADIO	3 ☒ BEST IN CREATIVE Activities	1,2,3 ☒ LIKED RESEARCH HIGH GRADES IN MATH + SCIENCE	2 ☒ DESIGNED NEW PROCEDURES
Planning	2,4 ☒ PARENTS ENCOURAGED HIM TO PLAN CAREER	3,4 ☒ See BELOW	1,2,4 ☒ WANTS TO BE TOP SYSTEMS MGR.	1,2 COURSES IN SYSTEMS ANALYSIS — GRADES - A	2,3,5 ☒ FEELS TIME FOR A CHANGE — —
Decision Making	1,2,4 ☒ SEE ABOVE	4 ☒ CHAIRMAN OF LOCAL SCHOOL BOARD	1,2 ☒ SEE ABOVE	1,2 ☒ SEVERAL COURSES IN MANAGEMENT	2,3,5 ☒ MAKES DECISIONS IN PRESENT JOB

Fig. 12 Completed page 3—Assessment Interview Report

she is being considered. Then review the selection plan for the position. In the interview summary section of the *Assessment Interview Report,* list all the traits to be measured by the assessment interview as indicated in the selection plan. Then fill out the column listings beside each trait to show whether the evaluation interview is a principal or a supplemental measure of that trait and to show the weight assigned to it.

Now on pages 2, 3, and 4 write each trait name listed on the front of the form on a line in one of the boxes on the left-hand side. There is space for fifteen traits on this form, more than enough for nearly every job. As Figure 12 shows, across the top of the page are listed column by column the five life-information areas and the topics discussed during the interview. For each trait, a separate box is provided in which to jot down interview notes under the appropriate life-information area headings.

Before the interview starts, you should check both the areas and the topics to investigate for each trait. Place a checkmark in the small square in each box to signify that a particular area must be discussed to obtain information related to the trait being measured. You then write the number of the particular topic to be covered. After you have completed this task, you have, in reality, prepared a detailed assessment-interview plan. The only task that remains is to determine the order in which you will discuss each topic.

DURING THE INTERVIEW. The life-information columns are arranged from left to right, but the order in which to conduct the interview during the information-getting sequence is optional. A good plan is to begin with work experience, then move to the educational area, then to the social and personal areas, and finally to conclude the interview by discussing the career and self-evaluation areas. While it is not necessary to follow this order, you should organize your interview so that you cover each area as a whole. During the interview, jot down notes under each heading as you desire, following the suggestions for note-taking made in Chapter 7.

During the interview, you should not hesitate to note other subjective impressions, additional questions that you may wish to ask, or subjects to be pursued in a later investigation. In your "Summary Comments" section you can include those impressions that will lend a personal touch to your final evaluation.

An open-ended form that does not limit the interviewer to any predetermined traits but provides space for a broad description of the applicant under four or five major headings can also be very effective. But if you wish to compare several applicants interviewed by two or more interviewers, the free form is somewhat inadequate. A structured form that permits the interviewer to include his or her own remarks and a free summary seems to us to be the ideal because it provides an interview guide, effects some standardization in interview, permits comparisons among interviewers, yields an objective appraisal in terms of a standard or anchoring point of the individual interviewer, and yet affords an opportunity to include the interviewer's unique impressions.

AFTER THE INTERVIEW. As soon as the applicant has left, complete the results column on page 1 for each trait. Place an X at one of the four columns—U (Unacceptable), M (Marginal), A (Clearly Acceptable), or S (Superior). This rating is based on the notes you made in the boxes to the right of each trait on pages 2, 3, and 4.

After reviewing the profile you have drawn of the applicant, considering both the test scores and the employment-interview report results, complete the decision part of the report on page 1. Completing this section deserves further consideration.

The Final Synthesis and Decision   The last and by far the most important step in the assessment-interview process is the determination of the final decision. If you have performed your task well, you will possess a varied accumulation of information that requires synthesis. This synthesis, however, must be based on a sound foundation of fairly objective assumptions concerning the selection process.

First, if you have conducted the interview properly, you will have discovered a great many imperfections and weaknesses in the applicant. This unfavorable information can be quite misleading and can create a halo effect in reverse when compared to the job requirements.[4] You must remember that job requirements usually describe the ideal incumbent. But the ideal person, even though perfect, is inferior to a real person with a number of imperfections—the ideal person does not exist while the real person does, and only a real person can perform the job function.

Failure to recognize this deception constitutes a major reason why so many companies recruit outside their own employee forces rather than promote from within. By dint of continuing experience with their own employees, they become aware of their weaknesses and imperfections. Since it is seldom possible to acquire the same degree of familiarity with outside applicants, they almost always appear much fresher, more attractive, and with none of the faults displayed by present staff members.

The shrewd evaluator weighs a person's weaknesses against his or her strengths to arrive at an overall judgment and does not use the selection plan as a template to lay over the evaluation of the applicant. Rather, he or she employs a system of checks and balances to determine which asset of the interviewee will compensate for which weakness. There is no set pattern of requisite human attributes for any job. Lack of formal education can be more than offset by an unusually varied and broad life experience; deficiencies in intellectual depth can be compensated for by an abundance of persistency, dedication, and energy.

Some defects, of course, cannot be compensated for. A lack of ambition or drive can never be offset by a high level of intelligence or by a scintillating personality; job knowledge and skill cannot overcome personal maladjustment. To sum up, since an employee's success can be attributed to his or her own unique combination of personal characteristics, no job specification that merely lists a series of personal traits and the minimum requirement on each is sufficiently flexible to be adequate.

Second, the final evaluation and synthesis should concentrate on life facts, on incident, anecdote, accomplishment, and achievement. What a person has done in the past is always the best indication of what will be done in the future. That is to say, the previous habits and behavior of a person afford the most solid foundation for speculation about future actions, provided, of course, that conditions in the future are similar to the past environment. We have a right to infer from a person's record

[4] See, for example, W. J. Crissy and J. Regan, "Halo in the Employment Interview," *Journal of Applied Psychology*, 35:338–341, 1951; B. I. Bolster and B. M. Springbelt, "The Reaction of Interviewers to Favorable and Unfavorable Information," *Journal of Applied Psychology*, 45:97–103, 1961.

of chronic tardiness that he or she in a new job will continue this practice. It may be socially desirable to argue that people do change, that they do learn from experience. But the evidence seems to suggest that unless the changes are wrought by intensive therapy or by a traumatic experience, they will be very gradual and rarely reflect a basic reorientation of values and attitudes.

Third, wherever possible, the final decision should represent the pooled judgment of competent evaluators. Multiple assessments, by themselves, are not superior to an individual appraisal unless each is made independently and unless each represents mature, experienced judgment. These pooled evaluations should also cover all the data in reference to the environment in which the individual is to be placed.

One final word needs to be reemphasized at this point. Implicit in the discussion of the employment and the assessment interviews, perhaps, has been the idea that the primary goal of the selection process is to obtain efficient, useful, and productive employees. In part, this is true. But if it were the whole truth, the selection task would not be so complicated, so interesting, or so important. The other side of the coin, the other major goal of the selection process, perhaps in terms of lasting values, the more important goal, is to place people in positions in which they will be able to grow and to develop toward the ultimate objective of self-realization and from which they can draw a full measure of satisfaction and stimulation.

In the last analysis, perhaps, this is really the challenge we face in looking for better and more reality-oriented ways of assessing people—for their own best interests, for the interest of the organization they serve, and ultimately for the common good of society in general.

chapter 9

Selection Interview Variations

> The materials of action are variable, but the use we make
> of them should be constant.
> —EPICTETUS, *How Nobleness of Mind May Be*
> *Consistent with Prudence*

As the essential feature of their selection strategy, most organizations permit the supervisor of the unit in which the vacancy occurs to have the final say in the hiring decision. In these organizations, therefore, the supervisor interviews every applicant to pass judgment on his or her fitness for the position in question.

To validate the usefulness of this procedure, the author has conducted many studies to determine what supervisors look for in an employment applicant and on what basis they make their final decisions. The results have been largely negative. Most supervisors frankly admitted that they did not have a clear idea or notion of what to look for. Some said they used the interview to stress how boring the work was and to gauge the applicant's expectation level to determine how long he or she was going to be interested in poor physical working conditions. Others said they saw the interview as an opportunity to explain the job to the applicant and to point out where he or she was going to work. A few said they went into elaborate detail, mentioning such qualities as appearance, a friendly smile, technical qualifications, aggressiveness, and ability to take pressure as things they looked for. But most supervisors agreed that they turned down very few applicants, accepting approximately nine out of ten referred. It would appear, then, that the supervisor's role in the selection process is quite minor. Nevertheless, in many situations it is essential.

In Chapter 1, we defined the interview as a communication between two people, comparing it to a game of tennis. To introduce a third party to the interview or to shorten it to ten minutes, we have implied, would be just as ludicrous as adding a third person to a tennis match or reducing the usual number of six or more games in a set to one or two. Perhaps to prove once more that nothing in life is really that fixed or absolute, we are about to hedge a little on our position.

In the selection program, there will be situations in which the basic interviewing pattern cannot be followed. There are occasions when the thirty-minute interview is out of the question. For example, a college recruiter visits a university campus only to find that the college placement officer has scheduled applicants every twenty minutes and the time allotment must include review and write-up between interviews; or the employment office reception room may be jammed with applicants responding to a newspaper advertisement. In each case, you have no alternative but to modify your interview technique to handle the situation.

There will be times when you will be unqualified to judge certain aspects of an interviewee's background or when practicality requires an appraisal by a third person. It will then be necessary to introduce another party to the interview situation.

Although these variations are necessary, they create unique problems. It can be argued that shortening the interview or introducing a third party, while absolutely necessary, may so materially alter the situation that it is no longer an interview. If these alterations are confined to technique or strategy and if in execution the principles expounded in Part 1 are adhered to, the essence of the interview as a process will not be completely destroyed.

Variations are deliberately introduced into the interview context to offset its major limitations of unreliability, inconsistency, subjectivity, and excessive time requirements. When two people meet on a given date to discuss the qualifications of one for a specific job, many factors can contribute to an erroneous outcome.

Three sources of error—the interviewer, the interview, and the interviewee—combine to attenuate the reliability of the process and to lower its predictive power.. Not every person can learn to control these variables. Sometimes the situation does not permit it, and sometimes a particular trait of an interviewee cannot be evaluated completely in the usual interview format. Hence, there is a need for variation.

Interview variations can be introduced by restructuring the format, by severely limiting the interaction, by adding a second or third interviewer in sequence or in tandem, or by interviewing more than one interviewee at the same time. There are many interview variations: some that are almost identical with the selection interviews as we have described them, and some that more closely resemble group-discussion tests. These variations boil down to two classes: the limited format and the multiple-appraisal techniques.

The Limited-purpose Interview

In certain situations, the interviewer is restricted either by time or by the applicant traits being assessed. The first type of interview is referred to as a *screening* interview; the second is a common *supervisory* or departmental interview.

The Screening Interview   In large-volume interviewing, you have little time to do more than classify each applicant roughly and reserve for later and fuller consideration those who survive the first coarse screening. The screening process usually begins with the completion by the applicant of a short application blank (the qualification form prepared by many college students in the college placement office is a good example). You begin the procedure by examining the completed form for an applicant's possession of such bedrock qualifications as hours available, craft-skill and salary requirements. Those who do not meet these base-line standards are excused quickly. The rest are given a highly structured fifteen-minute interview. In this interview, described below, only the high spots of the applicant's qualifications are reviewed. Qualified applicants are given a "score" on the interview, and those with the highest scores are invited to return later for fuller consideration.

To be used effectively, the screening interview requires careful planning based on empirical research and analysis in which the traits essential for job effectiveness have been identified. These are carefully described so that they can be recognized and minimal levels of acceptability can be determined. Variations of the degree to which people possess the trait are derived and a suitable rating form is constructed. Figure 13 illustrates a twenty-minute interview-report form for the campus interview developed by a discriminant analysis of the characteristics of effective and ineffective trainees, between those who stayed and those who terminated quickly, and by referral to certain minimum standards of appearance, diction, behavior, and decorum required by the job.

The interviewer can complete many of the items on this report form by referring to the application blank and is limited to a few basic personal judgments. Since time is critical, the interviewer confines the inquiry to a few elementary questions and records a quick overall impression of the diction, poise, and appearance of the applicant. There is little interaction and no opportunity to establish rapport or to discuss personal problems.

This approach is most effective in large-scale recruitment when a volume of applicants can be anticipated, or it can be incorporated into the routine of the daily employment operation in which a number of applicants are processed each day for entrance-level positions. This

INITIAL INTERVIEW REPORT

Name ___JOHN M. BROWN_____ School _Hale University_

Local Address ___416 Edwards Hall_____ Date _2/5/74_

Program Recommended: ☒ Management   ☐ Accounting   ☐ Engineering   ☐ Sales

Why did he apply?

Referred by Professor _____ Referred by Placement Director _Mr. Jones_
                          name   name

☐ Curiosity   Other Reason _Highly recommended by Mr. Jones._

Age	☐ Below 20 ☐ Over 30	☐ 26-30	☒ 21-25 23 years
Citizenship	☒ U.S. Citizen		
Marital Status	☒ Single	☐ Married	
Physical Requirements	☐ Meets Requirements	☒ Intramural Athletics Basketball	☐ Varsity
Level of Degree	☒ Bachelor's	☐ Master's	☐ Ph.D.
Undergraduate (Mgmt. Pro. only)	☐ Other	☐ Bus. Admin. Govt.	☒ Broad, Liberal Arts A.B. Economics
Standing in Class	☐ Upper 1/2	☐ Upper 1/4	☒ Upper 1/10 Magna Cum Deans List Laude
Undergrad. Schlng. Situation	☐ Part Time	☐ Full Time	☒ Full time flshp or sclshp National Merit
Undergraduate extra-curricular activities	☐ Minimal	☐ Active participation in 2 or more org.	☒ Active leadership in 1 or more org. Class President
Military Service	☐ None	☒ Enlisted Infantry 6 mos	☐ Senior non-comm. or comm.
Employment	☐ Spotty or None	☒ Consistent summer work Outdoor - unskilled	☐ Pertinent experience
Reason for applying	☐ Wants tng. prog. or job	☒ Wants career in business	☐ On basis of studies Wants a carrer in this Co.
Appearance	☐ Meets Requirements	☒ Well-dressed, clean-cut	☐ Faultless grooming
Bearing and Poise	☐ Meets Requirements	☐ Alert, poised	☒ Impressive, mature
Speech and Diction	☐ Average grammar and vocabulary	☒ Good vocabulary, Clear diction, Good grammar	☐ Extensive vocabulary, polished speech

OVERALL RECOMMENDATION

☐ ☐ ☐ ☐ ☐ ☐ ☐ ☒ ☐
Not Recommended 0   1   2   3   4   5   6   7   8   9 Strongly Recommended

Wants plant management, plans to go to graduate school

Signature ___James Andrews___

FINAL DISPOSITION _Invited to Corporate Headquarters for final tests and interviews will report 3/16/74 J.A._

Fig. 13   Initial interview report: campus interview

method has no value beyond the classification stage of the selection sequence, but when it is appropriately and correctly employed, it can be very efficient and efficacious.

The Supervisory Interview   It is customary in many companies for all applicants to be interviewed by the supervisor of the unit in which the vacancy exists as we have indicated earlier. The average, uninstructed interviewer or supervisor who sees the applicant after "screening" by the personnel representative conducts only a conversation, that is, a completely nonsystematic interview following no particular plan, utilizing no particular style, and with no rationale determining what must be included and excluded as part of the interview content.

When queried as to what they look for in such encounters, most supervisors admit they just want to take a look at the applicants, see what kind of people they are and show them the physical location of the work area. In some companies, the supervisors try to conduct very intensive interviews. A supervisor may have accumulated an interesting array of "standards" which he or she relies on completely, standards that may be invalid, discriminatory, or discourteous. The fact that he or she has never been instructed in or exposed to proper interview techniques and, therefore, has little understanding of the interview components does not discourage the supervisor. Believing in an ability to "size a person up in five minutes," the supervisor applies rules for interviewing which are usually the result of a few dramatic occurrences in the past. These occurrences, although they stand out vividly in the memory of the supervisor, may vary with the day, the month, the job, or the applicant.

If an applicant has been interviewed in the personnel department by a competent professional, there is little need to duplicate the process in the operating department. Unless they are thoroughly trained in employment and/or assessment interviewing, supervisors should be restricted to inquiries and decisions in just two areas: technical and interpersonal competence. In other words, all a supervisor should be required to judge is whether an applicant has the skill and knowledge to do the job effectively and get along with fellow workers and superiors. And even for these traits, the supervisor may not be the most competent one to judge.

By restructuring the amount of supervisory interviewing, the employer can control both the quality and the uniformity of the interview more effectively. This employer will also permit supervisors to devote more of their time to their own job functions and to their subordinates. Of course, the prerequisite for this course of action consists of a highly professional and competent personnel staff that is completely familiar with the demands of the job for which it is responsible. Figure 14 illustrates a supervisory interview-report form that limits the supervisor's judgments to technical and interpersonal competence. This form may also be useful for a similar technique described later—the serial interview.

The Multiple-appraisal Technique

As we have just indicated, it is often necessary to evaluate an applicant's qualifications in a person-to-person situation. The personnel interviewer may be unfamiliar with the knowledge of a particular technology

SUPERVISOR'S EMPLOYMENT INTERVIEW REPORT

APPLICANT'S NAME MIRIAM WILSON DATE 6-4-75 POSITION APPLIED FOR SECRETARY

INTERVIEWER'S NAME GEORGE OLSEN TITLE MANAGER DEPARTMENT PURCHASING

YOUR EVALUATION OF THIS APPLICANT

INDICATE YOUR RATING BY CHECKING THE APPROPRIATE BOX

	Rel	U	M	A	S		Rel	U	M	A	S
TRAINING (SCHOOLING & TRNG.)	✓			✓		MANNER (POLITE, FRIENDLY)	✓				✓
EXPERIENCE (JOB RELATED)	✓			✓		SPEECH (UNDERSTANDABLE)	✓				✓
CRAFT KNOWLEDGE	✓			✓		INTEREST IN POSITION	✓			✓	
CRAFT SKILL	✓			✓		OTHER					

COMMENTS: Excellent candidate

OVERALL RECOMMENDATION

NOT RECOMMENDED ☐ 1 ☐ 2 ☐ 3 ☐ 4 ☐ 5 ☐ 6 ☐ 7 ☑ 8 ☐ 9 STRONGLY RECOMMENDED

ALTERNATE JOBS QUALIFIED FOR:

INTERVIEWER'S SIGNATURE George Olsen

Felix M. Lopez & Associates, Inc. 1974 FOR INSTRUCTIONS, SEE REVERSE SIDE TTA-20

INSTRUCTIONS

1. Before you see the applicant, look over his application and any other information you have on him. Fill out the top of the form and, in the relevancy (Rel) columns, check those areas important to effective performance of the job.
2. When you meet the applicant, greet him warmly and do your best to establish a positive atmosphere.
3. Once rapport is established, begin interviewing the applicant, asking questions only in areas you have checked as relevant. Follow questioning techniques in interviewer training program and in Chapter 3 of our Decision Making Employment Manual.
4. Give the applicant sufficient information about the job involved to enable him to make a decision.
5. Close the interview, using the techniques described in the Manual.
6. Rate the applicant in each of the relevant areas by checking the appropriate boxes under U (unacceptable), M (marginal), A (acceptable), and S (superior).
7. After the applicant has left, make your overall recommendation by checking the appropriate box in the nine point scale from "Not Recommended" to "Strongly Recommended."
8. Make any comments necessary in the space provided. This is particularly essential in the case of "Not Recommended" applicants.
9. If, in your estimation, the applicant is better qualified for positions other than the one for which you were interviewing him, list them in the space provided.
10. Send all material on the applicant, including this completed form, to your Employment Center to the attention of the original employment interviewer.

© Felix M. Lopez & Associates, Inc. 1974 TTA-20

Fig. 14 Supervisor's employment interview report (Copyright © 1974 by Felix M. Lopez & Associates, Inc.)

or the concepts of a discipline and may need more expert assistance. Besides technical support, however, the axiom that "two heads are better than one" constitutes another reason for a second or third interviewer. There is no question that an interview by two skilled people can contribute to more effective selection simply because variations in perception and evaluation tend to cancel out the effect of unconscious bias in each separate assessment. But as we shall describe further, the use of more than one person in the selection process also brings with it certain problems. We can identify four multiple-appraisal techniques that approximate the interview situation to some extent: the serial interview, the panel interview, the group interview, and the leaderless group discussion.

The Serial Interview The necessity of talking to an employment applicant is based on two needs: to decide what kind of a person he or she is and to determine the applicant's technical qualifications for the job. The larger agencies rely on the personnel specialist to evaluate the applicant's personal attributes and social skills because this specialist is usually more experienced in this task and because the organization wishes to ensure uniform personal standards. The personnel specialist's inability to evaluate the applicant's technical qualifications gave birth to the serial interview, a technique more widespread than is supposed because it is utilized even where it is not recognized.

After the employment interview, or even after the assessment interview, the employment interviewer may refer the applicant to a supervisor for whom the incumbent will work, who conducts another interview. The latter may refer the candidate to a third supervisor or to another colleague for additional conversation. Thus, by the time the applicant has completed the program, he or she will have undergone a series of interviews each of which is referred to as a "serial" interview. Even when the initial interviewer is quite conversant with the technical requirements of the job, the serial interview has value. A company that wishes to minimize the parochial aspects of its hiring practices will enlist the services of as wide a cross section of its management group as possible to select new employees. Some companies, mindful of this salutary effect, require an applicant to be interviewed by at least one representative of a department, plant, or division other than the one in which he or she is expected to work in order to eliminate the narrow personal compatibilities that result from exclusive selection by one unit head.

Thus the serial interview gives the employer a broader evaluation of incoming applicants and permits the applicant to obtain a wider exposure to company managers. The value of the serial interview is realized only when it is administered correctly. All those in the interviewing chain meet beforehand to discuss the basic requirements of the position and to decide what each is going to do in the selection sequence so that each individual interviewer in the series contributes a unique bit of information to the total product.

Next an interview report form similar to Figure 13 or 14 is used by each interviewer so that when combined they form a continuous whole. For example, the personnel representative's evaluation covers the applicant's drive, energy, stability, interpersonal skills, and personal adjustment; the department X interviewer evaluates the applicant's technical qualifications for that department; the department Y interviewer stresses technical ability for work in that unit; and the department Z interviewer might examine the applicant's potential for future managerial positions. Each of the four interviewers includes in the report a personal evaluation of how the person came across as a person and as a prospective subordinate or associate.

Then, immediately after the interview, each interviewer completes the rating form and makes a decision before conferring with the other interviewers. After the last interview, the applicant returns to the personnel representative for information on what actions are expected to take place next and can also take the opportunity to convey his or her impressions of the experiences in meeting the other interviewers and to ask questions that may have occurred in the interim. After the interviewee has departed and on the. same day, the four interviewers meet to discuss the applicant and to complete a joint report.

This is the proper way to administer the serial interview, and although it may not always be possible, it is always desirable. If, as is often the practice, the applicant is seen on different days by different interviewers and if they comment beforehand to each other, the contaminating effect will so affect the perceptions of the later interviewers that the real value of the technique, separate and independent evaluations, will have been lost.

The serial interview, when used as described above, may represent a substantial gain in information over a single interview. Since it also gives the applicant a wider view of the company, it may increase his enthusiasm and interest in it, particularly if he or she has been treated cordially and efficiently by each interviewer. But it requires an unreasonable amount of the applicant's time.

If interviewed by three people, each of whom devotes forty-five minutes to the interview, the applicant has spent three times the ordinary time allotment to pursue a job that may not materialize.

There is also an unnecessary duplication of interview questions. One after another, serial interviewers ask the same questions and cover the identical areas of an applicant's background. This tedious repetition not only discourages but also fatigues an applicant, and the last interviewer in the chain may find that everyone he or she sees is surprisingly deficient in enthusiasm and alertness.

If there is an executive within the chain whose judgment is highly respected and viewed as most influential, the other interviewers will hold their own evaluations until they have learned how he or she thinks. In addition, there is ample evidence to show that the interviewers' evaluations may vary widely. The reconciliation of their variations is a question for which there is really no pat answer other than continued discussion which demands additional investment of time.

Because of these problems, many agencies and companies resolve them by recourse to a panel or board to conduct the interview.

The Panel Interview   The panel interview, consisting of three or more interviewers, enables them to base their decisions on the same sample of behavior, and it provides the applicant with an opportunity to discuss his or her background and qualifications with them simultaneously. In the public service, this interview is usually referred to as an "oral test," and the interviewing panel, the "oral board of examiners."

The panel interview permits an applicant to tell his or her story once and thus saves considerable time. It is also expected that with additional interviewers more comprehensive coverage of the applicant's background can be obtained, fewer personal areas will be investigated, and therefore the more relevant facets of qualification assessment will be discovered. It is also contended that this technique tends to minimize bias and prejudice because as a panel, interviewers are less likely to be influenced by stereotypes or to allow their own personal beliefs or convictions to affect their appraisals.

The use of the panel interview procedure starts with the careful selection and education of the panel members. Ideally, a company or agency should maintain a slate of panel members who have completed a course of instruction on interviewing techniques and on the obligations and duties of a panel member and who have been furnished with a prepared manual of instructions describing their duties, the various rating forms used, and the meaning and significance of the terms included in these forms.

A panel includes at least three members and usually no more than five, the chairman of which is normally the personnel representative. Each panel member must be familiar with the duties, the responsibilities, and personal requirements of the job or jobs to be filled as described in the final selection plan. At least one of the panel members must be a technical expert in the field in which the job is situated. No more than two of the panel members should be from the same unit, division, or department in which appointments are expected to be made, and these departmental representatives should constitute a minority on the panel.

Preparation for a panel interview is exactly the same as for an assessment interview with a few additional chores thrown in. Before the actual interviews take place, the panel meets to plan the specific courses of action, to review questions (ordinarily the personnel member supplies the questions), to determine who will ask which question, and to clarify the rating method and the standards.

At the beginning of the interview, the chairman of the panel greets the interviewee, introduces the person to the other panel members, and spends a few minutes in general social conversation to relax her or him. The applicant naturally will be more anxious in this situation. To avoid the appearance and the solemnity of a board of inquiry or a general court-martial, the interview should be conducted in a pleasant room devoid of the usual desk or large table. Ideally, the panel members should sit in a loose circle around the applicant, much in the style of a friendly meeting in a living room.

The style of the interview simulates informal group discussion. It begins when the chairman asks the interviewee to run through his or her qualifications briefly. The interviewers, of course, have briefed themselves beforehand and have copies of the applicant's biographical questionnaire in front of them. In turn, each of the interviewers asks at least one question so that all are drawn into the interview conversation from the very beginning. The questions can be prepared in advance but must never be read to the applicant unless the affair is a highly formal oral examination. The chairman, being the personnel representative, asks most of the questions, but all panel members contribute to the conversation in a pleasant, lively fashion.

As much as possible, the panel interview adheres to all the principles of effective interviewing. One interview topic flows into another as unassumingly and as naturally as possible. Additional questions are built on the interviewee's responses. It is quite permissible, even convenient, for the interviewers to take notes during this interview; one of the panel interview's chief advantages lies in the opportunity to do this unobtrusively while another panel member is carrying the brunt of the conversation. Each panel member must guard against dominating the conversation, against boring in, against probing too intensively. These actions are not appropriate to this technique since the interviewee is quite outnumbered and may feel, if pushed too hard, that he is being "gang" tackled.

Panel interviews vary in length from forty-five minutes to an hour-and-a-half, depending on the usual factors of job level, purpose, and material to be covered. It is terminated by the chairman with the usual question as to whether the interviewee wishes to ask any questions, after which the applicant is informed of the next step in the selection procedure and when a decision may be expected; and the meeting is closed cordially with handshakes all around.

As soon as the candidate leaves the room, the panel members complete their rating forms. After this, they compare evaluations and resolve major deviations by discussion and compromise. In the first few interviews, it is advisable to hold free discussions of each interviewer's ratings and rating standards to reach closer consensus on the meaning of rating form terms, question purposes, and typical applicant responses.

Individual ratings must then be pooled, and there are many ways of doing this, some mathematically derived, and some arrived at subjectively. An interviewer modifies his or her own rating only in unusual cases where wide variations are conflicting, contradictory, or embarrassing, or where there is no other way of reaching a decision on the applicant. Needless to say, if the interview panel is always composed of an odd number of judges, the possibility of irreconcilable deadlock is reduced. For some positions, the interviewers' decisions should be unanimous with no dissents accepted. This is not always necessary, but in instances of internal selection it may be advisable from the standpoint of applicant acceptability.

When conducted properly, the panel interview can achieve results superior to the serial interview and even to the individual interview. But as a selection technique, it has its disadvantages.

It introduces a note of formality into the interview atmosphere that tends to inhibit interaction and hence communication. Consequently, the more intimate and personal aspects of the applicant's background cannot be discussed, and there is virtually no opportunity for counseling and problem-solving action if either is required. Since rapport is hard to establish, since the personality interaction is far less spontaneous and natural, and since many of the more valuable insights afforded by the regular interview are lost, the information capacity of the panel interview is actually less than that of an individual interview conducted by a skilled practitioner. And, finally, there is always the very real problem of the dominant and influential member of the panel, a problem that is far more serious and difficult to handle than in the serial interview situation.

The Group Interview   The group interview is a technique in which two or more applicants are interviewed simultaneously. There are situations where this is desirable and effective; there are many others where it is quite out of place.

Normally, employers go to great lengths to keep applicants apart, to prevent them from conversing with one another, from comparing notes, and forming adverse impressions. But, sometimes when there are a half-dozen applicants being considered seriously for a job, all possessing the basic qualifications, it may be helpful to bring them together with one or several interviewers to engage in a group discussion to observe how they behave in a competitive situation, to determine how aggressive, how retiring, or how sociably they may act.

There are no set rules for this technique. Everything and anything goes. One way it is done is by bringing them together over coffee or over a meal. A question is presented to the group and the interviewer notes who responds first, who provides the best answer, who says nothing, who competes with whom.

The group interview deviates radically from a regular selection interview. Naturally, very few personal questions are discussed in front of the other candidates so the interview focuses upon the more objective, impersonal subjects. An applicant may interject personal feelings into the discussion, but only when he or she feels that they are likely to be self-enhancing.

There are many ways a group interview can be of advantage to a potential employer, but usually if it is deemed desirable to bring candidates together for such a session, it can be accomplished far more objectively and successfully by means of the leaderless group discussion technique.

The Leaderless Group Discussion Technique The leaderless group discussion technique, also referred to as "LGD," known in public personnel administration parlance as "the group oral performance test," and as employed by the author, the "group interaction test," stems from a desire to employ multiple interviewing techniques under controlled conditions. The LGD technique has become an integral component of the assessment-center approach simply because by means of it, it is possible to obtain a wide range of information about the overt behavior, the manifest attitudes, the expressed values, and the social skills of applicants in a detail not possible when the number of applicants is large and each has to be interviewed individually. Research has strongly suggested that the results of this technique are highly significant in terms of obtaining a representative sample of the applicant's behavior that is predictive of those qualities that make for effective leadership in small-group situations. When properly structured, the observers witness human interaction among a group of applicants as each attempts to influence and to change the behavior of the others and is in turn influenced and changed by the others. The applicant does not merely tell the interviewer what he or she would do in a specific situation but actually does it.

Principally, the LGD technique requires a group of applicants to act as a committee or task force to discuss and to solve a problem under the observation of company representatives. The problem can be structured or unstructured. In the highly structured version, the group is required not only to explore the problem but also to make a decision as a group on the problem. Each applicant may be assigned a specific issue to defend, thus ensuring considerable conflict and debate among the participants. The size of the group can vary between five and nine; smaller or larger groups are impractical.

Essentially, LGD is a device by which a person is placed in a situation that will stimulate behavior along the lines most resembling the behavior required in the job for which he or she is being appraised. In other words, when employers wish to learn whether a person can act in a certain way or how he or she will react under a given set of circumstances, they can structure a situation with all or most of the aspects of the real-life role, place the person in this role, and carefully observe the resulting behavior.

The behavior best elicited by the LGD technique has been shown to be that associated with small-group leadership ability. This ability, however, is not a unitary trait but is rather a complex set of responses called into play when the leader attempts to influence or to change the behavior of one or several individuals. In LGD, a goal is posited for each member of the group and for the group as a whole. These goals may not necessarily be in harmony and, in fact, may conflict. To resolve the conflict, each individual in the group must attempt to change the behavior of the several group members. In so doing, he or she will manifest behavior that is typical of his or her usual life style and pertinent to the objectives of the situation. Since the behavior employed will be self-defeating if it is socially unacceptable, the candidate must temper it with a recognition of group needs and group goals and the personal needs of the other group members.

The LGD technique is essentially a situational test and, as such, is one of the most promising instruments for the appraisal of an applicant's leadership and social skills. It is, however, a very far cry from the interview as we have described it in this book. It is presented here only to demonstrate the types of observable behavior that are relevant to job-success prediction that cannot be obtained in the interview. Frequently, the behavior observed in the interview is representative only of the applicant's interaction with that particular interviewer and may be quite atypical of his or her normal interpersonal behavior, particularly in peer group encounters. Since the latter are more the rule than the exception in business, it is quite an omission to neglect to sample this behavior objectively.

In LGD format, the average, well-adjusted applicant loses his or her self-consciousness and sense of artificiality very quickly; because of the intriguing nature of the problem, and its built-in conflict, he or she can only work with the group by resorting to real-life behavior. The author's research tends to confirm the fact that the behavior displayed in a group interaction, role-playing situation is quite similar to the behavior displayed on the job.

But LGD still remains a highly unique and specialized tool for the measurement of certain skills important in many management jobs.

Problems with Interview Variations

While interview variations tend to control interview error by standardization and by multiple appraisal, they create other problems.

First, by delimiting the interaction and the content, important elements of the communication process are excluded, and the interview fails to account for unique characteristics of the applicant that may be critically predictive of success or failure in the job.

Second, by adding additional interviewers, the interview's essential format as a face-to-face encounter is materially altered. It is no longer a "you-I" situation; it is a committee or task force engagement with a whole new set of conditions and parameters that must be accounted for and controlled.

Third, since the basic interview structure has been modified, there has to be a new formulation of role dimensions and expectations. Not only do the interviewers have to know who will do what, but the interviewee will have to know which interviewer is playing what role, a question that cannot arise in an individual interview. Unless this question is soon clearly resolved, one interviewer may tend to dominate the situation. Frequently, the interviewer with the most extrinsic power and authority in the organization will, knowingly or unknowingly, superimpose his or her judgment on that of the others participating in the decision-making process, an event that the cointerviewers will be only too delighted to encourage. Hence, while the other interviewers may possess greater astuteness, sophistication, and skill, the dominant power figure will nevertheless so influence the final decision that the supposed gains growing out of the multiple-appraisal technique will have been effectively dissipated.

The most vexing problem is the inability to establish rapport in any of the interview variations that we have described. Like a psychotherapeutic interview between a patient and three psychiatrists, the net result is a loss of a sense of intimacy, a diminution of empathy, a confused interviewee, and a consequent inhibition of communication. For very special reasons and in unique situations, interview variations may and do have their value, but when they are employed, the personnel administrator must recognize that one is giving something to get something, and what one gives must be less than what one gets.

part 3

Problem-solving Interviews

Most of the personnel literature and nearly all of the psychological research dealing with the personnel interview focuses on the selection situation. There are two reasons for this emphasis: first, a selection interview terminates in a decision, that is, in a tangible outcome whose accuracy can be verified; second, in the employment sequence, the selection interview's functional utility is obvious.

There is, however, another type, the problem-solving interview, where the outcome is not so neat, nor is its usefulness so apparent. Yet, this interview can be a very powerful management tool. Every day on the job, an employee confronts obstacles that interfere with effective performance or frustrate personal needs. Whether the barrier is trivial or overwhelming, it calls upon the employee to adopt some form of problem-solving behavior.

Left to his or her own devices, the employee can blindly thrash about like an animal caught in a trap, attempting many different solutions. Or, acting as a rational human being, the employee can develop insights into alternate solutions to the problem by logical analysis. One way of facilitating this analytic process is to seek the advice and the counsel of another interested person, if for no other reason than to think it through aloud. Somehow or another, the verbalization of an inner conflict makes it more amenable to solution because it appears to diminish in size and intensity when it has become audible and perhaps, visible. This "thinking out loud" represents the broad framework of the problem-solving interview—the joint attack on a situation that is of concern to the interviewee.

Two heads will be better than one only if the second person understands his or her proper role as a consultant and a change agent— to help the person with the problem, to avoid or clear up cloudy thinking, to amend otherwise inflexible attitudes, and to clarify the psychological atmosphere by releasing emotion and reducing anxiety. Of course, ultimately, the person with the problem has to be the one to solve it, to work it through on his or her own, or it will simply not stay solved satisfactorily.

It is quite important, at this point, to note that a problem need not be distressing, nor does the person who has it have to be unhappy, depressed, and ineffective. A lottery player, for example, who wins a million dollars has a "delightful" problem deciding what to do with the money. An exceptionally effective employee, to cite a more pertinent example, may have many "problems" usually referred to as "challenges"—how best to continue his or her progress, how to ensure maximum growth and self-development, or how to perform more effectively on the present job.

In Part 3, we examine the problem-solving interview in the occupational context as it applies to four situations: improving job performance, increasing job satisfaction, dealing with complaints, and exercising authority. The interview in each situation has the central theme of problem solving and the immediate intention of changing the interviewee's behavior by removal of obstacles to job effectiveness.

chapter 10

The Dimensions of Job Effectiveness

> To travel hopefully is a better thing than to arrive, and
> the true success is to labor.
> —ROBERT LOUIS STEVENSON, *Virginibus Puerisque*

In recent years, much has been written and spoken about the productivity problem and about the crisis in motivation. In fact, besides the fair employment problem, the major concern of American management has been to find ways of motivating workers. We have already indicated that underlying the equal employment opportunity issue is the deeper and more complex criterion problem, the widespread acceptance of the assumption that job effectiveness is a unitary end-result variable. A similarly false assumption contaminates and confuses the motivation problem.

The difficulty begins with equating job effectiveness with "job success" and then misinterpreting the latter term. The word "success" can be defined variously as (1) specifically, gaining money, position, or other advantage; (2) the favorable or prosperous termination of anything attempted; or (3) a termination that answers the purpose intended. It will be noticed that these three definitions have distinctly different applications to the term "job success." The first definition, which might be viewed as the popular social norm, treats job success solely as the acquisition of wealth, high position, and the admiration of one's peers; the second is used most frequently by managers to describe high productivity and efficiency. Although both definitions are so narrow as to be unrealistic, they have influenced profoundly the conduct of most personnel programs, have colored the vocational aspirations of young people entering the labor market, and have inevitably shaped our whole social system.

One review of the psychological literature, for example, reported the following wide variations in objective indexes of executive success:

a combination of salary, investments, debts, and club memberships; position in the managerial hierarchy; job performance ratings by supervisors and peers.[1] A Carnegie Tech study, analyzing the early careers of a group of young executives, defined success in terms of a person's income and status, the characteristics of the people for whom he or she works, the superior's estimate of the person's long-run advancement prospects, and the number of unstructured tasks he or she was assigned.[2] While admitting that these criteria were somewhat superficial, the authors defended them as a reasonable basis on which to judge the "success" of anyone's career.

More recently, however, motivational and occupational research indicates that the third definition cited above—"a termination that answers the purpose intended"—is the most appropriate meaning to employ as a concept of job success. According to this interpretation, "job success" is a term encompassing the satisfaction, via the occupation, of a broad spectrum of human needs—needs first of all of the individual, of the employer, of supervisors, coworkers, and subordinates, and ultimately, of the community. To underscore this understanding of job success, therefore, we have used in its stead the term "job effectiveness."

As we stated in Chapter 6, since job effectiveness has many dimensions, it is imprecise to use simple measures of job performance as success criteria. It is equally imprecise to speak of employee motivation in global, unitary terms. The failure to recognize this fundamental error has had serious consequences for organizational theorists, as well as personnel practitioners. As Hackman has pointed out, no single motive or motivational pattern is sufficient to account for the work of men and women in industry.[3] In the past decade, dozens of motivational models have been proposed by scholars, but the results of efforts to put these models into practice have not been impressive. The dominant management philosophy of motivation is the "jackass fallacy" which Levinson describes as the assumption that workers are essentially jackasses to be controlled or manipulated by the stick and the carrot.[4]

After a survey of the various theories, models, and research results dealing with motivation, job performance, and job satisfaction, it is hard to fault management for sticking with the jackass theory. A practical way of dealing with the subject and one that has some support in the literature is to consider job satisfaction and job performance as two

[1] Charles Bulin, "The Measurement of Executive Success," *Journal of Applied Psychology,* **46**:303–306, 1962.

[2] W. R. Dill, T. L. Hilton, and W. R. Reitman, *The New Managers: Patterns of Behavior and Development* (Englewood Cliffs, N.J.: Prentice-Hall, Inc., 1962), pp. 139–140.

[3] Ray C. Hackman, *The Motivated Working Adult* (New York: American Management Assn., 1969), p. 15.

[4] Harry Levinson, *The Great Jackass Fallacy* (Boston: Graduate School of Business Administration, Harvard, 1973), p. 10.

separate but interrelated end-result variables. In this view, job performance consists simply of the contribution the employee makes to the employer's goals; and job satisfaction is the fulfillment of the employee's needs. Admittedly, this model is oversimplified, but it has its usefulness in the development of a comprehensive human-resources personnel program. While the two variables are treated by some theorists as independent or causal variables and are also definitely interrelated, they do not necessarily vary in perfect harmony; that is, high performance is not always associated with high satisfaction. But together they constitute what is referred to as organizational behavior, and a high degree of both constitutes organizational effectiveness.

Job Performance

Performance is simply behavior in a system role and in a system activity. An employee's performance is viewed as his or her actual accomplishments as they are influenced by role functions, ability, adaptability to the environment, and the organizational milieu, i.e., leadership style, organizational structure, values, and reward system. These influences can be grouped into three major categories, personality, role, and organizational milieu which in our model of organizational behavior are referred to as the independent or causal variables.

The two major approaches to the analysis of job performance used by students of worker motivation consist of job analysis and accountability. In Chapter 6, we have dealt with the first approach through Threshold Traits Analysis, which relates to the first task of management, proper employee placement. Accountability deals with the motivational properties of *intention* and such related ideas as purpose, goals, objectives, and standards of performance. It is this notion that we will deal with in Part 3. The evaluation interview is designed to improve job performance by establishing individual accountability. But first let us explore what we mean by accountability.

Accountability   Accountability refers to the process of expecting each member of an organization to answer to someone for doing specific things to accomplish tangible performance results according to specific plans and timetables. The process assumes (a) that every member of an organization has joined to help it achieve its purposes, and (b) that when his or her performances contributes to these purposes it is functional and when it does not, it is dysfunctional. Accountability insures that every member's performance is largely functional.

Accountability is often confused with responsibility and authority. Responsibility, in its core meaning, denotes answerability for the performance of an office, a charge, or a duty. Answerability implies both authority and accountability. In recent years, indiscriminate use of the term responsibility has tended to reduce its effectiveness as a practical concept. The term accountability has been widely substituted to specify a more definitive delegation of assignments.

Since some results are achieved by group effort and others by individual effort, there are basically two types of accountability: institutional and individual.

GOAL SETTING. Institutional accountability is established by goal-setting programs frequently referred to as "management-by-objectives," "results management," or "work planning and review." The programs are by no means uniform. In the United States, many MBO programs represent no more than individual accountability activities. In Europe, in contrast, they tend to represent ways of managing.

The underlying concept of the goal-setting approach is simple: the clearer the idea you have of what you want to accomplish, the greater your chance of accomplishing it. Goal setting, therefore, represents an effort to inhibit the natural tendency of organizational procedures to obscure organizational purposes in the utilization of resources. The central idea is to establish a set of goals in a company, to integrate individual performance with them, and to relate all corporate activities to their accomplishment.

The goal-setting or MBO approach not only seeks to take advantage of the motivational consequences implied in purposeful, results-oriented performance, but also provides an opportunity for the consultative, participative practices that insure high commitment to the organization. It thereby integrates successfully a number of theoretical principles advanced by organizational and social scientists.

Unfortunately most MBO programs are either designed as individual performance-evaluation systems or violate a fundamental principle of goal setting, that those who are to achieve the goals established must participate in their articulation.[5]

PERFORMANCE EVALUATION. Individual accountability is generally established by performance evaluation, a system of instruments and techniques to evaluate how employees are performing their assigned duties. *Evaluation* is a broad conclusion concerning the value of an employee's past performance. It differs from the *assessment* process described in Part 2 which is a conclusion concerning a person's qualifications for future performance. An assessment is a judgment of potential and refers to the level and degree of the personal traits possessed rather than to past performance in a specific role.

Since evaluation touches the employee directly, it is the most delicate and difficult to handle. If it is carried out properly, it can accelerate

[5] See, for example, Harry Levinson, "Management by whose objectives?" in *The Great Jackass Fallacy*, pp. 87–107.

organizational development. If it is executed poorly or indifferently, problems of employee motivation and productivity will persist. The central vehicle of the evaluation process is the interview which we will describe in detail in Chapters 11 and 12.

As a key component of the personnel system, a performance evaluation program has three broad purposes:

First, it must directly assist each member in improving his or her current role performance.

Second, it must furnish those in authority with information concerning individual performance and provide a basis for making sound decisions concerning such other personnel transactions as appointments, transfers, reassignments, and retirements.

And third, it must furnish information to the individual on how well he or she is doing.

Very few persons ever perform their appointed tasks at maximum potential, but it is both possible and desirable to continue working toward this goal. In this way, the person *optimizes* his or her level of performance. A well-conceived performance-evaluation program assists each member to reach this *optimum* level because:

1. It demonstrates that those in authority really care about the person's performance.

2. It furnishes the assistance that the person needs to grow, and personal growth is a key to achieving maturity.

3. As he or she grows, personal potential also grows.

4. Continued growth and achievement are normal human needs that constitute powerful motivating forces when satisfied by organizational activity.

These three purposes—information, motivation, and development—require quite different approaches, but the fact is that very few programs, public or private, fulfill even one of them.

It is difficult, moreover, to establish a performance-evaluation program without a goal-setting program to give it a frame of reference. An employee's job function must flow from an organizational statement of purpose, goals, and accountabilities. When a goal-setting program is established, the entire performance-evaluation program will operate within a network of consultative interviews among managers, supervisors, and employees in which each person receives ample opportunity to participate in the establishment of work unit goals.[6]

Employee Development   The implementation of a total accountability program depends to a large extent on the attitudes and the skills of both managers and employees. If they are skeptical, anxious, or hostile to

---

[6] For an amplification of these ideas see Felix M. Lopez, "Accountability in Education," *Phi Delta Kappan*, 52:231–235, 1970.

the plan, it will fail no matter how well it is conceived. Another essential step in introducing accountability into an organization, therefore, is to establish intensive development programs. Such programs must be practical and primarily participative in nature. Their purpose is not merely to disseminate information but rather to change attitudes and to impart specific skills, particularly the skill of conducting evaluation interviews. This will not be easy. Most managers and supervisors have had little experience with such programs to prepare them for the tasks involved. The specific objectives of the program should be:

1. To emphasize the influence process in handling employees and to deemphasize the formal authority-power-coercion approach to supervision.

2. To provide a deeper understanding of the communication process itself. Such a program must heighten the awareness of the employees as to how they relate best to others and should develop the individual's flexibility in dealing with the broad spectrum of personalities encountered in the fulfillment of his or her responsibilities.

3. To emphasize the sociopsychological realities that management faces today. The program should make managers and supervisors aware that they simply cannot rely on authoritarianism to get results with people.

Complete understanding of the significance of these objectives requires a review of the other major division of job effectiveness, satisfaction.

Job Satisfaction

Accountability is concerned with organizational needs and goals. But the members of the organization, as we pointed out in Chapter 2, possess a rich and varied assortment of personal needs and goals. Simply put, they join an organization fundamentally because they see that by attaining organizational goals, they will reach some of their own goals. To the extent that they do this, they will be highly motivated. Management, therefore, must not only evaluate employees, they must also counsel them.

The performance-evaluation process is aimed at the satisfaction of the employer; the counseling process, at the satisfaction of the employee; and the two in tandem, at the ultimate target of job effectiveness. The conduct of a vocational counseling interview requires a precise definition of what constitutes job satisfaction and an answer to the questions why people work, why they become satisfied with their work situation, and why they seek to "get ahead."

Defining Job Satisfaction   The need to define job satisfaction is particularly important at this point in the discussion because there are two ways of viewing it—operationally and intuitively. In the operational view, job satisfaction is a hypothetical, empirically derived construct that provides the rationale for most employee surveys because it limits it to the sum total of a worker's favorable or positive attitudes toward various aspects of the occupational environment. In the intuitive sense, job satisfaction is a much more subjective, more pervasive, almost mystical concept that is best defined by contrasting it to the more limited operational definition and to the idea of employee morale.

In its most profound, deeply personal sense, job satisfaction is the spontaneous feeling of well-being and pleasure that the worker derives from the free and successful pursuit of an activity that requires not only ego involvement but the total commitment of the self. This intuitive definition has many implications. In the operational sense of the term, most employees have a reasonably high degree of job satisfaction; in the intuitive sense, only a handful enjoy true job satisfaction. In the limited meaning, satisfaction with one's work can be unrelated to job performance; in the more profound meaning, it cannot.

Operationally, job satisfaction is a complex variable composed of many independent subvariables—attitudes toward pay, toward the place and hours of work, toward the supervisor and fellow workers, toward corporate policy, and toward the duties of the job itself. In its deeper implications, job satisfaction is a unitary trait gauged by one standard—self-fulfillment. In the more limited meaning, job satisfaction is an appropriate measure of the inner state of those occupied with the satisfaction of the physiological, security, and affiliation needs. In its more personal meaning, it describes the interior peace of those whose needs for understanding, for beauty, and for self-realization have become salient.

Job satisfaction in the intuitive sense differs also from the phenomenon known as "morale," even though the two terms are often used interchangeably. Morale is a group characteristic referring to the cohesiveness of a collection of people, the relationships of the various members of the unit to one another, their common view and acceptance of total group norms, values, and goals, and the urgency they feel to defend and extend these values and purposes. Job satisfaction, in contrast, is a very individual, personal, and intimate quality. It is conceivable, for example, that a group of workers can have low job satisfaction individually, but high morale collectively. An infantryman, plodding along in the mud, may have very low job satisfaction, but together with his platoon members, he may possess a high degree of morale. A group of research scientists, on the other hand, may have high degrees of job satisfaction individually but, collectively, little or no morale.

Morale, therefore, refers to the relationship between a person and a group, and the group to other groups. But job satisfaction describes the relationship between a person and his or her work. Its presence or absence will depend on the fundamental reason why people work at all.

Theories of Job Satisfaction   In recent years, there has been an abundance of theoretical speculation and research dealing with employee motivation and job satisfaction.[7] In some instances, the ensuing discussion has been marked by acrimony and intense debate. The two most widespread and controversial systems are those of Abraham Maslow and Frederick Herzberg.

Maslow's Need Hierarchy   Since a need, biological, psychological, or social, seems to be at the root of all behavior and since we have defined success in terms of need satisfaction, we must examine the structure of different human needs a little more closely. There are many ways to classify and to typify them, but many occupational theorists have found that the system proposed originally by psychologist Abraham Maslow provides the most convenient classification.[8] A brief summary of Maslow's need theory, therefore, will not only help us clarify our concept of job effectiveness but will provide us with a framework for the consideration of the problem-solving process later.

Human needs can be ordered into eight hierarchical categories according to the level of their prepotency, that is, according to the order of their primacy and urgency as motivators. Only after the more prepotent needs are satisfied will other higher-level needs emerge as the main motivating forces of a person's behavior. Naturally, the *physiological* needs constitute the starting point for all human motivation. As they tend to be satisfied, the *safety* needs, the demand for protection from bodily danger and the continued maintenance of physiological need satisfaction, become dominant.

On the next higher level are the needs for *belonging and love* which include the need for group relationships, the desire to affiliate and to be a part of something or someone. Since the next higher need, for the *respect and the esteem* of others, stems from the affiliation need, the thwarting of both produces feelings of inferiority, weakness, and helplessness.

After the physical and social needs are satisfied, the need for *information* emerges. This need represents the desire to know more about the surrounding environment and to acquire knowledge. The next higher need, for *understanding*, is based on the satisfaction of the need for

[7] For a summary of these see John B. Miner and H. Peter Dachler, "Personnel Attitudes and Motivation," *Annual Review of Psychology*, 24:379–402, 1973; and Edward E. Lawler, "Job Attitudes and Employee Motivation: Theory, Research & Practice," *Personnel Psychology*, 23:223–237, 1970.

[8] A. H. Maslow, *Motivation and Personality* (New York: Harper & Row, Publishers, Incorporated, 1954).

knowledge. This is the wish to extract meaning from the events in the environment and to understand the purpose of one's existence.

When knowledge and understanding have been achieved, a higher need emerges, the need for order, symmetry, loveliness, and *beauty*. And finally, when all these needs are satisfied, man copes with the highest of all human needs, the need for *self-actualization*, that is, the desire for self-fulfillment, for self-realization and the wish to become everything that one is capable of becoming.

Thus, as a person grows and matures, he or she desires to satisfy an increasingly higher order of needs; when the basic needs for food, shelter, and clothing and physical safety are assured, the person becomes concerned with social and esteem needs, and seeks, therefore, to affiliate with mutually supportive others. When social needs are gratified, he or she becomes concerned with questions of autonomy, of knowledge, of understanding, and of freedom of expression, and, ultimately, reaches the pinnacle of self-fulfillment in the need to be what he or she must be.

The application of this need system to the world of work is, we believe, quite relevant. In modern society, there is really no single situation as potentially capable of satisfying all human need levels as a person's occupation. When the question "why do people work" is asked, the time-honored reply, "for their daily bread," is true if it implies more than the mere satisfaction of bodily hunger; it must refer more truly to the bread of life. Therefore, as we attempt to identify the criteria of job effectiveness, we must refer the end product to the need levels of different groups of workers. For some, as in the lower socioeconomic groups, the satisfaction of physiological and security needs will represent success. For executives, on the other hand, the self-actualization and the autonomy needs seem to be the most significant for success.

No matter at what level a person's needs are operating, it is quite obvious that they cannot always be met. As a matter of fact, some of them are quite unamenable to, perhaps, incapable of, being satisfied.

Unsatisfied needs mean frustration or conflict, and in organization life, an individual who behaves consistently in response to frustration or conflict is known as a "problem employee," a chronic complainer, a person who cannot get along with anyone, or simply as an ineffective employee.

When a larger group of workers is continually frustrated, the very fact of the goal interference will serve as a rallying force for organization and unified effort, and the resulting collective behavior is likely to follow a pattern of aggression. An organization can quickly recognize frustration and conflict in the form of absenteeism, grievances, complaints, high turnover, and eventually, labor strife.

Although in the occupational world, frustration and conflict are inevitable because the needs of the organization and individual needs do not always coincide, not all their disequilibriums are necessarily disturbing or undesirable. Conflict between an individual and an organization can lead to growth, and a person can use conflict as a "lever" to promote personal development. And an organization can also develop and mature as it learns to cope with conflict.

Not everyone is content with this hierarchy of need theory as a framework within which to define job success, nor are they disturbed by the idea of conflict between the individual and the organization. George Strauss has stated that the absence of gratification in work is not a serious deprivation because most people find ultimate life satisfaction in the community and the home, that many workers accommodate themselves to the demands of the organization without too much psychological discomfort, and that it is only the professional scientific fraternity that places such a high value on the need for autonomy and self-actualization.[9]

Despite its widespread influence on management and organizational behavior, Maslow's theory has only recently been tested experimentally. The results have been inconclusive leading to the inference that the research evidence does not support the theory or that the theory has not been articulated with sufficient specificity for precise testing. It is probable that the latter is the more likely explanation because the theory itself is quite reminiscent of the core of the major philosophical systems developed by civilization.

Herzberg's Two-factor Theory   Much more controversial and, perhaps, even more influential has been the theory of job satisfaction formulated by Frederick Herzberg and confirmed by more recent findings. This theory identifies two mutually exclusive sets of satisfactions that can be obtained from the job: *context* factors, involving the financial reward system, supervision, and the work environment, and *content* factors, stemming from the intrinsic nature of the work.[10] Herzberg suggests that since the context factors—salary, working conditions, supervision, personnel policies, and management climate—are addressed primarily to people's avoidance needs, that is, to their needs to avoid pain and discomfort, the inability to gratify these needs will cause a great deal of dissatisfaction, but their fulfillment will be satisfying only briefly and only up to the point where the satisfaction stimulates even more pressing demands. They are therefore insatiable. For example, on the day employees find that they have been awarded a salary increase, they become quite elated even though inwardly they may feel a sneaking

---

[9] L. R. Sayles, *Individualism and Big Business* (New York: McGraw-Hill Book Company, 1963), chap. 8.
[10] Frederick Herzberg, "One More Time: How Do You Motivate Employees," *Harvard Business Review*, 46:53–62, 1968.

sense of annoyance that the raise was not just a little bit more. Despite this, they are normally quite happy and content—for a few weeks. When they become adjusted to the new salary scale, and that takes but a fortnight, they begin to look forward once more to another salary increase, and their attitude is just about what it was before they received the raise.

The other job-satisfaction factors, related to the job content, its meaning, recognition, opportunity for growth, for challenge, and for mastery of the environment, which Herzberg terms "motivators" and which we have described as the elements of a more profound interpretation of job satisfaction, do not dissatisfy a person when they are absent but can really serve to stimulate and to satisfy him or her over a long period of time as the higher needs are gratified.

The motivators cater to people's need to explore the mystery of life and in some small way to come up with a few answers for themselves. These answers are directed toward healthy people's fascination and curiosity about the external reality of the world about them and permit people somehow to identify with their work and to see it as an extension of their ego in the same way that artists look at a painting and see themselves in it.

It is readily apparent that most jobs in American industry, because they are structured around the economic and social reasons why people work and because they are designed to eliminate the mystery and the fascination, become drab, boring, and uninviting to the degree that they become more routine and "efficient." The industrial engineer works very relentlessly to achieve this end by simplifying a job so that its variability is minimized and so that the standardization of duties and depersonalization of requirements is maximized. Because he or she perceives man as an object, the industrial engineer views human qualities as sources of potential error and thus expends great effort on the task of controlling them. In the process, he or she engineers the fun out of the job and makes it a truly tedious task, not so much in the physical sense, but in the consequences for human dignity and self-respect.

Most psychologists seem to divide themselves into opposing camps with respect to Herzberg's theory. There is no denying that it has spawned a wealth of research, the conclusions from which can be used to support a position either for or against the theory. It is probable that, as with Maslow's theory, the present state of psychological research is inadequate to settle the issue conclusively.

Job Enrichment. The two-factor theory has given rise to the job-enlargement and job-enrichment movements in American industry. The fundamental hypothesis underlying these movements is that people are more productive and more satisfied with their work after their jobs have been enriched. An enriched job is one characterized by increased responsibility for one's work, a chance for personal achievement and the recognition that goes with it, and a chance for psychological growth and advancement.[11]

Job enrichment, however, cannot constitute a panacea for the motivation problem as the evidence attests. To facilitate job effectiveness requires a total program involving concerted effort both by management *and* the individual employee.

Ways of Facilitating Job Effectiveness

There is no doubt that the question of individual needs versus organizational goals is vital to an adequate definition of job effectiveness. Its resolution requires an understanding of the spheres of preeminence appropriate to the organization and to the individual and an appreciation of how the two can be harmonized. Within such a conceptual scheme, we can acquire a realistic view of job effectiveness on which to build a program that will satisfy the individual worker, the organization, and the community.

Job-effectiveness Model   Management people have long been aware of the vital roles played by both job satisfaction and job performance. Their deep misunderstandings have stemmed from the assumption that the two variables are congruent, that is, that a satisfied worker is a productive worker and the low producer is a dissatisfied employee.

The best way to develop an understanding of the interplay between these two factors is to treat them as though they were independent of one another, as two separate outcomes of job activity. The result is a model depicted in Figure 15.

QUADRANT I includes those employees who enjoy high degrees of job performance and satisfaction. While this quadrant constitutes the area of job effectiveness, many studies suggest that no more than 15 to 20 percent of workers are situated here.

QUADRANT II includes those employees whose performance is acceptable but who are dissatisfied with either the job content, job context, or both. Such employees generally constitute placement problems due usually to underemployment or misplacement. Employees will not remain for very long in this quadrant. They will either change their job functions or leave them. If they cannot do either, they will develop the symptoms of frustration. The net result will be a rapidly diminishing performance level that will move them to *Quadrant IV.*

QUADRANT III includes those employees who are fairly content with their jobs but whose performance is low. These employees are satisfied

[11] See John R. Maher, ed., *New Perspectives in Job Enrichment* (New York: Van Nostrand Reinhold, 1971).

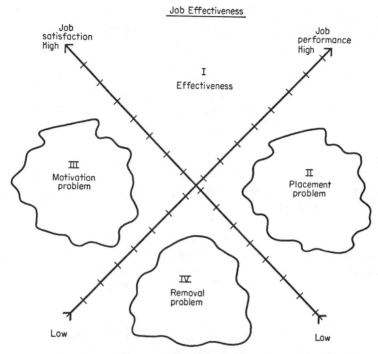

Fig. 15   Job effectiveness

to put in their eight hours without worrying about such items as high output or performance excellence. Most workers occupy this quadrant, and this is the heart of the current motivation problem. Traditional management efforts to alleviate motivation problems have concentrated on such rewards as pay, vacations, a shorter work week, and increased recreation that can only be enjoyed off the job. Current motivation research seems to characterize these efforts as inadequate. In time, workers in this quadrant will fall into *Quadrant IV*.

QUADRANT IV includes those employees who exhibit both low job satisfaction and low job performance. Since these employees cannot be tolerated for very long in an effective organization, we refer to them as removal problems. The average personnel manager spends most of his or her time working with this group instead of with the group in *Quadrant I*.

We have drawn Figure 15 in a way which indicates the gravitational forces of misplacement, poor job structure, and an indifferent or hostile environment that serve to pull employees out of the job effectiveness quadrant. It takes effort, deliberate and concerted effort, on the part of both management and the individual employee to rise into and remain in *Quadrant I*.

The Personality-role-milieu Transaction   In the job-effectiveness model, therefore, effective performance is viewed as the dynamic outcome of the transactions that occur among three major causal variables: personality, role, and organization milieu.

These transactions determine the unique characteristics of the end-result variables, job performance and job satisfaction, which taken together constitute job effectiveness. Consequently, an effective program of selecting and motivating employees must be based upon a dynamic model that includes careful consideration of each of these variables.

PERSONALITY.   This variable includes the physical, intellectual, emotional, moral, and motivational characteristics of the person performing the job. As we indicated in Chapter 2, an occupation or vocation is the chief means of acting out one's self-concept according to modern theories of vocational choice.

These principles have led occupational psychologists to project theories of personality based upon vocational choice.[12] Essentially, these theories rest on the idea that people are happy and effective only in certain specific organizational roles; that, within the limits of the labor market, they will seek their favorite roles as persistently as water seeks its own level.

Vocational choice, therefore, is a cumulative process of decision making which is begun in childhood and largely irreversible. Whatever the decision, the fact remains that by the time he or she reaches adulthood, each person is able to function effectively in only a few of the wide assortment of occupational cells in the three-way matrix provided by society.

ROLE.   This variable includes the functions and the demands of the job established to achieve the organization's goals.

Roles flow from the organization's purpose; they are independent of the personalities who enact them. A person can change roles only by modifying or ignoring organization purposes and goals which is a common practice. But unless tasks are clearly defined and roles clarified, there is no way of establishing criteria of effective job performance.

ORGANIZATIONAL MILIEU.   This variable includes the structure, governing style, values, and rewards of the organization in which the role is enacted. The organizational milieu is a product of the personalities that inhabit the organization and the roles that have to be performed in it. The combination of these two factors creates a value system, a structure, and a climate that is conducive to both. We use the term "milieu" rather than environment to include all the environments—physical, psychological, and social, as well as internal and external. This milieu consists of two separate aspects: the way the organization is structured

---

[12] See, for example, J. L. Holland, *The Psychology of Vocational Choice* (Waltham, Mass.: Blaisdell Publishing Co., 1966).

for decision making and the value and reward climate surrounding its activities.

Rensis Likert has pointed out that research tends to support the principle that the leadership and other management policies and processes must be so developed as to ensure the maximum probability that in all activities and relationships with the company, each employee will, in the light of personal background, values, and expectations, view the experience as supportive and will build and maintain a sense of personal worth and importance.[13] Job effectiveness, then, based on this principle, consists of a rather delicate blend of policies, procedures, and practices that will create an organizational climate that tends to satisfy individual, organizational, and community needs ranging from the lowest order of survival needs up through the higher-order needs of autonomy and self-realization.

Job effectiveness is a result requiring the combined efforts of all company members—stockholders, managers, union leaders, and employees. It cannot be attained without deliberate and conscious effort; it is achieved through a careful balance of many programs, policies, and techniques rather than by the introduction of one brightly conceived artifice. Since job effectiveness is the responsibility of the organization *and* the individual, it proceeds simultaneously and intermingles at two distinct levels of operation—the organization-wide level and the personal level.

The Organizational Effort   To assure an individual's membership in the group and "on the team," to place the person properly, management must develop and implement four major personnel programs.

PROCUREMENT.   The first program, which we have already discussed, is selection, which provides for the adequate recruitment, selection, and advancement of people with ability and character.

DEVELOPMENT.   An employee education and development program is the second activity that management fosters to ensure job effectiveness. When able people are brought into an organization, the means must be provided to enable them to work toward a greater sense of self-worth by learning, by increased understanding, and by self-development.

PROGRESSION.   A third major management activity designed to facilitate job effectiveness consists of a comprehensive progression program designed to provide for an objective and orderly upgrading of employees in accordance with their capacities, demonstrated achievement, and the organization's needs.

REWARDS SYSTEMS.   The final activity consists of programs and

[13] Rensis Likert, *New Patterns of Management* (New York: McGraw-Hill, 1961), p. 101.

policies that satisfy human physiological and security needs by providing workers with just and fair compensation, social insurance benefits, and a disciplinary program through which uncooperative employees, after suitable warning, receive appropriate sanctions and penalties.

The Personal Level   Often the most soundly conceived and conscientiously applied program fails to live up to the promise anticipated in its preparation and initial announcement. For some reason or another, its goals are not reached because it fails to appeal to employees as individuals. There is a very logical explanation for this failure—the program prepared by a specialist in a staff department may overlook the vital importance of the contact point, the place where the worker confronts the management representative, the supervisor, and where the program assumes the aura of reality.

Personnel policies are designed for people collectively, sometimes for large numbers of people who differ in many ways. Sooner or later there must be a private face-to-face encounter between supervisor and subordinate, between counselor and counselee, or between personnel representative and employee to discuss the implementation of these organizational policies, to apply them in the light of the immediate here-and-now situation. There is no effective substitute for the validity of this traditional person-to-person function.

There is ample evidence to support the assertion that the quality of supervisor-subordinate relationships has a deep effect on the quality of labor-management relationships in the overall corporate structure. Rensis Likert reports that the supervisors in favorable work groups are much more interested in subordinates as persons than supervisors in work units with unfavorable job-related attitudes. Close personal contact with frequent discussion between supervisor and subordinate tends to enhance the job satisfaction and the job performance of employees, although Dr. Likert cautions that no simple set of supervisory practices will always yield the best results.[14]

This person-to-person encounter, the handservant of the organization-wide and small-group communication processes, usually takes place in a problem-solving interview of three possible forms: coaching, counseling, or admonition.

COACHING.   The term "coaching," more apt than the traditional term "performance appraisal," although still not completely descriptive, is the process by which the supervisor periodically discusses the performance of each individual subordinate to help him or her work through job-related problems.

COUNSELING.   From time to time, employees, no matter what their degree of effectiveness, will need advice, suggestions, and guidance from an independent, impartial source. These problems will be concerned with personal difficulties, worries, or perhaps fears. In the latter case the supervisor is not always the most qualified or the most appropriate person to whom the employee may bring a problem. As part of a company's overall communication network, a formal program of counseling interviews in which both specialist and supervisor work hand in hand is not only desirable but really essential.

ADMONITION.   There comes a time when an employee who cannot or will not abide by group norms, whose behavior becomes sufficiently deviant to be characterized as a nuisance, whose problems are so pressing and so urgent as to disrupt group performance must be properly admonished.

Since we propose, therefore, to facilitate job effectiveness on a person-to-person level by means of coaching, counseling, and admonition and since we view these practices as essentially problem-solving ventures, our final step must be the exploration of the nature of the problem-solving process itself.

The Problem-solving Process

In the introduction to Part 3, we mentioned that there were two types of problem-solving approaches: that common to the animal world, involving blind trial and error, and that unique to human beings, requiring insight and intelligence. The latter process will be our concern in the problem-solving context of the interview. Psychologists, mathematicians, and philosophers have been intrigued and challenged by this distinctively human activity for many years. Such men as John Dewey, Max Wertheimer, Frederic Bartlett, and Karl Duncker have developed generalized schemes that describe the series of mental steps a human being undergoes to solve a problem.

The Five Steps   To begin with there must be a problem and the question is, what is a problem? As Karl Duncker put it in his monograph, "a problem arises when a living creature has a goal but does not know how this goal is to be reached. Whenever one cannot go from the given situation to the described situation simply by action, then there has to be recourse to thinking."[15] The problem can be a frustrating situation, where the person has no adequate response to reach the goal, or a conflict situation, where he or she has too many responses or too many goals and adjustment must be on a selection or compromise basis. In either situation, to arrive at a satisfactory, integrative, and self-

[15] K. Duncker, "On Problem-solving," *Psychological Monographs,* 58(5) (whole no. 270), 1945.

enhancing resolution of the problem, the person has to proceed through the five logical steps of the problem-solving sequence.

BECOMING AWARE THAT A PROBLEM EXISTS. Problem-solving behavior can begin only when the person believes that some state of affairs is not completely satisfactory, that things are not as they should be. The belief may be only a feeling, vague and ill-defined, but enough information has to be on hand to alert the person to the general nature of the problem and to motivate the person to do something about it.

PROBLEM DEFINITION. Once a problem is perceived, the next step is to think it through, to define it clearly and accurately, to develop information concerning it as it exists presently and concerning how things should look once the problem is solved. Feelings of dissatisfaction are symptoms, and symptoms have causes. The next question, therefore, is to determine the source of the symptom formation. Many people are led astray at this point by emotional reactions that interfere with clear thinking. To define a problem accurately, a person must not only think clearly and logically but must also try to avoid *autistic* thinking, that is, thinking that is determined by and bounded by one's own needs, wishes, and feelings.

The problem solver must also avoid *cloudy* thinking and watch out for past experiences and generalizations that on the surface appear to be similar to the present problem. Rigid continuation of actions that have been successful in the past but are inappropriate to the present conflict effectively hinder its solution.

IDEA PRODUCTION. After a problem has been recognized and its dimensions clearly delineated, the next step is to produce as many ideas as possible that may prove helpful in solving it. In the group problem-solving process, this procedure is referred to as "brain-storming"; but an individual can storm his or her own brains or can engage in the process with another person. The object is to produce as many ideas as possible before evaluating them because many of the ideas will be silly and evaluation will tend to inhibit the germination of not only silly but of different ideas.

EVALUATION. Evaluation follows the production of a number of ideas, some good, some poor. It consists in thinking through each alternative solution, examining its consequences, and weighing its advantages or disadvantages. Sometimes, what first emerged as a silly idea, is seen imperceptibly as a rather ingenious solution to a problem even though its implementation may involve certain risks. A set of alternative outcomes from the accumulated information is compared with the originally defined desirable outcome, and a solution is selected that promises to yield the greatest advantage and least disadvantage. This process of selecting the best alternative is greatly facilitated by the original analysis of the situation and the desired goal.

TESTING THE SOLUTION. When a decision has been made and a course of action decided upon, it should be put into practice in a limited manner to determine whether it is truly the best solution. A solution is tested by verifying its merits objectively and then by feeding the evaluation back to the solution-planning stage. When the decision is made to test the plan, the problem solver must stick to it; if not, it will never be proven whether the plan was workable. If the first attempt is successful, the problem of course no longer exists; if it is not, the problem solver must reject the solution, but the resulting feedback should give additional information to enable him or her to "backtrack," to redefine the problem, or to reevaluate the original goal. This process of reapplication can occur many times until the problem is solved or until the problem solver decides that there is no solution.

Problem solving is a difficult, taxing process in its own right, particularly if the problem is of major proportions with many ill-defined or ambiguous elements such as the choice of and progress in an occupational career. But thinking through perplexing problems on one's own is much more hazardous because of individual tendencies to engage in autistic thinking, that is, to decide upon a course of action with incomplete information or before the problem is really defined, because of "all or nothing" thinking, because of being influenced by emotional ideas that mask clarity, and because of inconsistent thinking. Thinking a problem through out loud in the presence of another level-headed, emotionally uninvolved person is an excellent antidote for these pitfalls and hazards to clear thinking, and this is precisely the objective of the problem-solving interview.

The Problem-solving Interview In the context of personnel administration, a problem-solving interview is initiated when an employee is prompted to seek and to accept advice from a credible source because of a perception of a situation that requires finer discriminations than he or she is capable of or because the problem demands special information not at his or her disposal. Both interviewer and interviewee confer on an equal plane so that they can work through the identification of the problem, its relevant features, alternate solutions, and their evaluation and can reach a conclusion about appropriate action.

The interviewer must assume the responsibility for the conduct of the interview by remembering that although employees are especially susceptible to influence by the interviewer whom they see as being in a position of authority emanating from the power of the office or from possession of specialized talent, no effective solution can be worked out unless the interview is characterized by the following points.

1. The interviewer is skilled in the role functions required for effective interaction in this type of interview.

2. The experience the participants have had with each other outside the interview enables them to develop a relaxed working relationship in the interview.

3. The interviewee is attracted to and has respect for the interviewer and has a high degree of confidence and trust in him or her.

4. The interviewer's values do not inhibit the understanding of and expression of the relevant values and needs of the interviewee.

5. The problem-solving activities of the two interview participants occur in a supportive atmosphere characterized by mutual understanding. All the suggestions, comments, ideas, or criticisms offered by the interviewer are intended to be helpful and are received in the same spirit by the interviewee.

The properties of a successful problem-solving interview and the expectations of the interviewee spell out the dimensions of the interviewer's role. Overall the interviewer must be helpful and permissive, and his or her behavior must be marked by patience and understanding, by an unselfish concern for the interviewee's welfare on and off the job, by a sincere desire to obtain and to use the interviewee's ideas, and, finally, by a continued awareness of the ultimate values implicit in the genuine model of job success described earlier in this chapter.

The interviewer's task role actions will address themselves to the rational aspects of the problem-solving process and will help define the problem and generate ideas by information exchange, by clarification, by testing hypothetical solutions, and by summarizing the interview results.

The rapport role behavior will dwell on the interviewee's emotional life, on his tensions and anxieties. Thus, the most effective style of problem-solving interviews will be largely nondirective to permit the interviewer to reflect the thoughts and feelings of interviewees, to listen carefully to what they say and do not say, and to help them clarify their thoughts by verbalizing them in the presence of another person.

THE AUTHENTIC PERSONALITY.   Regardless of the problem, the interviewer's main object must be to increase the interviewees' sense of self-acceptance and consequently their ability to accept other people. In Chapter 1, we pointed out that the self-concept is at the root of the interaction process. Chris Argyris refers to this sense of self and other awareness and acceptance as "human authenticity," suggesting that at the root, people seek deeply satisfying "I-Thou" relationships that will enhance their self-regard in such a way that others will do the same.[16]

When the problem-solving interview is conducted by a skilled, insightful, and empathic interviewer, the employee, as problem solver, can so develop a sense of self-esteem, that he or she will move at least

[16] C. Argyris, *Organizational Effectiveness and Interpersonal Competence* (Homewood, Ill.: Richard D. Irwin, 1962), pp. 21–22.

a little way toward the goal of self-actualization. This, then, is the proper function of the problem-solving interview: to enhance the interviewee's sense of personal dignity and self-respect, while at the same time providing him or her with the opportunity to act as a free human being regardless of the circumstances that occasioned the interview.

Toward Organizational Effectiveness   Personal authenticity is a major goal of the problem-solving interview, but in the context of personnel administration, it is only one side of the coin—the other side is marked by the idea of organizational effectiveness. This "two-factor" concept of job success implies, then, that as a substantial number of the members of the organization grow in personal effectiveness, interpersonal competence, and personal authenticity, in the precise meaning of these terms, the organization cannot help thriving and prospering and making a significant contribution to the social system of which it is a unit. Both parties to the interview must be aware, therefore, that they have obligations to the larger group and that the problem-solving interview is only a means by which the common good of all is attained. Research by Maier and Hoffman demonstrates that the more formal authority relations in organizations inhibit creative problem solving.[17] We suggest that greater emphasis on problem-solving interviewing skill is needed.

By means of the problem-solving interview, multiplied many hundreds and thousands of times annually throughout a company or an agency, the forces of misunderstanding, personal conflict, and emotional immaturity making for organizational conformity and ineffectiveness are modified and inhibited, and the forces of mutual understanding, confidence, interpersonal competence that further growth and accomplishment are expanded, channeled constructively, and lead the organization and its people to greater heights of valid job success. Every interview is, as we have said, a two-way street; the problem-solving interview is no exception. It is one of the main routes by which an organization learns about its members, about itself, and about its role and status in society, and it is a process by which the person grows in personal authenticity, self-esteem, and effectiveness and contributes to the total effort of the organization.

[17] N. R. F. Maier and L. R. Hoffman, "Organization and Creative Problem-solving," *Journal of Applied Psychology*, 45:277–280, 1961.

chapter 11

The Performance-evaluation Process

> We must touch his weaknesses with a delicate hand. There are some faults so nearly allied to excellence that we can scarce weed out the faults without eradicating the virtue.
>
> —OLIVER GOLDSMITH, *The Good-natured Man*

Not long ago, the president of a multidivisional corporation was deeply frustrated by the steady decline in profitability and efficiency of one of his major divisions despite opposite trends in other divisions of the company and in the industry. Yet each year, on the basis of an elaborate performance-evaluation plan, the superiors gave high ratings and substantial salary increases to the operating managers of this division. On two occasions, with the help of outside consultants, management-by-objectives programs were installed in this division. Both times the effort failed dismally. While every key manager met the objectives superbly, the division's performance continued to slide, a result the plant managers attributed to plant obsolescence and to the rising prices of raw materials.

The problem this president encountered is rather common in industry. His managers viewed performance evaluation in terms of activities rather than results and as a justification for an automatic annual salary increase keyed to the cost of living. The idea that performance evaluation should relate to organizational results and should change individual job behavior in a positive direction simply never occurred to them.

This is the nub of the performance-evaluation problem. Whatever the method used to evaluate an employee's performance, it will be of little value unless, as a result, it changes the employee's behavior in some way. But the problem goes deeper than that. Without a sound objective estimate of the value of an employee's contribution to the work effort, it is impossible to develop valid selection and promotion tools, training programs, or equitable salary plans. In lieu of objective criteria of performance, management is left with such arbitrary and randomized indexes of worth as seniority, supervisory opinions, or pure prejudice. In most cases, management opts for supervisory opinion as the best of the lot.

Since the majority of these performance evaluations are uninformed and subjective, they are biased and inconsistent. In view of this and because correct evaluations of people's job performance are so invaluable, efforts to standardize and to systematize them began as soon as engineering techniques were first applied to the employer-employee relationship. A rather heated controversy over the merits of the different systems introduced to accomplish this task has ensued. But at this point, it is worth noting that the argument relates to the mechanics of performance evaluation and not to the process itself. The question of whether a subordinate's effectiveness should be evaluated is really quite irrelevant—it happens. And the issue of the propriety of communicating these evaluations to the subordinate is equally pointless, for it occurs, with or without the supervisor's awareness. The only proper questions open for discussion are how job performance is to be evaluated and when, how, and for what purpose the results are to be transmitted to the employee.

As we have already implied, the answers proposed to these questions have been subjected to such considerable dissent that we find it necessary to consider the history of the performance-evaluation problem briefly, then review the more salient objections to the problem, and finally to present a possible solution.

The Performance-evaluation Problem

Performance-evaluation programs have had a long history dating back to the Greek mathematician, Pythagoras. In modern times, the practice has been widely tried but with varying degrees of success as attested to by the fact that annually almost as many companies abandon plans as adopt them. A National Industrial Conference Board Survey in 1964 reported that 72 percent of the respondents maintained formal performance-rating plans.[1]

A later survey of over 300 public and private agencies conducted by the author indicated that 75 percent maintained a performance-evaluation plan of some type.[2] But less than half indicated that their plans were achieving their objectives.

It is reasonable to conclude that employee-performance evaluation is a common practice in the United States, Canada, and in many Latin

---

[1] *Personnel Audits and Reports to Top Management,* Studies in Personnel Policy No. 191 (New York: National Industrial Conference Board, 1964).

[2] Felix M. Lopez, *Evaluating Employee Performance,* Public Personnel Association, 1968.

American countries and the trend is toward its increased use. Progress, however, has been halty, marked by little theory, by even less research, and by a flood of explicative literature, not all of it illuminating and much of it quite critical.

Objections to Evaluation Interviews   The systematic evaluation of job performance reached a plateau in the middle 1950s. Riding high on the new wave of enthusiasm for management education and development, company after company introduced its staff to what appeared to be a keystone of progressive management—performance evaluation. It was not long before the inevitable reaction set in against these ill-considered ventures. When supervisory interviewing skills were found deplorably wanting and evaluation techniques quite subjective and unreliable, their devotees became disillusioned. Management literature, initially lauda-tory, became increasingly scornful, and business journals devoted pages to criticism of evaluation programs in general and to the evaluation interview in particular.

These objections were, at first, soundly expressed and well taken; if correctly construed, they would have resulted in constructive improve-ments in the process. But the vehemence of the more disillusioned led to abandonment of performance evaluation as a management tool and its position of disdain among personnel managers.

The critics emphasized four main points: the evaluation and inter-viewing inadequacies of the supervisor, the emotional stress of the evaluatee, the ineffectiveness of performance evaluation to effect change, and its irrelevancy for the attainment of either personal or corporate objectives. In effect, the critics concluded, the performance-evaluation interview forces the supervisor to "play God" and embarrasses the employee, achieves, at best, inconclusive results, and is excessively time consuming.

"PLAYING GOD."   One serious contention stated that by placing undue stress on a subordinate's personality traits in the performance evalua-tion, the superior must encroach on the preserve that is itself the center of considerable controversy and in which he or she has little compe-tence. In doing so, it was alleged, the superior is really "playing God" which in Douglas McGregor's classic review "constitutes something dangerously close to a violation of the integrity of the personality."[3] Others asserted that while "playing God" the supervisor must become, in effect, an amateur psychiatrist.

EMBARRASSING THE EMPLOYEE.   A second objection stems from the first. Given the supervisor's naïveté, the evaluation interview is likely to be a very embarrassing experience for both parties, but especially for

---

[3] Douglas McGregor, "An Uneasy Look at Performance Appraisal," *Harvard Busi-ness Review*, 35(3):89–94, 1957.

the employee. Consequently, most subordinates view the evaluation interview with considerable apprehension and as a painfully awkward experience. It was argued that the supervisor could not be the subordinates' counselor because of his or her position as boss. Since the subordinates were thus hard put to it to discern whether they were being advised or directed, they would experience anxiety so intense as to interfere with the constructive thinking that the supervisor was trying to encourage.

INCONCLUSIVE RESULTS.   A third criticism was directed at the apparent ineptness of the evaluation interview to effect any permanent change in an employee's job behavior. No practical action program emerged from many interviews, and the improvement plans that did emerge were really perfunctory because of the supervisor's inability or unwillingness to see that they were implemented. This criticism was compounded by the controversy among the proponents of the performance evaluation program over whether it should be tied to an organization's reward system.

One group argued very strongly that evaluation interviews must be completely divorced from any management action such as salary review or promotion administration. Another group contended that the two must be tied together because the only meaningful process was the one that paid off in a salary increase or promotion.

TIME-CONSUMING.   Managers themselves criticized the evaluation process most strongly on the grounds that they simply did not have the time that any well-thought-out plan required. They claimed that the evaluation of even one subordinate, if done conscientiously, could take several hours. When the interview follow-up time was added in, the complete sequence represented an impossible demand on the manager's time. If the supervisor had a dozen subordinates to evaluate, he or she could easily spend most of the working day on this task. Because top management did not look with favor on this expenditure of time, the supervisor had to accomplish it in the leisure hours.

Answers to the Objections   The advocates of performance evaluation have replied to these criticisms by stating that while the objections are valid they constitute incentives to improve rather than to abandon the process. The issue, says Winston Oberg, should not be whether to scrap them; rather, it should be how to make them better.[4]

RESEARCH DATA.   However much critics may allege that the supervisor in conducting the evaluation interview is "playing God" or engaging in pseudopsychiatry, there is reason to believe that employees welcome these encounters even when they are less than skillfully

---

[4] Winston Oberg, "Make Performance Appraisal Relevant," *Harvard Business Review*, 50(1):61–67, January–February, 1972.

handled. Robert Finn, describing a study of his company's evaluation-interview program, stated that employees believed that if there were no appraisal interview program, few supervisors would ever sit down with their subordinates for such discussions.[5] He concluded that it was evident from the comments of the subordinates "that the kind of discussion carried out by supervisors in the routine performance of their job did not satisfy the employee's need for communication and contact with them. The employees were in favor of some kind of periodic interview because it gave them the opportunity to talk things over with their supervisors more thoroughly—though admittedly not all employees were anxious to take advantage of this opportunity."

In a study of the differences in two performance evaluations systems, Cummings reported positive shifts in attitudes where subordinates were involved in decision making related to the evaluation system. From the study, he found support for the psychological involvement of subordinates in the process.[6]

MISUSE AND ABUSE. As we have indicated, criticisms of the performance-evaluation interview almost always refer to misuses and abuses. The failure to focus the evaluation upon job performance, the neglect of a problem-centered approach, the misunderstanding of the components of the interview process, and ignorance of communication principles all constitute abuses.[7] When a relatively unskilled and uninstructed supervisor, unaware that the interview is a highly intricate communication tool with its own unique set of rules, engages in a clumsy conversation with a subordinate, it is little wonder that the employee may feel that he or she is being talked to by an amateur psychiatrist, and a poor one at that.

Clarification of meanings, definitions of terms, and clear distinctions among the various elements in the total system are important virtues in discussing so overworked a concept as the evaluation process. Even a superficial review of the adverse literature impresses the reader with the bewildering confusion in terminology, the lack of precise definitions, and the interchangeability of words that represent ideas that are not interchangeable.

The object of the evaluation process is improvement in present job performance, not mere information exchange. As a problem-solving technique, it is quite different from the counseling interview; as a kind of consulting relationship, it differs according to the nature of the client,

---

[5] R. H. Finn, "Is Your Appraisal Program Really Necessary?" *Personnel*, 37:16–25, January–February 1960.

[6] L. L. Cummings, "A Field Experimental Study of The Effects of Two Performance Appraisal Systems," *Personnel Psychology*, 26(4):489–502, Winter 73.

[7] See G. A. Riede, "Performance Review—A Mixed Bag," *Harvard Business Review*, 51(4):61–67, July–August 1973.

whether effective or ineffective, management or nonmanagement, administrative, technical, operating, or professional. When these distinctions are observed, most of the abuses can be so minimized that the interview becomes a most satisfactory experience for both participants.

Supervisors must be educated to view the evaluation interview as an integral part of their job. They must look upon the evaluation of a subordinate as so vital a responsibility that to neglect it or to eliminate it places them in the position of nothing more than an overseer.

A more realistic, saner concept of supervision casts the superior in the role of coach, consultant, communicator, and catalytic agent around whom the work and the workers center. To fulfill this far more demanding role, supervisors must establish a trustful and confident relationship with subordinates, and for this they need careful development. As a critical part of this development, they need to increase their interpersonal communication skills. Therefore, when people are promoted to supervisory positions, it is best to assume that they are so ignorant of evaluation interview skills that they will require meticulous and lengthy schooling before they are equipped to handle all the phases of this function. But when they become skilled in the art of performance evaluation interviewing, they will be not only more effective leaders of people but keystones in the arch of successful management.

This, then, is the view to be elucidated in this chapter. We shall not be concerned with the evaluation process as an administrative technique designed to provide a legitimate basis for making promotions and setting salary increases, or even with the question of whether it should be related to these transactions. Our hypothesis is that the performance-evaluation interview, when properly conducted, provides the supervisor with a significant opportunity to establish rapport with subordinates and, thereby, to create a more productive, more cohesive work group.

Essential to the conduct of a performance-evaluation interview is a clear understanding of the problems involved in evaluating human performance, the procedures available to accomplish this task, and the elements of an effective program.

Evaluating Human Performance

Most people are so accustomed to judging the intentions and actions of other people in everyday situations that they naturally assume they do so with considerable accuracy. The fact is that the evaluation of human performance in any activity is so complicated that even when it is done conscientiously, the evaluation will contain many uncertainties. When the complexity of the task is underrated and the evaluation is performed casually, the chance of error increases and the degree of uncertainty is extended. Every evaluation, therefore, has to be considered in terms of the width of its "zone of uncertainty," that is, by the degree of error implicit in the final evaluation.

The Evaluation Chain   A genuine performance-evaluation process combines a series of essential activities that occur in the following order: performance, observation, evaluation, communication, influence. Each activity constitutes a link, a weakness in any one of which affects the entire chain of events.

PERFORMANCE.   A person's performance consists of actual accomplishments as they are influenced by an understanding of job functions, ability and motivation, the environment surrounding the job, and an error component due to chance. The first task for the employee, therefore, is to develop an adequate understanding of what he or she is expected to do. The employee accomplishes this not merely by learning what must be done but by appreciating what constitutes an effective standard of performance for each job function.

OBSERVATION.   Accurate and controlled observation is the second link in the evaluation chain and is influenced by four factors: (1) the position of the observer, (2) the frequency of observation, (3) the predisposition of the observer, and (4) random errors. If the observation is to lead to accurate evaluation, each factor has to be controlled insofar as it is possible. Observation is subject to the perceptual process that we described in Chapter 4.

EVALUATION.   The actual evaluation task, which is really a comparison of observations to performance standards, is a function of *recall* and *measurement.*

Recall is subject to the same biases toward the individual and the situation as the observation process and also contains random errors. Although the ability to remember can be improved considerably by instruction and practice, it is a weak link in the chain of evaluation unless it is strengthened by such aids as written records and frequent reviews over relatively short time spans.

Measurement, as the assignment of a class of numerals to a class of objects, includes three operations: (1) the observation of certain phenomena, (2) the selection of appropriate methods of discriminating among them, and (3) their explanation in numerical terms.

Even in the physical sciences, however, measurement fails to realize perfection. From time to time, for example, distances between continents have to be corrected as newer astronomical methods of measurement are developed. In the social sciences, precise measurement is hardly likely because there will always be an indeterminate degree of interaction between the observer and the observed. The recognition that social measurements have a high residue of uncertainty is crucial to the performance-evaluation task. To be accurate, performance evaluation must be reasonably reliable and closely associated with actual performance characteristics.

As we have pointed out in Chapter 6, the difficulty of demonstrating the accuracy of evaluation instruments is known in the psychological literature as the "criterion problem." It constitutes the heart of performance evaluation—How do we really recognize a person who is doing an effective job?

COMMUNICATION. The fourth link, communicating the evaluation, constitutes "the moment of truth" for the performance-evaluation program because it determines its success. Only when an employee becomes a full working partner in the evaluation can it be effective. If the evaluator handles this situation properly, the program will go well. If not, it is better that it not be tried at all.

Skill in performance-evaluation interviewing is not easily acquired. There is ample evidence in the literature, not to mention in everyday experience, to suggest that most supervisors do this job poorly, so poorly, in fact, that many observers strongly recommend that the practice be discontinued or left to professional counselors. Since this is such a drastic solution, the only alternative is to teach supervisors how to interview effectively.

INFLUENCE. The last and probably the most important link in the evaluation chain is influencing. Whatever the method used to evaluate performance, it will be of little value unless it changes the employee's behavior in some way. A real change occurs in people only when their pattern of response to events in the work environment is so modified that they begin to behave consistently in ways quite dissimilar to their usual behavior. Because this problem is so important, methods of communicating an evaluation to people and of influencing them to undertake to change their behavior must be clearly understood.

Reducing the Zone of Uncertainty The five links in the evaluation chain constitute ways of reducing the degree of uncertainty in the evaluation process. Essentially they minimize three major sources of error: the person being evaluated, the evaluation situation, and the evaluator.

THE EVALUATEE. With respect to the person being evaluated, the requirements for effective performance evaluation are:

1. The characteristics judged must be relevant to effective job performance. There is no point in evaluating traits that have little to do with success on the job. A clear specification of job functions and standards has to be developed, agreed upon, and put into writing by both parties.

2. The employee must be evaluated on a representative sample of his

or her total job effectiveness rather than upon isolated events that have occurred from time to time or only upon the more unusual activities that have come to the attention of the supervisor. Provision must be made for a systematic, representative sample of the person's on-the-job performance.

3. There must be ample opportunity for personal interaction between supervisor and subordinate. The evaluator must know and understand the person being evaluated and have a good idea of his or her abilities and interests.

4. Finally, subordinates' attitudes toward the evaluation process must be positive. They must see it as helping them, as something that they want to have happen to them, something in which they have faith and confidence.

THE EVALUATION SITUATION.   With respect to the evaluation situation, the following conditions must prevail:

1. The purpose of the evaluation program must be clearly specified, and the uses to which it is to be put must be explained to all who are to be affected by them.

2. Administrative conditions must be clearly supervised, controlled, and standardized. Each person must be evaluated under the same conditions and opportunities; adequate procedures must be devised; training programs initiated; promotional literature distributed and the entire plan conducted in an open, receptive climate.

3. Finally, appropriate measurement techniques that meet as closely as possible the specifications for reliability, validity, and relevancy must be developed and utilized.

THE EVALUATOR.   The evaluator is the most important cog in the evaluation machinery. Unless this job is done right, the whole program will go down the drain. Essentially an evaluator needs three basic skills —the ability to observe people, the ability to judge them, and the ability to communicate the results of these judgments to them empathically.

Not one of these skills is innate; each is the product of careful selection and intensive cultivation. The evaluator must have the emotional and intellectual predisposition to perceive, describe, and judge another's performance as honestly and as objectively as possible and, in addition, must take the opportunity to observe the person's performance frequently. This means direct observation over a representative period of time, probably about six months. Naturally, evaluators who are responsible for people scattered over a wide stretch of territory are hardly in a position to give a good account of their performance. Evaluations that are based on a small slice of an employee's total performance will include a high degree of uncertainty.

Evaluators must also be favorably disposed toward the process and see it as an important part of their responsibility. They must take the time to evaluate their subordinates, do it meticulously, and give it a good deal of thought, time, and energy.

Finally, they must consider this task as a primary area of their accountability and be willing to be judged on the way they evaluate those assigned to them.

Evaluation Procedures

There are two approaches to the task of evaluating human performance. The *person-oriented* approach assesses the person directly, focusing upon unique traits and style of performance. The second, the *results-oriented* approach, emphasizes the person's accomplishments. Admittedly, this classification is broad and extremely tenuous because there really are no clear lines of demarcation separating the various procedures.

But for our purposes, this is a logical and convenient classification. The *person-oriented* approach, explained in detail in Chapter 6, is based on the idea that a worker's traits determine job effectiveness. The *results-oriented* approach, currently in vogue among most management theorists, is based upon the idea that job effectiveness is determined by what is accomplished.[8]

Evaluating The Person   Despite a spotty history of success, person-oriented procedures have dominated the performance-evaluation process from its inception and have proven extremely resistant to eradication. As indicated in Chapter 6, a good case can be made for the emphasis upon the person in evaluation procedures. Performance ineffectiveness stems mainly from personal deficiencies rather than from insurmountable working conditions. Authorities usually assume, therefore, that an employee's unique combination of personal traits determines the caliber of personal job performance.

There is such a wide assortment of person-oriented evaluation methods available that any attempt to classify them has to be tentative. We have subdivided them into three major groups: (1) performance scales, (2) performance comparisons, and (3) performance descriptions.

PERFORMANCE-SCALE PROCEDURES.   A performance scale subdivides job performance into a series of separate performance factors such as "quality of work," "honesty," and "reliability." A scale of values, ranging from "poor" or "below average" to "excellent" and "superior," is provided for each factor to enable the rater to indicate the level that the employee possesses.

---

[8] For a detailed presentation of these procedures, see Felix M. Lopez, *Evaluating Employee Performance*, Public Personnel Association, 1968, chaps. 9 and 10.

These procedures are popular because of their simplicity, ease of administration, and the facility with which they can be completed. But their attractions are more than offset by the transparency, accommodation to conscious and unconscious error, and quick reducibility to rote completion of the method.

PERFORMANCE-COMPARISON PROCEDURES. Essentially, the performance-comparison method places a group of comparable people in rank order in terms of their overall work performance, future potential, or other characteristics. A more recent development in the ranking method is known as the *paired-comparison system* by which the name of each employee in a work group is paired with that of every other employee. Another variation of the ranking technique is the *forced-distribution method* by which employees are ordered according to perceived merit into a bell-shaped normal frequency distribution.[9] There are four major difficulties with the performance-comparison method:

1. It is tedious—the task of ranking a group of individuals becomes imposing for one supervisor when his or her group includes more than fifteen subordinates.

2. It is misleading—the magnitude of the differences in ability between ranks is not equal at different points in the array.

3. It is nonevaluative—it says nothing about satisfactory performance because it provides no cutting point to indicate a minimum level of acceptability.

4. It is noncomparative—there is no way that rank in one work unit can be compared to rank in a similar work unit.

PERFORMANCE-DESCRIPTION PROCEDURES. Performance-description methods range from completely open-ended, unstructured reports through a series of checklists to the more complicated and probably the most sophisticated method—the *forced-choice technique.*

Essentially, in the forced-choice technique of performance evaluation, the rater is required to judge which of several alternative statements is most descriptive of an employee's job performance. The alternative statements are established after experimental application to a number of employees at specific levels in the organization. The device "forces" the rater to discriminate on the basis of concrete aspects of the subordinate's work behavior, rather than to rely on a general impression of the person's total worth.

More importantly, the method yields a numerical index by which persons throughout the organization in a variety of occupations can be compared on the basis of factors that have been found by empirical investigation to be a significant part of job performance. Since the

---

[9] For a detailed analysis of the paired comparison procedure, see P. H. Thompson and G. W. Dalton, "Performance Appraisal: Managers Beware," *Harvard Business Review*, 48(1):149–157, January–February 1970.

evaluator is aware of neither the relative weight nor the significance of the forced-choice alternatives, the final product is less influenced by conscious bias or social pressure, and even errors of recall and observation are to some extent reduced.

The adherents of the forced-choice method are attracted to it by the following advantages:

1. It tends to minimize some of the subjective elements that complicate the evaluation process.

2. It reduces the rater's ability to produce a desired outcome.

3. It provides a wider, more normalized distribution of ratings and is relatively free of the usual pile-up at the top of the scale.

4. It can produce a standardized, objective index.

5. It can be adapted to the computer.

6. It produces results that correlate positively with other variables associated with effective job performance.

While the forced-choice technique probably is the most objective method of person-oriented evaluation, it has its disadvantages. First, it is difficult and time-consuming to construct, and it involves a good deal of expertise and, usually, the availability of a computer.

Second, supervisors dislike it. One psychologist referred to it as an abortive device to outwit human nature, alleging that it frustrates the rater because he or she doesn't know whether the rating is turning out high or low.

Wherry points out that what happens in the forced-choice method is that the evaluation function is taken away from the rater who becomes responsible only for an accurate and fair description of the subordinate's performance.[10] This, Wherry thinks, is perfectly sensible.

In summary, a strong case can be made for the conclusion that, in terms of the measurement principles developed in Part 2 and in the light of current research findings, a well-constructed forced-choice performance-description report enables the evaluator to describe performance in such a way that it minimizes the effects of environmental influences, performance errors, observational errors, conscious bias, and social pressure.

Evaluating Results   Largely because of dissatisfaction with performance scales and ranking methods, American managers turned to results-oriented procedures, particularly to evaluate managerial performance. The results-oriented approach is based upon the assumption that people's accomplishments, rather than the people *themselves*, are the proper object of evaluation.

[10] R. J. Wherry, "Problems in the Evaluation of Personnel," in *Social Science Research Reports*, vol. 1, "Introduction and Review" (New York: Standard Oil Company, New Jersey, 1962).

In some cases, the evaluation is based upon an analysis of events that occur while the job is in progress or on pure output measures, such as sales or other measurable indexes of performance. While there seems to be a broad consensus that this method is the soundest measure of performance, the road to its effective implementation is by no means a primrose path; there are many difficulties and problems that have to be resolved.

Results-oriented evaluation procedures range from simple, direct measures of output and accomplishment, such as sales recorded, cases handled, goods produced, and complaints resolved, through narrative reviews of performance to the consultative and participative goal-setting procedures usually referred to as "management-by-objectives."

QUANTITATIVE PERFORMANCE MEASURES. A quantitative-performance measure is often the most direct indication of effectiveness. The number of sales made, cases closed, items produced, people interviewed, or positions filled have always been considered ideal measures of proficiency that ought to be used whenever possible. But only the briefest experience will disclose the fact that another correlate of productivity, quality, that is, the number of items rejected, complaints received, sales returned, or errors made, must be combined with production figures to obtain a really accurate view of a worker's effectiveness. The care exercised in setting such targets determines how valuable they will prove to be as tools for the objective measurement of performance. Personal judgment plays such a very vital part in this process that it is generally recognized that the targets are usually no better than the people who set them.

NARRATIVE MEASURES OF PERFORMANCE. Because of the shortcomings of quantitative measures of performance and their impracticality for many occupations, such as that of a teacher, an interviewer, or a lawyer, researchers have turned to narrative measures of performance.

Essentially, this procedure attempts to evaluate performance qualitatively but with an underpinning of factual information to support it. Of the many ways of doing this, there are two that have received the most attention: the *field-review method* and the *critical-incident technique*. In the field-review method, a member of the central personnel staff conducts an informal but structured interview with the immediate supervisor of the person to be evaluated, usually in the supervisor's work area. The critical-incident technique relies upon the collection of specific observable job incidents that are judged to be critical because they are related directly to either good or poor job performance.

Both are thorough procedures that insure that the evaluation is based on concrete events relevant to job effectiveness. Each is a way of making sure that supervisors observe subordinates' work and single out the important facets of performance for comment. These methods, however, have one serious but not insurmountable defect: in form and procedure, if not in intent, they resemble the "little black book" of the authoritarian supervisor.

CONSULTATIVE PERFORMANCE MEASURES.   After years of experience with performance-evaluation methods, many administrators and behavioral scientists have come to the conclusion that a performance-evaluation program can fulfill its purpose of improved job performance only when the evaluatee (1) participates in establishing the criteria by which his or her performance is to be judged, (2) helps plan future improvements in that performance, and (3) discusses openly with his or her supervisor their mutual responsibilities with respect to improving performance.

Although the evidence for their validity is neither abundant nor completely positive, in recent years these assertions have profoundly influenced performance-evaluation methodology. There has been a noticeable trend toward the adoption of programs that call for greater participation and consultation between supervisor and subordinate in defining precisely what is expected of the subordinate and that emphasize the results of performance. This trend has proceeded in two stages, the first of which is referred to as the performance-standards method, and the second, the management-by-objectives method.

A standard of performance is a precise description of what a job incumbent must do under existing work conditions to perform a specific duty in a manner fully satisfactory to the supervisor. Ideally, performance standards complement job descriptions of what the employee is to do and distinguish his or her responsibilities from those of workers of other types and in other positions.

The standards of performance method, however, is neither simple nor does it constitute a panacea for every evaluation problem. Successful implementation demands fulfillment of a number of particular requirements:

1. A sound position-classification program must be established under which all jobs are described and allocated equitably to appropriate salary ranges.

2. Supervisors must be trained intensively in this method. If the standards arrived at are not clear, fair, and specific, they will be no more helpful than the ambiguous rating scales they have replaced.

3. It must be accepted from the very beginning that the method is difficult and time-consuming. Supervisors must believe in its value and be given time to conduct it.

4. It must also be recognized that employees with high dependency needs or limited capacities must have their standards set for them and be given clear-cut instructions on what they should do.

A variation of the performance-standards method has emerged that concentrates more on short-range objectives. This performance-objectives method is usually known by the term *management-by-objectives*.

Although management-by-objectives programs are widespread in industry, a careful analysis of them suggests that the only element they have in common is the name. The term has been used in five separate contexts—as a management philosophy, a budgeting technique, a planning technique, a system of long-range forecasting, or as an alternative to performance evaluation. The management-by-objectives method is also referred to under such other names as "programmed management," "work planning and review," and "goal-setting."

A Multitrait, Multimethod Evaluation Program

It seems safe to conclude that neither a person-oriented nor a results-oriented procedure can stand as a complete answer to an organization's evaluation problem. The solution appears to lie in an integrated, multitrait, multimethod, and multipurpose effort that is the product of a participative-action research program.

The Organization View For the organization, performance evaluation is primarily a tool to determine the quality of its manpower resources and to improve its current level of performance. As in the communication of financial results, information flowing up to the decision and policy levels must be presented in a form that enables those who review it to form a broad and accurate picture of the total system activity. For example, if at the end of a year, detailed two-page descriptions of the performance of each of 1,000 subordinates were given to a company president, he or she would be so overwhelmed with details that, in fact, he or she would obtain almost no information at all. For the president's purposes, therefore, the data must be presented in a convenient summary form that enables them to be grasped by a single human mind in the space of an hour or two of study.

The information must also apply uniformly across people and across groups of people. To be comparable, therefore, it must be standardized and objective, that is, it must be independent of the person reporting the information and it must be reduced to units that have applicability to many groups of people. For example, if budget-performance data depended upon the qualifications and the point of view of each reporter, and the units varied from dollars to francs, the summary statement would be difficult to interpret.

Standardized and summarized information must be encoded in symbolic form. The most convenient and dependable symbols are numbers.

These, then, are the requirements of a performance-evaluation system designed for organizational effectiveness and efficiency: standardization, objectivity, quantification of results, and orientation toward the decision-making process.

The Individual View   Information presented to an individual employee in the format described above will be of little assistance because it lacks the specificity and individuality that is required to apply it to the individual's own performance. A constructive performance-evaluation program must be designed to secure the cooperation of the employee. When we view the organization from the bottom up, the perspective is so different that the communication network takes on a totally different appearance. The employee who views the organization in this way develops a self-image not of one employee among a great many almost anonymous workers, but of a unique person in a specific position and views job performance in terms of opportunities, relationships to associates and supervisors, and in terms of personal career aspirations. In evaluating personal performance, the employee is interested not in rigorously objective standardized data but in concrete tangible particulars. Employees want to know how they did, how they can do better, how they can obtain a larger share of the system's rewards, and how they can, through their positions, achieve their life goals.

The reports that are submitted to them about their performance must relate quite directly to their specific positions and their environment—to their supervisors, to their fellow workers, to their accomplishments or lack thereof, to their instructions, to the standards established for them, and to their potential for improvement. Such reports have to be subjective to reflect what an immediate supervisor, with whom the employees work every day, thinks of their performance in the light of the particular problems and situations they encounter in their daily experience.

These subjective reports must be qualitative, that is, descriptive, narrative, and anecdotal rather than symbolic and comparative. Employees may, in a general way, be interested in how they compare to other workers but only in terms of how this comparison will affect their status. The evaluation's efficiency consists of the degree to which it helps them solve problems, to meet obstacles and challenges successfully in the drive to secure a happier and a fuller existence. Employees will certainly be comforted, of course, by the knowledge that the performance program is organizationally effective and efficient, that the information given to them is also flowing upwards, that it is objective, standardized, and impartial, and that it is being utilized to make fair decisions about pay, promotion, and other personnel actions. But when it comes to applying this information to *them,* it will be meaningful only if it is individualized to the maximum extent possible so that each employee can comprehend its significance and apply it to his or her performance.

An acceptable and efficient performance-evaluation program must be individualized, subjective, qualitative, and oriented toward the problem-solving process. These divergent criteria for the effectiveness and acceptance of a performance-evaluation program suggest their broad features and the procedures and practices necessary to make the program most useful. These specifications also indicate why so many plans fail. The conflict between organizational and individual needs places such severe stress on a single plan designed to meet both objectives that it usually collapses under the strain. If the program emphasizes employer needs, individual employees will be so frustrated that they will withdraw their cooperation and conspire to defeat the program's objectives. If the plan is designed primarily to gain acceptance by stressing personal growth, its irrelevancy for organizational objectives will, in the long run, so undermine its administration that it will be followed more in form than in substance.

A Managerial-Performance Evaluation Program   To illustrate how these various requirements can be combined into one complex but workable plan, we shall end this chapter with a brief description of an actual managerial-performance evaluation program. This program, as depicted in Figure 16, requires five documents, twelve distinct steps, and overall coordination by the central personnel office of the company.

It combines the forced-choice, person-oriented method with the results-oriented, performance-standard method and involves not only the manager's immediate superior as coach, but also provides for a separate stream of information from associates and subordinates.

STEP 1. DEFINING THE SCOPE OF ACCOUNTABILITY.   The program begins when the personnel director or other central administrative official defines the "scope of accountability" of the manager's job. The scope of accountability is more than a mere job description; it defines precisely the functions the manager is expected to perform. In essence, it constitutes the mission with which he or she is entrusted by the company. It usually is divided into three areas of accountability: functional, administrative, and financial.[11]

The scope of accountability is written in reasonably broad terms to provide for flexibility in implementation, depending upon the unique circumstances of each geographical area. Thus, it is generic in nature, fairly permanent, and reviewable only occasionally as circumstances warrant.

[11] See Phil N. Scheid, "Charter of Accountability For Executives," *Harvard Business Review,* 43(4):88–97, July–August 1965.

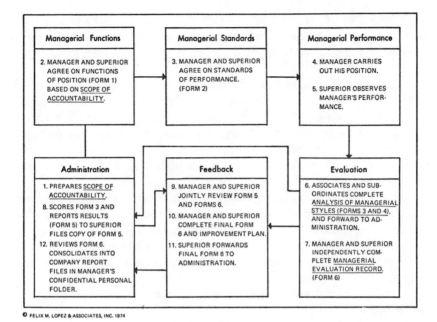

© FELIX M. LOPEZ & ASSOCIATES, INC. 1974

Fig. 16   Managerial evaluation program

STEP 2. ESTABLISHING POSITION REQUIREMENTS.   The next step is to agree on the job to be done in a specific unit. Perhaps the most common basis for misunderstanding between a superior and a subordinate consists of the differences between what each thinks the latter's position entails. It is essential that these differences be resolved at the outset because misunderstandings can only be magnified and compounded from here on. The scope of accountability forms the basis for this agreement but it lacks the detail necessary to reflect the specific and unique nature of particular positions. But it does serve as a control by establishing parameters within which specific position requirements can be defined.

This task is best performed by both supervisor and manager, first independently and then jointly. The requirements are put into writing and are signed by both parties.

STEP 3. AGREE ON PERFORMANCE STANDARDS.   The idea here is to develop mutually acceptable standards of performance for all of the more important or more time-consuming tasks listed in the position-requirements agreement. It is essential that standards of performance be (1) mutually acceptable to both, (2) related to the scope of accountability, (3) within the control of the manager, (4) meaningful and realistic, (5) specific and observable.

Developing standards of performance is a rigorous exercise requiring intensive effort and a good deal of patience. It may require two or three meetings between superior and manager, and after a period of time, a number of the standards of performance might even prove to be totally unrealistic.

After preparing a tentative list of standards, both parties decide which performance factors or traits are particularly required to meet each standard. One set of six used in some companies includes such factors as *initiative, technical competence, dependability, emotional maturity, interpersonal competence,* and *organizational identification.*[12] Meeting standard A, for example, might require a high degree of technical competence. Standard B might require emotional maturity.

Completing this exercise has two purposes. First, it gives both superior and manager an opportunity to review their standards to see that all the relevant factors of managerial performance are covered. If, for example, no standards call for initiative, one might question the comprehensiveness of the standards set. Second, by assigning each standard to a performance factor, an opportunity is later created to identify the manager's personal traits that contribute to or inhibit the meeting of his or her standards.

Ordinarily, the first three steps described above are carried out only in launching a performance-evaluation plan for an individual manager. After the first year, it is unlikely that substantial modifications in the scope of accountability, position requirements, or performance standards will be necessary. But by taking these three steps, both superior and manager will have gone a long way toward accomplishing their objectives. The accrued benefits will include:

1. Knowing that the superior really is concerned about the manager's performance.

2. The discovery of misunderstandings or overlapping accountabilities.

3. The resolution of misunderstandings between manager and supervisor about the tasks and the demands of the position.

4. The identification of potential problems where there is incomplete agreement on the job to be done.

5. The superior gains commitment or recognition of accountability on the part of the manager.

6. The rest of the evaluation task is made easier.

STEPS 4 AND 5. OBSERVING MANAGERIAL PERFORMANCE. Once the standards of performance have been completed, the manager performs his or her job with the help and the advice of the superior. It is the superior's responsibility to make certain that he or she is in a position to observe first-hand the manager's performance. This means the

---

[12] See Lopez, op. cit., pp. 210–211.

superior must set aside adequate time for observation, must review periodically the list of standards established, must take notes, and, finally, must give frequent feedback to the manager on those observations which can contribute to the achievement of standards.

STEPS 6, 7, 8 AND 9. COMPLETING ANALYSIS OF MANAGERIAL STYLES. About a month before the manager and superior plan to confer on the official evaluation of the manager's performance, the superior distributes to associates and subordinates copies of the *Analysis of Managerial Styles,* a forced-choice instrument depicted in Figure 17. This form is completed and returned directly to the personnel office where it is scored

---

ANALYSIS OF MANAGERIAL STYLES

Instructions

This questionnaire consists of 120 statements descriptive of managerial styles and behavior, divided into 30 sets of four. You are to rate each statement on how well it fits or describes the behavior of the individual in question on a zero to nine scale as follows:

1. In each group of four, decide which one statement is most descriptive and in the space provided at the right (Degree of Fit) enter a number indicating how well it describes or "fits" the individual. A rating of nine (9) indicates that it is very descriptive, or a perfect fit, and lower numbers indicate lesser degrees of fit.

2. Then select the statement in the same group of four that is next most descriptive and indicate the extent to which it fits by entering the appropriate number in the box corresponding to it. Continue doing this until you have filled in all the boxes for each group of four statements. Then continue on to the next group of four statements until you have completed all 30 sets (one hundred & 20 statements).

3. Note that you are not to use the same number twice to describe degree of fit in any set of four statements. In other words, there are to be no ties within each set.

18. A. Understands the functions of the organization ___
    B. Is capable of handling more responsibility ___
    C. Can separate vital details from trivia ___
    D. Has confidence of people in other departments ___

19. A. Can work well with anybody ___
    B. Is consistent in relations with others ___
    C. Is a clear thinker ___
    D. Is unruffled in emergencies or crises ___

5A		11A		17A		23A	
5B		11B		17B		23B	
5C		11C		17C		23C	
5D		11D		17D		23D	
6A		12A		18A		24A	
6B		12B		18B		24B	
6C		12C		18C		24C	
6D		12D		18D		24D	

Fig. 17 Analysis of managerial styles

```
┌─────────────────────────────────────────────────────────────────────────────────┐
│ MANAGERIAL EVALUATION PROGRAM                    ANALYSIS OF MANAGERIAL STYLES     │
│ SUMMARY REPORT    (FORM 5)      12/1/75                                            │
│                                                                                   │
│ JOHN M. BROWN                                                                     │
│ SECTION SUPERVISOR - MANUFACTURING, EASTGATE PLANT                                │
│                                                                                   │
│ TOTAL NUMBER OF RATERS:  8                                                         │
│ PEERS:  4    SUBORDINATES:  4                                                      │
│                                                                                   │
│                     R A T I N G S   I N   P E R C E N T                            │
│                                                                                   │
│                                                             AVERAGE   PERCENTILE   │
│ RATER           1   2   3   4   5   6   7   8   9   SELF              DEPT    CO    │
│                                                                                   │
│ INITIATIVE      75  80  67  62  60  74  76  71   -   75     70.6      92      90   │
│                                                                                   │
│ TECHNICAL       80  75  80  84  79  70  72  76   -   80     77.0      96      95   │
│ COMPETENCE                                                                         │
│                                                                                   │
│ DEPENDABILITY   65  60  74  71  70  62  75  70   -   65     68.4      80      82   │
│                                                                                   │
│ EMOTIONAL       80  80  75  64  83  81  80  87   -   75     78.8      90      91   │
│ MATURITY                                                                           │
│                                                                                   │
│ INTERPERSONAL   72  74  80  85  80  78  75  88   -   72     79.0      94      97   │
│ COMPETENCE                                                                         │
│                                                                                   │
│ ORGANIZATIONAL  67  68  75  80  59  75  80  72   -   65     72.0      79      81   │
│ IDENTIFICATION                                                                     │
│                                                                                   │
│ OVERALL INDEX   80  81  74  78  72  70  75  72   -   70     75.3      93      91   │
│                                                                                   │
└─────────────────────────────────────────────────────────────────────────────────┘
```

Fig. 18   Computer print-out—analysis of managerial styles

either by hand or by computer. The resulting profile, shown in Figure 18, is forwarded to the parties concerned.

STEPS 10, 11 AND 12. COMPLETING THE MANAGERIAL-PERFORMANCE EVALUATION RECORD.   While the *Analysis of Managerial Styles* is being processed, the manager and the superior begin the process of evaluating the former's performance. The superior initiates it by giving a blank copy of the final evaluation report to the manager to complete in pencil. The superior also completes one independently. This procedure will be discussed in more detail in the following chapter.

There are inherent problems in this aspect of the total program. The idea is to avoid a "report card syndrome," that is, the mere act of committing a rating to paper. To minimize the problems and assure maximum effectiveness, the evaluation report should be designed to help both parties by considering not merely behavior and not merely results but rather performance characteristics, that is, work results compared to performance standards that take into account the unique style and the behavioral-performance characteristics of the individual manager.

The first step is to look over the list of performance standards agreed upon to determine which have been met (the manager is not expected to meet all standards), which have not been met, and which have been surpassed. Each standard is placed under an appropriate performance factor. Then, after all standards under each performance factor are reviewed, it is possible to assign an overall "rating" to that performance factor. This rating is now not exclusively subjective because it is supported by factual information based on actual job performance. If, for example, a manager is rated as above standard on technical competence, it should be relatively easy to pinpoint the reasons for this rating. And, conversely, if an employee fails to meet certain performance standards, it is easy to pinpoint the personal factors that account for this result.

The next and most important step in the entire process is the interview between the manager and superior to review their separate evaluations of the manager's performance and profile based on the associate's ratings. This is a major value of the *Analysis of Managerial Styles*. Because it provides an independent check of the superior and manager's evaluation on each performance factor, the profile of the *Analysis of Managerial Styles* is quite helpful. During the interview the manager and the superior go over their individual reports and then complete the official version in ink which they both sign.

The object of the interview is to develop an overall rating of the manager's performance and to prepare a specific performance-improvement plan. It is at this point that the fruits of the whole process are realized. The improvement plan must be specific, with concrete time tables and built-in measures to indicate whether the plan has been successful. It is simply insufficient to suggest to a manager whose interpersonal competence has been judged substandard that he or she read a book or try to be more friendly. The superior must know and have available a range of resources, furnished either by the company or outside agencies, to help the manager to realistically improve performance.

STEP 13. CENTRAL PERSONNEL OFFICE ACTION.   After the interview has been completed and the official report has been signed, it is forwarded to the personnel office for permanent file. Both the superior and the manager retain a copy with their own guidance and consultation.

Top management will then possess a carefully considered and quite specific evaluation of each manager to enable it to assess the company's managerial assets. This information, at the very least, should make possible more effective promotions and other assignments. In this way, the program provides adequate controls to keep the central administration informed of what is happening in the system and to facilitate remedial action when needed.

chapter 12

The Performance-evaluation Interview

Not failure, but low aim, is crime.
—JAMES RUSSELL LOWELL, *For an Autograph*

In training workshops on performance evaluation, the participants, all experienced supervisors, are first asked to complete the following interview script between an employee, Jim, and his supervisor, Mr. Manager:

JIM: "You wanted to see me, Mr. Manager?"
MANAGER: "Yes, Jim. I would like to talk to you about your work over the past year."
JIM: "Oh, fine. (Pause) Has it been OK?"

In over 90 percent of the scripts turned in by the participants, the manager gives negatively critical information to his subordinate, Jim. At the end of the script, the participants are asked to describe the probable outcome of this interview. They almost invariably report that the interview had little positive effect on Jim's performance and many attach an unhappy ending, dismissal or resignation, to the whole process.

While hardly scientific, this informal survey pretty well describes the prevailing attitude of supervisors toward the evaluation interview. It is an attitude that has been earned by past experience. Usually supervisors are given an inadequate procedure to work with and receive little or no training in the techniques of the performance-evaluation interview. Most of them, making the fundamental error of treating the interview as an information-giving medium, proceed to tell their subordinates of their deficiencies. Since criticism leads only to defensiveness, they obtain little or no improvement in their subordinate's performance. The improvement of an employee's performance requires consideration of the differences in communicating evaluations to effective and ineffective employees, the performance evaluation interview as a problem-solving technique, and the best ways of conducting the interview.

The Components of the
Performance-evaluation Interview

Whatever the method used to evaluate subordinates' performance, it will be of little value unless it changes their behavior in some way. Real change occurs in people only when their patterns of response to events in their environment are so modified that they begin to behave consistently in ways quite dissimilar to their usual behavior.

Structural Aspects In all subordinates' eyes, their supervisors are focal points of the company communication network. As group leaders, they are the principal channels through which the word is passed down on what must be done and through which the word is passed up to higher levels on what has been accomplished. They are the nucleus of the work cell, the organizing forces, the catalysts, the agents, the initiators who set group goals, get action started, and keep things moving; they are also consultants to whom the workers come for advice and assistance on technical matters and job problems; and, hopefully, they are the only people in the organization upon whom the workers can depend to learn what is expected of them, how well they are doing, how they might improve, and what rewards or penalties they might expect.

There is, however, substantial evidence in the literature and in the everyday experience of most people to suggest that this ideal description of fully communicative supervisors is rarely fulfilled on any management level. Yet practically all the recent studies of supervisory and organizational behavior reach the same conclusion that supervisors who achieve better job performance as measured by productivity, earnings, costs, and quality differ in leadership style from those who achieve poorer performance. Among the major ways in which supervisors of superior performing units differ from the leaders of poorer performing units, the area of personal communication with individual employees stands out most sharply. The former seem to make clearer to their subordinates what has to be accomplished and then allow them the freedom to do it.

Supervisors in lower-performing units communicate too, but with a difference. Since the latter in their feedback mechanisms emphasize the one-way transmission of instructions, they must rely upon the worker's job behavior to tell them whether their messages were received completely and accurately. The trouble with this kind of feedback is the time lag between transmission and report.

When it comes to the question of how well the subordinate is performing, the need for communication feedback is even more critical. Unless told otherwise, a worker who is doing very well can become quite convinced that the supervisor is dissatisfied with his or her efforts, and a thoroughly ineffective worker can believe that he or she is performing at a highly satisfactory level. The supervisor of the better performing unit is much more likely to tell subordinates how they are doing.

Simple feedback is not fully representative of the supervisor's responsibility in this area. The supervisor has to communicate so that a *change* occurs in the subordinate's behavior. This can be done only by convincing the subordinate, first of all, of the need for change by showing alternative ways in which he or she might change and ways of evaluating the change. The supervisor cannot, of course, compel the subordinate to change or issue an ultimatum to force the employee into a mold of supervisory imagination or personal preference. The change must emanate from within the person, but the supervisor can be an *agent* of change.

Although effecting change in a subordinate toward increased effectiveness is a supervisor's highest obligation, it is not an activity that comes naturally. It requires careful thought, proper instruction, and an appreciation of the entire context in which it takes place. The process by which a supervisor evaluates subordinates' performance, feeds it back to them, and coaches them in ways of performing more effectively is what we shall refer to as the "performance-evaluation interview."

The evaluation interview centers on current job performance in the specific position held by the subordinate at the time of the interview. Discussion of job satisfaction or discussion of past performance in other jobs is a function of the counseling interview, and the supervisor is not a *counselor*. The role of the supervisor is that of a consultant and nothing else. Spencer Hayden says that coaching is work-centered, fact-centered, and thing-centered but counseling is person-centered rather than work-centered. It takes in the whole person, including home life, goals, fears, hopes, history, and self-concept.[1]

The supervisor as coach and consultant has four objectives:

1. To help subordinates do their present jobs better by pointing out even higher standards of performance to which they can aspire, that is, to encourage them to excel.

2. To give subordinates a clear picture of how well they are doing at present by commending them for it and by showing sincere appreciation for it.

3. To build an even stronger, closer relationship with subordinates by eliminating misunderstandings, sources of anxiety, or insecurity, by

[1] S. Hayden, "Getting Better Results from Post-appraisal Interviews," *Personnel*, 32:541–550, 1955.

listening to and accepting feedback on how well he or she is supervising, and by discussing any personal job problems the employee may wish to bring up.

4. To develop practical plans for improvement jointly, and to launch projects designed to utilize the employee's total abilities more completely.

Functional Aspects   The role relationship and personality interaction of the performance-evaluation interview depend on whether the supervisor is speaking with an effective or ineffective subordinate.

The former requires much greater skill and is less emotionally demanding but is richer in personal satisfaction for the supervisor. It is like the coaching given to an accomplished actor or to a professional athlete—a discussion of fine points, of improved technique, of ways of sharpening already highly developed skills. But it is far more than this. This interview enables the supervisor to build a closer working relationship with subordinates by getting to know them better, by letting them know that they are respected and that their contribution to organizational goals is appreciated. It guarantees employees an opportunity to tell their supervisors how they view their jobs and progress; and it permits employees and supervisors to develop jointly a program in those areas that subordinates want and that supervisors think is practical.

While a supervisor fulfills his or her highest duty by fostering the personal growth of a highly talented subordinate, the sternest test comes in coping with an ineffective employee. There is no doubt that, for every supervisor, the test is bound to come. Even in the most well-managed company, there will be people who perform their duties in a perfunctory or less than acceptable manner. Inadequate initial selection, improper orientation or on-the-job instruction, misdirected or indifferent supervision, dissipated interest in the job, or the interference of personal problems can reap a heavy toll in performance quality.

The inevitability of these circumstances is no reason to accept inferior deportment with resignation, or, at the other extreme, to react with indignation and hostility. The fact that an employee is unable to function satisfactorily in a given job is not necessarily an indication of general inadequacy, nor is discharge the only way to deal with the problem. If either alternative were effective, millions of workers would be dismissed from their positions annually, other millions would be added to the already high rate of unemployment, and all of us in the course of our careers would experience the humiliation of being fired.

Interviewing the Effective Subordinate   In the previous chapter, we stated that the sequence of the problem-solving process begins with an awareness that a problem exists, is followed by a definition of the problem and the delineation of alternative courses of action, and is concluded by the selection of the most suitable and practical solution. The performance-evaluation interview follows the same sequence. The specific problem concerned involves the attainment of excellence—what it consists of and how it may be achieved. Because the effective employee by our definition is one who is already performing his or her duties in an exemplary fashion, and not merely one who is just "barely getting by," the problem may be a bit obscure and frequently overlooked.

Although it is an opportunity to exchange information, to mutually define and delineate the problem, it is not primarily an information-exchange interview because if it were, there would be little or no change in the subordinate's behavior. Since it is a problem-solving technique, once the problem has been specified, the interview content focuses upon idea production, even brainstorming, and then shifts to evaluation of the ideas to determine a specific course of future action.

Essentially, therefore, the two participants try to answer three questions: What is the present situation? What can management do to improve it? What can the employee do to improve it? The main thrust of the interview is self-analysis and the immediate outcome must be a practical plan of action pointed toward the goal of excellence.

Whether the interview achieves this purpose as a problem-solving technique dealing with the challenge of excellence depends on its functional factors because the dynamic qualities of a critique make it or break it. Under current concepts of organization, you as a supervisor have a power relationship with your subordinate all year round. Everyday you give orders and instructions to your subordinates, lay out their work, correct them, reprove them, and in general, oversee their activities. But, suddenly, on a particular day at a specified time, you cast off the mantle of authority for an hour or two and don the robes of a consultant. Although many respected authorities declare that this shift is so unnatural as to be impossible, we believe otherwise. We believe that it becomes unnatural only when you, because of a lack of proper instruction or insight, fail to shift roles sufficiently and present your employees with too many reminders of your usual authoritarian role. It is true, however, that when you overemphasize the power aspects of your position in your day-to-day relationships, a shift to a consultant role will be almost impossible. Effective interviewing presupposes a more democratic relationship between you and your subordinates on a continuing basis and the employment of absolute authority only in time of crisis.

INTERVIEWING THE INEFFECTIVE SUBORDINATE.   Of all the personnel interviews described in this book, communicating with the ineffective subordinate via the performance interview is the most difficult. Few supervisors who attempt it can really put their messages across. It is not uncommon for a supervisor to speak to a subordinate about his or her deficiencies for over an hour, only to find at the end that the subordinate failed to comprehend the message. Worse yet, there are cases in which, after such a meeting, subordinates believe that they have just been commended for their work, while the supervisors are convinced that the subordinates have really been "told off."

The principles outlined in Chapter 2 will suggest to you the reasons for the communication breakdown that occurs so frequently during this particular interview. Because the structural aspects have been over-looked or misperceived or because the functional aspects are so emo-tionally loaded, the consequent noisy interference or psychological "static" prevents the message from getting through clearly or distorts it altogether.

The receiver, then, through the process of selective perception and a personal filter system, can hear only what he or she wants to hear and can fill in the gaps in the message from personal ideas drawn from the self-attitude system. Helping this dynamic process are the feelings of uneasiness and guilt and embarrassment and distress in you which un-wittingly cause you to garble your message in its transmission and thereby to sabotage your own intentions. Insensitive and unaware of the need for feedback, you will be certain that you have communicated when actually you have not.

Since the interview, to be effective, has to be structured carefully, there is only one possible approach—the problem-solving approach. There must be an explicit intention on the part of both parties to work through *mutual* problems and to determine whether a solution is pos-sible. The goal is to effect a change in the behavior of your subordinate and perhaps in you. Any other approach to this interview may be ade-quate "for the record," if that is what you have in mind, but it will serve no other end.

The content of this interview consists in exploring the forces that determine the employee's level of performance, to identify them, and to decide how best they can be modified to bring about a change in be-havior. You are first an information giver, then a consultant, and then a change agent as you describe as specifically and graphically as pos-sible what constitutes an acceptable minimum level of performance, how the employee fails to meet these standards, and what can be done about it. These are tasks demanding the clearest communication.

The functional aspects of the interview constitute its essential distin-guishing characteristic because they represent for most supervisors an anxiety-inducing situation. It is never very pleasant to inform another person of his or her inadequacy. But when these shortcomings constitute a real threat to the person's livelihood, the "telling" is even more dis-tasteful. To overcome these indelicate side-effects and to repress your anxiety, you may conduct the interview on a strictly impersonal, objective plane, as though you were going over the malfunctioning of your automobile with a garage mechanic. But this approach is bound to be fruitless because of the interactional effects that will inevitably break down the icy mask of rationality that you attempt to wear. Since interaction, as we have defined it in our model of the interview, is really an engagement of self-concepts and because in this interview the self-esteem of one of the parties is under siege by intimations of unworthiness, the employee will react by drawing upon his or her repertoire of defense mechanisms. Such behavior, as we have already noted, is designed to reduce tension and the pervasive discomfort the employee feels, and the interviewee's resulting actions are not likely to be purposive, constructive, or even polite.

This will, in turn, call for a reaction from you that will be exaggerated by the guilt that you are trying to suppress. Tensions will increase, emotions will boil over, and the interview can deteriorate into a common quarrel.

To prevent such an occurrence, you have to understand your role in this situation. Unless you play down the dimensions of your primary role that identify you with management and hence with authority, noisy interference will begin the minute you start the interview. To counteract this you must indicate that you have temporarily shifted roles to that of a consultant and a change agent. You must inform the employee of the standards that you expect.

There are two kinds of consultant relationships, voluntary and involuntary. The former is referred to as a *counseling* situation in which the client is disposed to accept help and the consultant is to give it. The second is referred to as the *evaluation* situation in which the client besides not asking for help is unaware that it is needed.

You must impress upon the employee the precise nature of your role —that as a consultant, you are an educator, an adviser, and an information source; you are not an order giver, a judge, nor a decision maker. Only when the potential of this role is exhausted without any change in the employee's behavior do you shift back to a more superordinate relationship and conduct a disciplinary interview in which you admonish, warn, and threaten.

Improving Job Performance

Improvement in job performance, like reducing a golf score, is extremely difficult to bring about, much less to predict. Change in behavior is relatively easy to recognize after it happens; it is a different matter to observe it while it is going on or to influence its direction or tempo significantly while a person is reorganizing habitual response patterns during the learning phase. It is even harder to predict potential change before it happens.

The first step to improve performance is to *identify* clearly the forces affecting an employee's behavior. The second step is to determine the *possibility* and the *probability* of change. The third step is to *influence*, that is, to convince the person of the need to change.

It is important, therefore, to understand the proper method of communicating an evaluation to a subordinate and of influencing that person to undertake a change in behavior. This process involves *first*, understanding the interviewer's role; *second*, determining approaches available to influence the subordinate; and *third*, appreciating the evaluation situation.

The Role of the Interviewer As a management representative, you as the supervisor have the responsibility of sustaining and improving your subordinate's performance. You have no direct responsibility for your employee's development, assignment to other positions, the resolution of personal problems, or the attainment of his or her life's goal.

You can, of course, play a role in these development areas if the company provides you with proper support. Since they are really beyond the scope of your accountability or perhaps of your competence, you have the obligation only to communicate your recommendations to higher authority.

Your task is to compare your observations and recollections of the subordinate's performance for the prescribed time period with the standards of performance you both have established for that position. You must then discuss this comparison with the employee in a way that will facilitate the acceptance of it and its application to future performance. Then, by joint consultation, you both formulate new plans and standards for that position.

Approaches to Influencing Current behavioral science and the management literature on performance evaluation strongly support the problem-solving approach. Norman Maier was among the first to point out that there are different ways of approaching the performance-evaluation interview, each with a different objective and based on different assumptions that call for different skills and role relationships.[2]

How many times do you find yourself in an influencing situation? For example, have you tried to "sell" your supervisor recently? Have you been disappointed that your associates did not accept your suggestion for improvement? Have you ever wondered why your idea was rejected by another person or why your offer of service was not accepted?

The matter of influencing another person to accept one's ideas, services, or techniques is an integral part of most management positions. There are many ways by which one person can influence another.

[2] N. R. F. Maier, *The Appraisal Interview* (New York: John Wiley & Sons, 1963).

Best known, of course, is the "hard sell" approach to influencing which often comes through as commanding or giving directions, using status, or name dropping. However, many people today are experimenting with approaches other than the hard-sell, approaches based on the quality of their ideas, their expertise, and/or personal relationships. The need to influence through empathy and understanding is becoming more critical as people become better educated and are less impressed by status alone.

It is difficult for a person to be influenced in a way that does not make him feel inadequate or resentful. There are many reasons why:

▪ People struggling to become independent do not like the idea of having to depend on someone else for a service or an idea.

▪ It is hard for us to admit our needs even to ourselves, much less to someone else, for fear some inadequacy may be identified.

▪ People often feel their problems are so unique that no one else can understand them.

There are also reasons why it is difficult to influence anyone effectively:

▪ Since giving advice makes people feel important, they don't ask whether the advice is in the best interests of the other person.

▪ When the person getting the advice becomes defensive, it is natural to try to argue or pressure that person—and to meet any resistance by applying more pressure.

Questioning, listening, restating, or summarizing the other person's position are ways to become more influential. This kind of *self-evaluation strategy* is the direct opposite of the hard-sell approach that tends to make people defensive and lead them away from acceptance. It is much more effective.

Only a few people, about 5 percent, are consistently influenced by fear, but everyone is sometimes influenced by fear. Persuasion is effective approximately 25 percent of the time for everyone and for 25 percent of people all the time. But understanding the other person, seeing his or her needs and responding to them is a form of influence that is always effective with 75 percent of us, and with everyone nearly 75 percent of the time.

From this basic assumption about human behavior, psychologists have evolved three approaches to performance-evaluation interviewing: the hard-sell, the soft-sell, and the self-sell.

THE HARD-SELL.   In this approach, the most commonly used, as we suggested at the outset of this chapter, you rely primarily on fear as a motivator, play the role of a judge, and tell employees what you think of them and what they must do to improve. This method is effective mainly with those employees who are highly dependent, fearful, anxious to please, and who can and want to improve.

THE SOFT-SELL.   In this approach, you play the role of salesperson and rely on your ability to persuade subordinates of the merits of your evaluation and of their ability to improve. You give them the opportunity to speak candidly, to freely express their feelings. Your hope is that such ventilation will lower their defenses and encourage them to explore areas for improvement. This approach tends to create better relationships with subordinates, but its effectiveness depends to a great extent on the subordinates' perceptions of what you tell them and on your sales ability.

THE SELF-SELL.   In this approach, which is the most effective, you play the role of coach and depend on your subordinates' ability to evaluate themselves. You permit them to develop their own improvement plans on the assumption that most persons will make a sincere effort to change their behavior only after they convince themselves they need to do so and can. The problem-solving or self-evaluation method as it is sometimes called is most effective, but it takes a great deal of skill and effort. It also implies some risk because you may hear things that you did not expect about your own performance and the outcome may result in behavior changes you were not expecting.

In comparing the three approaches, note that the purpose of the self-sell method is to stimulate growth rather than to inform, to persuade, or to reduce defenses. The basic assumption underlying it is that openness and understanding will lead to improvement; the reaction that will be generated by the first two methods is that of defensiveness. In the hard-sell method, hostility is suppressed; in the soft-sell method, the hostility is expressed and accepted by the mentor.

The skills required in the first two approaches are those of sales ability, patience, listening, and reflecting feelings, whereas in the self-sell method the key skills are knowing how to analyze a problem and to generate ideas for solving it. Improvement is insured in the self-sell method while there is real doubt of it in the other two approaches. In the hard-sell approach, there is a risk that the employee will become increasingly dependent and his or her behavior will generate deeper problems. In the soft-sell method, the need for improvement may never be realized.

The values underlying the first method are authoritarian; in the second, they are democratic; and in the third, they are consultative.

How to Conduct the Evaluation Interview

The performance-evaluation interview consists of two types of meetings according to the model we developed in Chapter 11. The first, which is sometimes called the pre-evaluation interview, concentrates on developing *expectations*, that is, of reaching agreement and mutual understanding concerning position functions, standards, and objectives. This interview involves negotiation, a process of give and take, and is based on the principle that to be accepted and implemented, standards must be set by subordinates and not imposed upon them.

Unless this first meeting takes place, it is nearly impossible to conduct an effective feedback interview which is referred to by some as the post-evaluation interview. In actual practice, however, after the first pre-evaluation interview the two types are combined into one meeting. You first review how well your subordinate has met the standards based on all the information collected. Then you review and revise the functions and standards previously set. Finally, you combine the whole evaluation into an improvement plan.

The following suggestions apply to the combined interview, although they can be used effectively in either type of evaluation interview. It is important to stress here that the material presented in Chapters 2, 3 and 4 is particularly pertinent to the evaluation interview. Here we wish only to add a few thoughts that apply particularly to the performance-evaluation interview. This interview consists of three phases: interview plan, sequence, and follow-up.

Interview Plan   As with every interview, the success of the performance-evaluation interview depends upon careful planning. First of all, you must be trained thoroughly in the skills necessary to conduct the interview, as we have repeatedly stressed. In other words, you must know how to supervise, how to evaluate, and to how to communicate with your subordinates. In addition, however, your plan must encompass setting the stage, completing your own evaluation, and arranging the physical setting.

SETTING THE STAGE.   The success of this interview is directly related to the way the stage is set. First, you must prepare yourself by gathering as much information as you can that bears on the interview, by developing a careful plan of the points you wish to cover, and by constructing an outline of your approach to these points. You should not, as suggested by some, develop an improvement plan, for that is the function of the interview and is the *responsibility of the subordinate*. You must have resource material on hand—training programs, college catalogs, job descriptions, organization charts, and other material—that may be of use in constructing a workable plan.

Accumulating information about the employee's job performance is your most important preparatory step because only on that basis can you organize your thinking and plan your interview. To do this, of course, you must complete a performance-evaluation report for the current period. A review of the functions and standards established for the position is essential here. Only after this has been done should you review your subordinate's personnel record and previous performance evaluations and consult with other staff members who can comment constructively on the subordinate's work performance.

Your subordinate must also prepare for the interview. To summon the person unexpectedly one afternoon and casually announce that an evaluation interview is about to take place is quite unfair because it will be such a surprise and will permit no chance for reflection. Notify your subordinate a week in advance where and when the annual or semiannual evaluation interview will be held. Encourage your subordinate to review the job descriptions, performance standards, job accomplishments, and problems and to be ready to discuss them with you. Make it clear that the interview is initiated mainly for the subordinate's benefit and that you hope he or she will find it a rewarding and an enjoyable experience. Ideally, you should ask the person to complete, in pencil, the evaluation record and let him or her know that you will do the same.

COMPLETING THE EVALUATION RECORD. Accumulating information about a subordinate's performance is your most important preparatory step because only after this can you organize your thinking and plan your interview. To facilitate this task, you must complete some type of official record such as that shown in Figure 19. In this illustration, the numbers in the column at the far left refer to the standards previously set. The letters B, M, and A in the column to the immediate right signify "Below," "Meets," or "Above" the standards set. As indicated earlier, each standard is listed under the two trait clusters or performance factors required to meet it. The final evaluation of that factor is thereby supported by factual, observable data.

If your subordinate has also completed the same form, your interview discussion can be conducted in an organized, objective, and mutually understandable fashion.

THE PHYSICAL SETTING. The time, day, and place of the interview are selected with a great deal of care. Remove it as far as possible in time from any incident that might have occurred on the job or from any promotion or salary-increase periods, and whenever possible conduct it on a day when the relationship with your subordinate is the most favorable and you both are likely to be in your best moods.

The length of the interview varies with the level of the subordinate's job. Interviews with clerical, production, and maintenance workers can be conducted in an hour or less, but with management or professional persons, two- or even three-hour interviews are not uncommon. Usually, an afternoon is the most advisable time of the day to set aside for this interview. Some prefer to do it over lunch, but this can lead to complications. The late afternoon is usually ideal because calendars are freer, and if both are willing, the interview may continue without deadlines or interruptions.

TECHNICAL COMPETENCE: The intellectual and professional knowledge and skill needed to perform position functions. It includes ability to plan, organize, communicate and analyze.

STANDARD NO.	PERFORMANCE B	PERFORMANCE M	PERFORMANCE A	COMMENTS
2			X	Exceed all phases of this standard
4			X	Received very favorable responses
5		X		Meet (a); exceeded (c)
6 & 7	X			60% of target; missed deadline
11		X		Just about on target; standard can be improved
13		X		About 25%-30% positive response
16			X	Suggest raising standard to 200 calls

SUMMARY

1   2   3   4   5   6   7   (8)   9   10

BELOW STANDARD   MEETS STANDARD   ABOVE STANDARD

DEPENDABILITY: The ability to fulfill responsibilities with a minimum of follow-up; efficiency and diligence.

STANDARD NO.	PERFORMANCE B	PERFORMANCE M	PERFORMANCE A	COMMENTS
1 & 9		X		Standard just a little too tight
8			X	Spent on average two hours; raise standard
12		X		(a) 80%; (b) 60%; (c) received "excellent"
19		X		Records about perfect
20 & 21	X			Attended about 50%; too many meetings, lower this standard
22		X		Met (a) and (c); earned $1200 per week
23			X	Included nearly all activities - suggest new standard
24	X			Attended only 60%; not enough time
25	X			Attended about half; lower standard
29		X		Met standard - just about right

SUMMARY

1   2   3   4   5   6   (7)   8   9   10

BELOW STANDARD   MEETS STANDARD   ABOVE STANDARD

Fig. 19   Evaluation record—standards (Copyright © 1974 by Felix M. Lopez & Associates, Inc.)

The interview takes place in a private room, free of distractions, interruptions, phone calls, or other business. Because the supervisor's office will have psychological connotations of authority, because it usually is under surveillance by other employees, and because it is unlikely to be distraction-free, a neutral meeting place is most desirable. In the room, there ought to be no desk or large conference table since these set up a barrier between the two participants. To facilitate paper passing and to emphasize the "togetherness," it is desirable that both sit side by side, as in a conference, to work on the same plan conveniently.

Interview Sequence There are four sequences to this interview: establishing rapport, exchanging information, developing the improvement plan, and concluding the interview.

ESTABLISHING RAPPORT. Beginning the interview and getting it off the ground is half the battle because if done correctly, you will arouse the employee's interest, allay all apprehensions, and permit more natural employee behavior. Begin the interview promptly, let the interviewee know that you will devote your undivided attention to the interview and that you are in no hurry.

The purpose of the introductory phase is to relieve the tension, to break the ice, and to get the person talking. To accomplish this, begin by discussing something of mutual interest, as though the purpose of the meeting were purely social. But do not overdo the social amenities. If you set the stage properly, your subordinate will know very well why he or she is there; the main anxiety of the person at this point will be to ascertain the interview climate. Emphasize the rapport dimensions of this interview. If at the outset you adopt a lighthearted approach in the misguided belief that you are putting the interviewee at ease, you may fall into a trap. When you get to the reason for the interview, which may not be so frivolous, the contrast will hit the interviewee with the impact of a pile driver. On the other hand, do not begin with a somber, mournful countenance, as though you were about to inter the employee; you will frighten the person to the point where he or she can hardly hear anything that is said in the remainder of the interview.

EXCHANGING INFORMATION. This phase constitutes the main sequence of the interview. To broach the subject of performance most gracefully, ask the interviewee to evaluate personal achievement, to describe the job from a personal viewpoint, and to appraise the results achieved. Frequently, the subordinate will describe the performance in realistic, unflattering terms, and if so, this self-evaluation provides an excellent springboard from which to begin an analysis of the forces determining employee behavior. If the performance is described in favorable terms, it will give you additional insight into the subordinate's attitudes, standards, and understanding of the requirements of the position. In either case, this approach provides an excellent way to open the main part of the discussion.

THE EFFECTIVE SUBORDINATE. Start the main sequence by asking a comprehensive question, such as "Tell me how you've felt about your job in the past year." By building upon the employee's answer and by using the techniques previously described—interaction, listening, role enactment—you quietly and unobtrusively withdraw from active conversation and play the role of participant-observer with emphasis on attentive listening.

Your main task at this point is to communicate to the subordinate a clear idea of how well he or she is doing, to show your appreciation of his or her efforts, and to suggest ways of improving. The most effective way of transmitting these ideas is by two-way communication and by having it appear as though the employee is interviewing you. It is best accomplished in a climate of friendliness and warmth. To create this climate, adopt a nondirective, employee-centered approach that emphasizes the task-role dimensions of clarification, testing, and summarizing. This enables you to think and to listen attentively and avoids the appearance of authority, dominance, cross-examination, argument, pleading, or instruction. This is not to say, however, that you say nothing. At the right time, feed your own evaluation into the conversation—the good points and the weaknesses—so that they are perceived as somehow an indistinguishable part of the stream of interview continuity.

Meyer and Walker found that the way in which a supervisor handles this feedback is related to whether the subordinate took constructive action to improve performance.[3] Even though you do the least talking, you still guide the interview, dwelling only briefly on past behavior and directing the conversation to future plans and activities.

Many performance-evaluation manuals advise you to enumerate your subordinate's good points first in order to prepare for discussions of failures and of areas of necessary improvement. Upon reflection, however, this is not such a good idea. Since most employees are aware of this device, they scarcely heed the enumeration of their good points as they wait "with bated breath" for what they believe to be the main idea of the interview—a catalog of their inadequacies.

This raises the question of the relative effects of primacy versus recency. In feeding back to an employee an estimate of performance, when and how gently do you touch upon weaknesses? Such is the primacy of even the mildest reproof by a supervisor that a sensitive employee may forget all but the criticism. Since it has been demonstrated that the interviewee will retain longest what is presented toward the latter part of the interview and since the most crucial aspect of the interview with the effective subordinate is the transmission of the idea of his or her good performance and relatively small need for improvement, it is far better to discuss any weaknesses first and then move on to those areas of good performance. The more recent information thus becomes of the highest primacy and the employee will tend to carry away a more favorable recollection of the interview.

THE INEFFECTIVE SUBORDINATE. After rapport is well established, penetrate to the heart of the interview, the variance between the employee's job behavior and an acceptable standard of performance. The

---

[3] H. H. Meyer and W. B. Walker, "A Study of Factors Relating to the Effectiveness of a Performance Appraisal Program," *Personnel Psychology*, 14:291–298, 1961.

presentation of this information is the critical point in the interview. How you handle yourself here will determine the success or failure of your efforts. It is vitally important to speak in concrete, simple terms, to illustrate your main points by actual examples, by incidence, and by facts and figures. Generalizations, vague impressions, or broad descriptions of your subordinate's personal traits are likely to ensnare you in a tedious exercise in semantics, in a discussion of personal standards and points of view.

When the employee realizes the negative aspects of the evaluation, he or she will react defensively and perhaps emotionally. You have to handle this effect constructively and use it to good purpose. The best way of reducing a subordinate's tension and anxiety is first to accept it and remain composed, second, to show a willingness to share some responsibility for the substandard job performance, and finally, to suggest that you both explore possible solutions to the problem.

Your subordinate's response to your evaluation of work performance will depend upon personality. One person will react defensively by disagreeing with your description of his or her performance and may attempt to give evidence to show that your evaluation is, in many respects, inaccurate. You must not try for complete acceptance at first, or even in the first interview. Indeed, you should be properly suspicious if you do win the employee's immediate assent, as we shall explain below.

Your aim is to establish your position and to gain at least partial acceptance of your point of view; complete understanding and insight may require several interviews. Careful listening to what the subordinate has to say is important in dealing with a defensive employee. Not only will you learn a great deal from the arguments advanced but you will gain the interviewee's respect.

In any event, it is a healthy sign when subordinates feel confident enough to put forth their own ideas. There is no point, however, in engaging in a debate in an attempt to answer their arguments. Valid or not, the point is that, in their eyes, these arguments *are* and must be accepted on this basis.

It is just possible that by listening and by not trying to force your own ideas down the throat of the interviewees, you will learn enough to modify your original evaluation. This willingness to compromise and to come halfway is, as the reader will recall, one of the key role dimensions of rapport behavior—"unblocking." When conflicts occur, you must be willing to meet them and not run away from them. By removing these obstructions, these differences of point of view or of fact, communication will flow freely enough to permit the main thrust of your message to get through.

A second type of employee will agree wholeheartedly with your report.

But agreement does not constitute acceptance. The assent of such employees may simply mean that they do not grasp the significance of the evaluation and its implications for future status, or they may be so insecure that they have to believe that you may be "just out of sorts" that day. The interviewees may be so anxious to minimize any disagreement that they go along just to get out of the interview situation as quickly as possible; or they may be so deferential and so submissive that they must always agree with you, even though they have little insight into their real problems or can conceive of no practical way of solving them. When there is easy concurrence, make certain that it is sincere, that it represents understanding as well as affirmation. The best gauge of this sincere comprehension is drawn from the self-evaluation made at the beginning of the interview.

A third personality classification includes those employees who may be so discouraged by the criticism that they offer an immediate resignation. This is by no stretch of the imagination a desirable interview outcome. Possibly, after an unemotional discussion of the employee's problem from every angle, you both agree that the employee is in the wrong job, should be transferred, or perhaps should resign. But such a deliberate conclusion is far different from a hastily arrived at impetuous flight from what appears to be an unbearably embarrassing situation. And admittedly, with some employees, you may be tempted to assent to this impulsivity, to accept what is patently an ill-considered resignation. True enough, you get rid of what is for you an immediately vexing problem. But, because the outcome will only serve to destroy the confidence of other employees in the evaluation process, you simply cannot afford to accept a resignation submitted under such circumstances.

If the employee suggests leaving, find out why he or she wishes to leave. It may only be an emotional release, an attempt to show you how little the job really means. If you concentrate on the employee's ability and show by your manner and by your words the respect you have for it, you will persuade the employee to reconsider.

A fourth personality classification includes those employees who may react by becoming surly, impassive, or unresponsive. No rapport can be established; you find yourself doing all the talking but are rewarded with little more than monosyllabic grunts. This reaction can be very disconcerting, particularly to a new, conscientious supervisor who has taken the evaluation responsibilities quite seriously, has prepared well, and is ready for the interview.

But interviewing savoir-faire can come to your rescue, especially when you are dealing with a sphinxlike subordinate. First, all questions are phrased in the form of declarative statements calling for open-end responses to force the person to respond more freely. Coupled with the judicious use of silence, open-end questions that build upon previous answers will force the issue, and a thread of conversation is started. At the outset, you may have to depart completely from your interview plan, but by going far afield, you may discover an area of great concern to the interviewee that will provide important clues to the root of the problem, and as he or she talks, the employee will feel more comfortable.

The final personality classification includes employees who have come to be known as "buck passers" who have to displace the responsibility for their inadequacies on someone else. They will try to avoid any blame, or at least the onus for their actions, by shifting the criticisms to others —their own subordinates, associates, the company, or you. This blame shifting is merely another defense mechanism. By astute questioning and by listening carefully, you can uncover the reasons why these employees cannot accept the burden of their failures. When it is made clear to them that you are not judging them, are not likely to chastize them, and, at the same time, are not "taken in" by their alibis and excuses, they may timidly and gingerly try admitting some minor faults. If these are accepted noncommittally, they may be encouraged to try a little more realistic self-evaluation until they arrive at the point where they are ready to explore ways of improving performance on their own.

Most often, after working through their initial emotional reactions, the subordinates will accept the evaluation and express a genuine willingness to attempt improvement and to change behavior in the direction indicated. When this stage is reached, and for some employees, it will take considerable patience, understanding, and time to get there, you can turn to the idea production phase of the problem-solving process, to an evaluation of alternative solutions, and the interview then follows the same course as that prescribed for the effective subordinate in the preceding chapter and ultimately climaxes in the construction of a realistic, practical, improvement plan.

As we mentioned earlier in this chapter, the way in which you handle the evaluation feedback is directly related to whether the subordinate takes constructive action to improve performance. The more criticisms or "improvement needs" you cite, the more defensive the subordinate will become and the less performance improvement will be achieved.

In view of this, the problem-solving technique using the open approach is the most fruitful way to complete the evaluation. As Figure 20 illustrates, when you encounter a barrier situation, i.e., a failure on some performance standard, follow these steps:

1. *Problem definition.* Get the full picture. Explore for viewpoints and feelings as well as facts. Take the initiative in listening and understanding to find out what attitudinal problems and roadblocks exist. Then determine a course of action.

2. *Reflection.* Express your understanding of your subordinate's point of view. There may be a possibility of a new understanding or interpre-

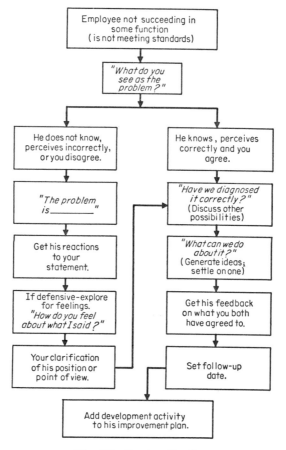

Fig. 20 Barrier situation

tation on your part. Ask open questions to clarify what you heard. Summarize the person's viewpoint and feelings as you see them to make sure you are interpreting them in the way intended.

3. *Clarification.* Get full clarification and mutual agreement on what the problem is. Then restate the problem and check whether you both accept and agree that this *is* the problem.

4. *Problem analysis.* Now, after clarifying and defining the problem and getting attitudes concerning it, analyze the work situation. Explain your viewpoints and encourage your subordinate's participation in making a decision.

5. *Commitment.* Get the subordinate's participation and commitment to working up an action program.

6. *Feedback.* Get the subordinate's reactions again to give you an indication of the understanding and acceptance of decisions reached and the motivation to carry them through.

THE IMPROVEMENT PLAN. Since the object of the evaluation interview is always performance improvement, an improvement plan has to be the interview outcome. Remember that criticism breeds defensiveness and that the more defensive an evaluatee becomes, the less improvement is effected. On the other hand, it has been found that the use of praise has no measurable effect on a person's reaction to criticism nor on subsequent job performance. To effect change and maximize the results of your evaluation effort, emphasize improvement planning. Appreciable improvement in performance is realized only when specific targets with time deadlines and ways of measuring results are mutually established.

When the subordinate's self-evaluation and your own appraisal have been completed, the nature of the problem should be clearly outlined. Although the problem-solving task will be directed at the goal of greater self-fulfillment, of satisfying higher-level needs, and of performing in a more exemplary way, the problem must be stated in pragmatic, tangible language. The problem may be that the employee cannot improve without additional education, or without counseling, or without a different occupational experience, or more challenging responsibilities, or even without a new supervisor.

Then, together you should develop ideas for the solution of the problem and select from them the most practical to form the nucleus of an improvement plan for the immediate future. Your plan, of course, must be manageable, specific, and practical. Instead of entailing the pursuit of a wide range of activities, narrow it down to the two or three most significant and attainable. Construct a timetable for the implementation of the plan and set up ways of measuring tangibly how well it is fulfilled. Then commit the plan to writing. Figure 21 illustrates a write-up of an improvement plan based on the managerial-evaluation program referred to in Chapter 11.

This form is typed and signed by you and your subordinate. Copies are retained by each with a third filed in the employee's personal folder in the central personnel office.

It is distinctly possible that the plan might require the assistance of the personnel unit or the management development section or even of an outside counselor. It is up to you to see that these auxiliary services are enlisted.

CONCLUDING THE INTERVIEW. When you feel that you have covered all the points previously incorporated in your interview plan, when you sense that the subordinate has had ample time to air his or her views, when a plan for future action has been drawn up, and when each person has a feeling of satisfaction with interview accomplishments, the interview is concluded as swiftly and as smoothly as courtesy permits. It is terminated by summing up all the main points; it is especially

Managerial Evaluation Program

Managerial Evaluation Record

POSITION   : Section Supervisor   LOCATION : Eastgate Plant
PREPARED BY   : John M. Brown   AND BY   : James P. Bartholomew
DATE   : 12/6/75   DIVISION : Manufacturing

Overall Evaluation

☐ Outstanding   ☐ Exceeds Standards   ☐ Meets Standards   ☐ Below Standards   ☐ Inadequate

DEVELOPMENT PLAN: List specific plans for improvement, objectives to be achieved, schedule of activities to be undertaken, manager's interests and aspirations, and general reaction to evaluation.

Remarks: Brown is enthusiastic about his position. Pleased with the evaluation by his associates and subordinates. Felt that the program and the interview were informative and helpful.

His strengths are in problem analysis, report writing and systems design. He needs to improve in the organization and administration of his section and in instructing and supervising his staff, areas in which he has less interest.

Following plan was developed for 1976:

(1) Change performance standards as indicated in this Record.

(2) Change his position functions to eliminate accountability for monthly departmental technical report.

(3) Enroll in February in Company Human Relations Program for supervisors.

(4) Complete courses in Organizational Behavior and Psychology Applied to Management at State University this Spring and next Fall.

(5) We will meet last Friday of each month for 1 hour to review his section's progress.

Fig. 21   Improvement plan (Copyright © 1974 by Felix M. Lopez & Associates, Inc.)

desirable that the employee summarize from his or her notes, mentioning specifically the plan of action and the agreed upon follow-up procedures. Then, you end the session with a handshake and an expression of appreciation for the subordinate's efforts.

Immediately thereafter, write for your own file a complete, concise, but detailed report of the interview, noting not only what transpired but also the subordinate's mood, opinions, and attitude. Finally, you should include the developed plan in the report for future action.

The Follow-up of the Evaluation Interview   If the interview has been even reasonably successful, a definite program with explicit action and a precise timetable for implementation will have emerged. If this outcome has meant anything, if the interview was intended to be anything more than a pleasant exercise, you must see that the program is followed. The follow-up may take the form of such extended activities as company training programs, outside educational programs, attendance at management seminars, or enrolling in conventions or technical meetings, or even simply reading a few books. Whatever it is, you should pursue it religiously and not leave it to your subordinate to carry it out alone. If you ignore this follow-up, your subordinate can hardly be expected to view your next invitation to a performance-evaluation interview with anything but skepticism. The true story of the demise of many performance-evaluation programs may lie in this sin of omission. Follow-up of interview plans is one of the most neglected aspects of the evaluation function because it is even more time-consuming than interview preparation or conduct. Follow-up might require you to keep records and notes, hold brief progress reviews with your subordinate at monthly intervals, and above all, live up to the commitments made during the interview.

Because of the tide of events and a busy schedule, we are often inclined to forget that we have incurred a serious obligation. If you have conducted interviews with a number of subordinates, retention is even more difficult. But each subordinate, concerned only with his or her own program, will remember and will be watching and waiting, even though he or she does not mention it to you. On the other hand, follow-up is so rewarding that it is difficult to understand why a supervisor should neglect it. The very fact that you show practical interest in your subordinate's plan for progress will encourage greater effort. The net effects are improved performance, an enthusiastic employee, and high morale in the work unit.

The chief hazard to avoid during the follow-up period is a compulsion to seek quick results. You may feel a need to demonstrate your ability to effect improvements in your subordinate. The employee, on the other hand, now under pressure to solve a serious problem of substandard performance, may feel obligated to change overnight. To offset this, your improvement program should be modest and long-range, and you should treat your urge to see quick results as unrealistic.

Since "the best-laid plans . . . often go astray" even when sincerely followed, they can be modified, corrected, or changed in the future performance-evaluation interview. The second and subsequent interviews can include a review of previous goals and plans established in preceding interviews, as well as an accounting of how many of them were accomplished and why some were not. This conscientious follow-up provides a healthy frame of reference within which the whole performance-evaluation system prospers. If adequate records are maintained to enable new supervisors to review the content of the evaluations and plans of the previous supervisors, the program will be even more popular and profitable for management and employees. It should not be long before all employees, both effective and ineffective, who participate in such a positive program will look forward to the evaluation interview as the single most important event of the work year. Then there would be no need to criticize or to "re-examine" performance-evaluation interviews.

chapter 13

The Career-counseling Interview

Blessed is the man who has some congenial work, some
occupation in which he can put his heart and which affords
a complete outlet to all the forces there are in him.
       —JOHN BURROUGHS, *Wake-Robin*

Not so long ago, the top officer of a bank with national influence in
financial and monetary matters became deeply concerned with the
turnover rate among its clerical employees. This officer, therefore, conducted an attitude survey to determine the probable causes of the dissatisfaction among this occupational group. Nearly 80 percent of those
surveyed indicated that they were most unhappy with the lack of promotional opportunities in the bank. Yet, the personnel office figures
showed that more than 20 percent of all clerical employees had been
promoted annually for the past five years. This misunderstanding was
due to the fact that neither the promoted employee nor his or her fellow
workers were aware that the personnel transaction was a promotion. It
was often looked upon as no more than a salary increase.

In a similar vein, Lawrence Ferguson pointed out that there is considerable confusion among junior managers about what it takes to get
promoted.[1] About half the managers in the 30 to 40 year age group who
were considered highly promotable declared that they did not know
what the promotion process was in their companies. This was because
it was not uniformly administered and they could not aim for a particular job due to their inability to discern any consistent pattern in the
promotions made.

These situations underline the widespread but ill-met need for something more than a performance-evaluation process to round out an effective personnel program. What is urgently needed is an employee-
counseling program.

[1] Lawrence L. Ferguson, "Better Management of Manager's Careers," *Harvard
Business Review,* 44(2):139–152, March–April 1966.

Performance-evaluation interviews are concerned with the explicit problem of improving job performance and, as such, are manifestly compatible with organizational goals. But the attainment of the reciprocal aspect of job effectiveness, the satisfaction of the employee's personal needs, even though it is only indirectly related to organization objectives, can pose equally challenging and just as essential tasks for both the employer and the employee.

We refer to an interview initiated for the purpose of solving the latter problem as a *counseling* interview. It differs from an evaluation interview in several important respects: first, it is not usually conducted by the immediate supervisor; second, it focuses on job satisfaction and life adjustment rather than on explicit job performance; third, it is usually initiated by the employee rather than by a member of management; and fourth, the parties involved have no continuing relationship outside the interview.

The Need for an Employee-counseling Program

It would be very convenient for a company to employ only well-adjusted, healthy, young workers, and when, because of the vicissitudes of time, they are no longer such, to dispense promptly with their services. Society, however, no longer permits an employer to retain only the fit and to relegate the remainder to the tender mercies of public and private charity, and even if it did condone such an inhuman policy, there are not enough people in the labor market who are free from emotional, physical, or mental handicaps to meet the manpower needs of all employers. Management must live, therefore, with the unavoidable fact that among its employee population there will be, at any one time, a given number of people with problems that affect job performance indirectly, but whose resolution is beyond the authority and the competence of the immediate supervisor.

Since these difficulties are usually personal, the employee must take the initiative to cope with them, but management will see that he or she receives help on company premises through an employee counseling program. The establishment of such an activity is neither an altruistic nor a paternalistic endeavor. If it is organized on sound principles, it will prove to be a hardheaded, financially profitable venture and an important arm of the corporate manpower and placement program which has as its objective the maximum utilization of its human resources.

Whether intended or not, counseling will be carried on in the plant, office, or shop. Employees with problems will come to the attention of those in authority under one disguise or another. Someone, somewhere, must and will talk to a troubled employee about grievances, career plans, the care of a sick spouse, retirement policies, or the possibility of a two-week leave of absence, and when this person does so, he or she is engaging in a counseling interview, even though quite possibly ignorant of formal counseling practices. But a more orderly system of dealing with these situations through an organized counseling program will prove more satisfactory and effective in the long run.

Such a program does not require the formal adoption of a program that utilizes special counseling methodology and professional counselors. In a study of industrial counseling practices, Eilbirt reported that although approximately 87 percent of the responding companies' personnel staffs engaged in counseling activities of some type, only 18 percent employed a specialized counselor, and few used outside specialists.[2] Eilbirt concluded that although the use of counseling specialists in formal programs was not widely accepted, many of the ideas and the techniques offered by counselors, psychologists, or psychiatrists have been adopted for use by the industry's regular personnel staff and by its supervisory personnel.

The evidence seems to indicate that most companies have some counseling program conducted by either the personnel administrator or the supervisor. The following two sections describe ways in which these two representatives can participate most effectively in the company employee counseling program; we have no intention of trying to add to the expertise of the professional counseling psychologist.

The Role of the Supervisor in the Counseling Effort   The supervisor's role in the counseling effort consists in the main of sensitivity to the needs of subordinates and an approachability that encourages them to consult him or her about their personal problems. Without prying, a supervisor must ever be on the alert for signs that an employee is experiencing some difficulty.

Of course, the behavior of particularly troublesome employees will be forced upon the supervisor without invitation or solicitation. But an employee who is in a rut and who is perplexed about the proper career path and where he or she is heading is apt to be so uncommunicative that a preoccupied supervisor may be unaware that a problem exists until the employee either becomes a behavioral problem or resigns.

Many employee problems can be dealt with successfully by the supervisor, but after consultation, it often becomes apparent that the solution is beyond the supervisor's competence because it involves specialized knowledge and professional skill. The alert, sensitive supervisor also knows when the problem is beyond him or her and to whom to refer the troubled employees. In referring the subordinate, the supervisor does not

---

[2] H. Eilbirt, "A Study of Current Counseling Practices in Industry," *The Journal of Business*, 31:28–37, 1958.

avoid the ultimate responsibility for the solution of the difficulty but by cooperation with the specialist and by follow-up on the job, maintains a continuing, active interest. In this way, he or she remains personally involved in the subordinate's welfare and fulfills the responsibility as a supervisor.

The Role of the Personnel Specialist in the Counseling Effort   In every organization, large or small, there must be a specialist who possesses the education and the experience to deal artfully and helpfully with employee problems. In some of the larger organizations, the number and the diversity of specialists is quite broad, ranging from attorneys for legal and financial matters to psychiatrists for emotional difficulties; but even though a company cannot afford such an array of talent, it must provide for a well-rounded, versatile, and able personnel specialist who knows the fundamentals of employee counseling, is familiar with the organizational environment, and can recognize the more obvious symptoms of behavioral maladjustment.

A company just *cannot* afford to be without such a specialist because this person facilitates by skillful counseling the economic and efficient utilization of personnel in four ways.

1. Because of the specialist's specific knowledge and skill, he or she has the ability to counsel and to advise employees at the level described in this and the following chapter.

2. This person works hand-in-hand with the immediate supervisor and, insofar as the confidence of the employee permits, keeps the supervisor fully informed of the progress of each relevant case.

3. As a specialist, he or she can win the confidence and respect of the employee and encourage self-help.

4. Finally, as a result of relevant findings and observations, the specialist is in an excellent position to recommend policies to higher management that will aid employees to adjust to the demands of their jobs.

The personnel specialist has then, truly, a catalytic role in influencing action on the part of others—the employees themselves, the supervisors, and top management—to modify the job environment.[3]

This concept of the personnel specialist as employee counselor requires that the person be much more than a "listening post." The more common interpretation, wherein the counselor conducts nondirective interviews and makes no recommendations and has no authority to effect change in the employee's environment in any way, has some merit in certain special situations, but it is, in our opinion, a rather sterile process overall. Most troubled employees are not interested solely

[3] See M. D. Salinger, A. L. Tollefson, and R. I. Hudson, "The Catalytic Function of the Counsellor," *Personnel and Guidance Journal*, 38:648–652, 1960.

in venting complaints; they do not perceive the counseling interview as an instrument of catharsis; their supervisors refer them to a counselor neither for therapy nor analysis. Lurking beneath the surface of most employee problems are legitimate difficulties growing out of their work situations. To resolve these conflicts, the industrial counselor must have upward influence in the management structure.

Whatever authority or influence the counselor does possess will always be limited so that there is little danger that he or she will either become a crutch on whom employees will lean or undermine a supervisor's authority. On the contrary, if he or she works closely with the supervisor and enjoys the confidence of top management, the counselor can win sufficient respect throughout the organization to attract continually a wide range of employee problems. Operating in this way, counselors represent a very sensitive and informative management barometer of employee feelings, troubles, and attitudes.

There is one limitation governing this enterprise—it is absolutely essential for the personnel specialist in industrial counseling to recognize when an employee's problem is beyond personal competence. Unless he or she happens to be a psychiatrist or a clinical or counseling psychologist, the specialist must not attempt to become involved in the deeper emotional problems. The practical employee counselor, therefore, must establish effective working relationships with professionals to whom he or she can refer employees for more specialized assistance. Finally, this brings us to the point where we must define more exactly the kinds of problems the industrial counselor can deal with. So far we have been discussing employee problems only in the broadest sense.

Although there are myriads of difficulties and conflicts that come to the attention of employee counselors, they can be grouped into two main classes—those involving inadequate job adjustment and those related to career progress. Although the greater portion of the literature on counseling deals only with the first class of problems (as the performance-evaluation literature stresses the task of prodding an ineffective subordinate), the truth is that the more significant but undoubtedly less dramatic employee-counseling effort is devoted to the second type of problem—to career guidance and placement.

Employees with Adjustment Problems In any organization, there will always be some employees whose behavior for one reason or another is such that their continued presence in the work force constitutes something of a bother and a nuisance to others. In a well-run corporation or public agency, the number of physically disabled, chronic malcontents, borderline psychotics, alcoholics, invalids, hypochondriacs, and irresponsible, insubordinate, and generally incompetent employees will be relatively small, representing perhaps no more than 1 percent of the total employee population. Despite their numerical insignificance, an inordinate proportion of management time must be devoted to deal with these people. Where union contracts are inflexible, where company policies are paternalistic, and where public relations people are hypersensitive, the individual first-line supervisor can exhaust patience and energy in the futile attempt to cope with these problem employees who cost the company a sizable sum of money in wasted time and effort. As we mentioned earlier, it would be convenient but wholly unrealistic to dismiss them summarily. Since this is usually not the best nor is it the most immediate solution, management must establish an orderly, rational program, with counseling at its core, to rehabilitate or remove these workers, or it will find itself hamstrung by an increasing load of problem employees. How this is done will be discussed in Chapter 14.

Employees with Career Problems   Up until a few years ago, it was believed that a person made a decision early in life to pursue a career, to which he or she remained committed until retirement or death. Indeed, this assumption still permeates the counseling practices in many secondary school systems. A more recent approach, developed by Donald Super and other vocational psychologists, views the process of occupational choice as continuous from early childhood until late middle age, encompassing a series of decisions at key points in the person's career.[4]

As Super sees it, the working career is divided into several stages beginning with the exploratory period of adolescence and continuing to the establishment period when the worker is well situated in a satisfying occupation. Occupational choice is therefore rarely a single decision; it is rather a series of conscious and unconscious choices determined to a great extent by uncontrollable contingencies, not excluding, as Eli Ginzberg has pointed out, the choice of one's parents.[5]

Since most of these points of choice are encountered in the organizational milieu, key occupational career decisions are made under the very nose of the employer, who, wittingly or unwittingly, may have a profound influence on each decision. People run into blind alleys; jobs that once constituted fascinating challenges become dull and uninteresting; young people find that they have neither the aptitude nor the taste for a field which they prepared for in college. Maximum use of the many excellent workers who fall or drift into career dilemmas requires the progressive employer to provide a program of employee guidance and placement. Such programs designed for mature adults on the job are still only in their infancies. There is little in the literature, and there are

[4] D. Super, *The Psychology of Careers* (New York: Harper & Row, Publishers, Incorporated, 1957), chap. 5, pp. 71–79.

[5] E. Ginzberg, "Guidance: Limited or Unlimited," *Personnel and Guidance Journal,* 38:707–712, 1960.

very few professionals engaged in this work. What little writing and research can be found is confined to the appraisal process.

Career counseling is still considered to be a technique to be pursued only in the schools and to be applied exclusively to adolescents. As a consequence, most vocational counselors and guidance workers have little first-hand work experience, particularly in private industry, and possess knowledge of the occupational world limited to the career literature found in the school or college library. As a result, says Ginzberg, "many young people aim too low, they fail to develop a flexible strategy, and they frequently have inadequate knowledge of the opportunities that are open to them."[6]

This gap between practitioner and first-hand experience places the issue squarely up to management, not only to adjust and to correct the errors made in initial choice, but also to assist experienced workers in exploiting their potential more fully through job or career shifts. The industrial counseling program must provide guidance to employees at each stage of their careers, from the early days of labor market entry through the career pinnacle when talents are fully utilized to the retirement-preparation years.

The person best equipped to function as the counselor in this program is the personnel administrator. In the remainder of this chapter, we shall try to spell out the broad elements of the personnel administrator's responsibility which must begin with a clear, unequivocal understanding of what Super refers to as the "psychology of careers."

The Psychology of Careers

Every living organism encounters crises in its journey from infancy to old age. A crisis is nothing more than a period of instability, a stage in a sequence of events during which future events are determined. The way in which the crisis is met represents the difference between growth and decline of the organism.

Human beings in their development pass through various crises, adolescence being the most widely publicized. So too, in our primary life activity, the occupation, we pass through a series of crises without realizing it. Peter Drucker focused on this problem in an interview in which he stated that at fifty-eight, he still didn't know what he was going to do when he grew up.[7] Emphasizing in the interview that one doesn't marry a job or an organization but rather manages one's own career, Drucker stated that the real career crisis today is the extension of the working life span. Noting that in our grandparents' time a per-

---

[6] *Ibid.*
[7] M. H. Hall, "A Conversation with Peter Drucker," *Psychology Today* 1(10):21–25, March 1968.

son's working life was over at age forty-five, Drucker pointed out that it is only half spent at that age today. But after twenty years in one organization or in one occupation a person may be psychologically drained—unable to contribute any more to it. The solution Drucker offered was to retrain these people as doctors, priests, lawyers, teachers, and social workers.

While Drucker's point of view may state the point too strongly, it sums up what Super refers to as the "psychology of careers," an approach that sees an individual as changing and growing throughout the course of his or her career, rather than as an incumbent of a series of occupations.

Basically there are four crucial decision-requiring crises that people encounter in their careers, each corresponding to one of the life stages described by Super.[8]

Career Choice   The first crisis takes place in the period of exploration when the young employee is concerned with the choice of an appropriate career. Much of the career-counseling literature is devoted to this crisis. The prevailing view is that the selection of a career is an expressive act that reflects a person's ability, attitudes, and drive and represents an active implementation of the person's self-concept. This crisis, which is perhaps the least critical, has received the most attention because it is usually encountered while the person is in school and under the supervision of educators and researchers. After leaving school, the person is hardly noticed by society unless he or she encounters mental or emotional problems. Only very recently have studies been made of the development of the mature adult.

Career Development   The second crisis occurs in the establishment period after a person has selected a career and is moving up in it. This is essentially the problem of promotion and upward mobility. As Theodore Alfred indicated, if individuals do not participate meaningfully in organization career decisions affecting them, they have a right to feel that they are being used in a "checkers" game.[9] Some companies, but not many, are responding to this problem by formal career planning and development. This process presents the young person with a frank and objective assessment of his or her talent, a clear view of career paths open in the company, and a statement of what the corporation has in mind for the person in the future.

Such a system, which represents a substantial modification of a manager's promotion authority, is the best antidote to the "Peter principle,"

[8] Super, op. cit., chap. 5.
[9] T. M. Alfred, "Checkers or Choice in Manpower Management," *Harvard Business Review*, 45(1):157–167, January–February 1967.

that in a hierarchy every individual tends to rise to his level of incompetence.[10] These new systems employ the assessment centers mentioned in Part 2, human-resources planning, and even job posting.[11]

Regardless of the programs, a key ingredient of all of them is counseling. At least one company is now developing what it refers to as its "career investment planning program" designed for a newly promoted executive. The objectives of this program are to help the executive become maximally effective in the new position in the shortest possible time, and to prepare an individualized development program for future progress that is consistent with the person's goals and those of the company. The counselor in this program is an outside consulting psychologist who serves in the role of resource person and adviser. The executive, not the corporation, is the client and is in complete charge of the program. The corporation's role in the counseling effort consists mainly of making the developmental opportunity available, and it receives information about the counseling relationship *only* from the client.

In establishing this program, the company hopes to reduce executive failure, provide an antidote for management obsolescence, broaden its top management pool, and identify management problems earlier. There is solid evidence that such a program may be needed in many situations. Hall and Schneider, in a study of career development in the priesthood, found that many positions contained the seeds of psychological failure.[12] An interesting corollary of their major proposition was the notion that the transition from a failure-oriented to a success-oriented work assignment is usually accompanied by the "psychological bends." If a person has grown accustomed to experiencing psychological failure, he or she will not be able to perform well under conditions making for success; realizing a personal inability to perform well under favorable conditions may only heighten a person's sense of failure and lead to further low esteem.

Career Maintenance   The third crisis occurs in the maintenance period when the worker reaches a plateau where he or she must accept the idea that further advancement is unlikely. This is the middle-age dilemma referred to by Peter Drucker. The crisis can be devastating for some people as they experience feelings of lost youth, failure, and uselessness. It is particularly traumatic to managers. Connor and Fielden refer to managers who have been passed over for promotion but kept on

[10] L. J. Peter and R. Hull, *The Peter Principle* (New York: Morrow, 1969).
[11] For a review of these techniques see F. M. Lopez, *The Making of a Manager* (New York: American Management Association, 1970), Chapter 12, "Moving Managers Up."
[12] D. T. Hall and B. Schneider, *Organizational Climates and Careers: The Work Lives of Priests* (New York: Seminar Press, 1973).

the payroll as "shelf sitters."[13] They report that in one company "shelf sitters" occupy a large area of one floor of an office building. They recommend that management either (*a*) demote the shelf sitter or (*b*) force an early retirement into a second career that the person has been prepared for at company expense.

This approach goes beyond a fairly widespread attempt in recent years to deal with the problem of obsolescence which Burack refers to as the growing discrepancy between a manager's expertise and the changing demands of jobs and work standards.[14] Known as the "selection out" or "executive transition program," this approach attempts to ease management's conscience by counseling and coaching a terminating executive in how to search for a new position or career.

While such programs are valuable in their own right, none deal with the heart of the matter, the personal adjustment required of every human being to the inevitable stage of life where he or she has "topped off." Many people attempting to push ahead to a job they really don't want, but to which they have been driven by family, peers, or supervisory pressure, can be helped immeasurably by a counseling relationship that enables them to restructure their views of the world and of themselves. Many stalemated employees can be motivated by encouraging them to break out of a rut and to venture into new fields more adapted to their real talents and aspirations. Employees can be shown the value of genuine job satisfaction and can be helped to find it, not in the external trappings of status, money, and prestige, but in the length and breadth of a challenging, stimulating activity that requires self-discipline and self-mastery and that, thereby, enhances inner self-respect and self-confidence.

Career Abatement   Finally, there is the fourth crisis, the onset of the decline, the point in a person's career where he or she must recognize that it is time to turn the job over to younger and abler men and women. This is essentially the problem of retiring, not from life, not from a career, but from active, full-time participation in an organization. We shall deal with this crisis again in the following chapter.

These four crises create a deep perplexing problem because they arise out of the social and cultural milieu, with its materialistic standards that push people to seek advancement for the sake of advancement and to be attracted to jobs with prestige and affluence. These issues are of particular significance to the career counselor in industry. Americans, by and large, acquire their social status from the type and level of

---

[13] S. R. Connor and J. S. Fielden, "Rx For Managerial 'Shelf Sitters' " *Harvard Business Review,* 51(6), 1973.
[14] E. H. Burack, "Meeting The Threat of Managerial Obsolescence," *California Management Review,* 15(2):83–91, Winter, 1972.

occupation which they pursue. They are also urged by the culture to strive for higher and higher social levels. These demands are brought to the job every day. Since promotions and salary increases are looked upon as primary roots of the satisfaction of these needs, employers find themselves in the very astonishing position of having to grapple with the upward mobility aspirations of their employees.

Counseling then becomes a task of exploring an employee's career aspirations and potential and discerning whether the drive for achievement and advancement is based on the search for true self-expression or is prompted merely by social pressure. As noted previously, the former can always be satisfied, and the latter cannot. The personnel manager who engages in career counseling must keep these background factors in mind while conversing with an employee who is in a quandary over the direction to follow in working out a career. The counselor with insight must appreciate the deeper, more personal aspects of true job satisfaction and the conflicts occasioned by social and cultural pressure. He or she must recognize the inevitable fact that every person has the power of self-fulfillment—but almost no one who strives for social status, or personal or financial affluence can achieve it satisfactorily. A constructive counseling program is based on this philosophy. In the words of counseling psychologist Cecil H. Patterson, changing human behavior by way of a counseling process has as its "purpose and result, to free the individual as much as possible from the control of external circumstances and to enable him to achieve control of himself and his environment. The goal of this approach—a goal which is outside of and not determined by science—is self-direction and self-actualization."[15]

How to Conduct the
Career-Counseling Interview

In the perspective of the problem-solving situation and of our broad definition of job satisfaction, we can now consider the structural and functional aspects of the career-counseling interview in industry. In the following pages, we shall consider the interview conducted by the personnel specialist in the company's central personnel unit. Supervisors, other company representatives, and outside specialists can also profit from the suggestions we will make, but they are intended primarily for personnel practitioners. Because of their unique view of the organization's career plan and procedures, their knowledge of current employment trends, their appreciation of the prevalent job market, their familiarity with the requirements of specific jobs, and their close cooperation with supervisors, these personnel practitioners are in the best

[15] C. H. Patterson, "Control, Conditioning, and Counseling," *Personnel and Guidance Journal*, **41**:680–686, 1963.

positions to provide counseling services to employees at critical choice-points in their careers.

Planning the Interview   The first rule governing this interview is that you, the counselor, almost never initiate it. Sometimes, the supervisor refers a subordinate to you after an evaluation interview in which it was agreed that the employee ought to get professional advice on career potential. Often, the employee comes to you directly—the most desirable beginning of all.

As the counseling interviewer, then, you are a third party serving in the role of resource person and adviser. Ideally, the counseling program is based on a general corporate policy encouraging employees to visit the personnel department whenever they have job or career problems. As the personnel specialist, you may be a staff member of the employment, training, management, or organizational planning unit. Your organizational identity is unimportant.

But what is important is that both you and the interviewee clearly understand that the interview purpose is to furnish the employee with information and insight—company organizational structure, career opportunities within the company, how promotions are made—and to help the employee think through ways of solving career problems. Above all, remember that the interview is not a therapeutic situation.

Sometimes, preparation for this interview is necessarily brief because the interviewee may appear at your office unannounced. But even when you arrange an appointment in advance, the first interview will be no more than an information-getting situation in which you ascertain the broad outlines of the interviewee's concern. After this "intake" interview, you can make careful preparations for the next meeting.

In the interim, you can accumulate background information about the interviewee—job experiences, educational qualifications, test scores, and supervisory performance evaluations. As a matter of routine, you will possess the basic information about jobs in the company and other occupational reference material.

Make the usual provisions for privacy and freedom from interruption during the interview and plan it to last between thirty and sixty minutes. Make provisions to take notes along the lines previously recommended. Generally, careful counseling requires a series of interviews, and sometimes it is helpful to review your notes of the earlier interviews.

Interview Sequence   As with performance-evaluation interviews, the sequence of this interview falls into four phases: establishing rapport, exchanging information, developing a plan of action, and concluding the interview.

ESTABLISH RAPPORT. The beginning sequence of the counseling interview can be brief because the interviewee is there voluntarily. Since he or she really wants to communicate, you can establish rapport quite readily. Begin with a broad question, such as "What brings you here?" if it is the first interview, or "How are you today?" if it is the second or later interview. Then, observe the usual social amenities before plunging into the main sequence. During this exchange of pleasantries, test the employee's moods and reactions. Sometimes, he or she may be apprehensive, particularly if it is the first or second meeting, or a little submissive, dependent, and waiting to be told and instructed. Patterson states that because of the social conditioning of prior experiences with teachers (and, in our opinion, with supervisors too), counselees expect to be told, to be informed, to be led, to be questioned, and to speak only in response to the counselor. In other words, they expect to be dependent upon the counselor's lead.[16] Since overdependency will block constructive thinking and problem solving, from the very beginning you should coach the interviewee in your respective role dimensions—you as the reflector and clarifier, and the interviewee as the thinker, talker, and decision maker.

Some interviewees will be unable to carry this burden entirely; they may be somewhat inarticulate or overly anxious. You must support and encourage them to take the first tentative steps in self-evaluation. Acquaint counselees with the idea that essentially the interview is a learning situation in which they think through a problem in the presence of an understanding observer who will participate with them in finding an appropriate solution.

EXCHANGING INFORMATION. When you have set the pattern and course of the conversation, move directly to the root of the problem. Devote your attention to the employee's perception of personal traits, aspirations, interests, and personality dynamics. Never give the client information about this material even though you can; rather help the person assess his or her own background, qualifications, and, especially, aspirations in the light of the objective evidence that has been accumulated about him or her. The emphasis is on the counselee's underlying attitudes and motivations. Using factual data as a base, guide the conversation to the substance of the interview, the employee's attitude toward various work situations and the reasons that prompt the exploration of new occupational goals. It may well be that the interviewee is interested in a particular career because of its extrinsic aspects, its prestige, privileges, or salary potential. The interviewee must realize that such motivation does not constitute a genuine interest in a vocational field, and that in the long run, it is self-defeating. Your task is to help

---

[16] C. H. Patterson, "Client Expectations and Social Conditioning," *Personnel and Guidance Journal*, 37:350–357, 1958.

CONFIDENTIAL

PERSONNEL DEPARTMENT

COUNSELLING INTERVIEW FORM

Name __John M. Brown__   Address __72 Salern Road, Morristown, N. J.__

Department __Manufacturing__   Unit No. __164__   Position Title __Staff Assistant__

Seniority in Grade __4/17/73__   Date of Employment __6/17/72__   Annual Salary __$15,000__

Date of Birth __1/17/49__   Referred by __J. P. Bartholomew, Eastgate Plant Manager__

PURPOSE OF INTERVIEW

☑ Career Guidance   ☐ Grievance   ☐ Transfer Request

☐ Employee Benefits   ☐ Disciplinary   ☐ Rehabilitation

☐ Personal   ☐ Other_____

Interview No. __1__   Supervisor notified   ☑ Yes   ☐ No

SUMMARY OF PERFORMANCE

Areas Requiring Improvement *Rated outstanding - Needs more direct experience in supervision of day-to-day personnel problems. - Considering a career in personnel & labor relations.*

THE INTERVIEW RECORD

Date of Interview __3/15/75__

Mr. Brown is on the last leg of a two year tour as staff assistant to Plant Manager, Eastgate Plant where he has apparently been quite successful. Now, he explained, he is not so sure that he wanted a career in manufacturing (his original idea when he graduated from college). Since last September he has been studying for his Master's degree in personnel at Columbia University. Shortly, after January, was assigned to personnel plant manager and has enjoyed the work very much.

He concerned about his long range career prospects if he were to shift to Personnel Department so early in his career. The "scuttlebut" has it that Personnel people don't get considered for top management positions. On the other hand, if he stays

Fig. 22   Counselor's report: career counseling interview

the counselee work through this idealized conception by assessing his or her capacities realistically and by relating them to the realities of the occupational world.

Avoid the trap of giving employees information to which they are not entitled—information about supervisory evaluations, test scores, or other personal evaluations. The purpose of the career counseling interview is to enable employees to establish reachable career goals and to determine the best course of action to follow to achieve them.

Since the fulfillment of this intent depends on the individual em-

THE INTERVIEW RECORD (Cont'd)

in manufacturing or shifts to some other field, he will miss out on the early training & experience he feels is necessary for success in personnel and labor relations.

The interview then turned to a discussion of John's career dilemma and the apparent conflict between doing what he wanted to do and his desire to "succeed." John stated that he enjoyed working with people and always found human relations problems particularly challenging. He believed he could make a real contribution to the company in this field. And there really was no reason why he could not advance to a position where he could make the most of his talent & ability.

I pointed out the respect and importance accorded personnel work in the company and the intensity of the selection procedure for Personnel representatives. I also noted the number of successful executives throughout the company who had spent a portion of their careers in Personnel.

John responded favorably to this information. He decided that he would apply for a position in personnel at corporate level. Since this involves an assessment interview he would let the company make the final decision. Then, if appointed, he would try the work out for a few years to determine whether he really enjoyed it

Signature *Mary Stephens*

ployee's perception of his or her problem, on the conflict or congruence between ability and aspirational levels, you must minimize the impact of your personality on the employee's thinking. Keep your views of life, your values, motives, and theories of motivation out of the interview as much as possible even though the interviewee seeks such information.

But your personal philosophy of human dignity and growth should shine through your interview behavior in an attitude of hopefulness, of kindliness, and of optimism. Maintain the characteristics of a helping relationship developed by Carl Rogers.[17]

[17] Carl Rogers, "The Characteristics of a Helping Relationship," *Personnel and Guidance Journal,* 37:6–16, 1958.

Personnel administrators or supervisors will find it extremely difficult at first to assume the mantle of a pure helping relationship as described by Rogers and to function solely as a catalyst and consultant. Interviewees, in turn, may have difficulty in sensing the dimensions of this role, even though you assume it quite readily. They will expect you to adopt a more direct posture toward them and may evidence some anxiety or hostility when they find that they are expected to do their own thinking and their own talking.

Most of this anxiety disappears quickly as you conduct the interview on the plane of an information-exchange interview. Be ready to furnish interviewees with objective data about the company's occupational world in which they are expected to function by having at hand facts and figures about the number of promotions and how they are made, the personal requirements of different positions, educational and developmental opportunities, transfer possibilities, and details of the retirement program. Here the personnel interviewer has a decided advantage over the usual counseling interviewer because the former knows first-hand the details of the organizational world and the practical realities of everyday business life.

Outside professional counselors are handicapped because their experience and knowledge of the occupational world is almost always second-hand, being drawn from occupational manuals, career literature, and the reports of other clients. If the clients are mature adults experienced in the business world, they will sense this unfamiliarity and perhaps unfairly discount the counselors' true value to them. This is one of the reasons why many adults rarely seek the services of the professional counselor. Clinical psychologists and psychiatrists treating employees for emotional difficulties also experience the difficulty of being unfamiliar with the demands of the patient's working environment.

The truly *professional* personnel specialist, widely experienced in every phase of personnel management, enjoying the confidence of top management and supervisors, and possessing a rich store of information about his own company, industry, and the community in which it functions, is a valuable reference source for a counselee (and for outside professionals, too, if they knew how to tap it). But a personnel administrator with limited counseling skill will effectively neutralize the advantages of his information.

If you adopt the approach of the nondirective, client-centered interviewer, leave the decision-making to the interviewee, and limit yourself to the roles of catalyst and resource person, you will perform as a most helpful counselor.

As with all problem-solving interviews, your goal is to arrive at a concrete practical plan of action for the interviewee which in Albert Thompson's words "helps the client not only to solve the immediate problem but to become better able to solve future problems."[18] As with the evaluation interview, the plan of action developed must be amenable to implementation and provide not only a satisfactory resolution of the interviewee's immediate problem but a foundation to cope with subsequent vocational decision-making situations.

CONCLUDING THE INTERVIEW. The counseling interview, unlike other personnel interviews, is not designed to attain its objectives in one session. More than likely, the problem will require a series of meetings extending over a period of time. When the forty or forty-five minute mark has been reached and no plan has been developed, it is time to end the session; when a plan has been constructed, it is time to end the relationship.

If no plan emerges, schedule another interview and terminate the session with a summary of what has been discussed. When the counseling process itself is being concluded, make arrangements for practical follow-ups to permit readjustment of plans if indicated.

Immediately after the conclusion of the interview, complete your notes and prepare a report similar to the one shown in Figure 22 as a record of what has transpired. This report can prove to be valuable for future sessions and in some cases become a confidential part of the employee's personal file. Where possible, make a report to the employee's supervisor to keep him or her informed of the counseling progress.

For the personnel administrator, the career counseling interview represents an unparalleled opportunity and a unique challenge. For the most part, you will be dealing with effective people whose careers are largely in the process of formation. You can aid that process by recalling the advice of Thompson: "What he [the counselor] contributes is his wisdom with respect to the problem-solving *process*. The client, in line with the principle that in most cases he is the best judge of what is best for him, has the responsibility for arriving at the ultimate solution."[19]

---

[18] A. S. Thompson, "Personality Dynamics and Vocational Counseling," *Personnel and Guidance Journal*, 38:350–357, 1960.
[19] *Ibid.*, p. 355.

chapter 14

The Problem-employee Interview

With his depths and his shallows, his good and his evil,
All in all, he's a problem must puzzle the devil.
—ROBERT BURNS, *Sketch: Inscribed to C. J. Fox*

A substantial financial institution in a large metropolitan center was deeply concerned by the absenteeism rate among its clerical employees. To remedy the situation, the management established an "absence control program," the heart of which consisted of a series of interviews between supervisors and employees with poor attendance records. Each interview became more extended and serious as the absence-frequency rate increased.

The program, however, had little impact on the attendance rate, but it did create considerable resentment in both supervisors and employees. The principal sources of the antagonism lay in the supervisors' ineptness in conducting these interviews and their stress on treating the symptoms rather than identifying the causes of the absenteeism.

Interviewing employees under potentially embarrassing or uncomfortable circumstances is quite difficult for the reasons we shall cite at the end of this chapter. Most supervisors avoid such encounters like the plague. Yet, problem employees and employee problems are company realities that must be confronted rather than swept under the rug. Supervisors must learn how to handle these situations effectively.

Long ago, society discovered that it must devote a considerable portion of its income and its effort to aid people caught up in the dislocations that are the inevitable price of civilization. It is only logical to expect, therefore, that the occupational arena, as a small corner of the battleground, will have its share of casualties.

Yet, this obvious outcome seems to disturb, and even shock many American managers who prefer to assume that all employees are, or at least if they had the decency, should be, contented and well adjusted. The facts, however, are otherwise. The most selective employment techniques cannot screen out completely the eccentric, the unstable, the antisocial, the alcoholic, the daydreamer, the chronic absentee, or the accident prone. And even if they could, management would still be involved with many problem employees. "No man is an island, entire of itself" said John Donne. The pressures of job, family, friends, and even of time itself can induce symptoms of distress in even the most well-balanced employee—symptoms that will retard production, increase operating costs, upset other workers, and lower the morale of the work group.

Recognize it or not, therefore, management must somehow confront the problem of employee maladjustment to control it and to minimize it but never to eliminate it. One way of minimizing its inevitable occurrence and even of capitalizing on it is to develop a program to deal with with it in an enlightened, constructive fashion.

Once management accepts this idea and moves to assume its obligation to help fellow people in trouble, it is likely to create an organizational climate that, paradoxically enough, will probably result in a lower incidence of employee maladjustment. A program of counseling, grievance, and disciplinary interviews helps establish this climate. These interviews have a common purpose of solving a problem in an area where authority, as it is usually defined, is virtually impotent. But before discussing them, we must first examine what we mean by a problem employee and why people are ineffective in their work, and then illustrate why authority cannot work in their cases.

What Is a Problem Employee?

It is insufficient to say, as some textbook writers do, that "a problem employee is an employee with a problem." We have already demonstrated that *all* employees have problems, but most are not only not problem employees but are, on the contrary, distinct company assets. It is equally inexact to refer to problem employees merely as ineffective workers. The problem employee in our view is a maladapted person who, for one reason or another within or beyond personal control, cannot meet the demands of the work environment. Dealing effectively with this person depends upon the nature of the deficiency and whether it is temporary or permanent.

Why People Are Ineffective in their Work   In a review of the relationships between absenteeism and turnover, Lyons found that most studies showed a significant and positive relationship between them.[1] On the basis of the data, he tentatively concluded that there was a progression

[1] T. F. Lyons, "Turnover and Absenteeism: A Review of Relationships and Shared Correlates," *Personnel Psychology*, 25(2):271–281, Winter 1972.

of behavioral withdrawal and turnover. In other words, absenteeism was a flag usually predicting termination. But Lyons could find little support for a set of common factors influencing the two forms of behavior. Turnover and absenteeism are apparently manifestations of different underlying causes.

Even though few managers realize it completely, there are many variables that must be controlled to assure effective job performance. Employees must first of all want to do a good job; then they must possess the necessary skills and knowledge; they must have a temperament suitable to the job environment; they must be fully instructed in the things they need to know; they must be given the proper tools, equipment, and working conditions; they must receive proper job direction; they must be granted rewards; and finally, they must be relatively free from distractions stemming from personal problems.

It follows, then, that with an ineffective worker, at least one of these variables is operating improperly. To diagnose substandard behavior, you must examine carefully each factor to determine which is the source of the difficulty, and having found it, decide upon possible remedies. Since there is a tendency to ascribe all poor performance to incompetence or uncooperativeness, it is useful to review the major causes of job ineffectiveness.

POOR INITIAL SELECTION.   A high proportion of job failures can be traced to faulty initial selection. Deficiencies in this area include not only inadequate job knowledge or insufficient education but other handicaps such as inadequate mental traits. Insufficient job knowledge can be remedied by training, but too much or too little innate ability is incurable. In fairness to the worker, the latter deficiency should be spotted *before* placement on the job. Most selection errors can be traced to improper motivational or social traits. These errors show up in tardiness, absenteeism, poor work habits, insubordination, inability to work with other people, or emotional instability. Most of these symptoms can be detected before employment through a systematic selection program described in Part 2.

INADEQUATE JOB INSTRUCTION.   Another cause of job failure lies in the quality of the instruction received by the employee, particularly during the orientation and probationary period. Although it is imperative that a new employee be informed in an orderly, comprehensive manner of things which must be known to do the job properly, this instruction is often carried out by another uninformed employee who merely passes on his or her own mistakes and misinformation.

POOR SUPERVISION.   Painful though it may be, the supervisor must honestly question his or her own behavior and, where indicated, admit responsibility for a subordinate's substandard performance. Poor supervision can be either misdirected or indifferent.

Misdirected supervision refers to the application of improper techniques and undue concentration on the wrong areas of an employee's performance. Indifferent supervision refers to the neglect of leadership obligations. Engrossed in their own problems, worried about their own security, viewing their jobs as technically oriented, indifferent supervisors pay scant attention to their subordinates.

PERSONAL PROBLEMS. The problems an employee encounters outside working hours may interfere seriously with performance on the job. Although a person is hired for only eight hours a day on company property, the company acquires an interest in his or her twenty-four hour day, whole family, personal habits, past, and, to some extent, future. Each day the employee carries into the plant or office along with a lunch pail or an attache case a complete set of personal worries, fears, joys, and hopes.

MANAGEMENT PROBLEMS. Problems off the job are not the only sources of lowered worker efficiency. Management can do a good job of creating its own problems. The industrial and labor relations climate and the general feeling of security pervading the organization have considerable influence on job performance. If the company is under stress, if it is operating at a loss, if profits are declining, if there is high turnover and "head-chopping" among executive personnel, if the company is pouring pressure on employees to decrease costs and increase production, if there is an atmosphere of hostility between management and labor, and if there is a general authoritarian philosophy in the company, then workers, particularly those of the marginal class, will perform in a mediocre or substandard fashion.

Types of Problem Employees   These problems, singly or in combination, create five types of employees who represent the "removal problems" in Quadrant IV of Figure 15, in Chapter 10.

1. *The Obsolete Employee.* There are employees in good health who are *permanently* unable to meet minimum job performance standards. Among such people may be the obsolete employees who were once able but who with technological advances or organizational growth can no longer handle the more complex duties their jobs entail. In Chapter 12, we discussed ways of dealing with such employees when the first signs of ineffectiveness are manifested. When an employee does not respond to a supervisor's evaluation and follow-up efforts, that person becomes a problem employee.

Two important characteristics of employees in this group deserve mention: their obsolescence is chronic and irreversible, and their work habits and general attitude are satisfactory. They simply cannot do the work required of them.

Studies of why employees leave a company are quite commonplace and will be referred to in Chapter 17. Flowers and Hughes, however, undertook to examine the reasons why employees stay.[2] Their brief answer was inertia and "golden handcuffs." These characteristics aptly describe the "shelf sitters" and the obsolete employees. They will not leave a company unless some external force is applied to them.

2. *The Reluctant Employee*. Some employees find it difficult or impossible to adhere to ordinary job discipline. Inability to adjust to reasonable regulations is manifested generally by excessive tardiness or absenteeism. Quite often, chronically poor attendance, which is as symptomatic of maladjustment as of alcoholism, constitutes a subconscious dislike of the job or a reluctance to work. We are not referring here to an employee in a poorly supervised, ill-disciplined work unit where no one seems to care very much about punctuality, but rather to a member of a well-ordered work unit where the practice of coming to work on time is firmly established, who has been cautioned, but who still finds it impossible to accept the standard.

Burke and Wilcox, who also found a positive relationship between absenteeism and turnover, emphasized the need of managers to identify and to deal with the factors underlying increasing absenteeism, to avoid treating symptoms (as in our illustration at the beginning of this chapter) and get down to fundamental causes.[3]

3. *The Disgruntled Employee*. In every large work unit and in many small ones, there will be at least one or two dissatisfied employees who attribute their unhappiness to their employers, supervisors, or even co-workers or subordinates. Feeling misunderstood, neglected, or persecuted, they distort or reject any gesture of management goodwill as an attempt to exploit them. They pour out their resentment into any receptive ear, particularly into the ears of new employees.

4. *The Disabled Employee*. Through the inexorable march of time, all employees are destined to become superannuated and hence, in a sense, disabled. There should be no stigma attached to the fact that one's reflexes grow slower, the vision is a little blurred, and the hearing is slightly less acute. The trouble is that most people find this process so disconcerting and so embarrassing that they refuse to admit it even to themselves. There is always a group of employees too old to do the job they have held for many years, too proud to admit it, and too financially impoverished to do anything about it. The employee then retires *on* the job, and this form of retirement is universally recognized as the most expensive and the least efficient pension plan available to an employer.

Another category of disabled employees includes those workers who

---

[2] V. S. Flowers and C. L. Hughes, "Why Employees Stay," *Harvard Business Review*, 51(4):49–60, July–August 1973.

[3] R. J. Burke and D. S. Wilcox, "Absenteeism and Turnover Among Female Telephone Operators," *Personnel Psychology*, 25(4):639–648, Winter 1972.

are unable to perform their full duties because of physical limitations due to injuries on or off the job or because of declining physical health. Often employees who are injured on the job and many loyal long-service employees injured off the job are carried by the employer at full pay on "light duty." Since health insurance coverage enables the employee to bear the burden of illness with little financial difficulty, the only hazard exists in the psychological sphere.

When people become physically disabled in our enlightened culture, they receive considerate attention and sympathy; they are encouraged to take things easy; and they receive all the comfort and care they require. For even average workers who never enjoyed such considerate attention before, disability becomes mighty attractive, so attractive that they are reluctant to abandon it to return to normal activities. When such workers finally return to full active duty, their perspective is restored and they enjoy once more the solid feeling of independence and self-sufficiency. But getting them back can be as real a problem as the task of reentry for orbiting astronauts, one that requires rehabilitation and firm handling via the counseling process.

Some employees, of course, will be handicapped permanently and will have to be encouraged to accept a position that, at first glance, appears unattractive or unperformable. Here again, sensitive and imaginative interviewing can aid these disabled workers to see things positively and in the long run will represent the foundation on which to build an effective rehabilitation program.

5. *The Troubled Employee.* As we have said before, employees bring to work with them the troubles and cares that they encounter off the job, and these worries influence the way they perform their jobs. The harping wife or the alcoholic husband can lower production just as much as a machine breakdown, and a night on the town can be just as costly to the company as to the worker. We can subdivide these "personal" problems into four major classes.

(a) *The financially embarrassed employee.* There are people in today's relatively easy-credit society who find it virtually impossible to stay out of debt. The chronic borrower is just as maladjusted as the alcoholic or the absentee. There are other employees who, for reasons beyond their control and in spite of health and accident insurance plans, incur heavy financial obligations stemming from serious illnesses, personal liability suits, property damage, or the debt of a friend or relative.

(b) *The domestically troubled employee.* There will be some employees with problems emanating from within the family circle, the most pressing of which usually involve marital discord. The contention that a person's private life is of no concern to an employer is, unfortunately, not as accurate as management would ardently prefer. When such domestic troubles as a sick child, a delinquent son, or a disintegrating marriage occupy a worker's attention to the extent that he or she cannot pay attention to work, it becomes very much the affair of the employer.

(c) *The alcoholic employee.* Alcoholism occupies a prominent place in the array of personal problems that management must attend to because of its traumatic impact upon job performance. An intoxicated worker is a menace to life and property. Since the alcoholic is usually unable to report for work, absences become so frequent that action is forced upon the supervisor. And the employee suffering from the after-effects of extended inebriation is in no shape to work safely, efficiently, or strenuously.

Because alcoholism is viewed as a pathological state, a great deal of attention has been paid to this problem in both the professional and the popular literature. Consequently, it is sufficient to note the fact that a counseling interview is only a small drop in the bucket of remedial action required to rehabilitate an alcoholic. Many employees who appear to be on the road to outright alcoholism can be helped by an understanding, patient, but firm interviewer; but referral to a specialist is the only effective course of action even with an incipient case.

(d) *The emotionally ill.* When an employee's usual pattern of behavior undergoes reasonably drastic changes so that, in a sense, he or she appears to be a different person, it is usually a strong indication that the person is a victim of severe anxieties that are beginning to get out of hand. The supervisor, noting that the behavior of an employee is atypical, should refer him or her to someone else within the company—the plant physician, a staff psychologist, or a personnel counselor. One of these specialists can determine better whether the employee is in emotional difficulty and, if so, can arrange with the person's family for therapy.

Other employees with emotional problems who may be under the care of a therapist even though they continue to work may require additional supportive counseling from time to time, with, of course, the knowledge and advice of the therapist. Such a coordinated program can aid in the restoration of a mentally disturbed employee to full duty and sound emotional functioning.[4]

How Does Authority Influence a Problem Employee?

It is widely assumed that managerial authority represents absolute power by which employees who do not do what they have been asked to

---

[4] For more on this, see Harry Levinson, "What Killed Bob Lyons?," *Harvard Business Review*, 41(1):127–143, 1963.

do can be punished arbitrarily and severely. In various ways over the past 100 years or so, however, the unlimited authority of the supervisor has been eroded by limitations and restrictions. Properly applied, these modifications give each employee a measure of security and protection against the uninhibited use of power by a supervisor. But they also enable problem employees to take advantage of the proper use of enlightened authority.

Even if exceptions could be made and problem employees could be dealt with on a punitive basis, their basic problems would remain unsolved. Power cannot cure an alcoholic; threats are useless with an incompetent worker; and an anxiety-laden subordinate cannot simply "pull himself together" on order. The plain truth is that authority by force just doesn't work with problem employees.

How can management assist problem employees? What is the scope of its responsibility? How fine is the line, and where is it to be drawn between proper concern for the welfare of an employee and paternalistic meddling in personal privacy? To answer these questions, we must explore the ways authority frequently is, and can be, exercised to approach and resolve an employee problem.

Discipline: Authority by Fear The most conventional way of dealing with problem employees is by fear and punishment. The assumption underlying such action is that when an employee is threatened with punishment, he or she will modify behavior to make it more acceptable to management. There are two difficulties with such an assumption: first, the employee may be unable to modify personal behavior; and second, since discipline does not make contact with the cause of the problem, the modified behavior is likely to represent mere public compliance without the essential private acceptance. Thus, despite the disciplinary effort, the employee's problem will remain, even though he or she may learn to screen its more objectionable aspects from the manager's observation. The employee's responses to the problem can be manifested in such subtle or indirect ways as apathy, indifference, arguments with customers, illnesses, or even, in the more extreme cases, by sabotage.

The three traditional disciplinary weapons are:

1. A reprimand, which is a kind of oral attack on the employee.

2. Forfeiture of certain privileges, which is a form of social punishment symbolic of the stock in the village square.

3. Dismissal, which is the capital punishment of organization life.

From the employer's point of view, dismissal is the most effective form of discipline because by ridding himself of the employee, the company eliminates the problem altogether.

Isolation: Authority by Repression   Since discipline is a very painful process and since its advantages are often very ambiguous and since most supervisors find that its proper exercise requires skill, patience, hard work, and time, they prefer to use other means of dealing with problem employees. Unfortunately, there are not a great many alternatives available. The supervisor can scold, threaten, or ridicule an employee, but such measures, at the worst, intensify the objectionable behavior, or, at the least, have no effect at all.

Sooner or later, the supervisor realizes that there is really only one other way to cope with problem behavior which he or she usually seizes upon eagerly. This is to forget that the problem employees exist by sending them into exile, by isolating them, or by surrounding them with psychological or even physical screens that effectively hide these "problems" from view. The supervisor begins this venture by sending an innocuous request to the personnel department to transfer or to reassign these employees to work that is "more suitable" for them. Transfer, as a method of solving the difficulty, is very impractical because even in large, multiunit organizations, the word gets around fairly quickly.

The supervisor must then resort to the next best step—isolation within the work unit. The supervisor relegates the subordinate to a corner of the office or shop, to a shift or phase of the work that will assure him or her minimum contact with other workers and, most importantly, with the supervisor. This is the technique of putting a person "on the shelf."

By removing these employees and their troubles from his or her level of awareness, the supervisor has more or less successfully repressed personal anxiety. But as with other forms of repression, the strategy is never quite successful. Ultimately, the problem will have to be faced more directly and probably when it is far more complex and more acute.

Persuasion: Authority by Salesmanship   A very popular way of dealing with employees is to try to sell them. Like the hard-sell and the soft-sell methods of performance evaluation, this approach works with some highly dependent, uneducated employees. The supervisor attempts to talk these employees out of their problems or appeals to their loyalty to the company. But in the end, it comes down to the hard question of just who is selling whom. The outcome is usually frustration for the supervisor and a fall back to isolation or discipline.

Understanding: Authority by Acceptance   The only effective exercise of authority is that based on the problem-solving approach. The employee has to be accepted and his or her problem must be understood. To achieve these ideals, you must initiate a fourfold program:

1. You must recognize that a problem exists.
2. You must deal with it intelligently and empathically.
3. You must refer the employee to a specialist when necessary.
4. You must be prepared to assume complete responsibility throughout until the employee's performance improves or until he or she is removed from your jurisdiction.

Hopefully, by means of the problem-solving approach, your employee may view the difficulties objectively, acquire insight into the realities of personal behavior, and come to accept or to choose a practical, self-enhancing solution.

Admittedly this is no easy task, nor do we suggest that it is likely to work in a majority of the cases. It is, however, the plan that has the most chance of success. The arbitrary dismissal of a problem employee, his or her early retirement, isolation, punishment, or reprimand will be perceived by other employees as a vague but nevertheless real threat to their own security. It could happen to them. Handling a vexing case with patience, tact, and diplomacy but with firmness and surehandedness may not be successful, but it will undoubtedly affect the other employees in a very positive manner.

Many companies have adopted this approach with encouraging results. Some larger corporations have industrial psychiatrists on their staff. Many others have company chaplains to give personal and spiritual counseling to employees on company time. Still others have established highly effective programs for alcoholic employees.

One of the most unique applications of the authority-by-understanding approach, is the on-the-family counseling program of the Xerox Corporation in Rochester, New York. In 1973, 105 families took part in the program and another 125 were referred to other agencies for help.[5] The counselors, whose salaries are paid by the company and are from an outside agency, report that 54 percent of the cases dealt with marital problems, others dealt with parent-child relationships, the second most common complaint, followed by financial difficulties, and then by personal adjustment problems.

As a method of handling problem employees, authority by understanding is not universally accepted. There are those who contend that kindness may be costly to both management and the employee because to engage in activities that more properly belong to medicine and psychiatry is distinctly none of management's business. It has been argued further that our concept of counseling in industry places an undue burden on the supervisor whose only responsibility is to get the work out and not to engage in psychotherapy with each of his or her workers.

As a reaction to the more vapid human-relations approaches advo-

[5] *The New York Times,* February 25, 1974.

cated in some quarters and for one specific type of problem employee, the emotionally ill, these objections are sound. Employers must be wary of the dangers involved in treating employees who are, in reality, seriously ill. As a universal principle of action, however, such a hard approach can be as hazardous as a soft line. Levinson states that, within certain limitations, a manager can render extremely important help to others in the company as well as self-help by understanding contemporary psychology better and by appreciating the complexities of the human motivations which must be dealt with.[6]

How to Conduct Problem-employee Counseling Interviews

Unlike the interviews described earlier, it is impossible to lay down a pattern of interview behavior for each problem employee. Each varies with the nature of the problem, the personality of the employee and, above all, interview objectives. These elements combine to form a pattern of structural and functional aspects that are held together by the employee's problem. The best way to describe problem-employee interviewing techniques, therefore, is to treat the structural aspects of each major interview type separately.

The Structural Aspects of Problem-employee Interviews   There are four types of problem-employee counseling interviews: grievance, placement, personal, and disciplinary interviews.

THE GRIEVANCE INTERVIEW.   Employees with grievances are considered to be something a supervisor could do without. But they can be quite constructive for maintaining sound employee relations. The "gripes" give valuable feedback on production, operations, and employee relations, and they should be treated very seriously, and handled expeditiously and compassionately.

The first person to hear a complaint should be you, the immediate supervisor, but this should not be the only open door for an aggrieved employee. Sometimes you are neither able to resolve the problem nor to appreciate it. Or, you may be the target of the grievance. A company must designate a place, therefore, where employees can lodge complaints without fear of reprisal. This place is normally the personnel department whose reputation for independence, fair dealing, and action should be such that both employee and supervisor have complete confidence in it.

The grievance procedures we are concerned with are quite different from the formal grievance machinery established by a collective labor

6 Harry Levinson, *The Great Jackass Fallacy* (Boston: Graduate School of Business, Harvard University, 1973), p. 178.

agreement. Complaints presented in the latter context are likely to be formal requests for interpretation of the provisions of the contract as applied to specific situations. The grievance interview deals with the treatment accorded to the employee as a person. First, it represents a catharsis for the employee. After the complaint has been vocalized, it somehow never seems to be as pressing as it did while the employee mulled it over internally. Second, by describing it to an interested listener, he or she may sense its unreasonableness, or a remedy might suggest itself.

Even though a grievance may be unreal—"Someone in management is out to get me!"—it is no less disturbing and upsetting than a real one. An imaginary grievance is often more difficult to handle because nothing tangible can be accomplished to redress it.

Regardless of the nature of the complaint, prompt action must be taken. The most legitimate employee criticism of grievance procedures is that remedial action takes an interminably long time, so long that supervisors seem to bury themselves under piles of "red tape."

Grievances and complaints, however, are not necessarily an indication of low morale or of poor supervision. One study has demonstrated that unreasonable pressure for greater performance on the part of the supervisor was associated with great reluctance by the employees to take grievances or complaints to the supervisor. Hence, a lack of grievances may not indicate that everything is going well; it may simply indicate that employees deem it futile to complain.

A grievance interview follows the pattern already set down in other parts of this book. It usually begins with aggression or an emotional outburst. At this point all you can do is listen and help release the emotion and reduce the tension. Once the atmosphere has cleared, once the employee has worked through all inner tensions, you can examine the problem more rationally to determine the best course of action to follow. Often, the grievance that occasioned the interview will prove to be groundless, but a real one will emerge. Sometimes the grievance is easily handled; sometimes it will be impossible to do anything about it. With a proper interviewing approach, the employee can come to understand why this is so and is likely to accept it. The important fact will be that he or she obtained a fair, interested hearing, and action was taken promptly on a valid grievance.

THE PLACEMENT INTERVIEW. The placement interview with the disabled, the superannuated, or the obsolete employee closely resembles the career counseling interview described in the previous chapter except that the problem is more urgent, the employee is permanently ineffective, and the interview has been initiated by management because there is a clear-cut need for immediate action. Generally, in cases of this kind, particularly with long-service employees, the climate is characterized by procrastination, uncertainty, and indecision. No one seems to be willing to inform the worker that removal from his or her present job is imminent.

The attitude is quite unfair to the employee. When it becomes apparent that an employee is unable to perform the functions of a job which was once handled well, management must inform the person and deal with the problem as expeditiously as possible.

Often, employees will recognize first that they can no longer handle their jobs and that they are being carried by fellow employees. Such a realization is hardly calculated to enhance feelings of self-worth. If, in a nonthreatening, supportive atmosphere employees are encouraged to explore their problems with an understanding, empathic, and knowledgeable adviser, a practical plan of action can be charted that will enable them to leave their present jobs with dignity and with hope. This interview, therefore, is conducted in the same spirit and along the same lines as that with the employee who has career advancement aspirations. Through the counseling interview and emphasis on life goals rather than upon social expectations, the employee may decide to accept a position which, at first glance, seems to be less attractive than the present position, but which holds out the hope for the employee of becoming a more useful and consequently a happier corporate citizen.

In our culture, unfortunately, it is considered a disgrace to be demoted, and both workers and management abhor the concept. Nevertheless, it can be a useful social tool that should be utilized fully. Once the employee realizes that the social stigma is illusory and more than offset by the satisfaction of doing a job well, he or she will accept a demotion fairly readily. For more than one person, a voluntary demotion becomes a "promotion" because it has placed the employee on a career avenue to full use of personal ability.

You can make an important contribution to the personnel-utilization program just by the way you deal with placement problem cases. You must approach the employee with firmness and unequivocation but with tact, empathy, and skill, and in this way you help management fulfill its corporate responsibility.

THE PERSONAL COUNSELING INTERVIEW.   In dealing with personal problems, management must realize that it is doing so quite gratuitously because, unlike with placement problems, it has no direct corporate obligation. If these cases are approached cautiously, however, the employer can help. Counseling employees in personal difficulty is limited to two main actions: listening and referral. Your primary function is to permit the employee to speak freely and in confidence and to listen to what is said. Your second step is to refer the interviewee to loan specialists in banks, family counselors, and other social agencies or to special clinics or therapeutic agencies, depending upon the nature of the problem.

Management's most critical task is to become aware that these problems exist. Unless there is a competent counseling agency in the organization to which these problems may be referred, most of them will lie hidden in the dark recesses of the company. Supervisors must know where to send troubled employees and then allow a proper professional to carry on from there.

In the grievance, placement, and personal-counseling interviews, the object is to help the employee adapt to and adjust to the working environment so that he or she can make a constructive contribution to organization goals. Figure 23 illustrates a counselor's report with a problem employee having difficulty with the complexity of his present job and demonstrates the counselor's conclusions with respect to a program of action to enable the employee to utilize his ability more advantageously. The emphasis is on voluntary cooperation—the counselor effects reasonable changes in the employee's environment, and the employee of his own volition modifies his behavior. Sometimes a change is brought about, and sometimes it is not.

Inevitably, there will be occasions when stringent measures become necessary. When the employee refuses to cooperate voluntarily, then resort must be made to admonition, to warning, to threats, and to the imposition of sanctions. These are the substance of the court of final appeal—the disciplinary interview.

THE DISCIPLINARY INTERVIEW. The interview with the employee to inform the person that he or she has so violated the standards of organization behavior that corrective action must be taken is quite different from the preceding interviews. This encounter is primarily an information-giving medium, the explicit purpose of which is "for the record" just as a judge pronounces the sentence in a court of law. For the record, then, this interview is essential, for it may be necessary to produce evidence of it in an actual court of law or arbitrator's hearing at some future date.

In relation to the principles developed earlier, however, the implicit purpose of this interview is much more significant—to impress upon the subordinate the unacceptability of past conduct and to encourage the person to change it. To achieve this goal, you need considerable acumen, empathy, and interviewing skill. First, you must communicate clearly and unmistakably; second, you must, by interaction, "reach" the employee to convince him or her of the possibility and desirability of change; and third, you must minimize the natural resentment that will trigger defense mechanisms to reinforce the undesirable behavior. Inability to accomplish these objectives underlies the ineffectiveness of most punitive measures.

Even in the disciplinary interview for the record, you utilize the problem-solving approach effectively. In an interesting role-playing experiment, Maier and Danielson found that the human-relations approach

CONFIDENTIAL

PERSONNEL DEPARTMENT

COUNSELLING INTERVIEW FORM

Name___Mark A. Greene_____ Address_11 10th Street, New York, New York____

Department___Marketing_____ Unit No.__621____ Position Title_Staff Assistant__

Seniority in Grade___4/17/73___ Date of Employment___6/17/72___ Annual Salary__$13,500__

Date of Birth___5/22/50___ Referred by__A. P. Matthews, Director of Marketing_____

PURPOSE OF INTERVIEW

- [ ] Career Guidance
- [ ] Grievance
- [x] Transfer Request
- [ ] Employee Benefits
- [ ] Disciplinary
- [ ] Rehabilitation
- [ ] Personal
- [ ] Other_____
    Specify

Interview No.____3____ Supervisor notified [x] Yes [ ] No

SUMMARY OF PERFORMANCE

Areas Requiring Improvement _Interpersonal competence, Reliability, observation of organizational discipline._

THE INTERVIEW RECORD

Date of Interview ___4/15/75___

Today Mark announced that Management-Development has approved his request for transfer to Eastgate Plant to replace John Brown who has been promoted to Personnel effective May 4.

He seemed quite enthusiastic and optimistic about his chances in manufacturing, pointing out how well John Brown had done there and how friendly everyone seemed to be.

He believes his assignment to the Marketing Department was an unfortunate assignment, that he is not cut out for staff work.

I suggested that he examine his experiences in Marketing to determine whether his own behavior influenced his apparent lack of success. He admitted, grudgingly, that he is

Fig. 23 Counselor's report: problem-employee interview

to discipline was more successful than the judicial approach because it tended to satisfy foremen, shop stewards, and workers more and because it was more positively motivating.[6]

Discipline, in its original sense, means to educate, to prepare by instruction. Only by derivation does it mean to correct, to chastise, or to punish. The disciplinary interview in its proper form can be an edu-

---

[7] N. R. F. Maier and L. E. Danielson, "An Evaluation of Two Approaches to Discipline in Industry," *Journal of Applied Psychology*, 40:319–322, 1956.

THE INTERVIEW RECORD (Cont'd)

sometimes tactless, but attributes this to his desire to cut through the red tape, and "get the job done." Admitted too (but I don't know how convincingly) that he tends to look down on detail, as "dirty, grimy work." Attributes this attitude to graduate school where one always "paints with a broad brush." and sees the "big picture."

In his new job, he said, he was going to get right down to the last grubby item, to understand the plant better than anyone else. "You can't really understand some of the problems until you really dig in."

I suggested that he might reassess his relationships with people and try to understand and to appreciate their feelings. He felt this would be no problem because the minute he laid eyes on Mr. Bartholomew, acting like a "real manager", he took an immediate liking for him. "He's my kind of boss— straight and to the point."

The interview ended with a review of our previous conversations, analysis of his weak points and strong points. I also pointed out the final probationary nature of this assignment— that if there was no improvement in the next six months, management would have to ask for his resignation.

He brushed this last comment off with the remark that it really was superfluous.

Assessing the three counselling interviews with this young man and in the light of his previous record, it is this interviewer's opinion that the outlook is not hopeful for any real change in job behavior.

Signature _Carl P. Wright_

cational medium if you have sufficient self-confidence and maintain an objective, guilt-free attitude. You can instruct an employee on the propriety of imposing penalties and explain why it is necessary to warn him or her of the imminent danger of even more serious sanctions. Because of its implications, you must transmit your message in no uncertain terms. You cannot mumble or double-talk. Your message will generate noise that will distort both its transmission and reception. Words of one syllable are not only desirable but essential.

While redundancy is valuable, there is such a thing as overcommunication. Do not belabor the subject until the interviewee is completely deprived of self-respect. Try to strike a proper balance between criticism and encouragement so that the employee can recognize the gravity of the situation but also may feel he or she can change, wants to change, and believes that you will help facilitate the changes.

The disciplinary interview is conducted only after all other remedial efforts have been exhausted. It forms an integral part of an overall written disciplinary procedure and is clearly understood by all. If an offense is such that an employee's retention is absolutely out of the question, the disciplinary interview should be brief and, depending on the employee's wishes, confined to the facts. In some cases, you may wish to counsel a dismissed employee to guide him or her toward a better work attitude. But, of course, the interview then is not so much a disciplinary as a personal-counseling interview.

The Functional Aspects of the Problem-Employee Interview   In a symposium on the impact of psychiatry on American management, Frederick Roethlisberger pointed out the role conflict experienced by the average American manager in dealing with problem employees.[7] Referring to it as "role shock," he said that the rational system within which the manager is required to order daily activities is in basic conflict with the social model which his or her conscience as a citizen impels the person to acknowledge. As a problem employee interviewer, you, too, unconsciously suffer role shock—the need to carry out the demands of the rational order but, at the same time, to experience the conscience, the feelings, and the moral sense of one human being dealing with another. The result is conflict, and since conflict breeds anxiety, to be effective, you must control it.

This would not be so difficult if you were dealing with a normal, well-adjusted human being with adequate ego strength to appreciate and to accept your ideas in a rational, detached fashion. But since the problem employee is usually troubled, he or she is also very anxious.

These are the very people who tend to resist social influence the most and who are the least susceptible to communication effects. This resistance will interact with your role shock to create a negative feeling in you as you conduct the interview. This negative set has a decided influence on interview effectiveness.

NEGATIVE INTERVIEWER SET.   Negative interviewer set refers to the emotional tone and the vague sensations that you experience which

8 F. J. Roethlisberger, "The Scientific and the Administrative Approach in Administration: The Relation of Ideas to Practice," in *The Impact of Psychiatry on American Management*, reprint series no. 129, New York State School of Industrial and Labor Relations, Cornell University, Ithaca, N.Y., 1962, pp. 26–30.

influence your conduct of the interview. There are five reasons for these sensations:

1. *Excessive self-blame.* Negative feelings usually are based initially on guilt, whether real or imagined. If you happen to be the supervisor, you will feel, with or without justification, that you somehow are at fault. Since employees must defend themselves, they are likely to behave in ways that confirm this ill-defined guilt feeling. The more you become convinced that you are to blame for the situation, the more negative and uncomfortable you will feel.

2. *Overidentification.* Guilt feelings lead to overidentification with the problem employee, to sympathy instead of empathy. You project yourself into the employee's position so that instead of appreciating the other person's feelings, you experience them. Because you must cope now with your own anxiety, your effectiveness is sharply reduced.

3. *Fear of strong emotion.* As the tension builds, you become apprehensive worrying that the interviewee may erupt into a fit of anger or tears. Since the American culture frowns on public emotional display, you experience a heightened sense of self-recrimination and embarrassment.

4. *Defensive need to justify yourself.* You then try to allay your discomfort by justification and self-defense. This unconscious need to obtain an acknowledgement from the interviewee that regardless of what has happened, you are not to blame is self-defeating because it does no more than reinforce your anxiety. If you take pains to suggest that the interview is more difficult for you than for the interviewee, that you wish you did not have to go through with it, and that you are doing your job, you will substantially undermine the interviewee's confidence in you. To ease your conscience further, you may act out one final fantasy, the typically American desire for a happy ending to every problem.

5. *The need for a happy ending.* If you approach every problem-solving interview with the fixed idea that, somehow or other, every obstacle can be overcome, that things always turn out well in this "best of all possible worlds," you are bound to be frustrated. Unjustifiable optimism is another way of repressing feelings of self-blame and of avoiding strong emotion. The foreknowledge that many interviews will have an unattractive ending is not likely to encourage very many interviewers to undertake them. Even some apparently triumphant endings will, on later observation, prove to be hollow victories. And even when an interview does turn out well, you will receive little credit for it.

THE POSITIVE APPROACH. To be effective, you must take steps to neutralize these feelings to develop a realistic attitude toward the problem-solving interview. This is also a five-step process.

1. *Take stock.* As a first step, take careful inventory of those feelings

that affect you the most. Do you have a compulsive wish for a pleasant ending? Are you overwhelmed by the need to defend or to justify yourself? Are you repelled by the thought of strong emotion? Or are you inclined to overidentify? By careful analysis, determine what bothers you the most in this type of situation.

2. *Live with your feelings.* After determining what bothers you the most, accept it and learn to live with it. As you adopt this attitude, you will find that your discomfort will abate.

3. *Study role implications.* Having accepted your feelings, study the role implications of being a consultant, counselor, or adviser to identify any conflict implicit in the job you have to do. By sorting out the actions appropriate to each role, you can behave in ways that build rapport and reduce self-centeredness.

4. *Be honest.* During your interview, be open, honest, simple, and direct. Do not equivocate by using such weak terms as "maybe," "but," or "perhaps," do not pass responsibility on to others or apologize in any way. If an emotional storm appears on the horizon, let it come, weather it, and try to give your best to help the employee with all your interviewing skill.

5. *Set clear limits.* Finally, recognize the very definite limits on what you can accomplish in a problem-solving interview. The situation may be at such a stage of deterioration that the interview cannot be too constructive. By your listening skill, communication ability, and knowledge of the situation and of management's responsibility and resources, you can be of substantial assistance to the employee; but at the same time, accept your limitations and don't try to exceed them.

Problem-solving interviewing, no matter what type, evaluation, counseling, grievance, or disciplinary, always leads you back to the selection process. When a good job of selection has been done initially and when the employee is suited for the job held, the problem-solving interview will be confined either to performance evaluation with a highly effective subordinate or to a career-counseling interview to guide the employee to a more rewarding, more meaningful position. Inadequate selection techniques breed interviews with problem employees and ineffective subordinates.

part 4

Information-exchange Interviews

Since the interview is basically an information medium, it can also be a vital component of the management communication network. When employed in such a direct way for the sole purpose of exchanging information, it is so relatively uncomplicated that the interviewer plays almost the same role as a questionnaire, a tape recorder, or a computer—almost, but not quite. The information that passes from source to destination over the interview communication system is far more complex than a mere electric impulse, a binary code, or a printed word and is far less tangible than a sound, a light beam, or a stroke of the pen.

The information passing through an interviewer ranges from vague feelings to intense emotions, from subtle attitudes to forthright convictions, each idea being quite different in outward manifestation but all sharing a common property of communicability only through the medium of a human being.

The information-exchange interviewer in the personnel management context represents a direct line between the employee and the management over which vital information can be exchanged. If the interviewer is competent, more reliable, accurate, and meaningful data become available to those responsible for the direction of the enterprise, and employees receive more detailed information that they must have to do their jobs properly.

Because of its unique message capacity, the information-exchange interview is an invaluable management tool. Although in purpose it is quite simple, the content of the information interview can be elusively complex. There is the ever-present danger of "overloading the circuit" by attempting to send or to receive too many bits of information unless "suitable equipment" is installed to carry the message load. This combination of complex content in simple context poses a trap for an unwary interviewer unless the information potential of the medium is understood.

The next three chapters, therefore, merit careful examination by those entrusted with the responsibility of establishing and maintaining an organization information system. In these pages we offer suggestions for the proper utilization of the information-exchange *interview in those personnel situations where it can do the most good for the total manpower and industrial relations program.*

Readers not immediately concerned with this specific application of personnel interviewing can still profit from careful attention to the next three chapters. Since every personnel interview contains information sharing as one of its basic elements, the supervisor, the counselor, and the employment specialist must also be adept at giving and getting accurate information via the interview.

chapter 15

Information-getting:
The Employee Survey Interview

So many men, so many opinions; his own a law to each.
—Terence, *Phormio*

A leading American corporation recently engaged a consultant to undertake a comprehensive study of its personnel activities. The corporate officers were intensely aware that their firm was in deep trouble. All the symptoms of employee malaise were there—excessive absenteeism, high short-term turnover, supervisory frustration, difficulties in recruitment, employee apathy, low productivity, and increasing customer complaints about the quality of the services they were receiving. But the senior and middle executives were mystified by the situation because they had made sincere but fruitless efforts to deal with the problem.

The consultant first conducted an extensive survey of the situation by collecting a great deal of relevant data, by compiling trends concerning employment activities—new hirees, transfers, promotions, and terminations—interviewing the officers, key managers, and supervisors in considerable depth, and administering an attitude questionnaire to a representative sample of employees.

After careful analysis of all relevant data, the consultant concluded that the situation was far worse than the company management realized. The corporation was in an advanced stage of what Rensis Likert describes as long-range organizational deterioration.[1] While many deep-seated difficulties and long-standing problems were uncovered by the study, the most glaring deficiencies unearthed were the two wide and deep communications chasms stretching on the one hand between senior management and first-line supervision and on the other between supervisors and the rank-and-file employees. First-line supervisors, for ex-

---

[1] R. Likert, *The Human Organization* (New York: McGraw-Hill, 1967), pp. 84–91.

ample, asserted that they were well aware of and appreciated *their* subordinates' job difficulties, but that senior management knew little and cared less about supervisors' problems. The nonexempt employees reported through the attitude survey that it was almost impossible to bring a grievance to the attention of a supervisor, and that even when they did, little action followed.

This corporation's inadequate employee communications is hardly unique. Blake and Mouton found that 74 percent of the managers sampled in their study cited communication breakdown as the single greatest barrier to corporate excellence.[2] The reason is not hard to identify. The establishment and maintenance of an integrated information complex require the utilization of many channels—oral, aural, and visual—each with its own unique applicability and special effectiveness.

Information must not only be handed down the levels of authority but up too. A communication complex must contain adequate retrieval mechanisms to provide for what Ralph Shaw calls "current awareness" and "retrospective research."[3] The valuable information that top management needs to make intelligent decisions always exists in the "memory drums" of its employees, many of whom are walking encyclopedias of information about day-to-day business affairs. But this information has to be retrieved to be useful, and this task is very hard.

Passing information up the channels of command is very much like trying to counter the force of gravity. It is easy to drop a heavy weight to the ground from the fifth floor of a building, but considerable effort and energy must be expended to move the same weight from the ground floor back up to the fifth.

Yet, as Fenn and Yankelovich have pointed out, it is impossible to exaggerate how healthy a planned system of upward communication for companies is, if it is carefully fashioned and sanely implemented.[4] In this chapter, we shall explore the elements of a healthy communications system that is structured around the supervisory-subordinate, face-to-face interview discussed in Part 3.

Communicating with Employees

Two basic principles apply to the management-communication model. First, communication is most effective when it is oral and face-to-face. A survey of corporation presidents showed that they preferred oral over written channels to transmit very important policies.[5] When the chips

---

[2] R. R. Blake and J. S. Mouton, *Corporate Excellence Through Grid Organization Development* (Houston: Gulf Publishing Co., 1968), p. 4.
[3] R. R. Shaw, "Information Retrieval," *Science*, 140:606–609, 1963.
[4] D. H. Fenn, Jr. and D. Yankelovich, "Responding to the Employee Voice," *Harvard Business Review*, 50(1):83–91, May–June 1972.
[5] P. E. Lull, F. E. Funk, and D. T. Piersol, "What Communication Means to Top Management," *Advanced Management*, 20(3):17–21, 1955.

were down and it was really important to find out what was really happening in the enterprise or to make sure that instructions were being transmitted accurately, they depended upon oral, face-to-face communication.

Second, an organization's main line of oral communication is the supervisor-subordinate channel. There are substantial grounds, however, to suspect that this channel is either misused or "rusted" from disuse. It is often poorly regarded and bypassed. One observer, A. S. Hatch, put it this way: "Feedback does not normally run through the supervisor-employee channel, for the filters in the line of communication are all funnel-shaped with the big end toward the top. Expecting communication to flow up through the line organization is comparable to directing a stream of water through the small end of a funnel."[6]

The Need to Know   Although the need for effective communication is vital to the operation of the whole corporate structure, we are concerned only with its use in the personnel management field. There is a formidable enough job to be done there. The history of the American labor movement is testimony to the problems that emerge from communication failure between management and employees. In the survey referred to earlier, nearly 80 percent of the presidents felt that there was a positive relationship between communication ineffectiveness and labor disputes.

A successful personnel and labor relations program, on the other hand, is based on a foundation of continuous and free information exchange between management and employees. In such a climate, the management group makes decisions with current awareness of what is happening in its enterprise and the employee groups labor under no false impressions of their respective roles in the corporate structure or their contribution to output and the consequent profit picture.

Today no true manager doubts these assertions, but faith and the need for communicative effectiveness do not guarantee its attainment. Management needs to know what information it must share with its employees. The question is, therefore, how can essential information be transmitted to employees and retrieved from them? This is indeed a good question that must be answered if we are to place the information interview in its proper perspective.

There are many things that happen in and to the average company that need to be known by members. It is the purpose of the communication network to pass these data around. One can assume that everyone does, in fact, know what is happening because the information is avail-

6 A. S. Hatch, "The Line Approach to Industrial Communication," in *The Personnel Function: A Progress Report*, Management Report 24 (New York: American Management Association, 1958).

able in official orders, circulars, and directives, in newspapers and business journals, in reports and memoranda.

The real manager, that is, one who is in constant and immediate contact with the realities of his or her operation, wants to know very definite things about what the employees are doing and wants them to know some very specific facts about corporate life. To achieve the former, the manager collects such personnel statistics as attendance, accident, termination, and promotion rates, reasons for and locations of terminations, community salary scales, and average hours worked. To reach the latter objective, he or she then reports facts about corporate finances, the company's plans and hopes for the future, and its rate of economic growth and progress to the employees.

But a real manager has to share more than facts alone with employees. He or she must have accurate information about employee opinions, feelings, and beliefs and must know why men work, what they hope to get out of it, and what they think of the company as a place to work. This information is not easy to come by. Surveys have repeatedly demonstrated that while foremen believe their subordinates work primarily for money, employees report that they work principally for recognition and appreciation.

Employees must understand management problems too. Studies underline their ignorance of the needs and the intentions of management personnel. To offset this unrealistic impression, management must give employees honest information about the reasons for decisions and clearly define corporate objectives and the assumptions upon which company policies are based.

True managers study employee attitudes and value systems. Top management should understand, for example, the basic employee attitude toward the free enterprise system, toward business ethics, and appreciate the employees' reasons for loyalty and allegiance to particular reference groups in the social system. It may be grossly false to assume that a worker's loyalty remains primarily with the union simply because of the economic protection that it affords. In any event, it is a matter of the utmost urgency for management to recognize the truth about employee attitudes, to know really "what makes the employee run."

The information obtained is necessary first of all to evaluate the efficacy of employee policies and programs. This information establishes a knowledgeable basis for intelligent collective bargaining and skillful contract negotiation. It is also helpful to design or revise programs for increasing employee morale and to help reduce costs, not only direct labor costs but overall costs stemming from waste and inefficiency.

The employee's need to know stems simply from the necessity of doing a job well, particularly when learning it. The employee also needs to know so that he or she may identify with a specific work unit and become part of the team. Without knowledge of the group of which he or she is a member, the employee cannot merge interests with it sufficiently to develop the feelings of ego involvement so essential to high morale. Ego involvement assumes effective job performance and, ultimately, job satisfaction.

Ways of Knowing The media for sharing information between management and employees cover a lot of ground and include oral and written messages; person-to-person, person-to-group, or group-to-group communication; and both formal and informal methods of getting the word around. For convenience, we shall lump them all into three very broad categories.

ONE-WAY MESSAGES. Modern management has developed and perfected a broad array of one-way communication media designed to transmit messages speedily to large numbers of employees. Some of these media are bulletin boards, employee newspapers, policy manuals, booklets, pamphlets, films, filmstrips, conventions, seminars, plant houseparties, and even public address systems over which a president may address the whole company. Such media have their purposes and their places in the corporate design and, if used correctly, are effective within their limitations.

Upward communication is often facilitated by attitude and opinion surveys and questionnaires. Suggestion boxes, "speak-up" columns in the plant newspaper, or "What I think about my job" contests are other examples of one-way upward information channels.

SMALL-GROUP MEETINGS. The obvious shortcoming built into one-way mass communication media, the absence of feedback opportunities, has forced American management to devote increased attention to another popular method of information sharing—the small-group meeting. Management by committee is now such an accepted fact of life that administering the modern corporation or government agency has become a problem of small-group leadership. A study of the structure and the customs of the average industrial or public enterprise will undoubtedly conclude that its dominant cultural trait is the exercise of responsibility through small-group control. Committees of four, five, six, or more executives and other officials situated at the apex of the pyramid and usually referred to as a "board of directors" or "cabinet" determine organization policy and objectives. Underneath this group there are found countless other committees and specialized task forces, staff groups, and clusters of people meeting informally for information-sharing and problem-solving purposes. Even in the labor union, shop committees and executive boards are key directional groups.

As a communication channel, the committee has become so vital to society that increasing scientific attention has been devoted to its processes. This led, for example, to the birth of "sensitivity training" and its extension to organizational development. In "training laboratories". and "management grid" programs, businessmen, educators, and social workers explore the inner anatomy of raw group processes to identify such phenomena as "hidden agendas," "invisible committees," and "nine-nine" management for the purpose of learning how to communicate more effectively in small-group situations.[7]

Other small-group communication techniques include the formation of special councils of workers and managers, "cracker barrel" meetings for first-line supervisors, and the formation of junior boards of directors.

THE INTERVIEW.   In a study of his company's internal communications, Louis Gelfand found that employees preferred to get information from their own supervisors.[8] Their responses indicated that too much information was coming from "the grapevine." The personnel interview is management's answer to the grapevine. It provides unparalleled opportunities for two-way communication, for immediate feedback, for the redundancy that makes certain that a message gets through. Because of its formal structure, it carries the aura of authority, and can be directed at pinpoint targets. Because of its transactional characteristics, it has an unlimited information capacity.

Although its use in the management communication network are many and varied, the interview also has distinct limitations, among which are the facts that it is time-consuming, expensive, and requires skill in application. But when it is vitally important to secure or to disseminate accurate and correct information, the one most-effective medium to do this job is the personnel interview. The fact that it is very often not effective is due to the lack of understanding and finesse with which it is employed. Referring to the President's study cited earlier, it is significant to note that they listed as the top three causes of "communication breakdown," inadequate use of communication media, lack of communicative ability in management personnel, and inadequate training programs.

But most importantly, the interview is the ideal way of facilitating communications between supervisor and subordinate. If it is supplemented by other communication media, including periodic and systematic sampling of employee activities, it will serve as an effective antidote to the ever-present, sometimes useful, but mostly pernicious "grapevine"—the informal communication network.

THE GRAPEVINE.   If the normal channels of communication break down or operate inefficiently, the word will still get around speedily and

---

[7] For an excellent review of these approaches see R. R. Golembiewski and A. Blumberg (eds.), *Sensitivity Training and the Laboratory Approach* (Itasca, Illinois: F. E. Peacock Publishers, Inc., 1970).

[8] L. I. Gelfand, "Communicate Through your Supervisors," *Harvard Business Review*, 48(6):101–104, Nov.–Dec. 1970.

efficiently, if not accurately, through the medium of the grapevine. Even where the communication network is healthy, the grapevine, as a phenomenon of organization life, usually carries information of a class that cannot pass through ordinary channels because it is spiced with colorful gossip, rumors, and half-truths that appeal to the emotional, fantasy-loving side of the average person. The more astute managers learn to take care of, to feed, and even to use the grapevine to good advantage. But it always remains a potentially dangerous mechanism that can backfire painfully.

Through the embedding process referred to in Chapter 2, the information that passes over the grapevine is leveled and sharpened. Important but prosaic details change or are lost, colorful aspects grow and increase in emotional implication as the original tale wends its way through the labyrinth of "information relay stations" from unfounded source to credulous destination.

The most effective way to control the grapevine, to keep it at a level of harmless "chit-chat," where common sense can recognize it as the medium of the interesting but the fantastic, is to provide a counter-system of interpersonal, face-to-face communication.

Determining Employee Attitudes

Information gathering is at the heart of every personnel interview. An employment interviewer can make the proper decisions if he or she obtains an accurate description of an applicant's character and previous life history; a counselor can advise an employee only after soliciting information to determine the substantive nature of the client's problem; a supervisor can improve a subordinate's job performance only by giving feedback on the way the person's job behavior conforms to company norms. But when the personnel interview is intended solely to collect or to give information, its information capacity, its modes of communication, and its unconscious errors must be reckoned with even more carefully. Since the collected information is summarized in such a way that the immediate sources lose their identities and a whole series of inferences must be drawn from the now anonymous data, the process by which this raw information is obtained must be rigorously examined and controlled. This is the essence of the science of determining employee attitudes.

Personnel management's concern with the termination interview is not based on the assumption that the departing employee is the most accurate information source of worker opinions and attitudes. Every personnel specialist agrees that the views of those who choose to remain on the job are more representative; but it is assumed that this information is far less accessible. The socioeconomic myth that, unless quitting, the average employee is afraid to express candid opinions about the job and the company is still very much alive today. For management to remain indifferent to the thinking and the feelings of its current employees is not only short-sighted, but also self-deluding. Even in smaller companies, where the work force is less anonymous and amorphous, top management should employ formal methods to assess the motives, the ideas, and the aspirations of its employees because these forces can have a critical impact on organizational effectiveness and output.

There is likely to be little argument with such a contention. But agreement on this point merely introduces the larger questions of where, when, and how to obtain the data, and how to recognize them when one has them. They exist in great abundance; management is anxious to seek them out; employees are eager to furnish them; but all sorts of obstacles, misunderstandings, and frustrations lie in wait for the naïve manager who attempts to collect them without careful planning and full awareness of what he or she is doing.

The Importance of Employee Attitudes   In a company's everyday activities, a surprising amount of employee relations feedback is turned up and left lying around unnoticed and unused because there is no plan for its systematic retrieval. When facts are assembled spontaneously, usually only bits and pieces of the total picture are used; the gaps are filled in with assumptions, hypotheses, and plain garden-variety biases. If the resulting patchwork is generalized to the overall employee population, the end product can be quite misleading. Many personnel managers have discovered to their chagrin that isolated stories, reports, or incidents do not necessarily provide a sound basis for appropriate inferences about employee attitudes.

Take, for example, the following sequence of events. An irate worker visiting the personnel office to discuss a grievance against a supervisor reports that fellow employees are equally unhappy; later, on the same day, a worker in a different unit quits abruptly; still later, a supervisor in a third unit fires a subordinate for insubordination. The personnel manager, in assuming that the three events are more than coincidental, concludes that first-line supervision is deficient in human relations skills.

More careful, more systematic investigation would have painted a far different picture by revealing that the first worker was a maladjusted, chronic complainer, the second received an unexpected appointment to the local police force and was ordered to report at once, and the third deserved firing months ago. The real underlying condition is not arbitrary and autocratic supervision but rather uncertain, lenient, laissez-faire leadership.

Valid conclusions can be drawn about employees' knowledge, feelings, and attitudes only when data are assembled by means of an organized approach that is an integral part of a broader upward communication system directed at two broad classes of information: what is actually happening in the here and now, and what lies beneath the surface that indicates what will happen in the future. To stay on top of the employee relations situation, the capable personnel manager must *know* not only what employees are doing but what they are thinking.

WHAT ARE THEY DOING? Now all executives worth their salt believe that they certainly know what their employees are doing at any given moment. The elaborate systems developed along traditional lines to report financial, sales, and production data keep them continually informed of what is going on. The trouble is that these yardsticks of employee output measure only part of the total organizational activity.

The astute manager takes additional measures to discover what is really happening within the walls of the plant or office. This manager makes provision for the compilation of factual and statistical information concerning terminations, absences, accidents, transfers, visits to the company doctor, waste rates, grievances, disciplinary actions, counseling interviews, and even suggestions dropped into the suggestion box. Further, the manager will be sensitive to every scrap of factual data, whether it comes from a supervisor, personnel manager, plant physician, or union delegate, that might develop insight into what is going on in the work force.

WHAT ARE THEY THINKING? Determining what has happened is, in a sense, an ex post facto exercise that omits the important question "why?" The answer to this question lies deep down in the feelings and attitudes of workers toward their working conditions, their supervision, their job duties, and their company management. Whether management adopts a hard line or a soft line toward its employees, whether it believes in the human relations approach or not, it simply has to have this information to function efficiently. One way of obtaining it is, of course, to simply imagine it; another is to infer it from the financial statement or the profit and loss sheet. A better way is to ask the employees themselves through an employee survey, a device that is nothing more than a formal method of mirroring the thoughts and feelings of employees about their jobs, their company, and its people.

Employee Attitude Surveys An employee survey is no idle pastime. When a company conducts one, it tells its employees that their ideas and their points of view on matters that affect them are wanted, and it promises them action on those items that dissatisfy them. This commitment has deterred some companies from undertaking the survey; the failure to honor it has destroyed employees' faith in many others.

Understanding the employee survey and its place in the overall communications system requires a brief look at the mechanics of making one. The first issue concerns the information sought.

ATTITUDES VERSUS OPINIONS.   Up to this point, we have been careful to qualify the employee survey by either the adjective "attitude" or "opinion." First, we refer the reader to the clear-cut distinction made in Chapter 2 between the two types of information, opinion and attitude. We classified opinions as subjective data because they refer to responses involving preferences or tastes, matters not likely to be so strongly held by respondents. We classified attitudes, however, as subconscious data because they are partly recallable, are interwoven in the worker's total personality, and have the most profound influence on employee behavior.

Because they are more consciously accessible and because a person feels less need to defend them, opinions are much easier to sample. By their nature, attitudes require more careful probing and deduction, and the results are subject to considerable error. The failure to make this important distinction has marked many survey attempts and accounts for their lack of acceptance as bona fide management controls.

For example, a company may obtain a wide range of opinions about the quality of the food in the cafeteria, the traffic flow in the parking lot, the value of safety shoes, or the need for a more liberal hospital plan. But such surveys afford no valid conclusion concerning the level of employee morale. To infer a degree of job satisfaction, which represents a positive attitude toward the total job, from a cluster of opinions that refer to employee preferences and tastes is a highly unreliable practice.

Often, however, the distinction between the two can prove to be academic because a more factual investigation may yield enlightening results concerning the amount and quality of the information possessed by employees. In a survey to be described in Chapter 16, new employees reported a very favorable view of the way they were treated in the orientation program, but their retention of the information conveyed to them was remarkably low.

SURVEY PROCEDURES.   Employee surveys are conducted to give management a clear idea of employee beliefs and, hence, probable responses to a wide range of policies and practices. When properly conducted, they underline policies that may be troubling employees, problem areas, communication breakdowns, and may suggest ways to improve job performance.

When employee surveys are conducted periodically, as they are in a number of companies, a tight, short lag in the feedback cycle is provided that enables management to cope with many problems before they grow costly and unmanageable. Conducting a survey is so complex that its full explanation does not belong in this chapter. The objectives of the survey have to be clearly established; the coverage, scope, and cost must be determined; and decisions should be made on such matters as which employee groups to include in the study, the type of techniques to adopt, whether consultants should be used, and the content of the survey topics.

Types of Survey The most common ways to survey employees are by the written questionnaire or the personal interview.

QUESTIONNAIRES. Being the most frequently used method of surveying employees, the questionnaire poses a series of items to which the employee responds by choosing one answer from a designated group, or by filling in a blank space with a few words. This method is a straightforward, direct way of obtaining information. It is a sophisticated measurement device, however, that requires substantial expertise to construct, administer, score, and interpret. The construction of a questionnaire is no job for an amateur, and even the professional has moments of self-doubt. The fundamental problem centers on the respondent's ability to comprehend the intent of a question. As with an objective test, it is assumed that the respondent understands perfectly the intention of the question. This assumption is far from certain. Although in a well-tested questionnaire a majority of the respondents will comprehend the intentions of the majority of the questions correctly, there are always a few who will misinterpret a "good question," and there will always be a few questions that the majority of the respondents will misinterpret. These distortions increase the error of questionnaire results and decrease their validity.

Since there is no way of reducing the transmission errors, the results of every survey conducted through a written questionnaire contain a systematic error that is either small or large depending on the competency of the survey specialists. Despite these problems, many companies administer questionnaires varying from a few questions hastily put together to a carefully planned and pretested instrument based on well-thought-out research designs. The major reason for this choice lies in the fact that the anonymity of the participants is preserved. How much of an advantage anonymity gives an investigator is debatable. The fact that the questionnaire assures the respondent that no response, regardless of how derogatory, or critical, or caustic it is, can be traced to its source appears to many investigators so important as to override any other selection factor in determining the survey instrument.

Despite the opportunity the questionnaire provides for free, frank, and anonymous responses, this method of surveying employees contains many difficulties. As an "open letter" to management reporting how employees feel toward significant aspects of their work situation, its chief limitation lies in the amount and the reliability of the information it elicits. A questionnaire constructed so that it will be interpreted uniformly by a large number of respondents will exclude an opportunity for individual expression that frequently provides valuable insights into employee attitudes. The solicitation of the latter kind of information must be reserved for a second survey tool, the personal interview.

INTERVIEWS. The survey interview mines the richest deposit of employee feeling when it is conducted by a skilled interviewer who understands the extensions and the limitations of this instrument. No assumptions have to be made about the questions included in the interview. After explaining briefly the purpose of the survey, you let the respondent speak freely. You obtain qualitative as well as quantitative information. With the opportunities to note emotional tone that accompany specific replies, you add another dimension to your findings—the depth of employee feeling about that topic. The most important advantage, however, lies in the feedback potential that permits you to phrase and rephrase your questions to make sure you are sharing the respondent's ideas. You can ensure that you are reporting the interviewee's thoughts and feelings of the interview accurately by the techniques of clarification, testing, and summarizing.

While the interview has many advantages as a means of obtaining employee opinions, it also has its disadvantages. Because it takes time, it is expensive; a survey interview may last an hour and, in many cases, longer depending on the depth to which you probe. Because the information obtained is qualitative, it is not amenable to the statistical treatment that provides convenient analysis and presentation.

This interview method is also subject to the unconscious errors described in Chapter 2. And since its value consists in the degree to which it reflects the subject's mood, emotional tone, and feeling intensity, the results are often submitted in a narrative style that makes interpretation more subjective.

Finally, since interviews are time-consuming, they frequently have to be conducted with a sample rather than with the whole population. Such a survey is more prone to sampling bias and error.

The richness and depth of the responses obtained by the interview can outweigh these objections. In a comparative study of questionnaire and interview, Jackson and Rothney found that the latter not only elicited significantly more complete answers than a mailed questionnaire, but a fourfold qualitative increase in the data for which the survey was initiated.[9]

The interview can be used most profitably to obtain preliminary information upon which to construct a written questionnaire. This will

[9] R. M. Jackson and J. W. M. Rothney, "A Comparative Study of the Mailed Questionnaire and the Interview in Follow-up Studies," *Personnel and Guidance Journal*, **40**:569–571, 1961.

ensure the inclusion of the more pressing concerns of employees. The interview and questionnaire techniques, therefore, are most artfully combined to provide maximum information getting.

Of course, in smaller work units every employee can be interviewed without the disadvantages cited above, and the questionnaire may be eliminated. In either smaller or larger surveys, the interview represents an important adjunct to the management information system.

How to Conduct a Survey Interview

As we have already indicated, the situational aspects of the survey interview are necessarily so detailed and diverse that we can treat them in only the most cursory fashion. If you plan to conduct such a survey, you are urged to consult other sources in the literature before trying your hand at this most complicated bit of personnel business. Since we consider the exit interview to be one of the most important applications of the survey technique, however, we'll have to consider some of its unique features in this book.

The Structural Aspects   The survey interview is unlike any other interview we have discussed so far. The relationship between the interviewer and the interviewee is reasonably neutral. In fact, the advantage is with the interviewee because he or she possesses information that the interviewer wants. But more importantly, nothing personal is likely to ensue from this encounter. The structure and the functional relationships of this type of interview are, therefore, quite unique.

CONTEXT.   The context of the survey interview includes consideration of the reasons for the survey, when it is to be conducted, who will do the interviewing, and who will be interviewed.

WHY.   The purpose of the survey interview must be clearly stated so that everyone understands why it has been proposed. The statement of purposes must declare explicitly that the survey findings will be shared with all who participate. Interviewees will speak candidly only when the interview is conducted in an open and frank climate.

The purpose of the interview may be general, that is, inaugurated to determine whether there are any grievances about which management is ignorant, or it can be specific, that is, undertaken to determine how employees feel about a particular situation, problem, or policy that has come to management's notice in one way or another. In either case, employees should be told enough to motivate them to communicate without influencing what they might say.

WHO.   After a careful formulation of survey objectives, the next most critical question is the determination of who conducts the interview. It is generally believed that outside consultants are best because they will be neutral and are emotionally uninvolved in the survey subject matter. An outside consultant represents no threat to the respondent and the information elicited will be of little personal interest to the interviewer. Because the consultant might be insensitive to many of the interviewee's more oblique references, on the other hand, he or she may miss significant undertones that have implications for employee job performance and job satisfaction. Because these by-products can outweigh the anonymity, it may be preferable for a member of the organization to conduct the interview. Such a person must not only be familiar with the customs and mores of the company but must also be able to inspire confidence in employees and permit them to speak frankly. The selection of such a person is an individual matter; preferably, the personnel-department representative can play this role. The only one definitely ruled out would be an official who occupies a position of authority in relation to the interviewee.

WHEN. The when of a survey interview is an easier question than the who. It is quite obvious that a survey of employee opinions must be conducted on company time, and most companies, when using the interview method, do schedule the interviews during working hours. When the questionnaire method is used, some companies ask the employee to complete it at home on his or her own time, a request that often defeats the purpose of the survey because it plants in the mind of the employee the suggestion that, if the company takes so dim a view of the procedure that it is unwilling to spend its own money to obtain the information, it cannot be important.

WHERE. It is essential to conduct the interview on company premises but not normally at the employee's desk, bench, or work space. Since there must be an atmosphere of privacy and dignity, the interview must be conducted in an area apart from the interviewee's normal work place, and out of the hearing of fellow employees.

WHOM. The determination of whom to interview has a significant impact on results. It is not enough to ask the foreman to send several employees to the interviewer or to select the first ten workers who enter the plant cafeteria. Systematic sampling methods must be followed so that each location, occupational group, and level of the employee population is proportionately represented in the experimental group. Of course, within location and occupational-level cells, the interviewees are chosen on a truly random basis to insure that the survey is not biased in favor of one group or another.

CONTENT. The content of a survey interview includes all information dealing with an employee's view of his or her job, its surroundings, its rewards, coworkers, supervisors, and subordinates, personal opinions of communication, reasons for working, beliefs about management, and even the worker's convictions about the free enterprise system. Most often, however, surveys concentrate upon three main areas.

Work. Questions in this category are directed at workers' attitude toward the content of their work—the interest they display in it, the satisfactions they derive from it, the opportunities for growth and realization of life goals, the degree to which it challenges their ability, and the opportunity it affords for self-expression.

People. The relationship between workers and their supervisors and coworkers is the second broad area covered. Questions may be directed at the employees' opinions of the direction and assistance that they get and do not get, the necessary information about their jobs that is given to them, the frequency, the quality, and the effectiveness of the discipline and correction they receive, and the credit, recognition, and praise for work well done that they obtain. This category often covers their relationships with coworkers, and their cooperation and support of one another.

Environment. The psychological and physical job environment constitute a third area for investigation. This dimension measures the employees' attitudes toward various elements that go to make up the total job environment: *rewards* such as pay, fringe benefits, or opportunities for promotion and development; *tangible elements* such as office layout, furniture, or expense accounts, and *intangible elements* such as the prestige and reputation of the company.

Many surveys dwell almost exclusively on these broader environmental questions, even though most recent findings tend to suggest that in the formation of a positive attitude toward the work situation, they are often the least influential.

Total. An overall attitude toward the job can be roughly estimated by adding together an employee's responses on each of the three dimensions. But this "total" must be qualified by the degree of importance each person attaches to each dimension. In any survey, it is necessary to ascertain the degree of significance a particular item has for a particular worker.

If an employee achieves a high score on the "work" dimensions, it means that he or she finds the job to be stimulating, but a low score on this dimension does not necessarily mean that the person is dissatisfied with the job. High scores, on the other hand, on the "people" and "environment" dimensions are not necessarily associated with a favorable attitude toward a job, but low scores on these two dimensions usually indicate that a person is unhappy with his or her present job.

But the true measure of satisfaction or dissatisfaction is best obtained by noting a discrepancy between the "importance" score, that is, the degree of significance a particular job factor has for the employee, and the "opinion" score, that is, the extent to which the employee feels personal expectations are being realized. Substantial discrepancies between the "importance" score and the "opinion" index on each dimension are indicative of the employee's disposition toward the job. A high "importance" score, for example, coupled with a low "opinion" score on the environment dimension, represents a high degree of dissatisfaction.

Functional Aspects   The structural components of the survey interview differ little from the survey questionnaire; the purpose, the people sampled, the content, the when, and the where all remain substantially the same. But what really marks the interview as a unique tool in the effort for meaningful information are its functional characteristics— the influence of the highly particular and individual role relationships and the dynamic quality of the personality interaction that ensues.

ROLE RELATIONS.   The dominant, overriding attributes of the survey interview, the quality that sets it apart and distinguishes it from the problem-solving interview, is its function as a measuring tool. As we have already mentioned, you as a survey interviewer are not a problem solver, a counselor, a disciplinarian, or a decision maker; you are a communications medium: a living, walking, talking questionnaire.

Your role determines not only the character and the dimension of your behavior during the interview but explains why, as a supervisor, you cannot conduct it. Your role also identifies a major problem that you must deal with. The problem is referred to by psychologists as "membership salience," the degree to which your role behavior triggers in the interviewee the reminder that he or she is a member of a particular group with specific norms which must be adhered to. If in your behavior, dress, or speech you project a high degree of salience, you will remind the interviewee continually that you represent a management group and that he or she must respond in a way that group members would approve. The reference group that becomes salient for the particular person will vary—it may be a bowling team, a union, a church, a veterans association, or just a morning coffee group. The information obtained, however, will not represent the interviewee's own thoughts, ideas, or beliefs. To minimize the effect of group salience, you have to employ "counter-norm communication," that is, to speak and to act in a way that will indicate, perhaps unconsciously, to the interviewee that there is no need to respond according to the group's values but that each individual can speak as he or she really thinks and believes.

You may wish to learn how employees feel about the automation of certain occupations in the plant, for example, and how best to retrain the displaced workers or to transfer them to other departments. The employee is unlikely to depart from the official union position or what is perceived as the group's attitude unless you convince the person that replies are being sought from each individual as a respected, independent thinker.

Some investigators are so wary of the problem of reference group salience that they have devised indirect methods of probing for employee attitudes. General Motors, for instance, launched a "Why I like my job" contest a number of years ago to find out what its employees were thinking. In his study of job satisfaction, Frederick Herzberg rejected the more conventional approach to attitude assessment and asked each respondent to describe incidents in his or her working life that were particularly satisfying and others that were especially dissatisfying. In this way, Herzberg could infer the situations and conditions that made for job satisfaction and dissatisfaction.[10]

PERSONALITY INTERACTION.   The success of the survey will depend on the personality interaction that occurs in the interview. Although your demeanor must be neutral, you can, by the quiet feelings of encouragement, by the force of your personal interest and empathy, and by your appreciation of interviewees' uncertainty, help them speak more fully and frankly. Always remember, however, that interviewees' responses are not necessarily true and accurate reflections of their innermost thoughts. Since it is quite possible that their opinions are really not their own but those of someone else, you must take into account respondents' suggestibility, emotional set, willingness to cooperate, and ability to articulate ideas. This is the major advantage of the interview as a survey tool—a subject's responses can be tested for sincerity and reliability as they are transmitted, can be discarded on the spot, and if necessary, you can deepen your probing to get true feelings and opinions.

Conducting the Interview   Except as modified by the unique characteristics of the survey, an employee-opinion or -attitude survey interview follows the pattern for the interview described in previous chapters. Preparation plays a more important and significant role, however; months of planning, testing, and experimental interviewing may have preceded the actual interview.

Before the actual interview, notify the employee of the time, the place, and the day that he or she is to be interviewed. To establish rapport, begin the interview by convincing the employee of the standards to be followed—complete confidentiality, freedom of expression, permissiveness, and your desire for his or her views.

To establish the proper climate, discuss the interviewee's feelings about the interview. Ask how the person feels that day, why the interviewee thinks he or she is there, what is his or her general opinion of the survey, and whether the person's participation is willing or unwilling. In this way, you draw the interviewee unobtrusively into the conversation by permitting the person to discuss personal events, feelings, and opinions. When you feel that rapport has been established, move into the interview's main sequence.

[10] F. Herzberg, *Work and the Nature of Man* (New York: World Publishing Company, 1966).

Begin with a broad, comprehensive question that focuses upon major interview objectives. You can build subsequent questions on the interviewee's responses. If the interviewee cooperates by speaking freely on the topic, you will only have to keep an eye on the time to be sure to cover your interview plan.

Be as informal as possible, using words understandable by the respondent. Use jargon unique to a specific craft as long as the terms are understood by the interviewee, but be quite certain of your terminology. Otherwise, you are apt to be marked as insincere and a "phony." Word your questions carefully so as not to suggest an answer. In particular, avoid leading questions. To guard against these errors, test your questions in advance. A question such as "Do you think your supervisor knows the technical details of his job?" is suggestive. Better questions are "What are your supervisor's strong points?" or "What do you think of your supervisor?"

Phrase questions to include one central idea—double questions are tricky and misleading. For example, the question "How do you think we can improve cafeteria food at the prices we charge?" is confusing and misleading. The respondent will not be sure you're asking for an opinion about the quality of the food or the prices. (One serious difficulty with the written questionnaire is the fact that many questions are influenced by preceding and succeeding questions that suggest an answer.) Needless to say, trick or catch questions are completely out of place.

To avoid direct questions that give the appearance of an interrogation, substitute, wherever possible, declarative statements. Instead of asking "What do you think of the overtime policy?" say "Tell me what you think of the overtime policy."

Even though this is an information-seeking interview, stress the interview techniques of clarification, testing, and summarizing. As with the termination interview, you may have to work through some emotional behavior on the part of the interviewee—especially hostility, anger, or resentment—before you can get to task-related matters.

Survey interview data has to be recorded in a standardized format. If a completely standardized style is employed, have a prepared checklist in front of you as you ask questions.

The content of this interview makes it quite natural to take notes during the conversation, but a structured interview report form, that is, one that combines a checklist with provisions for free comments, is most helpful. One thing is certain—the interview data must be recorded as soon as possible. A delay of even five minutes may alter the results appreciably.

After all the information has been collected, end the meeting with friendly dispatch. Reassure the interviewee that what was said will be held in confidence and that it will not affect employment status in any way. As a final note, invite the employee to ask questions or to add any additional comments that he or she may feel will be helpful to the survey.

In a well-planned, efficiently administered survey, many essential activities begin when the interviews are concluded. The data have to be reviewed, summarized, analyzed, coded, tabulated, reanalyzed, interpreted, evaluated, and reported. All of this is quite beyond the scope of this chapter, but to put the interview in perspective, a word or two is in order concerning the follow-up of survey results because it refers to a commitment that must be made by the interviewer.

Following Up Survey Findings   Following up survey findings is the key to subsequent interviews. When the final results have been compiled, the manner in which they are acted upon determines the success of future surveys. Effective follow-up of the type that convinces employees that the survey was sincere will include two major phases. First, the findings must be reported to the participants and to all employees who knew that the survey was being conducted. Besides a bulletin, a pamphlet, or an article in the employee newspaper, good feedback involves additional personal interviews with some or all of the participants, and it most certainly requires group meetings with all.

The survey findings are reported briefly, meaningfully, and simply, but truthfully and in language and symbols that the recipients can understand. Overburdening employees with statistical tables, charts, or graphs that are hard to fathom is a way of confusing the results. Unless they are strictly necessary, eliminate unnecessary details and use pictorial material wherever possible to help employees comprehend what they said to management. Many an otherwise effective and useful survey stumbles at this point because the final report looks like the annual federal budget to the average employee.

The second and final phase of the follow-up procedure is more difficult because it entails the adoption of the suggestions made by the survey participants or the remedying of conditions about which they complained. Even though the recommendations may be difficult or expensive to put into effect, it is quite essential that an effort be made because management is now "on the hook." The whole communication, and perhaps the entire employee-relations program, is at stake. When employees are confident that what they tell management will be treated with respect, that action will follow, they will be always ready to pass on to their supervisors accurate and valuable information. And this, after all, is the ultimate goal of the information-exchange interview program.

As a way of collecting information, the interview can be quite efficient and hence invaluable; it can be used effectively to locate and to identify situations and conditions affecting the lot of the employee group and to form the basis for more astute employee relations decisions.

chapter 16

Information-giving: Orientation and Coaching Interviews

> There is nothing makes a man suspect much, more than to know little. —FRANCIS BACON, *Of Suspicion*

Because of the tendency to consider the interview solely in terms of fact-finding, information-giving interviews are among the more neglected aspects of the art of management. In fact, many supervisors and personnel managers hardly ever think of the interview in this context. The results of one study, designed to find out how much new employees had learned about their companies when they were hired, how much they learned in the early days of employment, and the nature of their attitude toward the orientation process, were quite revealing.[1] The study showed that although new employees reported that they had received adequate information about their jobs and had been treated well, actually they were quite ignorant of such personally important details as the amount of vacation to which they were entitled, when they might expect a salary increase, and even the most elementary details of the health insurance program. The study also found that many respondents knew less three months after employment than on their first day of work.

In the same study, fifteen companies with a total employee population of approximately 90,000 reported orientation practices varying from a minimum of one forty-five-minute session during the first two weeks of employment to a full-time, two-week course. Most programs, however, tended to be less than one day in duration. The companies unanimously reported that their new employees did not remember much of the information given to them, but no company was quite sure of the direction in which to move to improve this situation.

The inadequacies reported in this study point up the hazards involved

[1] Enid F. Beaumont, *The Induction of New Employees into The Port of New York Authority* (New York: The Port of New York Authority, 1961).

in relying exclusively upon the efficacy of mass communication media to teach employees. In view of the inability of people to learn and to retain a mass of new details quickly, it becomes apparent that an effective employee instructional program must include the interview. This interview cannot be treated as a routine, matter-of-fact clerical procedure; rather, it must be considered a delicate responsibility involving the introduction of a person to a new climate and into a new culture.

The Interview as a Method of Instruction

It is fairly safe to say that most employers give little thought to the idea of the interview as an instructional medium. The reasons for this state of affairs are obvious enough. First, the average company is loaded with pamphlets and training manuals that describe in detail everything that employees need to know about their job, their company, and the benefits of working for it. All they have to do is read them. Second, training is conceived of as a group activity, in terms of a teacher standing in front of a class, of demonstrations, drills, exercises, lectures, guided tours, panel discussions, and conferences, but rarely as an individual encounter between supervisor and subordinate. Third, when it is apparent that a person-to-person approach is required, the information-giving function is frequently turned over to an "experienced" older employee who "knows the ropes."

The difficulty with these reasons is that most employees do not read the literature given to them by their employers, and even the few who do fail to comprehend or to retain what they have read. As for training, there are subjects and situations that cannot be taught effectively in a group. And finally, the experienced older employee all too often is either so untutored that he or she passes on the same old errors and misinformation or, lacking skill in instruction, is unable to get any message across to the pupil save indifference and the advantages of mediocrity.

The interview, therefore, is one of the tools by which management gives each employee, from unskilled worker to executive, the information needed to do a job effectively. The interview fits into this program when the interviewer knows how to impart ideas to another person and understands the need in information sharing of interaction and motivation.

If we view the interviewer as a private tutor and the interviewee as a pupil, the information-giving interview closely resembles the Socratic method of teaching, in which, by astute questioning, the teacher takes the pupil down the road to new learning. The particular advantage of this method consists in the opportunity it affords the teacher to consider the individual and unique problems of the pupil and to progress according to the pupil's learning speed. The group teacher must adopt a pace regulated by what he or she estimates as the class mean learning rate. Since no single student will learn at exactly the mean learning rate, the teacher's pace will be too slow for half the class and too fast for the remaining half.

Another feature of classroom learning is the inhibition of students' questions. Even though a particular point in the instruction may be unclear, a student will probably hesitate to ask a question for fear of interrupting the class or of being exposed to possible ridicule by the other students. Because of its privacy and the rapport established, a student interviewee will feel more free to ask for clarification of what has been said, to express doubts, and to discuss the personal implications of the subject matter.

These propositions may seem obvious, but it is surprising to note how frequently they are overlooked. New employees are inducted and instructed in the duties of their jobs principally through classroom techniques; changes in company policy and practice are announced via such mass media as bulletin boards and house organs; and older employees are instructed on new equipment by means of technical manuals and short lectures by service representatives. It is no wonder that the individual worker fails to comprehend what management wants to convey. Since even human nature abhors a vacuum, the inquisitive employee will turn to other sources for tutoring. In the informal atmosphere of the locker room or cafeteria, highly unofficial but nonetheless effective information-giving interviews will be conducted by other employees. Given the opportunity to discuss personal problems, employees will acquire inaccurate information to form a distorted image of the idea that management hoped to transmit to them.

The information-giving interview is not a substitute, of course, for other media of communication. It complements them and is most effective when used in conjunction with the other media. But there are at least two situations where the primary information medium *must* be the interview: the orientation of new employees and on-the-job coaching of current employees. Before considering how such interviews are to be conducted, we must examine briefly the significance of employee instruction.

The material presented in Chapter 4 on the learning process applies equally to the coaching interview. Here, it is necessary only to mention briefly some unique objectives and conditions that are involved in the information-giving interview.

Ego Involvement and Employee Placement   We have already discussed why an individual worker, who is suited for a specific job, can fail to do that job well. Such failure may be due to inadequate instruction, to poor supervision, or to personal problems, but in each case the person's ineffectiveness will be characterized by a lack of interest in what he or she is doing. Human interest in a particular task or set of duties is called by many names, all loosely applied, including instinct, appetite, drive, or motivation. The phrase we use to describe this positive attitude toward a job is "ego involvement." In the words of Gordon Allport, ego involvement is "a condition of total participation of the self as knower, as organizer, as observer, as status seeker, and as socialized being."[2] Its presence or absence makes a critical difference in job performance—without it, the worker will fail; with only a partial ego involvement, a worker will achieve at best only a consistent level of mediocrity.

In a study of oil refinery and electronic workers, Victor Vroom lends support to this assertion.[3] He reports that workers ego-involved in their jobs are rated higher than non-ego-involved workers by their supervisors and that the opportunity for self-expression which the ego-involved workers enjoy gives them greater satisfaction with themselves and their jobs than non-ego-involved workers.

An employee rarely becomes ego-involved in work without help from management. The employer must take steps to provide the employee with formal and continuous assistance with the problems of adjustment to the group—problems that will occur inevitably to every employee whether in one of the highest perches on the organization chart or down below in the ranks of the unskilled. We term this management responsibility for personal assistance and interest "placement" because it represents the ongoing adjustment of the worker to the demands of the job and because it is a continuing process that extends throughout the employee's career. It begins the very first moment an applicant visits the employment office to inquire about a job, and it continues throughout his or her employment career, extending even into retirement.

In this book we have discussed other aspects of the placement function—selection, performance evaluation and counseling. In this chapter, we shall deal with the orientation and induction of employees and their on-the-job coaching. Ego involvement with the job depends upon the information-giving process simply because apathy and indifference have their origin in the employees' ignorance of the things they are expected to know but actually do not. This ignorance is due primarily to the fact that they were poorly instructed, misinstructed, or were never instructed. Speaking of the plight of the ignorant, John Henry Newman said "Few, indeed, there are who can dispense with the stimulus and support of

---

[2] Gordon W. Allport, *Personality and Social Encounter* (Boston: Beacon Press, 1960), p. 78.
[3] Victor H. Vroom, "Ego-involvement, Job Satisfaction, and Job Performance," *Personnel Psychology*, 15:159–177, 1962.

instructors . . . and next to none, perhaps, or none, who will not be reminded from time to time of the disadvantages under which they lie. . . ."[4]

What Is Instruction? To understand the dynamics of the information-giving interview, you may try a little experiment that should take no more than ten minutes. All you need is a multicolored, detailed magazine illustration, a tape recorder, and a friend. Ask your friend to listen as you describe the picture, shielding it so that it cannot be seen and cautioning your friend that he or she will be expected to repeat the description shortly. Explain that he or she may ask questions during the description until satisfied that all the necessary details have been grasped.

Then turn the recorder on and describe the picture. Immediately after the description while the tape recorder is still recording, ask your friend to repeat what was said. When this task has been completed, show the picture to your friend as his or her description is replayed. You will observe two interesting results.

First, your friend will probably express amazement at the difference between the mental image of the picture and the actual picture. Second, after comparing the picture, your description of it, and the subject's reproduction of it, you will note many discrepancies among the three versions. Some of the disparities will be amusing, particularly if your friend's recollection is listened to by a second friend who repeats the process and relates what he or she has retained. Many details will thereby be lost in the succeeding reproductions, others will be exaggerated or embellished, and possibly many details will have been added.

This experiment illustrates the embedding process referred to in Chapter 4. It exemplifies the basic hazards that must be overcome in the information-giving interview, and unless you happen to be skilled in this type of exercise, it will illustrate most of the mistakes made by information givers.

RETENTION. Your ability to retain information is much more fragile than you realize and far less durable than you assume in your daily conversations. Laboratory experiments show that forgetting begins to take place almost as soon as something is learned, that the retention of nonsense items is much more difficult than meaningful material, that memory of an event is weakened by succeeding events that interfere with the original learning, and that it is easier to remember the first things learned than similar things learned later.

In experiments similar to that just cited, most information givers, anxious to give the listener as many details as possible, tick off the

[4] J. H. Newman, *The Idea of a University* (Garden City, N.Y.: Image Books, Doubleday & Company, Inc., 1959), p. 168.

objects and people in the picture in laundry-list fashion without relating them to each other and without organizing them meaningfully. Since the instructor perceives more details than he or she can possibly convey, the listener receives an incomplete series of poorly related "nonsense" words. Consequently, the listener fills in the gaps from personal experience, and the result is a caricature rather than a faithful reproduction of the original picture.

Management does not ordinarily require employees to memorize nonsense material, but such tasks as learning company rules, names of officials, job titles, and job functions may constitute for a new employee a "nonsense" or irrelevant learning task. Since he or she must somehow put meaning into the assortment of items that seem unrelated, the employee will do so in a way that tends to blur some of the details, to stereotype others, and to cause the parts retained to resemble objects and events already personally familiar. The final product, now, will be only a small and unrecognizable version of the learning that management was hoping for.

And what is worse, the subject matter may now be repugnant to the employee. Robert Mager says that an important goal of teaching is to prepare the student to use the learning and to learn more about the subject which has been taught. To reach this goal, the tutor must send the student away from the learning situation possessing a tendency to approach rather than to avoid the subject matter taught.[5]

To be an effective information-giving interviewer, you must clearly recognize that your subject can absorb and retain only just so much information and that which you want retained must be presented as meaningful, relevant, and interesting data to the interviewee. Use the interview, therefore, as a two-way communication process requiring the employee to feed back to you what has been heard so that you gauge how well you have transmitted your message.

LOGICAL EXPOSITION. Present the information in a logical sequence, proceeding from what the interviewee is familiar with to what he or she does not know and what is, therefore, quite unfamiliar. The use of the word "orientation" to describe the information-giving interview with a new employee is particularly appropriate, but it is also apt in every instructional interview. The employee must literally be *oriented*, that is, placed in a correct position with respect to the landmarks familiar to a personal mental landscape of known ideas. Once the person has his or her bearings, then the purpose of the new information being conveyed can be understood and the employee can proceed on the journey into the new and unfamiliar with a point of reference to what is already known.

[5] R. F. Mager, *Developing Attitude Toward Learning* (Palo Alto, California: Fearon Publisher, 1968), p. 5.

It is a common yet highly undesirable practice, for example, to explain the workings of the profit-sharing, pension, or hospital insurance programs to an employee on the first day on the job. Unless the person happens to be an actuary or an insurance analyst, he or she will be so overwhelmed by the information, so unable to relate it to what is already known, that little of the new information will be retained, and what is remembered will be grossly inaccurate. It is wiser to mention merely that there are attractive benefit plans available that will be explained in detail at another time when the person is ready to understand and appreciate them. A month or two later, when the employee has settled down on the new job, he or she can be taught what is necessary about these subjects.

Proper learning takes place only when the person is ready and motivated to learn. The "learning set" of the employee is another important aspect of this information-giving process. An applicant is more concerned with the requirements of a prospective job, its salary, and whether he or she will be hired than about the details of the pension plan or the company bowling team. After being hired, the person will be ready for and interested in more details about the new job and company. Logical exposition therefore calls for the orderly presentation of information in a meaningful, interrelated fashion to a learner who is ready and willing to comprehend it. When utilized in this fashion, the information-giving interview is a thinly disguised version of one of the oldest and still one of the most effective forms of teaching.

The Orientation of New Employees   The necessity of a formal employee orientation program is best illustrated by reference to a type of learning known as *imprinting* that is peculiar to such animals as ducks, geese, lambs, and other herd animals. "Imprinting" is the name given by psychologists to the early responses to vocal and auditory stimuli that an animal learns. A gosling, for example, learns to follow its mother around a few hours after hatching. If an experimenter substitutes a decoy for the mother at the time imprinting ordinarily takes place, the young bird will imprint on, that is, learn to follow the substitute. Such imprinting, however, must be learned at the right time in the bird's life, or it never takes place. Since all animals seem to have a critical period for their behavioral development, it is logical to suppose that human beings also have periods that determine the direction of their social, intellectual, and emotional development.[6]

If we think of new employees as newly hatched birds, we can visualize them as ready for imprinting, that is, ready to learn whom to follow for advice and guidance in their new situation. If they are imprinted on

---

[6] See J. P. Scott, "Critical Periods in Behavioral Development," *Science,* **138**:949–958, 1962.

a fellow employee or on a union official instead of on a supervisor or other management representative, they are likely to follow such a guide throughout their employment. Since experimental data suggest that the critical period for development is fairly specific and concentrated in early life, it is quite apparent that management must imprint new employees promptly, or else the opportunity will have been lost permanently. This is a cogent reason for new-employee orientation.

Reporting to a new job is an emotional experience, and impressions obtained under such conditions are generally quite lasting. Most people, each of us in fact, can recall vividly our first day of work or at any rate can remember it better than most days. The thrill of reporting to the new job in a new organization, the enthusiasm and the interest stimulated by this new experience, the desire to succeed, the hope of meeting congenial workers—all these aspirations and emotions can be molded into firm qualities essential to an efficient, satisfied, and loyal employee if the person is greeted warmly at the outset, is treated courteously, handled efficiently, and informed in logical sequence of the many things he or she needs to know about this new job in this new company. If, on the other hand, the new employee is welcomed perfunctorily, instructed indifferently, and required to flounder around to learn such essentials as where to hang his or her coat or where to find a suitable place to eat lunch, the person's original enthusiasm will be dampened considerably and the seeds of a cynical, skeptical attitude will have been planted.

Careless reception is less erroneous, however, than viewing the situation as an "indoctrination" procedure. There is an important distinction between indoctrination and orientation. The former implies an effort to mold the new employee to the corporation's point of view. Failure of most "free enterprise profit" stories in company magazines amply testify to the average employee's tendencies to reject all efforts of indoctrination.

Orientation implies acclimatization and adaptation. Without being actually aware of it, a new employee suffers from what anthropologists call "culture shock," an experience similar to that of being a traveler in a foreign country. The removal and the distortion of the familiar elements to which the person is accustomed in a home environment and their replacement by other people, places, and things are unsettling and uncomfortable.

New employees feel uncertain and ill at ease, and need reassurance to help them get their bearings in this new "country," the company environment.

Objectives The first objective of the orientation program is to provide a new employee with a pleasant atmosphere in which to adjust to the new surroundings. Since an employee is most impressionable at this early stage, it is important to help him or her form positive initial attitudes toward the company and to perceive it as a warm friendly neighborhood rather than a cold, indifferent wasteland or, perhaps, a menacing jungle.

A second objective is to establish the feeling that the employee really belongs and is a member of the work group. Feeling welcome, a person is apt to adopt attitudes that conform to the group and will be more disposed to receive, understand, and accept communications from management. When a genuine interest is shown in the employee, a reservoir of goodwill can be built up to offset the inevitable disappointments that are met in any job.

A third objective is to alleviate anxieties and to motivate and prepare the new worker for the learning that is to take place over the next few days, weeks, and months. It is well to bear in mind that to a new employee the job is apt to be, in the words of William James, "blooming, buzzing and confusing." The consequent insecurity and bewilderment will serve as effective mental blocks, preventing the person from learning the very things that must be known.

PROGRAM PHASES.   To discuss in detail the mechanics of a comprehensive orientation program is naturally beyond the scope of this book, but to place the orientation interview in proper perspective, we must sketch the broad outlines of a program in which it may be embedded.[7]

Ideally, there are four phases to the proper introduction of an employee to a new job in a new company. The first phase takes place in the employment department itself and begins when the applicant meets a company representative, is selected for a job, and is given, bit by bit, information about the job, the company, and its benefits.

The second phase begins when the new employee reports to his or her supervisor and to the immediate vicinity of the new job. Here the person meets fellow workers, learns where to eat, where to wash up, where to hang a hat and coat, and all the personal details that make working pleasant and convenient. During this phase the new employee decides whether he or she is going to be happy in the new job, and it is also at this point that the informal orientation conducted by fellow workers begins.

The third phase consists in the more extended program conducted by the company training unit, usually in formal classroom instruction, and lasting over a period of weeks and in some cases, months. In these sessions, the employee is given more elaborate information concerning company policies and products, employee benefits and privileges, and a word or two about recreational and social activities. The fourth phase

---

[7] See Joan E. Holland and T. P. Curtis, "Orientation of New Employees," in J. J. Famularo (ed.), *Handbook Of Modern Personnel Administration* (New York: McGraw-Hill, 1972), chap. 23.

consists of a final interview with the employee by a personnel counselor at the end of the formal orientation period which varies from job to job but usually covers a six-month period. In this last phase, the employee is given final details of some of the more complex aspects of the working environment that the person is now, hopefully, ready to assimilate; the newly initiated employee is also given an opportunity to discuss personal problems that may have arisen during the first six months of employment and that, now that he or she has become acclimated, an employee may wish to discuss.

There is a great deal of variation in the order in which this information is presented to employees in individual companies. The most general practice provides for a formal orientation interview on the first day of employment, conducted by an employment interviewer. In this interview the new employee receives a brief explanation of compensation, fringe benefits, and working conditions, enrolls in the company insurance program, authorizes deductions for union dues, lockers or uniforms, and completes the information that is required by the paymaster to put him or her on the payroll.

The employee then reports to the supervisor who greets him or her and conducts another orientation interview in which the requirements, the responsibilities, and the local ground rules of the working environment are discussed. Sometime later in the month the employee is asked to attend a group meeting lasting from two to eight hours in which he or she views films, hears lectures, is taken on a plant tour, and is instructed in various company-wide affairs affecting all new members of the organization. Then, finally, after six months, when it is assumed that the "new" employee has completed the probationary period, has a thorough understanding of job routines, and is considered to be an "old hand," he or she reports to the personnel department for individual counseling. The counselor may be a member of a training unit, or of the employment department, or from a counseling section—the point is that the employee is given full opportunity to settle personal problems, and at the same time, the counselor is able to gauge how well the employee has been oriented.

Conducting the Information-giving Interview

The instructional or coaching interview, then, is a focal point where management encounters employees, engages their interest, helps them with their learning problems, teaches them appropriate job behavior, and develops in them effective work habits and healthy job attitudes. In the orientation program, there are really three or four interviews: the first, conducted by the employment specialist after the applicant is hired; the second, conducted by the supervisor when the employee reports to the job site for the first time; the third, conducted by a department head or a general foreman a bit later on; and the fourth, conducted by an employee counselor months later when the employee has hopefully absorbed the complex details of the operation, philosophy, and organizational structure of the company. In such a sequence, the new employee receives necessary information at the appropriate time when he or she is ready for it and can relate it meaningfully to what is already known. The same logic holds true, of course, for any job-coaching or instructional interview. You must realize that the learner can accumulate information best if it can be related to previous learning. Information must be prepared in a lesson-plan form, reducing it to its simplest elements. Then it must be transmitted in a way that permits full opportunity for feedback. The art of job coaching lies in the tailoring of instruction to individual needs and in a question-and-answer format that binds teacher and learner into a single unit. A personal, almost intimate, relationship is thereby developed in which rapport can be established and in which the learner can form an attitude of trustful dependency on the teacher. When the interview approaches this stage of engagement, it becomes an effective method of instruction.

PREPARATION.   As with any interview, adequate preparation is a most important part of the information-giving interview. You must construct a lesson plan containing instructions, objectives, an outline or checklist of the information you wish to convey, the sequence in which you will present it, and references, audio-visual aids, and other material connected with the instruction. Suitable visual aids are particularly helpful, but they must be designed specifically for the interview setting. They must be desk or table size so that you can employ them naturally when you wish to illustrate a point, and they should blend into the interview area so that they will not appear artificial or distracting. Prepare reading and other home-study material to hand to the interviewee at the appropriate moment and explain it carefully when it is transmitted. Pamphlets, employee handbooks, rule books, and instructional manuals that are given to the learner at the wrong time or with little or no explanation usually remain unread.

The time and the place of the interview also affect the learning that takes place. Job-coaching interviews often must be conducted on the job site; orientation interviews are held in a place that is most conducive to learning and is free from interruptions and distractions. Conduct neither the supervisory nor the personnel department interview on the first day of employment because the employee is usually too excited and too confused to listen attentively. On the first day, it is better to welcome employees, to introduce them to supervisors and coworkers, and then to tell them that an interview will be conducted a few days later when they have had a chance "to settle down."

The Main Sequence   Although the information-giving interview is a teaching situation and your role is strictly that of a tutor, the interview departs markedly from the classroom atmosphere in flexibility of approach and in its relaxed, informal atmosphere. By your interest, enthusiasm, and skill, you encourage the learner to ask questions, to make comments, and to express personal reactions. And this is not so easy to do. Often, you are so accustomed to conducting such sessions that your material becomes stale and "old hat" to you. Unless you are careful, you are apt to present your information in such a rapid-fire fashion that it will assume the trappings of a sidewalk salesman's patter. Noting the canned approach, interviewees will feel that they have to play the game too by simply going through the motions of appearing to be interested in what they are obviously not learning. Since they now have the well-merited impression that the interview is no more than a formality to be undergone strictly for the record, employees' interest will dissipate and no learning will take place.

To be effective, each interview has to be as fresh and as different as possible from the preceding ones. The only way you can possibly do this is to center your attention on the learner's background and problems. Since these will differ from learner to learner, your interview is bound to be personally appealing.

Begin the interview with a discussion of some aspect of the learner's personal life history. As explained in earlier chapters, a friendly, sincere interest in the learner always helps to establish rapport quite quickly.

Next, guide the conversational flow to the task functions that have to be worked on. Introduce each subject logically with a series of questions to ascertain what the interviewee already knows about it. This tends to avoid repetition and establishes a foundation on which to build new ideas. For example, if the health insurance program is to be explained, you can begin by asking new employees what they know about group health insurance, whether they have been enrolled in a plan previously, or whether they have ever applied for benefits under a plan. Using this knowledge as a point of departure, slowly increase the employees' interest in this otherwise prosaic subject by personalizing it as much as possible. A young person, for example, is not apt to be interested in the details of a life insurance program, but the subject may be introduced by discussing first the provisions of the plan for conversion to a regular policy upon marriage.

It is also wise, wherever possible, to let employees express the new learning in their own words. Experiments in communication and persuasion strongly suggest that communication, comprehension, and retention are enhanced by eliciting verbalization from the learner.[8] An

[8] Carl I. Hovland, Irving L. Janis, and Harold H. Kelley, *Communication and Persuasion* (New Haven, Conn.: Yale University Press, 1953), p. 215.

ORIENTATION CHECKLIST

NAME ___John M. Brown___   Medical Exam Date 3/16/75

CLASS No. __1900__   TITLE: __Management Trainee__   Starting Date 6/17/75

DIVISION __Management Development__   DEPARTMENT No. AND NAME __721 - Personnel__

PHASE – A – Personnel Department   DATE INTERVIEWED 6/19/75

PENSION PLAN ___5_% HOSPITAL PLAN RATE _individual_   LIFE INSURANCE RATE $20,000

☑ APPLICATION COMPLETE   ☑ SECURITY CLEARANCE   ☑ RETIREMENT AUTHORIZATION
☑ FORM 1320 COMPLETE   ☑ CIVIL DEFENSE OATH   ☑ SAVINGS BONDS
☑ MILITARY SERVICE VERIFIED ☑ W-4 FORM   ☑ BENEFIT AUTHORIZATION
                            ☑ IDENTIFICATION CARD ISSUED

☐ DATE AND PLACE OF BIRTH VERIFIED FROM _Birth Certificate. City of Worcester, Massachusetts_
                                                     Document

☐ SCHOOL OR COLLEGE COMPLETION VERIFIED FROM _College Transcript - State University_
                                               Document

INDUCTION INTERVIEW. POLICIES EXPLAINED: Date 6-19-75

☑ FIRST PAY DAY   ☑ SOCIAL SECURITY   ☑ LIFE INSURANCE
☑ HOLIDAYS   ☑ RETIREMENT CONTRIBUTIONS ☑ PARKING LOT
☑ SICK LEAVE   ☑ HOSPITAL - SURGICAL
☑ VACATION   ☑ MAJOR MEDICAL

COMMENTS: _Mr Brown will require assistance in obtaining an apartment, now living in YMCA; plans to marry in September; requested two week leave of absence without pay; promised as a condition of employment_ Signature _James Andrews_
                                                                        Employment Interviewer

PHASE – B – Supervisor Orientation
(return this form to Personnel the day after employee reports to your unit)   Date 6/17/75

POLICIES EXPLAINED: JOB: PERSONAL:
☑ PAY INCREASES   ☑ DUTIES   ☑ FELLOW EMPLOYEES
☑ PERFORMANCE APPRAISAL   ☑ HOURS   ☑ WASH UP
☑ PROMOTION   ☑ WORK PLACE   ☑ LUNCH ROOM
☑ REPORTING ABSENCES   ☑ OVERTIME   ☑ COAT ROOM
☑ LEAVING JOB   ☑ TRANSPORTATION

EQUIPMENT ISSUED: OTHER:
☑ HANDBOOK OF RULES   ☑ GUEST PASS TO CAFETERIA
☐ TOOL
☐ LOCKER KEY   SENIOR EMPLOYEE ADVISOR _PAUL PETERS (former trainee)_
                                                       Name
☐ _____
                             COMPANY WIDE ORIENTATION 8/7/75
                             (not less than 30 days from this date) Date

COMMENTS: _Member of general management training program Class #27; scheduled for company management course 1 3 weeks of October - assigned to Paul Peters Class #35._ Signature _Timothy Philips_
                                                                     Supervisor
                                                    Management Dev. Director

Fig. 24   Four-phase orientation-interview checklist

information-giving interview should be structured to continue for no more than an hour because in this time span you will have presented all that employees can retain. You can cram much more into a two- or three-hour session and be quite satisfied that you have really "put it across," but if you later measure the retention of what you have put across, you will be disappointed with how little has really stuck with the employees.

Frequently, in conveying complex information such as the provisions of the seniority policy, the objective is not to give the employee all the

---

PHASE – C – Training Department: Company Orientation

DATE REPORTED _8/7/75_   GROUP _Management and Trainee Class #27_
PLANT TOUR _East Gate Plant_

WAS EMPLOYEE INTERVIEWED? ☐ YES ☑ NO

COMMENTS: _Very alert group; participated actively in discussion;_
Brown asked many very intelligent questions

Signature _Jack Homer_
                    Training Specialist

Date of final Orientation Interview (not less than 6 months from today's date) _3/8/75_

PHASE – D – Final Orientation Interview

☑ PENSION PLAN   ☑ PROFIT SHARING PLAN
☑ EDUCATIONAL REFUND PROGRAM   ☑ _Special Trainee Rotation plan_
☑ PROMOTION OPPORTUNITIES   ☐

PROBLEMS: _Mr. Brown is concerned about career choice; wants to_
apply for graduate school & select program in line with
Company's interests; seems attracted to personnel work

ATTITUDE OF EMPLOYEE: _Very enthusiastic, believes that his first_
nine months have been better than he expected; seems
well versed in Company policies and practices

Signature _Mary Stephens_
                    Employee Counselor

---

details but rather the broad highlights: that length of service governs vacation, sick leave, and transfer privileges, that the purpose is to give recognition for loyal service, and that the person will get additional information as required from the supervisor or shop steward.

Finally, the information dispensed should consist only of that information that the employee is likely to use in the near future. To fill a person up with items that are going to be of little immediate value will be a complete waste of time, will interfere with other more immediate learning, and will decrease the absorption of more important information.

CONCLUDING THE INTERVIEW. After the learning session has reached the point where the objectives of the lesson plan have been achieved, the interview is terminated as quickly as possible by asking the interviewee to summarize what has been discussed. It is well here to ask the interviewee what problems he or she may foresee in using the information acquired and then for you to try to help resolve these problems.

It is also a good idea just before the interview is over to make a brief note of the conclusions drawn from the interview and to check to see that all points have been covered.

RECORDING THE INTERVIEW. In developing the lesson plan or the program, it is well to construct a systematic form or checklist of information that must be conveyed to the employee, particularly when a number of "teachers" are involved in the total sequence. In orientation interviews, the design of a special checklist is especially useful. Figure 24 illustrates the four-phase orientation program as it would be completed by the different interviewers in the sequence. This checklist is initiated on the first day of employment by the employment division, follows the employee through the program over the succeeding six months, and finally, upon completion, is placed in the permanent personnel file as a record for later consultation when counseling or performance-appraisal interviews are conducted.

Properly executed by skillful personnel, conducted with a minimum of lost time and red tape, and individualized to the maximum, the orientation program will pay rich dividends to the employer, if only in the form of turnover reduction. Since the termination rate is highest among employees with the least service, an effective induction and job instruction program, complementing, of course, an equitable selection program, will constitute not only an integral part of the company's overall placement program, but it will also serve to reduce the number of early quittings and firings that occur because of inability to adjust to the new environment.

In the long run, a planned orientation program actually saves more time than no plan at all. The proper instruction of new employees constitutes a form of employee-relations preventive medicine because it tends to reduce disciplinary, grievance, and problem-employee interviews that often result from misinformation or inadequate instruction. The foreman or supervisor who spends his or her time in the careful instruction and orientation of employees will reap a rich harvest in better job performance but, more especially, will have fewer disciplinary and grievance interviews. The neglect of this aspect of the total placement program leads to the necessity of greater attention to another element in this program, the termination interview which is the subject of the final chapter.

chapter 17

The Termination Interview

> A moment yet the actor stops,
> And looks around, to say farewell.
> It is an irksome word and task.
> —WILLIAM MAKEPEACE THACKERAY,
> *The End of the Play*

A very large American corporation undertook a comprehensive psychological research program to identify the personal characteristics of their effective managers. The purpose of the study was to discover a trait profile to help them identify, select, and readily develop young women and men with management potential. Under terms of strict confidentiality, an outside consultant assessed, by means of a biographical questionnaire, a battery of tests, and interviews, every manager in the company. In turn, the company furnished the consultant with an enormous amount of data on the performance of each manager.

After the data were processed, a specific configuration of personal and life history characteristics emerged that correlated with effective managerial performance to a surprisingly high degree. Despite the fact that the managers who fitted this personality pattern contributed nearly 40 percent of the corporate profits, they represented only 15 percent of the management population. In the management group, there were far more managers of differing personality configurations who were less effective and even ineffective according to their contribution to corporate earnings.

To account for the relatively low numerical strength of the effective group of managers, the company decided to pursue this study further. After another year of analysis, they discovered that the potentially more effective manager was the most likely to leave the company, particularly in the early stages of his or her career. The organization climate was such as to drive these future winners out of the company with relentless efficiency.

Other investigators have arrived at similar conclusions. In his study of professional employee turnover, Farris found that 35 percent of those who left their organizations were judged to be among the top half in usefulness to these organizations and in one organization, 23 percent of those who left were judged to be among the top 10 percent in usefulness.[1]

Dunnette, Arvey, and Banas note that many companies lose 50 percent of their college graduates during their first four or five years of postcollege employment.[2] This turnover was significantly related to the sharp discrepancy between these employees' actual job experiences and their expectations at the time of recruitment.

As we indicated in Chapter 12, the "shelf sitters" and the candidates for the shelf do not leave a corporation as readily as would be desirable. There is a good reason to believe that a high percentage of the men and women marching out the company door are the most able. Unfortunately, like some types of internal bleeding in the human body, no pain is felt until the person collapses fatally.

To determine how effectively an organization is managing its human assets, you need to stand at "the gate" and note the number, the occupations, and the behavior of those employees who are leaving it for the last time. It is at this hypothetical gate that management's mistakes, from the selection to the performance-evaluation program, are added up and the bill paid.

There have been numerous estimates of the cost of the loss of a single employee who must be replaced, although the figures will vary according to the job, the qualifications, and the training time required. One authoritative estimate put the national figure at over 50 billion dollars yearly in 1974, up from 32 billion dollars ten years ago.

In one corporation with about 8,000 employees and a clerical employee turnover rate of 53 percent, it was estimated that at $1000 per termination, a very conservative figure, the annual loss was 3 million dollars or about 60 percent of the company's net earnings.

Another national employer, one of the largest and most prestigious, recently published a report entitled "I Quit," a study of short-tenure losses in one of its divisions. The report stated that each time those two words were spoken it cost the company between $3,000 and $4,000. In one department where they heard those words over 3,600 times in one year, it cost an estimated $13,500,000.

But these are really conservative estimates. There are termination-loss figures for some jobs of $10,000, $12,000, and even $15,000 per person, depending upon recruitment and selection costs, the develop-

[1] G. F. Farris, "A Predictive Study of Turnover," *Personnel Psychology,* **24**:311–328, Summer 1971.

[2] M. D. Dunnette, R. D. Arvey, and P. A. Banas, "Why Do They Leave?," *Personnel,* **50**(3):25–39, May/June 1973.

ment period required, and the number of instructors involved in the training program. For this reason, a termination control program seems to be an essential element in the corporate personnel program. The core of such a program is the termination or exit interview.

The Termination Control Program

According to national and local surveys, eight out of every ten large companies use some sort of termination control program. A formal program tries to provide orderly procedures that are set in motion as soon as an employee separation appears likely and at a date considerably prior to the actual departure. Establishing such a program cannot be haphazard. Its objectives must be understood by all concerned, particularly by supervisors, so that it can be conducted in a sequence that will ensure the collection of all information related to the employee's separation. At the same time, the program must be completely individualized to permit the departing employee full opportunity to settle any remaining personal questions.

A termination control program will naturally provide for the orderly and efficient separation of *all* employees, but in this chapter we deal only with those who are leaving the company voluntarily for other employment or who have been asked to leave because of unsatisfactory job behavior. We pass over employees laid off because of a lack of work, leaving for extended military service, retiring employees, or those leaving to become homemakers or mothers. Admittedly, these groups represent a substantial proportion of the departing population, and there is much to be said for the argument that even within this group, there are a great many serviceable employees who could be retained profitably by the company with a little effort. But the primary target of a termination control program is to reduce the number of employees who leave for other employment or who are dismissed for inadequate performance.

There are within a termination control program three different termination interviews: the first, referred to as a *preliminary* termination interview, is conducted with an employee who has signified an intention of leaving but who is not actually committed to a final decision. In personnel jargon, this interview is termed a "salvage" interview. Another termination interview, known in personnel circles as the "exit" interview is conducted with the employee who is definitely on the way out. We subdivide the exit interview into *voluntary* and *involuntary* interviews because each is decidedly different in context, content, role relationships, and personality interaction.

The Preliminary Termination Interview The preliminary termination interview precedes an actual resignation. The alert supervisor who notes that a subordinate seems depressed or disinterested may call the person aside to conduct a preliminary termination interview or refer the person to a personnel department representative for counseling. In theory, this should happen often; in practice, it almost never does.

Preoccupied with getting the work out, most supervisors are surprisingly insensitive to the job-hunting activities of their subordinates. And, even if a supervisor is on the lookout for dissatisfied employees, the task is made more difficult by employees who threaten constantly to resign but who really never do. It takes a very perceptive, alert supervisor to discriminate between the two species—the chronic complainer and the genuinely discontented worker.

If, however, you find out that a subordinate is thinking of leaving but is not actually committed yet, initiate a preliminary termination interview at once, provided, of course, that you consider the contemplated resignation undesirable.

Since the prevention of an employee's termination is the sole objective of the "salvage" interview, timing is important. An employee who has definitely accepted a position with another company and who has already announced it to others is too deeply committed to be talked out of it.

It is better to speak to an employee as soon as there are definite signs that he or she is "looking around" to change jobs. This talk cannot be just a casual conversation or a brief chat; it must be a formal interview structured to identify the underlying causes of the employee's unrest. If conducted properly, this interview becomes far more than an information-seeking exercise; it develops into a counseling interview. *The Wall Street Journal* reported that by having counselors dig deeper about job preference, work problems, and challenging responsibilities, companies are able to double the number of salvages and to hang on to good employees.[3]

THE COUNSELING APPROACH.   Since a counseling situation implies a problem, you must identify the difficulty motivating the employee to seek other employment. In exploring possible motives, proceed on the assumption that few persons leave a job situation that satisfies their psychological and social needs. Despite assertions to the contrary, an employee looking for greener pastures is really seeking to escape from a position that is frustrating in some way.

Remember that nearly always there are two reasons for a resignation —the stated and the real reason. The stated reason is usually the most socially desirable, while the real reason is often unrecognized by either the employee or the supervisor. Getting the truth in a preliminary termi-

[3] *The Wall Street Journal,* "Why Did You Quit?," June 17, 1966. P. 1.

nation interview is difficult, therefore, and will require careful analysis of the forces acting upon the employee to stay or to leave.

FORCE-FIELD ANALYSIS. At the preliminary termination stage where the employee is uncommitted either way, the person is in a state of dynamic equilibrium, wavering between the forces encouraging a job change and the counterforces pressuring the employee to stay where he or she is. When these opposing forces are of equal intensity, the employee unable to make a decision will experience considerable tension.

In this circumstance, to increase the pressure to stay by making promises or appealing to loyalty won't help much. It will only increase the tension and perhaps create more anxiety. Try to understand the employee's point of view; conduct the interview only to arrive at a satisfactory resolution of the problem by analyzing the forces which will play a part in the final decision, which must rest with the employee.

Among the factors influencing a person to stay may be, for example, an interest in his or her work, a fondness for fellow workers, and the convenience of the location of the plant. The pressure of family expenses, the fact that a neighbor was recently promoted, or the generally uneasy feeling of being in a rut may be the forces prompting an employee to look for another job.

Carefully identify as many of the forces working on an employee as you can, taking care not to leap to conclusions too quickly. Discontented employees may have real or imaginary grievances; they may feel sincerely that they are entitled to a higher salary, that they could get more responsible assignments in another job, or that they could advance further in a different line of work or in another company. Talk patiently and objectively and from the employee's point of view about each of these feelings. You will get nowhere talking about company plans, painting a picture of a bright tomorrow, or offering the employee a salary increase unless such a promise can be kept, the person is entitled to the raise, and it serves to resolve the basic conflicts.

After analysis of the total situation, you may conclude honestly that the employee will be better off in a new job. If that new job already exists within the company, it is your responsibility to help the employee get it. And even if it is not within the company, you still have an obligation to help the person make the shift to another organization by sympathetic understanding and encouragement.

Often, the change is in the best interest of neither the employee nor the company. People become restless and dissatisfied with their jobs for many reasons, sometimes not within the employer's control. The social standards prevalent in American society create discontent in otherwise happy workers. The employee who remains in the same job for four or five years acquires a social stigma of being either unambitious or inadequate. The theme of "onward and upward" taught from the early days of childhood accounts for more job dissatisfaction and personal discontent than most employers can handle on their own.

Actually, there should be little need for preliminary termination interviews. If you conduct performance-evaluation interviews regularly, if you maintain an open-door policy with respect to grievances, if the company has an adequate counseling program, and if the organization climate encourages employees to speak freely to management, problem situations that cause turnover will be solved before they reach the critical stage. If none of these communication tools or facilities are available, however, the preliminary termination interview will be a waste of time.

The Voluntary Exit Interview   The exit interview with the employee leaving an organization voluntarily can help eliminate potential or real grievances, influence personnel policies, and, ultimately, reduce further turnover. To be effective this interview must be placed in the proper setting, focus on appropriate sources and levels of information, and be conducted in a style that ensures the acquisition of accurate data.

An effective termination program does not consist merely of a requirement that supervisors and personnel interviewers, wherever possible, should conduct exit interviews with leaving employees. Such an approach is so haphazard that in a few years the company will conclude that the exit interviewing program does not tell them very much and they will abandon it.

An effective program is tailored to the specific company requirements, coordinated with other personnel programs, communicated throughout the company, and administered to ensure that all leaving employees are interviewed. If it is implemented by trained interviewers, both at the supervisory and the personnel department levels, the exit interview becomes a really fertile information source.

STRUCTURAL ASPECTS.   An appropriate procedure begins with the notice of resignation. The supervisor completes a report containing his or her own evaluations of the employee's job performance and the employee's reason for leaving which is forwarded to the central personnel unit where a final interview is conducted by a specially trained person on the last day of work. The exit interviewer completes a termination report containing all the relevant facts on the basis of which the termination is classified. Finally, at periodic intervals, statistical analysis of turnover experience are reported to management. Out of such a program emerges a stream of data, which when coordinated with other personnel statistics will bring problem situations to the attention of department heads and top management.

The program receives the support of top management by being established as a mandatory procedure. Then, it is up to the individual's superior to cooperate with the central personnel staff by turning in the report of the termination and by seeing to it that the employee appears for the exit interview. Immediately after notice, the supervisor reports the resignation to the central personnel staff. After interviewing the employee, he or she completes a report which contains two sets of information: a description of the employee's reason for termination and a final evaluation of the employee's job performance. Figure 25 illustrates a typical report. On one side of the form, the supervisor completes a checklist appraisal of the terminating employee's job performance and indicates whether the employee would be worthy of possible reemployment. On the back of the report, the supervisor describes in his or her own words the reasons for the separation. This explanation is quite meaningful and helpful to exit interviewers and is a distinct improvement over the practice of merely requiring the supervisor to classify the termination according to a predetermined code.

The supervisor's report is essential to the termination control program. Besides aiding the exit interviewer, it is used by the supervisor to analyze his or her general effectiveness and to increase sensitivity to problems within his or her jurisdiction. It also helps later when an ex-employee requests employment references or is being considered for reemployment.

After turning in the report, the supervisor must make sure that the employee shows up for the exit interview. A resigning employee might be somewhat reluctant to appear for this final interview, either because it is viewed as superfluous or because at this stage the person does not wish to "rock the boat." Perhaps, after months of soul-searching and many interviews with the supervisor, the employee has made this decision. Now he or she wants to leave in as pleasant and tranquil an atmosphere as possible.

Unless it is very inconvenient to avoid the exit interview, most separating employees will skip this step. And a hit-or-miss exit interview program yields very unreliable information. Fortunately, however, in this age of employee benefit programs, leaving a company is not accomplished simply by saying goodbye and walking out the door. The employee must obtain information about insurance programs, must sign papers, turn in the identification card, company tools and equipment, parking-lot pass, and locker key before receiving the final paycheck. This "debriefing" is performed logically by personnel department specialists who are nearly always better versed than the supervisor in the complexities of the benefit plans.

If employment interviewers conduct these interviews, they will find it quite useful for future employee hiring. If the terminee is interviewed by the person who hired her or him, the experience will be doubly helpful.

TERMINATING EMPLOYEE
APPRAISAL

Employee's Name ____Greene_____Mark_____ Date __9/1/75__
                        (Last)   (First)   (Middle)
Present Position __Staff Assistant_____   Dept. or Plant __Manufacturing - Eastgate__

INSTRUCTIONS TO SUPERVISOR (also see GC's 20-2.02 and 20-2.12)

Rate the employee on the basis of the actual work he has been doing for the past year before attempting to fill in report. It is necessary to have in mind the exact qualities on which the employee is being rated. For this information study this form carefully. In each quality compare the individual with other employees who have worked under you and have done similar work. Place a (✓) check in box below term which best describes the employee's standing on the quality.

Forward completed report to Personnel Director, attached to Appointment or Separation Payroll Notice.

Was the Employee INTERESTED in his Job and Company	Enthusiastic ☐	Gets Along ☑	Promotes Team Effort ☐	Indifferent ☐
Had Employee Satisfactory KNOWLEDGE of His Job	Meager ☐	Fairly Complete ☑	Unusually Detailed ☐	Well Informed ☐
Was the QUALITY of the Work Satisfactory	Rather Careless ☑	Work Free From Error and Waste ☐	Many Errors ☐	Often Has to be Corrected ☐
Did Employee Show Good JUDGMENT	Seriously Lacking in Judgment ☐	Fair Amount of Common Sense ☐	Makes Immature Decisions ☑	Unusually Mature Judgment ☐
Did Employee Show INITIATIVE	Occasional Effort ☑	Exceptionally Resourceful ☐	Needs Much Urging ☐	Resourceful ☐
Was Employee INDUSTRIOUS	Barely Meets Requirements ☐	All That is Expected ☐	Does More Than Is Expected ☐	Lazy ☑
Was Employee RELIABLE	Dependable Under all Circumstances ☐	Needs Close Supervision ☐	Needs Little Supervision ☐	Follow Ups Required ☑
PERSONAL HABITS	Seldom Subject to Criticism ☐	Actions on Job Bring Discredit to Company ☐	Ordinary Conduct and Manners ☐	Above Criticism ☑
Did Employee Enjoy Good HEALTH	Handicapped—Very Frequently Ill ☐	Frail—Frequently Ill ☐	Vigorous—Very Seldom Ill ☐	Reasonably Well Common Illness ☑
SUPERVISORY *(No Supervisory Responsibility)*	Stimulates Others ☐	Limited in Leadership Guidance ☐	Commands High Respect Gets excellent Team Work ☐	Dissension in his Sphere ☐

Length of Notice Given _Two Weeks_ Considering everything -- would you reemploy?   ( ) Yes   (✓) No

If Yes, for what type of work? _____

WRITE REASON FOR SEPARATION   Supervisor's
(DETAILED STATEMENT BY SUPERVISOR)   Signature *James P Bartholomew*
ON THE REVERSE SIDE.   Title *Plant Manager*

Fig. 25   Supervisor's report of termination

If the resigning employee must visit the personnel department for final clearance, 98 percent of the voluntary quits will receive an exit interview. Then, by structuring *explicitly* around fringe benefits and other final details with which the leaving employee is concerned, this interview will achieve the *implicit* goal of gathering data about the employee's opinions of and attitudes toward the job.

FUNCTIONAL ASPECTS.   The immediate objective of the exit interview is purely administrative—to enable the employee to separate gracefully and efficiently with all records completed and with all the informa-

SUPERVISOR'S REPORT OF TERMINATION

Mark was assigned to me last May after unsatisfactory tour in Marketing Department—Personnel thought he might work out better in a line department. He did not work out. Has many great ideas but doesn't have the follow through. I gave him three special assignments in a row which he messed up. He's bright but can't seem to work on a team. Wants to be the plant manager without first learning how it runs.

Submitted his resignation today. Plans to enter business of his father-in-law. Hope he straightens out.

James P. Bartholomew
SIGNATURE

Plant Manager
TITLE

9/1/15
DATE

tion required about financial and insurance affairs. Figure 26 illustrates a form that is most convenient for expediting these final procedures. This checklist enables you to process the group life and health insurance, savings bond, and retirement programs, ensures the transfer of the leaving employee's personnel records from the active to inactive files, and provides a means of obtaining information concerning the disposition of the final paycheck. You can use the completion of this form as a stepping stone to more sensitive areas. If you conduct the interview pleasantly and efficiently and furnish accurate information, you can establish a climate that will enable you to move gradually to

REFERENCE: GC 20-2.02

EMPLOYMENT TERMINATION CONTROL REPORT

NAME	ADDRESS	CITY & STATE
☑ MR. ☐ MISS ☐ MRS. MARK A. GREENE	11 10th Street	New York, N.Y.

DEPT./FACILITY	ORG.UNIT NO.	POSITION TITLE	ANNUAL SALARY	SENIORITY	DATE OF BIRTH
Manufacturing	123	Staff Assistant	$13,500	NA	5/22/50

DATE EMPLOYED	TERM. EFFECT. DATE	MOS. OF SERV.	TYPE OF ACTION		REASON CODE
6/17/72	9/15/75	39	☒ RESIGNATION ☐ RETIREMENT ☐ DISMISSAL ☐ LEAVE OF ABSENCE		242

EMPLOYEE'S REASON(S) FOR SEPARATION:

To enter business with father-in-law — dissatisfied with progress in Company — feels he was given poor assignments; believes he has a lot more to offer. Thinks management training program a waste of time — Company not living up to promises made in college recruitment program; No complaints about supervision, working conditions or salary. Submitted a 4 page memorandum analyzing his difficulties and how they could have been remedied by better personnel development program. (attached)

SIGNATURE *James Andrews*

FORMS COMPLETED BY SUPERVISOR & OTHER UNITS:
☑ TERMINATING EMPLOYEE APPRAISAL   ☑ SURRENDER OF EQUIP. AND PROPERTY (incl. certifications of Library & Cashier)

FORMS COMPLETED BY TERMINATING EMPLOYEE:
insurance withdrawal form, transfer of health insurance plan. Waiver of pension

INFORMATION FURNISHED EMPLOYEE:
☑ GROUP HEALTH INSURANCE ☑ GROUP LIFE INSUR. ☑ U.S. SAVINGS BOND REFUND

TERMINATION CHECK LIST:
☑ PROMOTION EXAM. RECORD   ☑ TRAINING & EXPERIENCE RECORD   ☑ ALL BENEFITS PROGRAM RECORDS

WAS TERMINATION DESIRABLE? ☑ YES ☐ NO   WAS RETENTION OF EMPLOYEE ATTEMPTED? ☐ YES ☑ NO (If yes, write details):

See supervisor's Report of Termination; counsellors report, Performance Appraisal Reports. This was a case of poor selection — suggest reanalysis of employment records and interview reports.

DISPOSAL OF FINAL PAYCHECK
(WHEN AVAILABLE): ☐ EMPLOYEE WILL CALL / / ☐ MAIL TO ABOVE ADDRESS ☑ OTHER: presented to employee

DATE OF INTERVIEW	CONDUCTED BY	TITLE	RELEASE OF FINAL CHECK(S)	IF DELAYED, SHOW REASON
9/15/75	James Andrews	Personnel Rep	☑ O.K. TO RELEASE ☐ DELAYED	

DISPOSAL OF EMPLOYEE'S FINAL CHECK(S)

Description	Check Number	Amount	Personally Accepted (✓)	Mailed to Res. (✓)	Mailed By	Date	Remarks
PAY CHECK	100234	$502	✓			9/15/75	
U.S. SAVINGS BOND REFUND						/ /	
						/ /	
						/ /	

Fig. 26   Interviewer's checklist of termination

questions that are most concerned to management—"Why are you leaving?," "Where are you going?," and "What do you think of us?"

Even before you get to this point, the discussion of administrative matters furnishes valuable clues about the employee's reason for leaving. The fact that an employee is quite well informed about the insurance benefits provided by a new employer is evidence of a carefully considered termination. Vagueness about the new company's benefits may indicate a more impulsive resignation, prompted perhaps by dissatisfaction with his or her present job.

The exiting interviewee's manner is another indication of inner feelings toward the company. If the employee is friendly, warm, and elated, the probabilities are that the person is moving up to a better job; on the other hand, a sullen and hostile demeanor may be a clue to dissatisfaction with the present job as the primary motive for change. It is important for you to keep in mind during the mechanical or information-giving phase of the termination interview that you must be alert to ways of pursuing your main objective. Avoid the common pitfalls of conducting the interview on such a strictly routine level that you miss vital information altogether. This is easy to do because the average departing employee is not anxious to stir up trouble. Concerned perhaps with the quality of the references he or she expects to get from your company, the person sees little to be gained by mentioning grievances. He or she will be noncommittal, and will simply state the reason for leaving is a "better job." Or, wishing to demonstrate how wrong the company has been in overlooking a good person, the employee may brag about the wonderful offer received and the opportunity to work for an employer who really recognizes ability. Another leaving employee may not even be aware of the reason for leaving. He or she may state simply that a more attractive job was offered and may fail to recognize that if he or she had worked for a more understanding supervisor or had found the present job more satisfying, the new job might never have been pursued.

Getting at the truth in the exit interview by digging beneath the surface of declared reasons for termination to obtain the real reason takes a good deal of patience, acumen, and interviewing skill. The opportunities for self-delusion and the acceptance of the obvious are widespread because most leaving employees will cooperate by offering such excuses as "better offer," "more money," "more responsibility," "closer to home," as the reasons for resignation.

It is deceptive for a company to believe that 80 percent of the preventable turnover is due to the offer of more money elsewhere. A higher salary offer is seldom the real reason an employee resigns; it is never the only reason.

A study of a large sample of Illinois industries compared the reasons quitting employees gave their employers with the reasons given to a team of university researchers later. The results indicated that ex-employees gave the full, real reason to their employers only 22 percent of the time.[4]

A company in the aircraft industry reported a 40 percent difference between the reasons given at the time of quitting and reasons given two

[4] Robert D. Loken, *Why They Quit* (Urbana, Ill.: University of Illinois, College of Commerce and Business Administration, 1949).

to eleven months later.[5] Interestingly enough, the latter study revealed that all the reasons given for quitting in the exit interview were related to factors beyond the control of the company, while all the reasons given later were related to such internal company problems as low pay, poor supervision, and slow advancement. The study also reported that 75 percent of those who had been out of the company two months and 67 percent of those who had been out seven months indicated that they would be willing to return to the company if a suitable offer were made.

Lefkowitz and Katz substantiated this result in their study of the validity of exit interviews.[6] Comparing exit interviewers' reports of reasons for termination with later questionnaire responses, 59 percent of the samples reported different "reasons" on the two sets of data. Interestingly, the investigators subdivided the terminees into involuntary, voluntary avoidable, and voluntary unavoidable classes. The smallest discrepancy between interviewers' reasons and questionnaire responses was in the last category. The object of effective exit interviewing, therefore, is to make an accurate statement of the real reason why an employee left the company.

The Involuntary Exit Interview   The dismissal of an employee for unsatisfactory behavior or for incompetence is a declining phenomenon in the American occupational world. The increased acceptance of the principle that a job is the personal property of its incumbent and the consequent importance of tenure have placed so many restrictions on management's right to dismiss an employee for cause that most supervisors are overcautious about exercising this prerogative. In one sense, this development is highly desirable, but in another, it is equally deplorable. Since few selection programs are more than 75 percent effective, at least one-quarter of the new employees hired in almost any organization are likely to be poorly placed. While some of these employees will perceive the situation and resign, there must also be a mechanism by which the remainder can be urged to leave for more conducive surroundings. The management that does not see to it that its supervisors dismiss unsatisfactory employees is not only lax in its responsibility, but is rendering a grave disservice to the employees concerned.

The difficulty, of course, is that everyone is inordinately sensitive to the injustice inherent in an arbitrary dismissal and in the unpleasant truth that when a person is fired his or her family is fired too. In Chapter 14 we discussed the negative feelings of those who exercise discipline

---

[5] Wayne L. McNaughton, "Attitudes of Ex-employees at Intervals after Quitting," *Personnel Journal*, 35:61–63, 1956.

[6] J. Lefkowitz and L. Katz, "Validity of Exit Interviews," *Personnel Psychology*, 22:445–455, Winter 1969.

and ways of overcoming the false sense of guilt that inhibits an otherwise good practice. An extremely low dismissal rate is one of the anomalies of American management and one of the most certain and most distressing symptoms of creeping bureaucracy.

Employees must be discharged for their own benefit, for the sake of other employees, and for the health of the organization. It need not be an unpleasant, guilt-ridden experience if the termination is handled properly in the context of an involuntary exit interview program and the procedures outlined in Chapters 12 and 14.

STRUCTURAL ASPECTS. The purpose of an exit interview with a dismissed employee is to permit the person to leave in as pleasant and as dignified an atmosphere as possible. If he or she has been asked to leave because of unsatisfactory performance, it is only natural to expect such ineffectiveness to be attributed to the company. You must try to counteract this tendency by persuading the terminee to accept the dismissal as fair and equitable.

Another objective of the involuntary exit interview is to give the terminating employee a "last day in court" by affording the person an opportunity to discuss fully and frankly the other side of the story. Finally, this interview can develop into a counseling session in which you give the terminating employee advice on a future course of action.

There are two categories of dismissed employees—those who are fired for improper conduct such as dishonesty, absenteeism, or flagrant violation of company rules and those who are discharged for incompetency or inability to adjust to job demands. The fact that the latter category is much smaller than the former is due not to the greater incidence of employee misconduct but rather to management's reluctance to dismiss a worker for ineffectiveness.

The interview with an employee discharged for improper conduct is highly structured and focuses merely upon giving information about the benefit programs. The employee will naturally ask questions about the type of character references which will be supplied when prospective employers make inquiry. Discuss company policy frankly at this point, but otherwise follow a formal pattern and handle the interview as expeditiously as possible.

In speaking to an employee who is being dismissed for incompetency, be more positive in outlook and adopt a more constructive, emphatic approach. You can, if you wish and have the time, explore with the departing employee the underlying reasons for dismissal and then embark upon career counseling.

FUNCTIONAL ASPECTS. The involuntary exit interview can cause you and the interviewee considerable discomfort unless it is carefully planned. It is always an awkward situation. Regardless of a person's opinion of the job or the employer, no one likes to be dismissed; it is an affront to one's dignity, a blow to self-respect. As an exit interviewer, therefore, you must try to respect whatever dignity the interviewee has left, even if dismissed for embezzlement and awaiting grand jury action. Whatever the reason for dismissal, there is no excuse to rub it in and thereby humiliate the leaving employee.

In listening to an employee's version of the termination, ascertain that his or her rights were respected and that, in cases of dismissal for incompetency or poor job adjustment, the person had ample notice of what was coming. Of course, if by company policy, a supervisor has the right to immediate, arbitrary, and unappealable dismissal, there really isn't any need for an involuntary exit interview. The more socially conscious companies, however, make sure that employees are dismissed only for serious reasons and only after the employee receives full and ample opportunity to correct deficiencies.

After completing the procedural part of the interview, ask the employee for his or her version of the termination to verify the circumstances that accompany the dismissal and to confirm the fact that the employee has had ample warning of unacceptable conduct. This fact is usually confirmed in a preinterview conversation with the supervisor. But being mindful of a rather common misapprehension of supervisors who believe stoutly they have carefully warned a worker when they have only reproved the person mildly, you should secure confirmation from the employee, too. A proper warning is unequivocal, explicit, and the final admonition is put in writing to be acknowledged by the employee.

After the employee acknowledges this proper warning, proceed to a discussion of the way the person feels he or she has been treated. If it is alleged that a grave injustice has been perpetrated, assure the employee that you will look into the matter, but there is no point in your feeling guilty or defensive or in arguing with the person.

You can adopt a much more constructive approach in an exit interview with an employee dismissed for incompetence. If he or she can accept personal inadequacies, you can suggest positive remedial action such as vocational counseling, guidance and testing, and, perhaps, additional schooling.

Your greatest hazard is a feeling of sympathy that may cause you to make a personal commitment to the employee with respect to reemployment, or references, or securing the person another job. A discharged employee will naturally be concerned about the employment record, and about what will be reported to prospective employers who inquire. Since each company has its own policy on this matter, it is best to inform the employee what that policy is. In any case, make no commitment without the full concurrence of management and in the light of the obligations you might be incurring.

Involuntary exit interviews are conducted and written up in the same way as voluntary interviews. In most cases, it is too late to do anything about the conditions or circumstances that have occasioned this particular separation, but if you do your job well, you can write an informative report of the termination that, when added to similar reports, can contribute to an accurate analysis of many terminations.

How to Conduct an Exit Interview

Getting the truth in an exit interview is a complex task. You, for one, are a source of error; the interviewee, for his or her part, reports highly unreliable information not only because of inability but because of a reluctance to talk; and finally, neither the interview situation nor the company's programs and policies may be conducive to a frank or open discussion of relevant material. To control these three sources of error, you will require a high degree of skill. You must handle not only the task functions of giving and getting information but the rapport functions as well. At the same time, you have to resist the temptation of trying too hard and of attempting to probe too deeply, and you must constantly be aware of certain personalities who are only too anxious to overwhelm you with extraneous, irrelevant, and perhaps untruthful information.

As with all personnel interviews, you conduct the effective exit interview by thorough preparation, beginning it in a low key, moving fairly quickly to the main sequence, bringing it to a pleasant conclusion, and carefully writing up your thoughts as soon as it is over.

Preparation As an exit interviewer, you must have a highly sensitive "third ear" to listen for main ideas, for patterns and trends, and for subtle cues. There is no mystery attached to this ability; it is simply the product of careful preparation and a readiness for listening. First talk with the supervisor to get his or her ideas or read the notice of termination. Then review the complete personal file of the departing employee. Make sure you have all the termination papers in readiness when the employee appears for the final interview—insurance forms, letters of recommendation, and final paycheck. Of course, be familiar with the resigning employee's job and work unit and with the overall company personnel and employee relations policies. See to it that your interview is conducted in a private room, free of interruption and distraction, and make certain that the interviewee is met promptly at the appointed time.

To facilitate discussion of relevant matters, some companies require the employee to complete a preinterview questionnaire which is used as a basis for discussion during the final interview. Most companies utilize the questionnaire, however, as a substitute for the exit interview and simply request the employee to complete it sometime after termination.

Main Sequence   From the outset, you must win the confidence of the terminating employee. You accomplish this by adhering first to the explicit task functions, that is, to the task of giving the employee any necessary assistance required and by discussing such items as length of service, job title, promotions received, and final salary. Then discuss arrangements for turning in equipment and passes, etc., and the provisions for converting group insurance and savings bond refunds.

Gradually lead up to the reasons for termination by saying, in a matter-of-fact way, "Can you tell me why you are leaving?" Explain to the exiting employee that you must determine a reason and would appreciate a frank answer. Explore the reasons given carefully and objectively but without expressing any evaluation or passing any judgment. Then ask if the terminee has anything to say about the company, indicating, of course, that anything reported will be held completely confidential and that the information obtained will be used only to improve present working conditions. You may even cite a few examples of improved working circumstances resulting from interview data. If the terminee does not wish to volunteer information, however, you may have to probe a little more skillfully.

Remember that you are a data collector, a fact finder who listens to and records what is said. Establish an atmosphere that assures the interviewee that what is said will be accepted and treated with the utmost confidence. As the information turns to these implicit goals, emphasize that you are asking for cooperation in order to improve conditions in the company, and show a sincere appreciation for help when you get it.

As the interviewee begins to talk, introduce positive strokes. Smile and by encouraging words demonstrate your acceptance of the person's cooperation. If the interviewee displays any emotion by being sharply critical of the company or persons in it, avoid defensiveness, do not retaliate or show any sign of displeasure.

Effective use of silence and question-phrasing may open up deeper levels of communication. Once conversation is flowing freely, guide it into more sensitive areas, but be prepared to deal with emotion, particularly with resentment and hostility. Watch the interviewee's anxiety level and reduce tension by shifting the subject to safer ground when necessary. Many seemingly unrelated or irrelevant comments may be made by an interviewee. At times, he or she may make statements that contradict previous statements. The complete picture of the termination will emerge not in one logical, continuous sequence but rather in a piecemeal, discontinuous mosaic you must assemble like the pieces of a jigsaw puzzle. Often, this has to be compiled from notes when you write your final report after the interview is over.

You should have a mental plan containing items you intend to cover during the interview, including every possible phase of the employee's working experience, from pay rate to the condition of the washroom, that might have contributed to a decision to quit. But this interview plan should not inhibit the exploration of a relatively minor point that may seem of importance to the interviewee.

Being highly structured, the first part of the interview is quite directed. When rapport is established and the conversation flows more freely, withdraw into a more nondirective style. At this point, concentrate on the categories of clarification, testing, and summarizing. If a really important and sensitive area is touched upon, you may have to resort to more subtle suggestions to explore it deeply, but take great care to avoid dissipating your relationship with the interviewee.

Basically, you seek an answer to the question "What is your opinion of the job you had with us?" The answer can cover a checklist of such items as: the employee's opportunity to use educational background, skills, and abilities; the technical know-how and leadership skill of the supervision; the personal recognition received; the opportunity for advancement; the amount of individual guidance received; the opportunity to participate in professional activities; the amount of job freedom; the planning and organizing in the section or unit in which the person worked; the extent to which his or her ideas were put to use; the amount of training received; the person's understanding of expected performance; contribution to the work of the unit; personal feelings toward management; the frequency of performance evaluation; the amount of work assigned; and the percentage of time spent in routine, repetitive work.

In addition, your interview plan should cover information about the job to which the employee is going—industry, size, salary increase, and opportunities for advancement. This list is not exhaustive, but it suggests the more important areas that ought to be included in a thorough exit interview.

A major obstacle to getting a thorough and frank report from an interviewee is your own overeagerness. Sometimes a resigning employee will enter the interview fully expecting to be interrogated, to be asked to inform on supervisors or coworkers. Many interviewees, therefore, will be very much on their guard and will deeply resent unnecessary pushing or probing. A terminee may say that he or she is leaving because of an opportunity in a job that will permit fuller exploitation of personal potential, that he or she was quite happy with the former job, and that the resignation is made reluctantly. Such an explanation must be accepted at face value and not brushed aside while you probe for the "real" reason. The exit interviewer who seeks a sensational or dramatic story from each resignee will only stimulate antagonism in many of them and will cause others to withhold any possible information that might have been given to the interviewer without prompting.

On the other hand, be wary of certain types who will look upon the exit interview as the perfect vehicle for the release of pent-up frustrations caused by supervisors or fellow employees. When a termination employee "tells all," disclosing how a supervisor has been cheating the company for years or how former colleagues have been loafing on the job all the time, you should accept this exposé noncommittally and avoid any manifestation of strong interest in it. Later, investigation usually proves that these allegations have little or no basis in fact.

Beware also of the braggart who, upon leaving, insists upon going into great lengths about the new job añd how for years in this company his or her light has been hidden under a bushel by a supervisor whom this person has had to "carry." Such behavior is the mark of a deeply frustrated person who is undoubtedly leaving for a job inferior to the one being terminated but is compelled to announce the achievement of well-deserved recognition.

Be alert to the person who says nothing, seems impatient and in a hurry, and wants nothing more than the final paycheck. Although this type is very difficult to start talking, he or she can be a storehouse of facts, if you can open the person up.

Take notes during the interview, a relatively easy task because you will have the termination report checklist in front of you and writing will be very natural. Written notes are a must in any interview, but in the termination interview they provide the basis for the final summary and the resulting statistical data.

When it becomes apparent that the interviewee has said all that is going to be said, has received all the necessary information, and has signed all the final papers, conclude the meeting by presenting the final paycheck and summarizing what has occurred. The interviewee is assured of the company's continuing interest in his or her welfare and is wished good luck and Godspeed.

After the terminee has left, immediately write your report in a format such as the one shown in Figure 26. Normally, exit interviews with quitting employees are conducted in a reasonably friendly, relaxed mood. The ex-employee has made a decision, is looking forward eagerly to the new venture, is anxious to cement favorable relations with the former employer, and thus the interview progresses smoothly. The situation is quite different with the involuntarily separated employee, and because of this difference, it requires more skill and tact and may call upon the most subtle and demanding techniques described in this book.

Selected Readings

There is a wealth of additional background material related to interviewing which the interested reader may wish to consult. Since the following list is meant only to be suggestive of the type of additional reading that can enhance interviewing skills, only a few of the more pertinent books and articles are cited, the criterion for inclusion being either recent publication or the significance of the message.

Part 1   Some Basic Considerations

Books

Berne, Eric: *Games People Play*, Grove Press, New York, 1964.

Carson, R. C.: *Interaction Concepts of Personality*, Aldine, Chicago, 1969.

Famularo, J. J. (ed.): *Handbook of Modern Personnel Administration*, McGraw-Hill, New York, 1972.

Golembiewski, R. R. and A. Blumberg (eds.): *Sensitivity Training and the Laboratory Approach*, F. E. Peacock, Itasca, Ill., 1970.

Hall, E. T.: *The Silent Language*, A Premier Publication, Fawcett, Greenwich, Conn., 1959.

Harris, Thomas A.: *I'm OK—You're OK*, Harper & Row, New York, 1969.

James, M. and D. Jongeward: *Born to Win: Transactional Analysis with Gestalt Experiments*, Addison-Wesley, Reading, Mass., 1971.

Jongeward, Dorothy: *Everybody Wins: Transactional Analysis Applied to Organizations*, Addison-Wesley, Reading, Mass., 1973.

Mager, Robert F.: *Preparing Instructional Objectives*, Fearon, Belmont, Calif., 1962.
McFarland, Dalton E.: *Personnel Management: Theory and Practice*, Macmillan, New York, 1968.
Morgan, Clifford T.: *Introduction to Psychology*, 4th ed., McGraw-Hill, New York, 1971.
Pierce, J. R.: *Symbols, Signals and Noise: The Nature and Process of Communication*, Harper & Row, New York, 1961.
Richardson, S. A., et al.: *Interviewing: Its Forms and Functions*, Basic Books, New York, 1965.

Articles

Anderson, R. P. and G. V. Anderson: "Development of an Instrument for Measuring Rapport," *Journal of Personnel and Guidance*, vol. 41, pp. 18–24, 1962.
Buchheimer, A.: "The Development of Ideas about Empathy," *Journal of Applied Psychology*, vol. 10, pp. 61–70, 1963.
Foltz, Roy G.: "Communication: Not An Art, A Necessity," *Personnel*, vol. 49, pp. 60–64, 1972.
Tesch, F. E., et al.: "The One-way/Two-way Communication Exercise: Some Ghosts Laid to Rest," *The Journal of Applied Behavioral Science*, vol. 8, pp. 664–673, 1972.
Uhrbrock, Richard S.: "The Personnel Interview," *Personnel Psychology*, vol. 1, pp. 273–302, 1948.
Whyte, W. F.: "Pigeons, Persons and Piece Rates," *Psychology Today*, vol. 5, no. 1, pp. 66ff., 1972.
Winograd, Terry: "Artificial Intelligence: When Will Computers Understand People?" *Psychology Today*, vol. 7, no. 12, pp. 59–68, 1974.

Part 2   Decision-Making Interviews

Books

American Psychological Association: *Standards for Educational and Psychological Tests*, Washington, D.C., 1974.
Byham, W. C. and M. E. Spitzer: *The Law and Personnel Testing*, American Management Association, New York, 1971.
Cole, N. S.: *Bias in Selection*, ACT Research Report no. 51, Research and Development Division of the American College Testing Program, Iowa City, Iowa, 1972.
Cronbach, L. J. and G. C. Gleser: *Psychological Tests and Personnel Decisions*, University of Illinois Press, Urbana, 1965.
Drake, John D.: *Interviewing for Managers: Sizing Up People*, American Management Association, New York, 1972.
Dunnette, Marvin D.: *Personnel Selection and Placement*, Wadsworth, Belmont, Calif., 1966.
Fear, Richard A.: *The Evaluation Interview*, 2d ed., McGraw-Hill, New York, 1973.
Guion, R. M.: *Personnel Testing*, McGraw-Hill, New York, 1965.
Hariton, Theodore: *Interview! The Executive's Guide to Selecting the Right Personnel*, Hastings House, New York, 1970.
Holmen, M. G. and R. F. Docter: *Educational and Psychological Testing: A Study of the Industry and Its Practices*, Russell Sage Foundation, New York, 1972.
Lopez, F. M.: *The Making of a Manager*, American Management Association, New York, 1970.
Rosen, D. B.: *Employment Testing and Minority Groups*, New York State School of Industrial Relations, Issue Series no. 6, Cornell University, Ithaca, N. Y., 1970.

Articles

Boehm, V. R.: "Negro-white Differences in Validity of Employment and Training Selection Procedures," *Journal of Applied Psychology*, vol. 56, pp. 33–39, 1972.
Fincher, C.: "Personnel Testing and Public Policy," *American Psychologist*, vol. 28, pp. 489–497, 1973.
Huck, James R.: "Assessment Centers: A Review of the External and Internal Validities," *Personnel Psychology*, vol. 26, pp. 197–212, 1973.

Lopez, F. M.: "Evaluating the Whole Man," *The Long Island University Magazine,* vol. 2, pp. 17–22, 1968.

Mayfield, E. C.: "The Selection Interview—A Reevaluation of Published Research," *Personnel Psychology,* vol. 17, pp. 239–260, 1964.

McCormick, E. J., et al.: "A Study of Job Characteristics and Job Dimensions as Based on the Position Analysis Questionnaire (PAQ)," *Journal of Applied Psychology,* vol. 56, pp. 347–368, 1972.

Miner, J. B.: "Psychological Testing and Fair Employment Practices: A Testing Program that Does Not Discriminate," *Personnel Psychology,* vol. 27, pp. 49–62, 1974.

Moore, L. F. and J. C. Craik: "Video Tape and the Screening Interview," *Personnel Journal,* vol. 51, pp. 173–178, 1972.

Prien, E. P. and W. W. Ronan: "Job Analysis: A Review of Research Findings," *Personnel Psychology,* vol. 24, pp. 371–396, 1971.

Shaw, E. A.: "Differential Impact of Negative Stereotyping in Employment Selection," *Personnel Psychology,* vol. 25, pp. 333–338, 1972.

Ulrich, L. and D. Trumbo: "The Selection Interview Since 1949," *Psychological Bulletin,* vol. LXIII, pp. 100–116, 1965.

Wagner, R.: "The Employment Interview: A Critical Summary," *Personnel Psychology,* vol. 2, pp. 17–46, 1949.

Wright, O. A., Jr.: "Summary of Research on the Selection Interview Since 1964," *Personnel Psychology,* vol. 22, pp. 391–413, 1969.

Part 3   Problem-Solving Interviews

Books

Barrett, R. S.: *Performance Rating,* Science Research Associates, Inc., Chicago, 1966.

Dowling, W. F. and L. R. Sayles: *How Managers Motivate: The Imperatives of Supervision,* McGraw-Hill, New York, 1971.

Hackman, Ray C.: *The Motivated Working Adult,* American Management Association, New York, 1969.

Herzberg, F.: *Work and the Nature of Man,* World, New York, 1966.

Holland, John L.: *Making Vocational Choices: A Theory of Careers,* Prentice-Hall, Englewood Cliffs, N. J., 1973.

Kellogg, M. S.: *What to Do about Performance Appraisal,* American Management Association, New York, 1965.

Levinson, Harry: *The Great Jackass Fallacy,* Graduate School of Business Administration, Harvard University, Boston, 1973.

Lopez, F. M.: *Evaluating Employee Performance,* Public Personnel Association, Chicago, 1968.

Mager, Robert F. and Peter Pipe: *Analyzing Performance or "You Really Oughta Wanna,"* Fearon, Belmont, Calif., 1970.

Maher, John R. (ed.): *New Perspectives in Job Enrichment,* Van Nostrand Reinhold, New York, 1971.

Maier, Norman R. F.: *The Appraisal Interview: Objectives, Methods, Skills,* John Wiley & Sons, New York, 1958.

Maslow, A. H.: *Motivation and Personality,* Harper & Row, New York, 1964.

Neff, Walter S.: *Work and Human Behavior,* Atherton Press, New York, 1968.

Odiorne, G. S.: *Management Decisions by Objectives,* Prentice-Hall, Englewood Cliffs, N. J., 1969.

Reddin, W. J.: *Effective Management by Objectives,* McGraw-Hill, New York, 1971.

Rowland, V. K.: *Evaluating and Improving Managerial Performance,* McGraw-Hill, New York, 1970.

Super, Donald E.: *The Psychology of Careers,* Harper & Row, New York, 1957.

Whisler, T. L. and S. F. Harper: *Performance Appraisal: Research and Practice,* Holt, Rinehart and Winston, New York, 1962.

Articles

Alfred, T. M.: "Checkers or Choice in Manpower Management," *Harvard Business Review,* vol. 45, pp. 157–167, 1967.

Flowers, V. S. and C. L. Hughes: "Why Employees Stay," *Harvard Business Review*, vol. 51, pp. 49–60, 1973.

Lawler, Edward E.: "Job Attitudes and Employee Motivation: Theory, Research and Practice," *Personnel Psychology*, vol. 23, pp. 223–237, 1970.

Lopez, F. M.: "Accountability in Education," *Phi Delta Kappan*, vol. LII, pp. 231–235, 1970.

Oberg, Winston: "Make Performance Appraisal Relevant," *Harvard Business Review*, vol. 50, pp. 61–67, 1972.

Reide, G. A.: "Performance Review—A Mixed Bag," *Harvard Business Review*, vol. 51, pp. 61–67, 1973.

Rush, Harold M. F.: "When a Company Counsels a Drug Abuser," *The Conference Board Record*, vol. 9, pp. 11–15, 1972.

Thompson, P. H. and G. W. Dalton: "Performance Appraisal: Managers Beware," *Harvard Business Review*, vol. 48, pp. 149–157, 1970.

Part 4   Information-Exchange Interviews

Books

Kahn, R. L. and C. F. Cannell: *The Dynamics of Interviewing*, John Wiley & Sons, New York, 1958.

Likert, Rensis: *The Human Organization*, McGraw-Hill, New York, 1967.

Mager, Robert F.: *Developing Attitude toward Learning*, Fearon, Belmont, Calif., 1968.

Morgan, John S.: *Getting Across to Employees*, McGraw-Hill, New York, 1964.

Stetson, Damon: *Starting Over*, Macmillan, New York, 1971.

Articles

Brumback, Gary B.: "Employee Attitude Surveys," *Personnel Administration*, vol. 35, pp. 27–34, 1972.

Dunnette, M. W., et al.: "Why Do They Leave?," *Personnel*, vol. 50, pp. 25–39, 1973.

Farris, G. F.: "A Predictive Study of Turnover," *Personnel Psychology*, vol. 24, pp. 311–328, 1971.

Gelfand, L. I.: "Communicate through Your Supervisors," *Harvard Business Review*, vol. 48, pp. 101–104, 1970.

Lefkowitz, J. and L. Katz: "Validity of Exit Interviews," *Personnel Psychology*, vol. 22, pp. 445–455, 1969.

Moore, Michael L.: "Learning Times: A Key Factor in Managerial Personnel Decisions," *Human Resource Management*, vol. 11, pp. 35–40, 1972.

Podnos, Ira: "The 'Consultative' Method of Training," *Personnel*, vol. 48, pp. 53–59, 1971.

Roberts, K. H. and C. A. O'Reilly, III: "Failures in Upward Communication in Organizations: Three Possible Culprits," *Academy of Management Journal*, vol. 17, pp. 205–215, 1974.

Urban, T. F. and H. Desai: "Both Sides of the Turnover Problem," *The Personnel Administrator*, vol. 17, pp. 34–37, 1972.

Name Index

Name Index

Alfred, T. M., 252
Allport, G. W., 305
American Psychological
    Association, 94
Argyris, C., 198
Arvey, R. D., 318

Bales, R., 43
Banas, P. A., 318
Bartlett, F., 195
Beaumont, E. F., 302n.
Benne, K., 31
Berne, E., 23
Blake, R. R., 284
Blumberg, A., 288n.
Boehm, V. R., 95
Bolda, R. A., 71n.
Bolster, B. I., 161n.
Bray, D. W., 139n.
Brune, H. L., 71n.
Bulin, C., 180n.

Burack, E. H., 254
Burke, R. J., 266

Carnegie Tech, 180
Chase, S., 35
Connor, S. R., 253, 254
Crissy, W. J., 161n.
Cronbach, L. J., 97n.
Cummings, L. L., 204
Curtis, T. P., 310n.

Dachler, H. P., 186n.
Dalton, G. W., 210n.
Danielson, L. E., 275, 276
Department of Labor, U.S., 92
Dewey, J., 195
Dill, W. R., 180n.
Donne, J., 263
Drucker, P., 251–253
Duncker, K., 195

Dunnette, M. D., 80n., 318

Eilbert, H., 247
England, G. W., 4n.
Equal Employment Opportunity
    Commission (EEOC), 91, 92

Farris, G. F., 318
Fenn, D. H., 28
Ferguson, L. L., 245
Fielden, J. S., 253, 254
Fincher, C., 97n.
Finn, R., 204
Flowers, V. S., 266
Funk, F. E., 284n.

Gelfand, L. I., 288
General Motors, 298
Ginzberg, E., 250
Glesser, G. C., 97n.
Golembiewski, R. R., 288n.
Grant, D. L., 139
*Griggs et al. vs. Duke Power
    Company*, 91n., 94–95
Guion, R. M., 95, 96n.

Hackman, R. C., 180
Hall, D. T., 253
Hall, E. T., 36
Hall, M. H., 251n.
Harris, T. A., 25
Hatch, A. S., 285
Hayden, S., 224
Hemphill, J. K., 100n.
Herzberg, F., 186, 188, 189, 299
Hilton, T. L., 180n.
Hoffman, L. R., 71n., 199
Holland, J. E., 310n.
Holland, J. L., 192n.
Hollingsworth, H. L., 4n.
Holloman, T. D., 131n.
Hovland, C. I., 313n.
Huck, J. R., 140
Hudson, R. I., 248n.
Hughes, C. L., 266
Hull, R., 253n.

Jackson, R. M., 294

James, W., 310
Janis, I. L., 313n.
Jeanneret, P. R., 100n.

Kaplan, L. B., 97n.
Katz, L., 328
Kelley, H. H., 313n.

Lanholz, L. N., 71n.
Lawler, E. E., 186n.
Lawshe, C. R., 71
Lefkowitz, J., 328
Levinson, H., 180, 182n., 268n., 272
Likert, R., 193, 194, 283
Loken, R. D., 327n.
Lopez, F. M., 70n., 183n., 201, 209n.,
    218n., 253n.
Lull, P. E., 284n.
Lyons, T. F., 263

McCormick, E. J., 100n.
McGregor, D., 202
McNaughton, W. L., 328n.
Mager, R. F., 307
Maher, J. R., 190n.
Maier, N. R., 71, 199, 229, 275, 276
Maslow, A. H., 186, 188
Maslow, A. P., 76, 77n.
Mattson, P. G., 23n.
Mayfield, E. C., 4n.
Mecham, R. C., 100n.
Meyer, H. H., 236
Miner, J. B., 186n.
Mouton, J. S., 284

NAACP Legal and Education Defense
    Fund, 94
National Industrial Conference
    Board, 201
National Training Laboratories, 31
New York Times, The, 271n.
Newman, J. H., 305, 306n.

Oberg, W., 203
Office of Federal Contract Compli-
    ance, U.S. Department of
    Labor, 92, 93, 95

Patterson, C. H., 255, 257
Patterson, D. G., 4n.
Peter, L. J., 252, 253
Piersol, D. T., 284n.
Prien, E. P., 99n.
Primoff, E. S., 100n.

Regan, J., 161n.
Reitman, W. R., 180
Riede, G. A., 204n.
Roethlisberger, F., 278
Rogers, C., 51, 259, 260
Ronan, W. W., 99n.
Rothney, J. W., 294
Rowe, P., 131
Russell, B., 33

Salinger, M. D., 248n.
Sayles, L. R., 188n.
Scheid, P. N., 216n.
Schmidt, F. L., 97n.
Schneider, B., 253
Scott, J. P., 308n.
Shaw, R. R., 284
Sheats, P., 31
Springbelt, B. M., 161n.

Straus, G., 188
Super, D., 24, 25n., 250, 252

Taft, R., 136, 137n.
Thompson, A. S., 260, 261
Thompson, P. H., 210n.
Tollefson, A. L., 248n.

U.S. Supreme Court, 91, 94

Vroom, V., 305

Wagner, R., 4n.
Walker, W. B., 236
Wall Street Journal, The, 320
Wertheimer, M., 195
Wherry, R. J., 211
Wilcox, D. S., 266

Xerox Corporation, 271

Yankelovich, D., 284

Subject Index

Subject Index

Absenteeism, 263, 264
Acceptance, authority by, 270–272
Accountability, 180–183
  scope of, 216
Activities, extracurricular, 126, 127
Adjustment problems, 249, 250
Admonition, 195, 274
  (*See also* Discipline)
Advertising, 87
Affirmative-action programs, 92, 93
Agencies, employment, 87
Aggression, 22, 28
  displaying, in interview, 48, 49
Aggressive talker, 150, 151
Alcoholism, 268
Analysis:
  job (*see* Job analysis)
  of management styles, 219–221
  threshold traits, 100–104, 181
  transactional, 23–25
  of turnover, 317–319
    and absenteeism, 263, 264
Analytic strategy, 137

Anticipation, listener, 60
Anxiety, 23
  in interview: assessment, 135, 136
  counseling, 260, 278–280
  employment, 111
  evaluation, 227, 228, 237
  termination, 321
Appearance of employment applicant,
  124
Applicant-processing flow, 104–107
Applicants, difficult, 150–152
Application blank, 84, 87, 105, 113,
  119–122
  content of: desirable, 121
  undesirable, 122
  gaps and inconsistencies in, 149,
    150
  weighted, 121, 122
Appraisal, performance (*see*
  Performance evaluation)
Approach to interviewing:
  negative, 55
  tell and sell, 55

Asking questions, 37, 38, 144–147
Aspiration, career, 252–254
  levels of, 254, 255
Assessment centers, 139, 140
Assessment interview, 106, 107, 133, 134
  components of, 134, 140
  conducting, 140–152
  functional aspects of, 135–137
  structural aspects of, 134, 135
Attention, listener, 62
Attitudes, 34, 35, 56, 289–292
Authenticity, 198, 199
Authority, problem employee and, 268–272
  of counselor, 248, 249
  of supervisor, 226, 228
  (*See also* Influence)
Autonomy, need for, 187
Avocations of applicant, 124

Behavior:
  conflicted, 22
  frustrated, 21, 22
  human, understanding, 18–25
  of interviewer, 124
  motivated, 19–21
  (*See also* Rapport interviewer
    behavior; Self-centered in-
    terviewer behavior; Task
    interviewer behavior)
Beliefs, 34
Biographical questionnaire (*see*
  Application blank)
Blocking, 49
Body language, 37
Brain-storming, 196

Campus interview, 165, 166
Career abatement, 254
Career advancement, 252, 253
Career choice, 252
Career counseling interview, 249,
  250, 272–280
Career crises, 252–254
Career development, 252, 253
Career-orientation area, 124, 125,
  154, 155
Career plan, 78, 252, 253
Careers, psychology of, 251–255
Category width, 131
Change, effecting, 223, 224

Channels, communication, 16, 17
Choice, occupational, 250, 251
Civil Rights Act of 1964, 77, 90–92,
  94
Clarification, 41, 42, 198, 300, 333
Classification phase, 87
Climate, establishing, 43, 44, 57, 58,
  114–116
Coaching:
  contrasted to counseling, 194, 224,
    225
  on-the-job, 71, 72
Coaching interviews, 302–304
Codes, communication, 16, 17
Committees, 287, 288
Communication, 15–18, 207
  breakdowns, 283, 284
  counter-norm, 298
  direct interview, 37–40
  employee, 284–289
    experimental results of, 313
    failure, 284
    media for, 287–289
    by supervisors, 223, 224
    upward, 284, 285
  engineering factors, 16–18
  indirect interview, 40–43
  media, 5–7
  modes of, 35–37
    basic, 16
    interview, 26
  oral vs. written, 284, 285
  psychosocial influence in, 25–29
  (*See also* Data; Information)
Competence:
  interpersonal, 199, 218
  technical, 218
Concentration, listener, 62
Conflict, 22, 23, 187, 188, 278
Content:
  of application blank, 121, 122
  of interview, 8, 10, 11, 54, 152–162
Content factors of job, 188, 189
Context of interview, 8–10, 55
Context factors of job, 188, 189
Conversation, 6, 7, 14, 15, 124
Counseling:
  career, 251, 252
  contrasted to coaching, 194, 195,
    224, 225
  in exit interview, 320, 321, 329
  objections to, 271, 272
  program, 245–247, 255

Counseling interviews, 10
  career, 249, 250, 272–280
  and evaluation interviews, 194,
    195, 224, 225, 245, 246
  personal, 274, 275
  with problem employees, 249, 250,
    272–280
Counselors:
  limitations of personnel, 248, 249
  outside professional, 247–249, 260
  use of, in industry, 247
Critical-incident technique, 212
Culture as communication mode, 36,
  37
"Culture shock," 309
Curriculum vitae, 122

Data:
  factual, 11, 33, 107
  subconscious, 11, 34, 35, 107
  subjective, 11, 34, 107
  (*See also* Interpreting interview
    data)
Decision-making employment system,
  98–103, 106, 107
Decision-making interviews, 10, 73,
  74
Decision theory, 89, 90
Decisions:
  interview: assessment, 160–162
  employment, 130–132
  premature, 55
  selection, 76
  unreliable, 55
  occupational, 250, 251
Decline stage, 254, 255
Defense mechanisms, 23, 24
  in interview: assessment, 135, 136
  counseling, 260, 278, 280
  employment, 111
  evaluation, 227, 228, 237
  termination, 321
Degrees, trait, 101–103
Delicate subject, discussion of, during
  assessment interview, 149
Demotion, employee, 274
Dependability, 218
Depth interview, 136–139
  (*See also* Assessment interview)
Description of applicant, 10, 80–83
Destination of communication, 16, 17
Development, employee, 183, 184, 193

Differences, individual, principle of,
  79–80
Difficulties, employee (*see* Problem
  employees; Problems)
Direct-observation measures, 84, 85
Directed interviewing, 13, 51
Disabled employees, 266, 267, 274
Disciplinary interviews, 90, 275–278
  and evaluation interviews, 195
Discipline, 269, 270
  (*See also* Admonition)
Discrimination, 93
Disgruntled employee, 266
Dismissal, 278, 328–331
Distraction, listener, 62
Domineering interview behavior, 50
Drives, 19–21
  anxiety, 23
  physiological, 20, 186
  psychological, 20, 186, 187
  social, 20, 21, 186, 187
  (*See also* Needs)

Educational-life area, 125–127, 155,
  156
Effectiveness:
  job (*see* Job effectiveness)
  organizational, 199
  personal, 198, 199
Embedding process, 63–64, 289, 306
Emotion:
  communication of, 23, 34, 36
  fear of strong, 279
  releasing, 45
Emotional illness, 268
Emotional maturity, 218
Empathy, 65, 66
Employment agency, 87
Employment department, orientation
  by, 310
Employment interview, 3, 105–109
  components of, 109–111
  conduct of, 111–119
  content of, 119–132
  decision, 130–132
  functional aspects of, 111
  sequence, 114
  structural aspects of, 110, 111
Employment office, 87
Employment policies, 77, 78
Encouraging interviewer behavior,
  44, 45

Ending, happy, need for, 279
Enrichment, job, 189, 190
Equal employment opportunity, 90–95
Equal Employment Opportunity Commission (EEOC) selection guidelines, 93, 94
Errors, interview, 54–57, 164
Establishment period, 252
Evaluation:
  of applicant, 10
  interview (*see* Performance evaluation interview)
  performance (*see* Performance evaluation)
  of problem, 196
Evaluator, performance, 208, 209
Examination, physical, 85
Exercises:
  performance, 85, 86
  placement, 106
  written, 85
Exit interview (*see* Termination interview)
Expectations, performance, 231
Experience:
  military, 127
  work, 127, 128, 156, 157
Exploration period, 252

Factual data, 11, 33, 107
Fear, authority by, 269, 270
Feedback, 16, 17
  face-to-face, 28
  by supervisors, 223, 224, 236, 239, 240, 285
Feelings (*see* Emotion)
Field-review method, 212
Filtering process, 27, 227
Fixation, 22
Force-field analysis, 321, 322
Forced-choice technique, 210, 211, 219
Forced-distribution method, 210
Forecasting employment needs, 78
Frustration, 21, 22, 187, 188

Game theory, 89, 90
Games as defense mechanisms, 23
Gaps, unexplained, 116, 149, 150
Gate-keeping interviewer behavior, 47
Global strategy, 137

Goal-setting, 182
Goals:
  affirmative action, 92, 93
  interview, 241
  life, 274
Grades, school, 126
Grapevine, the control of, 288, 289
Grievance interview, 10, 272, 273
Grievances, employee, 272, 273
Group discussion, 6
  leaderless, 174, 175
Group interview, 107, 173, 174
Group processes, 287, 288
Guidance, employee (*see* Counseling)

"Halo" effect, 132, 161, 162
Handicaps, physical, 266, 267, 274
Health of applicant, 123
Hostility:
  atmosphere of, 28
  of interviewee, 151, 237, 273
Hours of availability, 125, 127
Human resources planning, 76–79
Hypothesis testing, 42, 64, 147, 148

Idea production, 196
Identification, organizational, 218
Impact in role playing, 71
Imprinting, 308, 309
Impulsivity, listener, 60
Incompetency:
  dismissal for, 328
  handling of, 274
Indoctrination (*see* Orientation, employee)
Indolence, listener, 60
Influence, 207
  approaches to, 229–231
Information:
  improper, 55, 121, 122
  levels of, 11, 33–35, 107
  management's need to share, 285, 286, 291
  sources of, 11, 16, 17
  (*See also* Communication; Data)
Information areas, life, 122–130
Information-exchange interviews, 9, 281, 282
Information giving:
  in employment interview, 117
  as a sequence, 58
Information-giving behavior, 39, 40

Information-giving interview, 9, 302–304
and embedding process, 306
Information retrieval, 284, 290, 291
Information seeking:
in employment interview, 116, 117
as a sequence, 58
Information-seeking behavior, 39
Information-seeking interview, 9, 288
Information theory, 16–18
Initiating interviewer behavior, 38, 39
Initiative, 218
Instruction, 302, 303
inadequate job, 264
interview as a method of, 303, 304
in interviewing skills, 68–72
Integration, listener, 63
Intelligence quotient, 81
Interpersonal competence, 199, 218
Interpreting interview data, 53, 64, 65, 131
Interrogation, 7
Interview:
analysis of, 3–13
assessment (*see* Assessment interview)
career counseling (*see* Career counseling interview)
content of, 8, 10, 11, 54, 152–162
context of, 8–10, 55
depth, 136–139
directed, 51
employment (*see* Employment interview)
errors in, 54, 57, 164
group, 107, 173, 174
information capacity of, 32–35
learning to, 68–72
limited purpose of, 165–167
in management information system, 288
multiple-appraisal, 167–175
nondirective, 51, 52
panel, 107, 170–173
patterned, 107
performance evaluation (*see* Performance evaluation interview)
personal counseling, 274, 275
placement, 273, 274
record (*see* Record of interview)
screening, 165–167
serial, 107, 169, 170

Interview (*Cont.*):
stress, 52
supervisory, 166, 167
Interview conditions, 55
Interview function, 8, 11–13
Interview problems, 149–152
Interview sequence (*see* Sequence, interview)
Interview structure, 8–11
Interview styles, 13, 51, 52
Interviewee:
behavior of, 123, 124
hostile, 151, 237, 273
coaching, 12
Interviewer, 5, 56
attitudes of, 56
background of, 56
development of, 68–72
dress of, 112
in employment, 11
negative set of, 278, 279
in problem-solving, 197, 198
role of, 107
uninstructed, 54
Interviewer behavior:
rapport (*see* Rapport interviewer behavior)
task (*see* Task interviewer behavior)
Interviewer questions, 56
(*See also* Questions)
Interviewer techniques:
effective, 57–65
variations in, 56, 57
Interviewer traits, 65–68
Intolerance, listener, 59, 60
Intuition, 37
Involvement:
ego, 304–306
and job satisfaction, 185
and listening, 61
Isolation, authority by, 270

Job analysis, 99, 100
Job effectiveness, 96, 97, 179–181, 190, 191, 193
and individual differences, 79, 80
Job enrichment, 189, 190
Job environment, 297
Job performance, 96, 97, 131, 180–184
evaluation of (*see* Performance evaluation)
standards of, 213, 217, 218, 231

Job satisfaction, 96, 97, 180, 181, 184–191, 296–298

Knowledge of interviewer, 65

Language, 35, 36
　body, 37
　(*See also* Communication)
Leaderless group discussion (LGD) technique, 174–175
Learned traits, 80
Learning, 68, 69
　capacity for, 69
　critical period for, 308, 309
　distributed, 69
　of interview skills, 68–72
　massed, 69
　motivation for, 68, 69
Learning aids, 70
Learning passivity, 70
Learning rate, 69
Learning set, 308
Learning tasks, 307
Lecture, 6
Levels, trait, 101–103
Life-information areas, 122–130, 152–162
Life positions, 24, 25
Linking, listener, 62, 63
Listener:
　ability of, 306, 307
　linking, 62, 63
Listening, 40, 58–63
　in evaluation interview, 230, 231, 236
　obstacles that hinder, 59–60
　skillful, 58, 59
　steps toward effective, 60–63
Logical exposition, 307, 308

Maintenance period, 253, 254
Management by objectives, 182, 213, 214
Maturity, emotional, 218
Measurement, 206, 207
Measures:
　direct-observation, 84, 85
　self-report, 83, 84
　trait, 83–86, 101, 102
　work sample, 85, 86

Mental illness, 268
Mental traits, 80
Message, one-way, 287
Milieu, organizational, 192, 193
Moral character, 123
Morale, 185, 186
Motivation to learn, 68, 69
Motivational traits, 80
Motivators, 189
Motives (*see* Drives; Needs)
Multiple-appraisal technique, 167–176
Multiple-regression analysis, 97

Naïve empirical strategy, 137
Need:
　for affection, 186
　for affiliation, 186
　for autonomy, 187
　for beauty, 187
　for a happy ending, 279
　for information, 186
　for safety, 186
　for self-actualization, 187
　for understanding, 187
Needs, 19
　hierarchy of, 186, 188
　of interviewer, 48
　(*See also* Drives)
Noise:
　and communication system, 17, 18
　in disciplinary interview, 277, 278
　in evaluation interview, 227
　psychosocial, 27
Nondirective style, 13, 51
　in assessment interview, 143, 144
　in evaluation interview, 197, 236
Nontalker, 151, 238, 239
Normal frequency distribution, 81
Normality, 81
Notetaking, 57, 113, 114

Observation of performance, 206
Obsolescence, employee, 253, 254, 265, 266
Opinions, 34, 292
Organizational effectiveness, 199
Organizational effort, 193, 194
Organizational identification, 218
Organizational milieu, 192, 193

Orientation:
career, 124, 125, 154, 155
employee, 308–311
Overidentification, 279

Perception, 58, 59
influences on, 28, 29
selective, 59
Performance, job (*see* Job
performance)
Performance evaluation, 182, 183,
205, 209
Performance evaluation chain, 206,
207
Performance evaluation interview, 4,
10, 222, 223
components of, 223–225
and counseling interview, 194, 195,
224, 225, 245, 246
with effective subordinate, 225,
226, 235, 236
follow-up of, 243, 244
functional aspects, of, 225
with ineffective subordinate, 226–
228, 236–240
objections to, 202–205
Performance evaluation problem, 201,
202
Performance evaluation procedures,
209–214
person-oriented, 209–211
results-oriented, 209, 211–214
Performance evaluation program,
214–221
Performance evaluation purpose:
individual, 215–216
organization, 214, 215
Performance evaluator, 208, 209
Performance exercises, 85
Performance factors, 218
Performance standards, 213, 217,
218, 231
Personal-life area, 123, 124, 152, 153
Personality, 192
authentic, 198, 199
Personality interaction, 13, 14
in interview, 27–29, 237–239
Personnel interview, 3, 7, 8
Personnel specialist:
assessment of, 139
role in counseling, 247–249, 255,
256, 260, 261

Personnel specialist (*Cont.*):
in termination, 323, 324
Persuasion, authority by, 270
Physical examination, 85
Placement, employee, 273, 274, 304–
306
Placement exercises, 106
Placement interview, 10, 273, 274
Plan:
career, 78
improvement, 241, 242
for interview: assessment, 140–
149
career counseling, 256
employment, 112–114
exit, 331, 332
performance evaluation, 232–
234
selection, 103, 105
Planning, human resources, 76–79
Positions, sensitive, 137–139
managerial, 138, 139
personnel relations, 139
Post-evaluation interview, 243, 244
Prediction, 10, 73
of job effectiveness, 90
Prediction score, 122
Preparation:
for interview: assessment, 141
counseling, 256
employment, 112, 113
information, 299, 312, 313, 331,
332
performance evaluation, 232–
234
for listening, 60, 61
Primacy, effects of, 236
Primary interview, 11
Probation, 88, 106
Problem, criterion, 96, 97
Problem employees, 187, 263, 268
alcoholic, 268
anxiety in interviewing, 278–280
disabled, 266, 267
disgruntled, 266
domestically troubled, 267, 268
emotionally ill, 268
financially embarrassed, 267
obsolete, 253, 254, 265, 266
reluctant, 266
troubled, 267
Problem-solving interviews, 9, 10,
177, 178, 197–199

Problem-solving process, 195–197, 231, 239–241
Problems, 177, 178, 195, 196
  adjustment, employees with, 249, 250
  career, employees with, 250, 251
  evaluation of, 196, 240
  family, 267, 268
  financial, 267
  interviewer, 54–57
  management, 265
  personal, 265
Procurement, 193
Productivity, 179
Progression, 193
Promotion, 86
Psychologist, professional, 136, 247–249, 260

Qualification, 88
Quantitative-performance measure, 212
Questionnaire:
  biographical (*see* Application blank)
  survey, 293, 294
  termination, 328
Questions:
  asking, 37, 38, 144–147
  in assessment interview, 152–157
  interviewer, 56
  variability of, 54–55
Quotas, hiring, 93

Ranking in performance evaluation, 210
Rapport interviewer behavior, 12, 31, 32, 43–47, 57, 58
  in interview: assessment, 135, 136, 142, 143
  career counseling, 257
  employment, 114–116
  evaluation, 198, 235
  survey, 299
  termination, 232
Reassignment, employee, 274
Recall, 206
Receiver, communication, 16, 17
Recency, effects of, 236
Recognition, seeking, 49, 50

Record of interview, 57
  assessment, 157–160
  counseling, 258, 259, 276, 277
  employment, 113
  evaluation, 233, 242
  orientation, 314–316
  survey, 300, 301
  termination, 323–325
Recruitment, 86, 87
  college, 166
Redundancy, 17, 18
References, character, 121
Regression, 22
Rehabilitation, 266, 267
Relevancy, in interview, 8
  of experience, 129, 130
Reliability, statistical, 81
Report, interview (*see* Record of interview)
Repression, authority by, 270
Resentment, 151, 237
Resignation (*see* Termination)
Restatement, 41
Résumés, 122
Retention, 63, 64, 306, 307
Reward system, 193, 194
Role, 12, 192
  of evaluation interviewer, 229
Role dimensions, interviewer, 37–50
Role interaction, 12
Role shock, 278

Salary, 125, 194
Salesmanship, authority by, 270
Salience, membership, 298
Salvage interview, 319–322
Satisfaction, job (*see* Job satisfaction)
Screening interview, 165–167
Secondary interview, 11
Selection:
  effectiveness of, 264
  and job effectiveness, 193
  phases of, 86–88
  principles of, 79–83
  standards of, 78
  tools of, 83–86
Selection interview, 3, 84, 85
  in depth, 136–139
  (*See also* Assessment interview; Employment interview; Screening interview)
Selection out, 254

Selection plan, 103, 105
Selection ratio, 79
Selection strategy, 76, 89, 90, 95–98
Selection theory, 75, 76
Self-acceptance, interviewer, 280
Self-actualization, 187, 198, 199
Self-blame, excessive, 279
Self-centered interviewer behavior,
　12, 32, 47–50
Self-concept, 21–25, 198
　in interview, 28, 29
Self-confessing, 50
Self-evaluation, 235, 236, 241
Self-fulfillment, 187, 198, 199
Self-justification, 279
Self-report measures, 83, 84
Semantics, 35, 67
Sensitivity training, 289
Separation (*see* Termination)
Sequence, interview, 57, 58
　assessment, 141–144
　career counseling, 256–261
　employment, 114
　performance evaluation, 235–
　　242
Serial interview, 107, 169, 170
Shelf-sitters, 253, 254, 265, 266
Signs, communication, 17
Silence, use of, 40, 41
Skills:
　communication, 66–68
　interviewer, 65–68
Social-life area, 123, 124, 153, 154
Social traits, 80
Stages, career, 252–254
Standard score, 81
Standardized interviews, 51
Standards:
　decision, 130–132
　performance, 206, 213, 217, 218
Strategy, selection, 76, 89, 90, 95–
　98
Stress interviewing, 13, 52
Subconscious data, 11, 34, 35, 107
Subjective data, 11, 34, 107
Subjects, educational, 126
Subordinate:
　interview with effective, 225, 226,
　　235, 236
　interview with ineffective, 226–
　　228, 236–240
Success, job, 179–181
　(*See also* Job effectiveness)

Successive hurdle approach, 97
Suggestability, 60
Summarizing:
　as a dimension, 42, 43
　in employment interview, 118
　in performance evaluation
　　interview, 198, 236
　as a sequence, 58
Superannuated employee, 273
Supervision:
　assessment of candidates for, 138,
　　139
　poor, 264, 265
Supervisor:
　attitudes toward, 297
　as coach and consultant, 194, 195,
　　224, 225
　in counseling effort, 194, 195, 224,
　　225, 247, 248, 255, 256
　in employee orientation, 310
　in termination program, 322–324
Survey interview, 9, 295–301
Surveys, employee, 291–294
　follow-up of, 301
Sympathy, 66
Synthesis, final, 88

Taking notes, 57, 113, 114
Tape recorder, 70, 71
Task interviewer behavior, 12, 32–
　43
　in performance evaluation
　　interview, 198, 236
Technical competence, 218
Ten-minute interview, 165, 166
Tension, 22
　reducing, 45, 46, 237
Termination, 238, 254
　reasons for, 320, 321
Termination control program, 319
Termination interview, 9
　involuntary, 328–331
　preliminary, 319–322
　voluntary, 322–328
Tertiary interview, 11
Test guidelines, 93, 94
Test standards, 94
Testing:
　hypothesis, 42, 64, 147, 148
　as interview dimension, 42, 147,
　　148, 236
Tests, 85, 86, 93

Threshold Traits Analysis, 100–104, 181
Training, interviewer, 68–72
Trait levels and degrees, 101–103
Trait measures, 83–86, 101, 102
Traits:
    performance, 218
    the thirty-three, 100, 102
Transactional analysis, 23
Transmitter, communication, 16, 17
Turnover, analysis of, 317–319
    and absenteeism, 263, 264
Two-factor theory, 188–190

Unblocking, 46
Uncertainty, zone of, 207–209
Understanding, 270–272
    human behavior, 18–25

Validity:
    demonstrated, 93, 94
    differential, 94–96
    statistical, 81–83
Values, 34
Verification, 85, 106
Video tape, 70, 71
Vocabulary, 66–68

Warning of dismissal, 330
Work-experience area, 129, 130, 156, 157
Work sample measures, 85, 86

Zone of uncertainty, 207–209